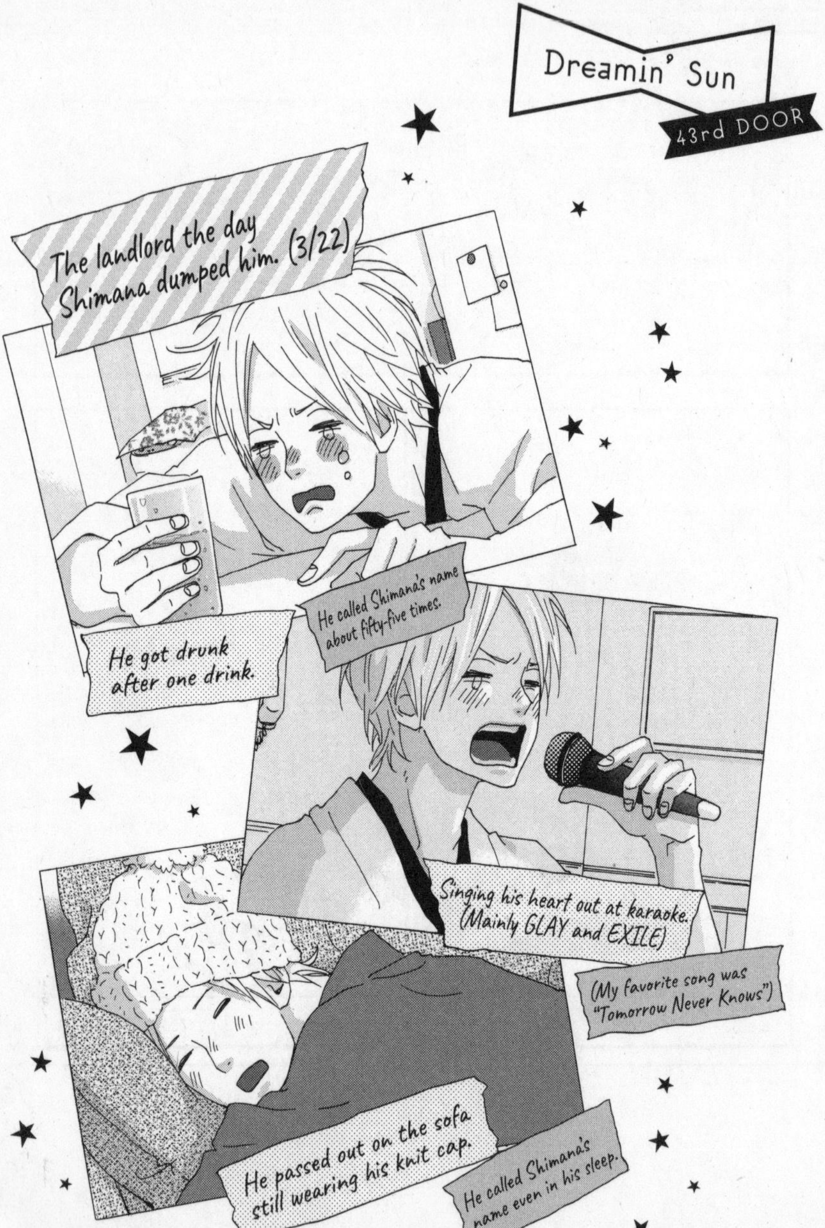
Dreamin' Sun
43rd DOOR
The landlord the day Shimana dumped him. (3/22)
He called Shimana's name about fifty-five times.
He got drunk after one drink.
Singing his heart out at karaoke. (Mainly GLAY and EXILE)
(My favorite song was "Tomorrow Never Knows")
He called Shimana's name even in his sleep.
He passed out on the sofa still wearing his knit cap.

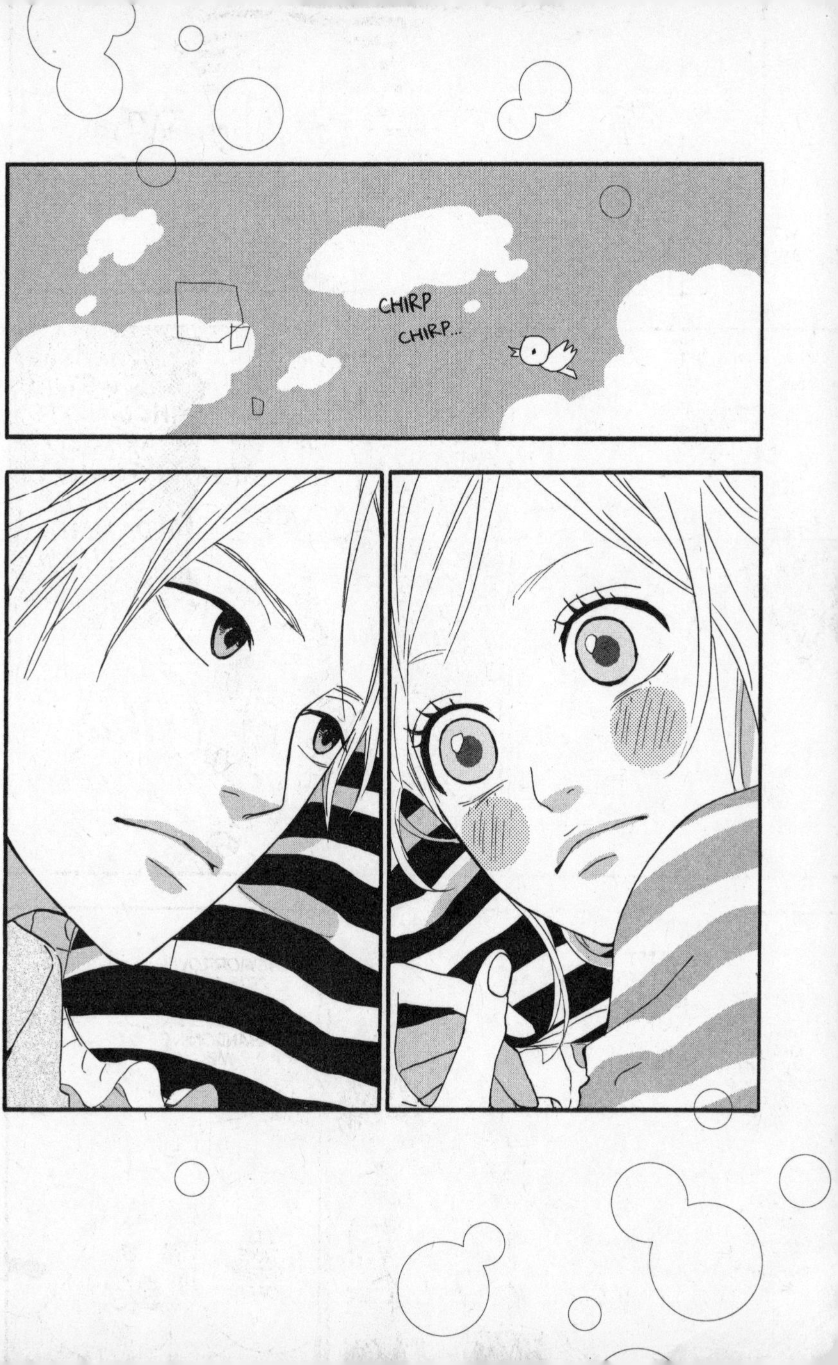
CHIRP
CHIRP...

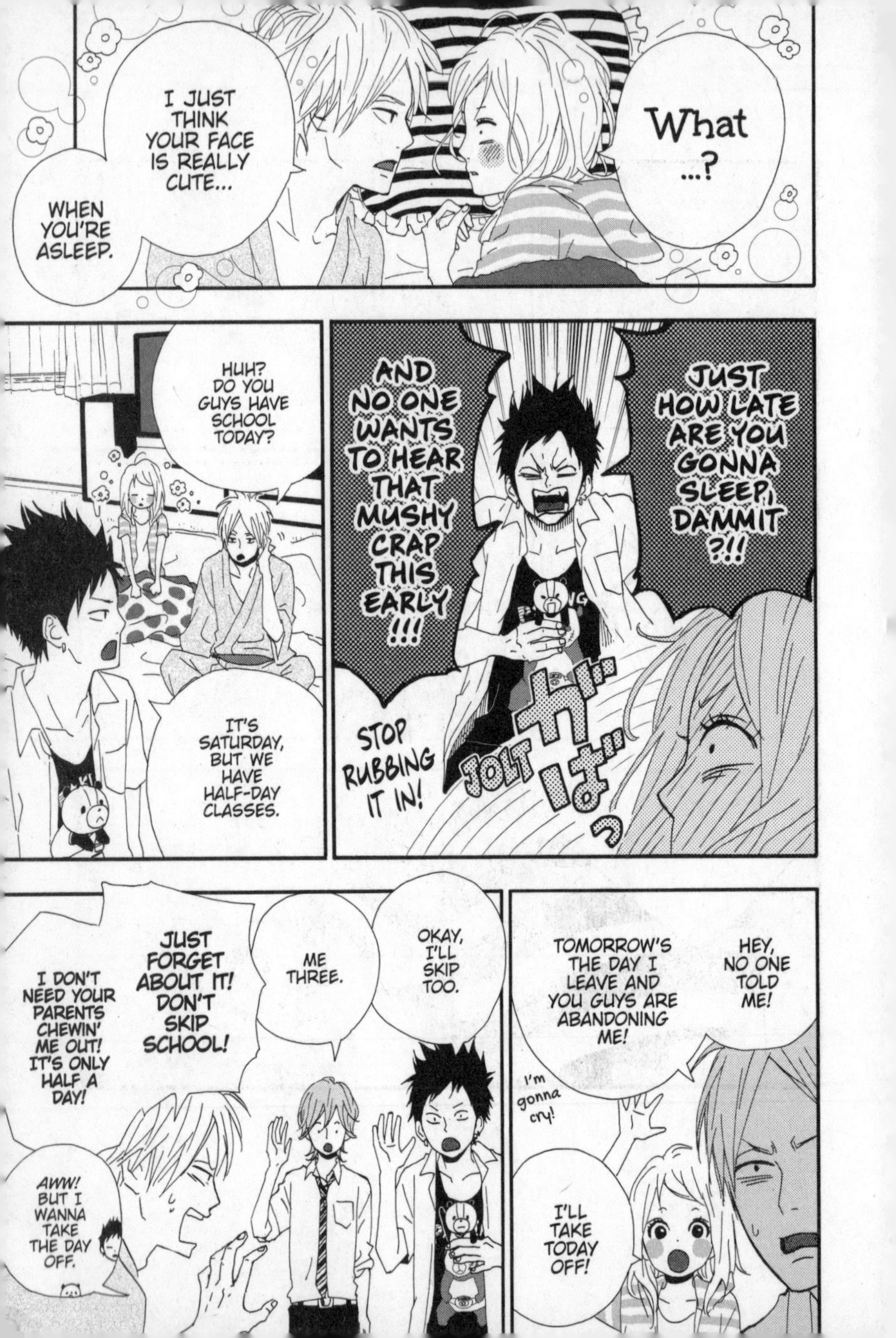
What ...?
I JUST THINK YOUR FACE IS REALLY CUTE...
WHEN YOU'RE ASLEEP.
JUST HOW LATE ARE YOU GONNA SLEEP, DAMMIT ?!!
AND NO ONE WANTS TO HEAR THAT MUSHY CRAP THIS EARLY !!!
JOLT
STOP RUBBING IT IN!
HUH? DO YOU GUYS HAVE SCHOOL TODAY?
IT'S SATURDAY, BUT WE HAVE HALF-DAY CLASSES.
HEY, NO ONE TOLD ME!
TOMORROW'S THE DAY I LEAVE AND YOU GUYS ARE ABANDONING ME!
I'm gonna cry!
I'LL TAKE TODAY OFF!
OKAY, I'LL SKIP TOO.
ME THREE.
JUST FORGET ABOUT IT! DON'T SKIP SCHOOL!
I DON'T NEED YOUR PARENTS CHEWIN' ME OUT! IT'S ONLY HALF A DAY!
AWW! BUT I WANNA TAKE THE DAY OFF.

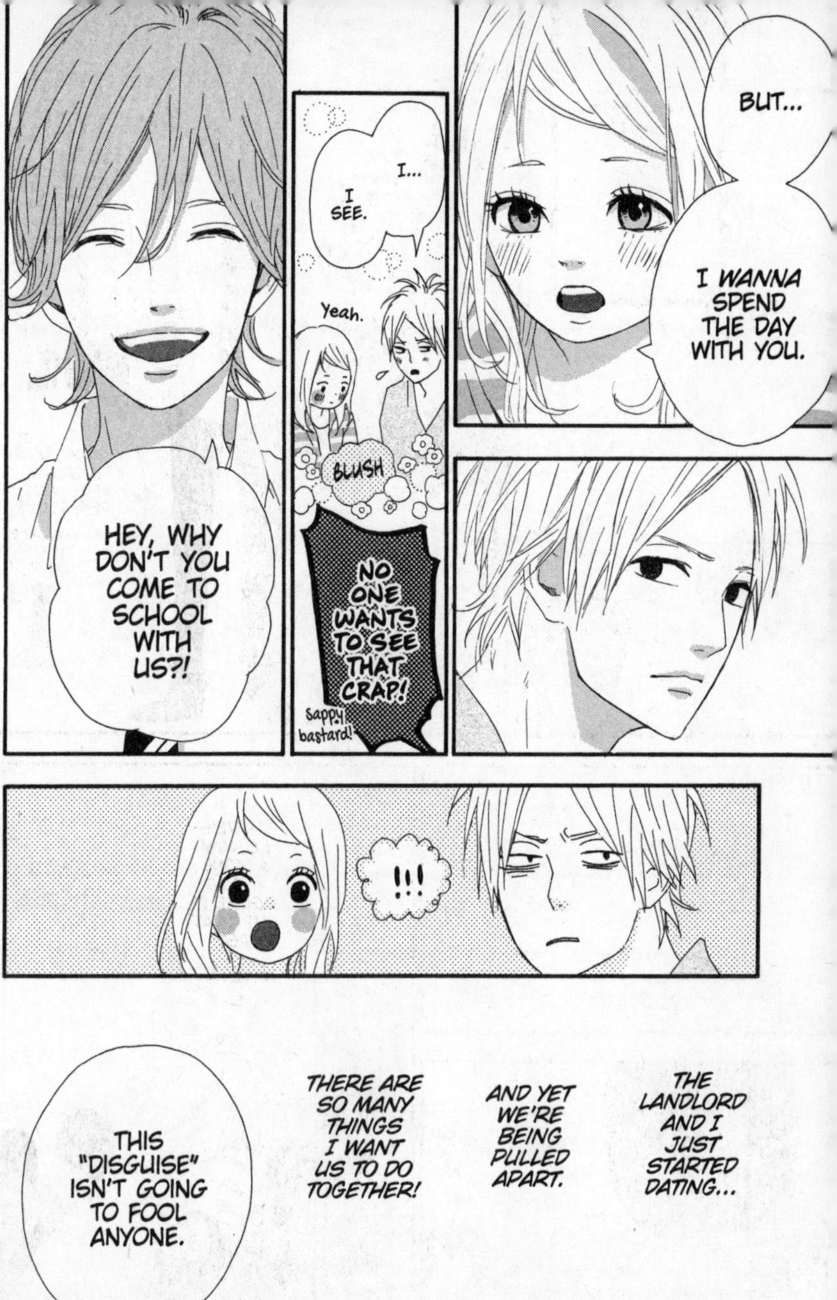
BUT...
I WANNA SPEND THE DAY WITH YOU.
I... I SEE.
Yeah.
BLUSH
NO ONE WANTS TO SEE THAT CRAP!
Sappy bastard!
HEY, WHY DON'T YOU COME TO SCHOOL WITH US?!
!!!
THE LANDLORD AND I JUST STARTED DATING...
AND YET WE'RE BEING PULLED APART.
THERE ARE SO MANY THINGS I WANT US TO DO TOGETHER!
THIS "DISGUISE" ISN'T GOING TO FOOL ANYONE.

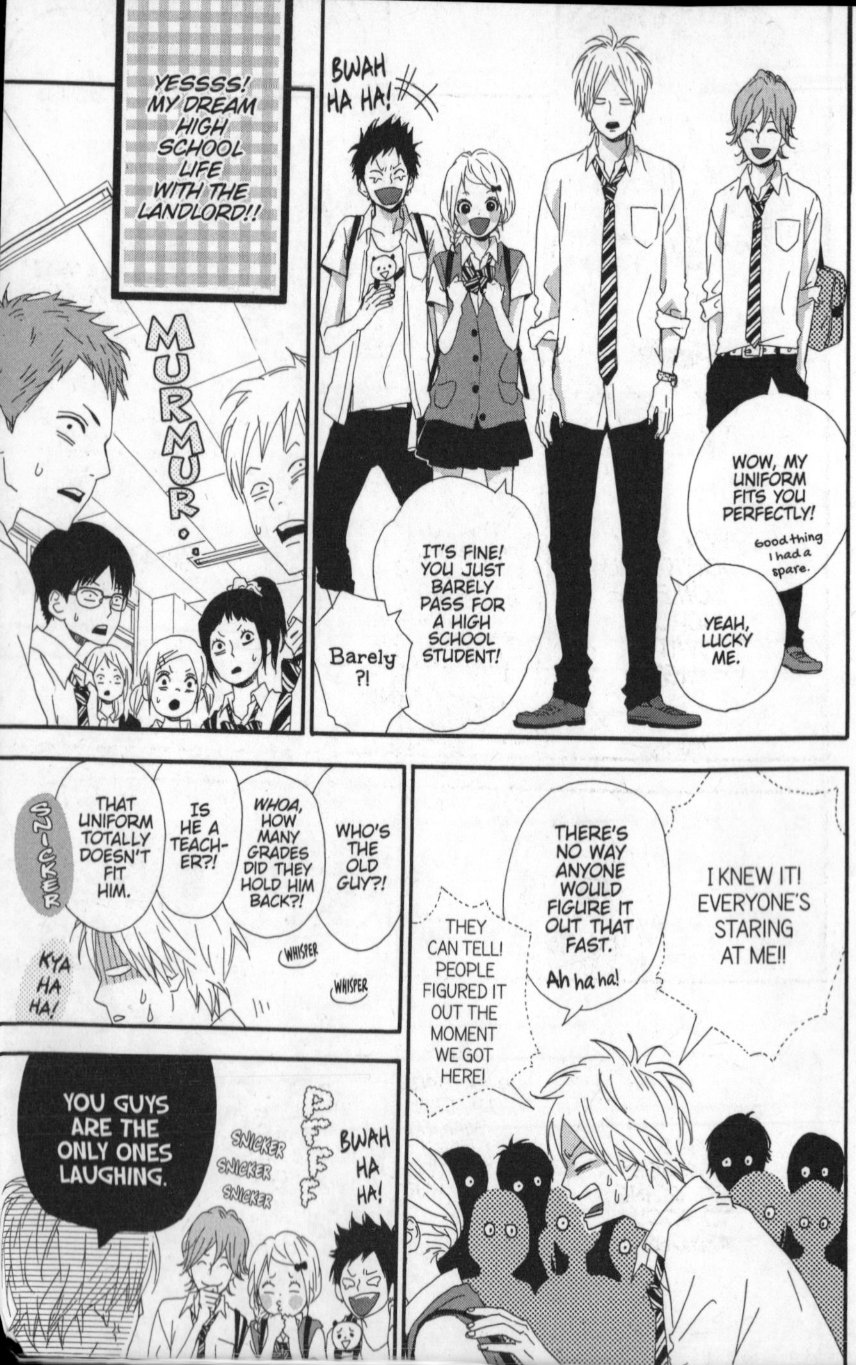
BWAH HA HA!
WOW, MY UNIFORM FITS YOU PERFECTLY!
Good thing I had a spare.
YEAH, LUCKY ME.
IT'S FINE! YOU JUST BARELY PASS FOR A HIGH SCHOOL STUDENT!
Barely?!
YESSSS! MY DREAM HIGH SCHOOL LIFE WITH THE LANDLORD!!
MURMUR.
I KNEW IT! EVERYONE'S STARING AT ME!!
THERE'S NO WAY ANYONE WOULD FIGURE IT OUT THAT FAST.
Ah ha ha!
THEY CAN TELL! PEOPLE FIGURED IT OUT THE MOMENT WE GOT HERE!
WHO'S THE OLD GUY?!
WHOA, HOW MANY GRADES DID THEY HOLD HIM BACK?!
IS HE A TEACHER?!
THAT UNIFORM TOTALLY DOESN'T FIT HIM.
SNICKER
WHISPER
WHISPER
KYA HA HA!
BWAH HA HA!
PFFF
SNICKER
SNICKER
SNICKER
YOU GUYS ARE THE ONLY ONES LAUGHING.

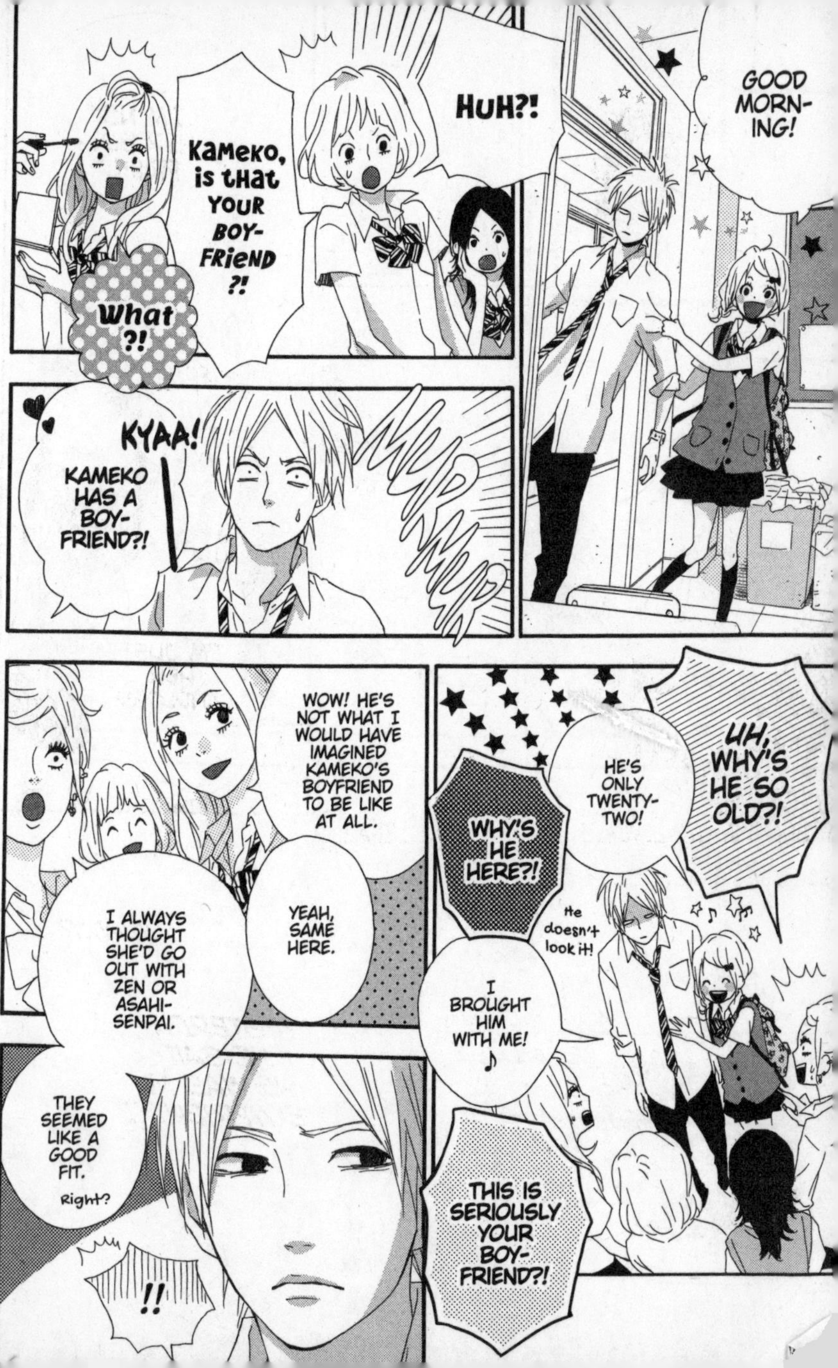
GOOD MORNING!
HUH?!
Kameko, is that your boyfriend?!
What?!
KYAA!
KAMEKO HAS A BOYFRIEND?!
UH, WHY'S HE SO OLD?!
HE'S ONLY TWENTY-TWO!
He doesn't look it!
WHY'S HE HERE?!
I BROUGHT HIM WITH ME! ♪
THIS IS SERIOUSLY YOUR BOYFRIEND?!
WOW! HE'S NOT WHAT I WOULD HAVE IMAGINED KAMEKO'S BOYFRIEND TO BE LIKE AT ALL.
YEAH, SAME HERE.
I ALWAYS THOUGHT SHE'D GO OUT WITH ZEN OR ASAHI-SENPAI.
THEY SEEMED LIKE A GOOD FIT.
Right?
!!

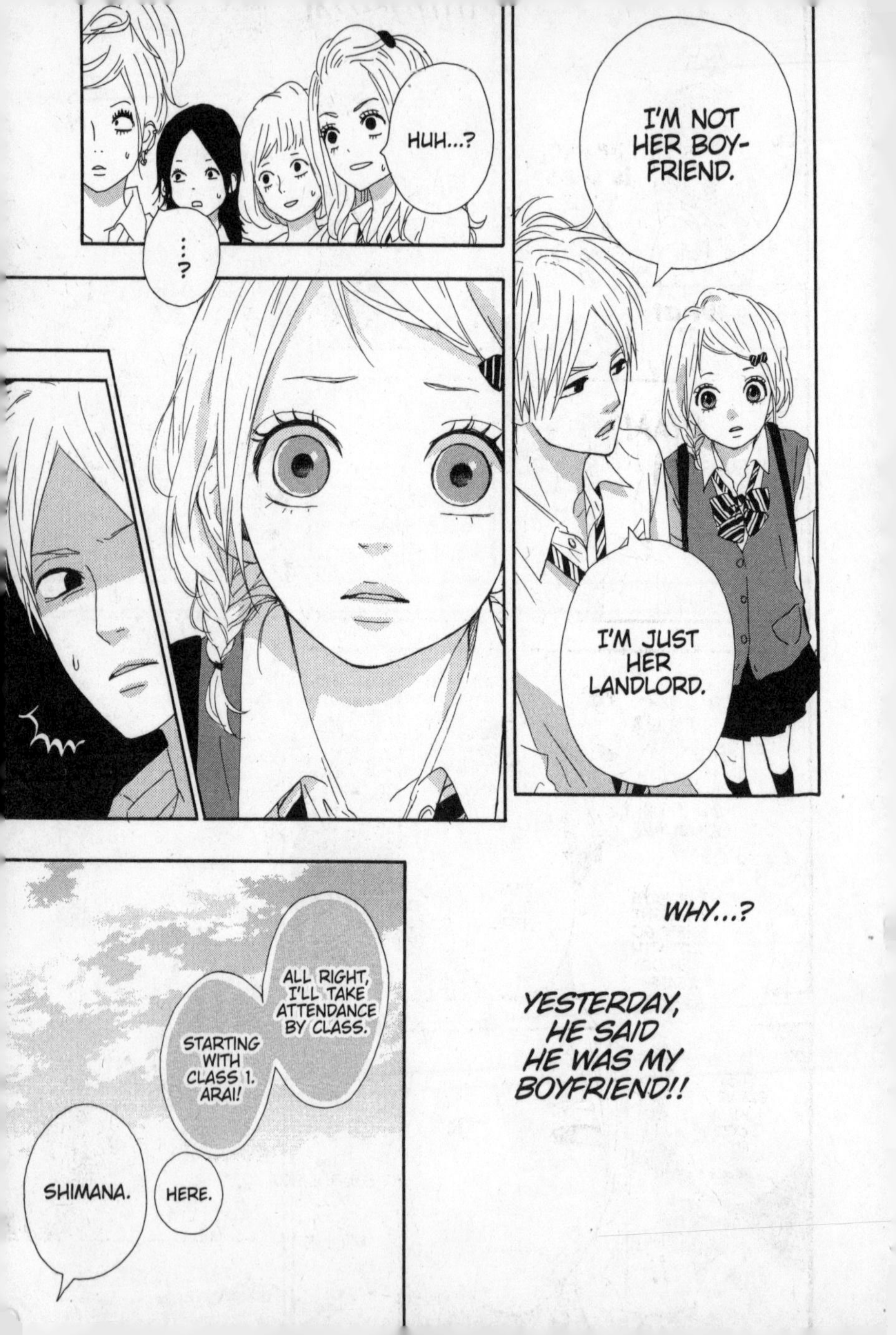
I'M NOT HER BOY-FRIEND.
I'M JUST HER LANDLORD.
HUH...?
...?
WHY...?
YESTERDAY, HE SAID HE WAS MY BOYFRIEND!!
ALL RIGHT, I'LL TAKE ATTENDANCE BY CLASS.
STARTING WITH CLASS 1. ARAI!
HERE.
SHIMANA.

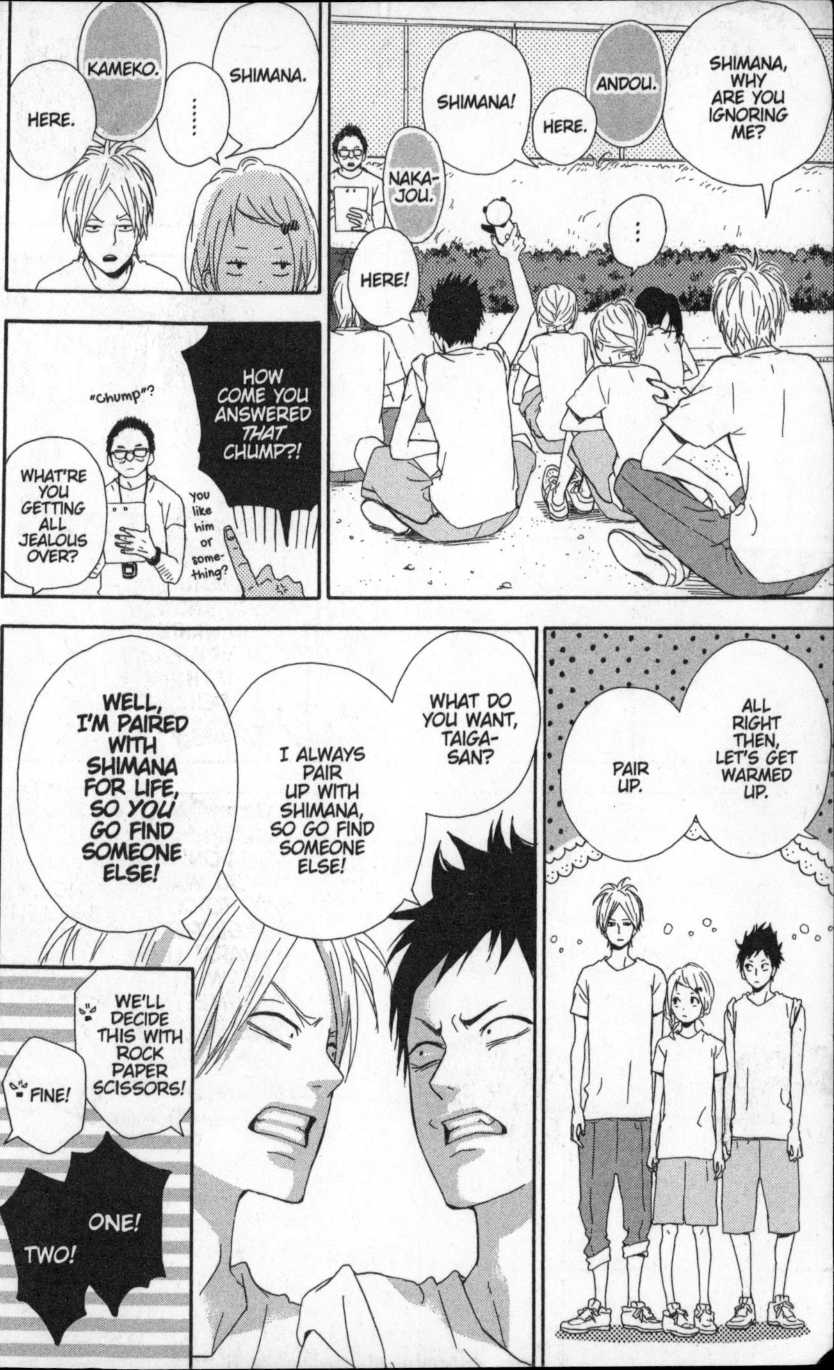
SHIMANA, WHY ARE YOU IGNORING ME?
ANDOU.
...
HERE.
SHIMANA!
NAKAJOU.
HERE!
SHIMANA.
......
KAMEKO.
HERE.
HOW COME YOU ANSWERED *THAT* CHUMP?!
You like him or something?
"Chump"?
WHAT'RE YOU GETTING ALL JEALOUS OVER?
ALL RIGHT THEN, LET'S GET WARMED UP.
PAIR UP.
WHAT DO YOU WANT, TAIGA-SAN?
I ALWAYS PAIR UP WITH SHIMANA, SO GO FIND SOMEONE ELSE!
WELL, I'M PAIRED WITH SHIMANA FOR LIFE, SO *YOU* GO FIND SOMEONE ELSE!
WE'LL DECIDE THIS WITH ROCK PAPER SCISSORS!
FINE!
ONE!
TWO!

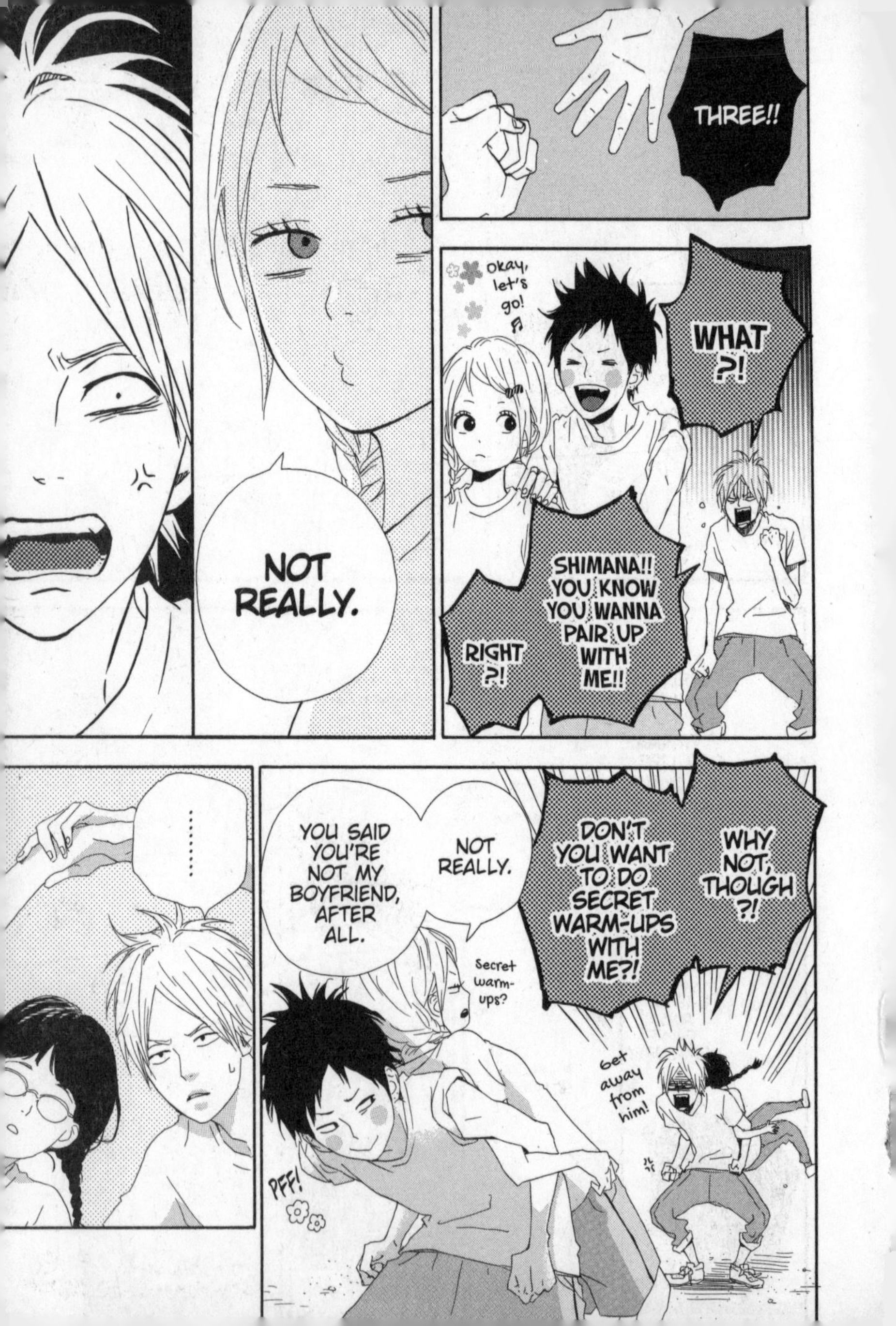
THREE!!
WHAT?!
okay, let's go!
SHIMANA!! YOU KNOW YOU WANNA PAIR UP WITH ME!!
RIGHT?!
NOT REALLY.
WHY NOT, THOUGH?!
DON'T YOU WANT TO DO SECRET WARM-UPS WITH ME?!
NOT REALLY.
YOU SAID YOU'RE NOT MY BOYFRIEND, AFTER ALL.
Secret warm-ups?
Get away from him!
PFF!
......

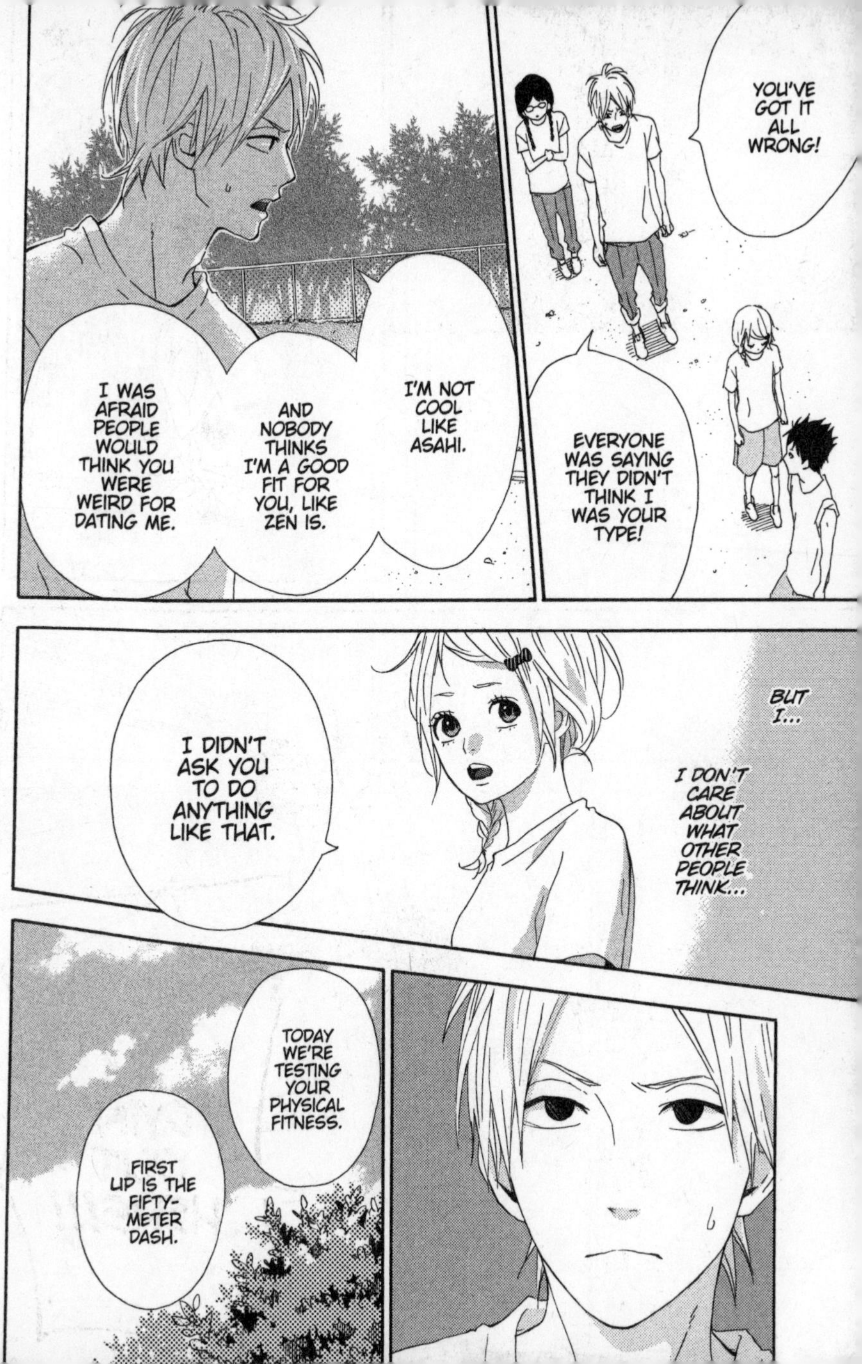
YOU'VE GOT IT ALL WRONG!
EVERYONE WAS SAYING THEY DIDN'T THINK I WAS YOUR TYPE!
I'M NOT COOL LIKE ASAHI.
AND NOBODY THINKS I'M A GOOD FIT FOR YOU, LIKE ZEN IS.
I WAS AFRAID PEOPLE WOULD THINK YOU WERE WEIRD FOR DATING ME.
BUT I...
I DON'T CARE ABOUT WHAT OTHER PEOPLE THINK...
I DIDN'T ASK YOU TO DO ANYTHING LIKE THAT.
TODAY WE'RE TESTING YOUR PHYSICAL FITNESS.
FIRST UP IS THE FIFTY-METER DASH.

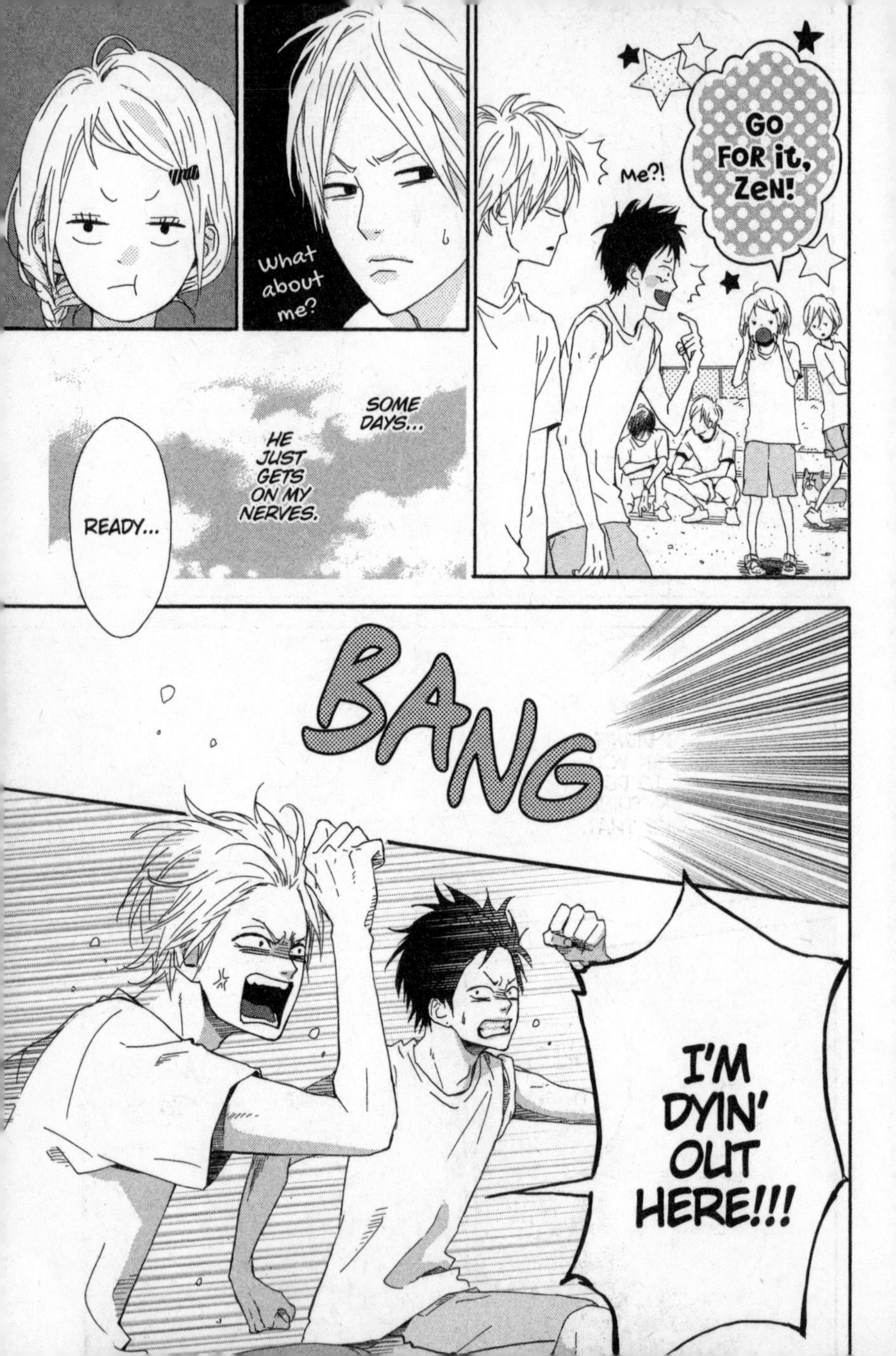
GO FOR it, ZEN!
Me?!
What about me?
SOME DAYS...
HE JUST GETS ON MY NERVES.
READY...
BANG
I'M DYIN' OUT HERE!!!

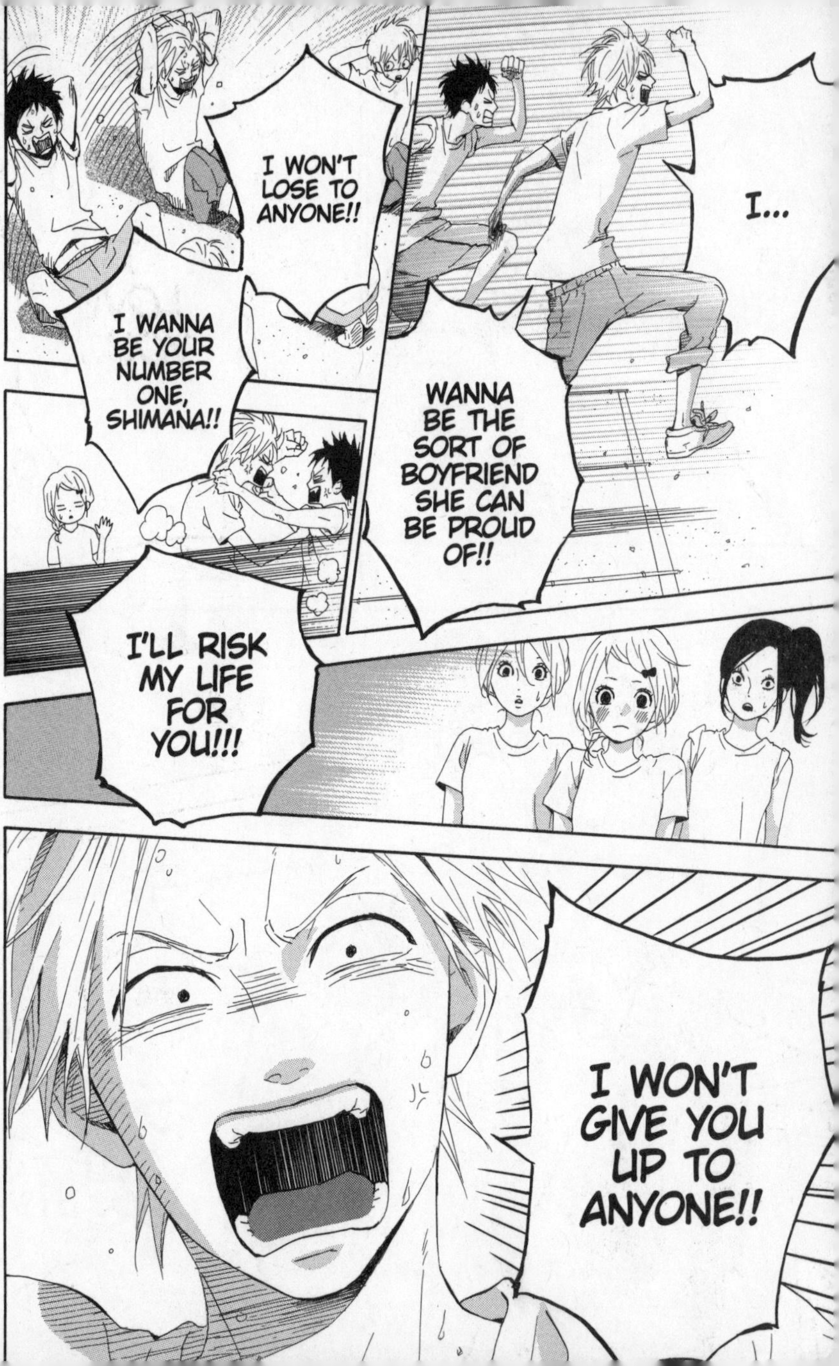
I...
WANNA BE THE SORT OF BOYFRIEND SHE CAN BE PROUD OF!!
I WON'T LOSE TO ANYONE!!
I WANNA BE YOUR NUMBER ONE, SHIMANA!!
I'LL RISK MY LIFE FOR YOU!!!
I WON'T GIVE YOU UP TO ANYONE!!

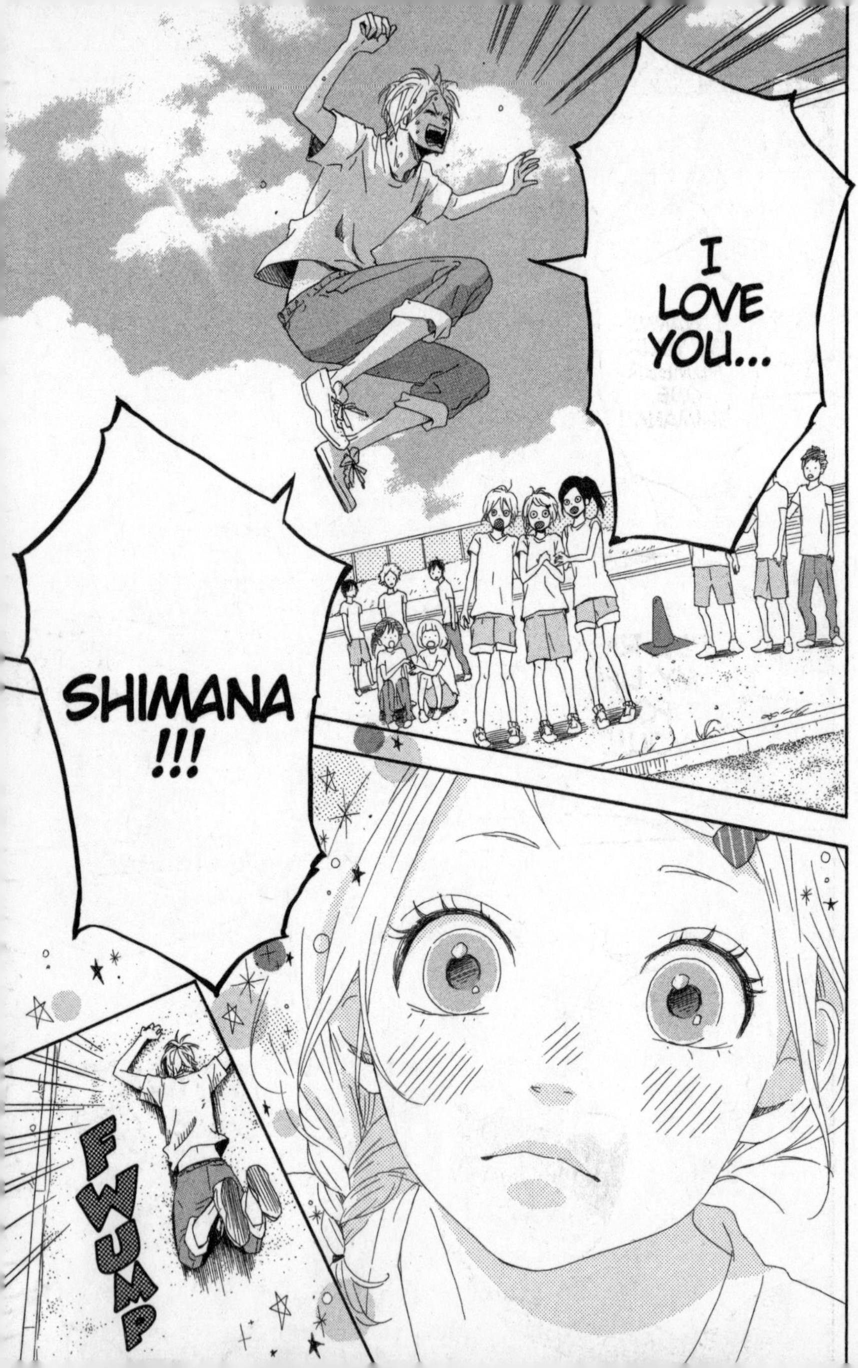
I LOVE YOU...
SHIMANA!!!
FWUMP

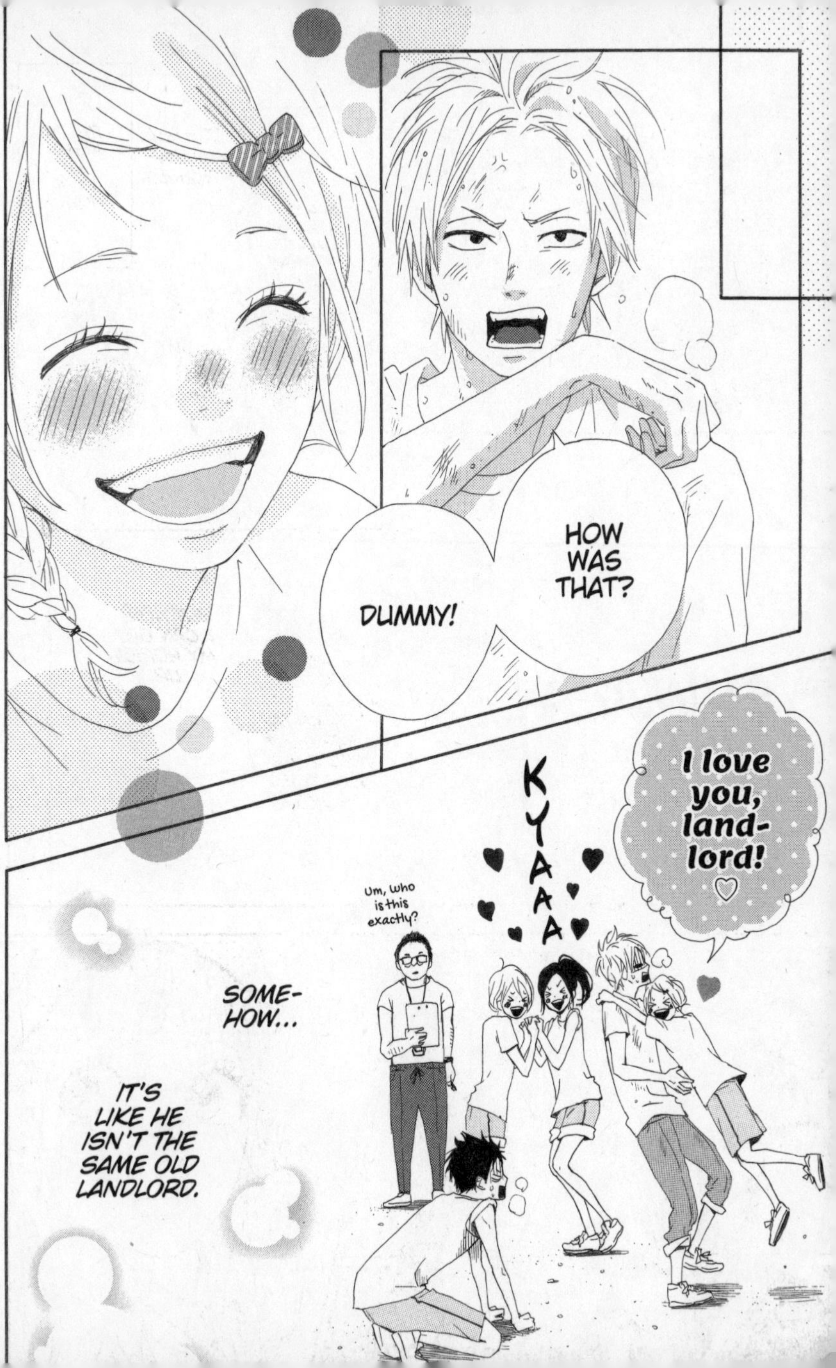
HOW WAS THAT?
DUMMY!
I love you, landlord! ♡
KYAAAA
Um, who is this exactly?
SOME-HOW...
IT'S LIKE HE ISN'T THE SAME OLD LANDLORD.

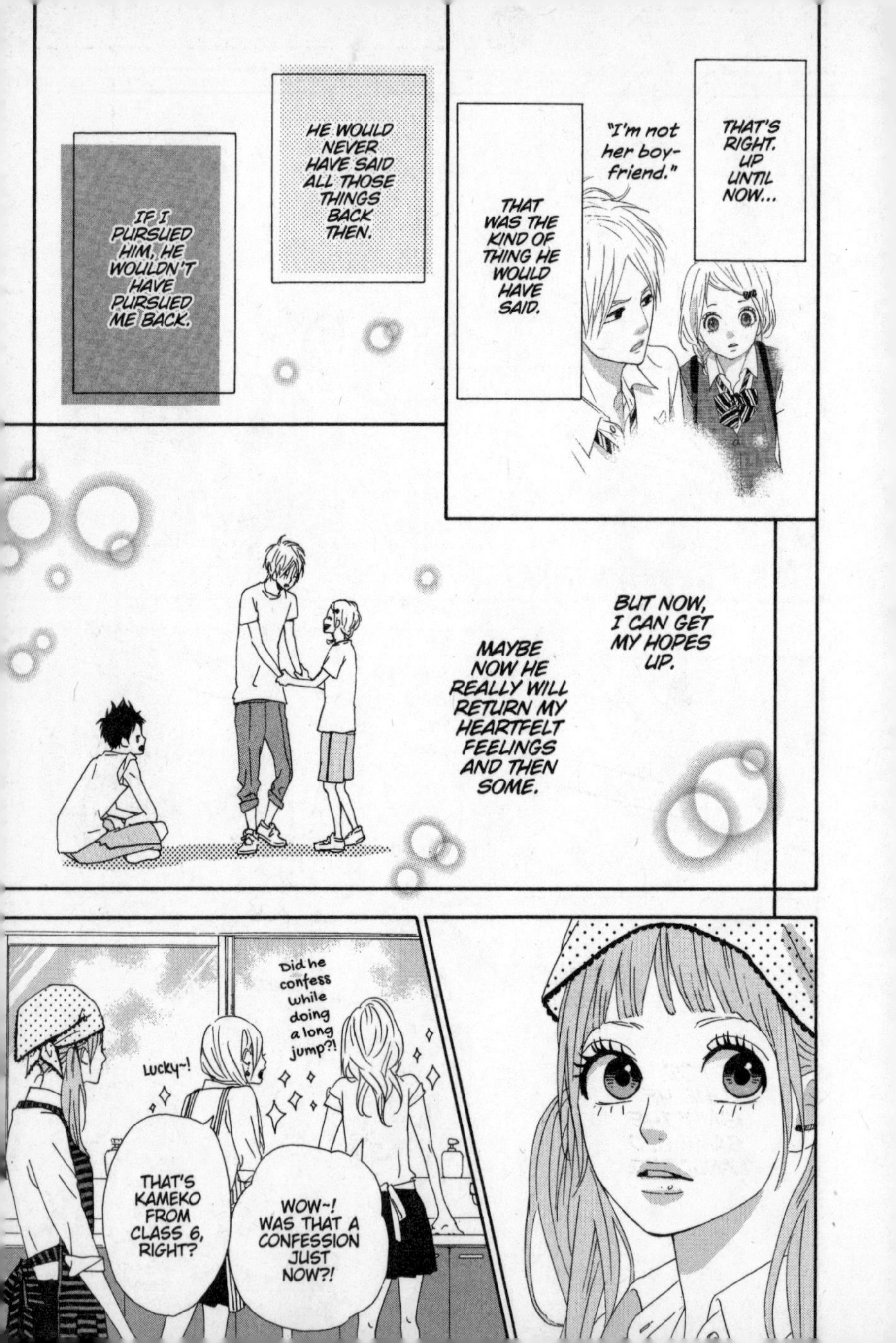
THAT'S RIGHT. UP UNTIL NOW...
"I'm not her boy-friend."
THAT WAS THE KIND OF THING HE WOULD HAVE SAID.
HE WOULD NEVER HAVE SAID ALL THOSE THINGS BACK THEN.
IF I PURSUED HIM, HE WOULDN'T HAVE PURSUED ME BACK.
BUT NOW, I CAN GET MY HOPES UP.
MAYBE NOW HE REALLY WILL RETURN MY HEARTFELT FEELINGS AND THEN SOME.
Did he confess while doing a long jump?!
Lucky~!
WOW~! WAS THAT A CONFESSION JUST NOW?!
THAT'S KAMEKO FROM CLASS 6, RIGHT?

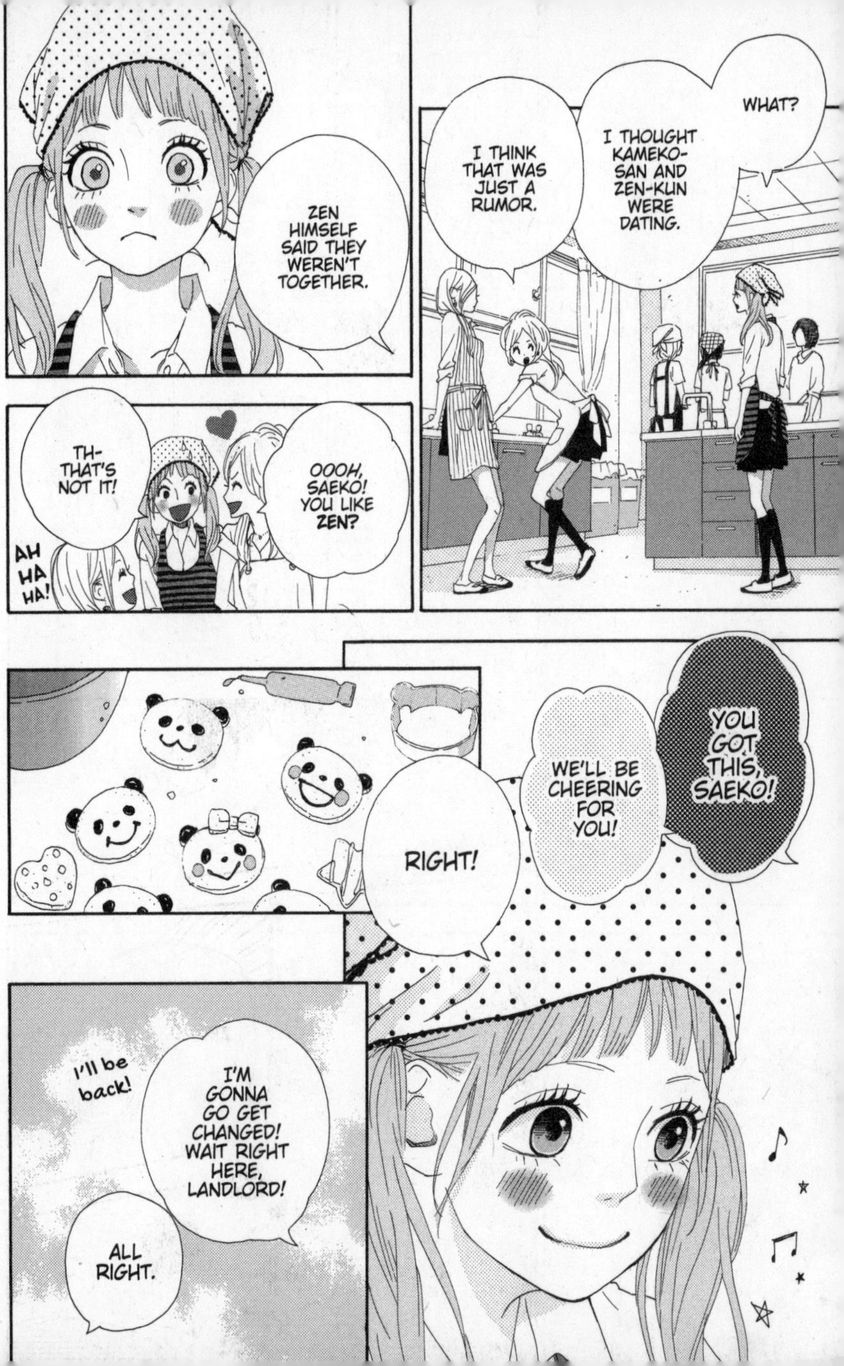
WHAT?
I THOUGHT KAMEKO-SAN AND ZEN-KUN WERE DATING.
I THINK THAT WAS JUST A RUMOR.
ZEN HIMSELF SAID THEY WEREN'T TOGETHER.
OOOH, SAEKO! YOU LIKE ZEN?
TH-THAT'S NOT IT!
AH HA HA!
YOU GOT THIS, SAEKO!
WE'LL BE CHEERING FOR YOU!
RIGHT!
I'M GONNA GO GET CHANGED! WAIT RIGHT HERE, LANDLORD!
I'll be back!
ALL RIGHT.

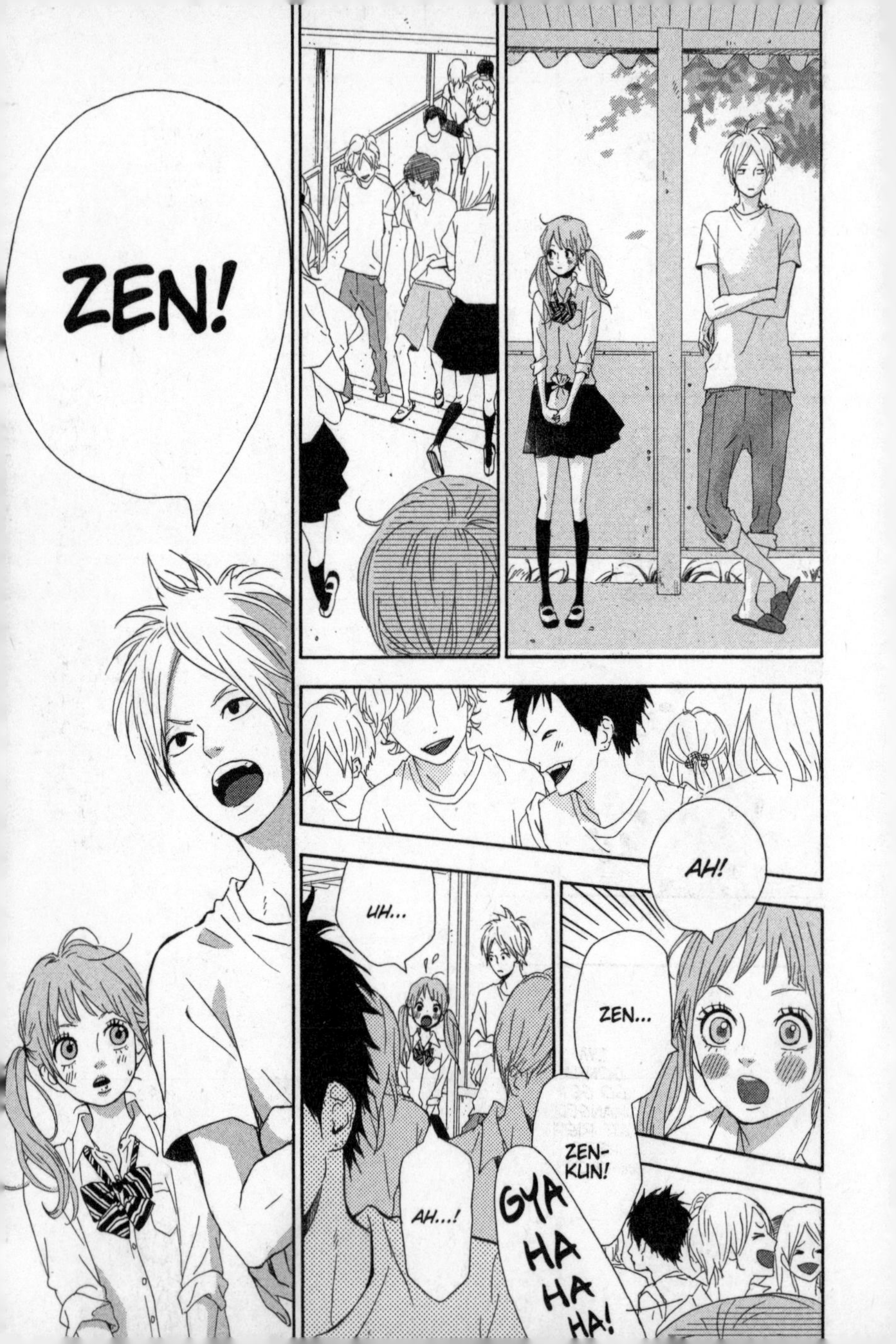
AH!
ZEN...
ZEN-KUN!
GYA HA HA HA!
UH...
AH...!
ZEN!

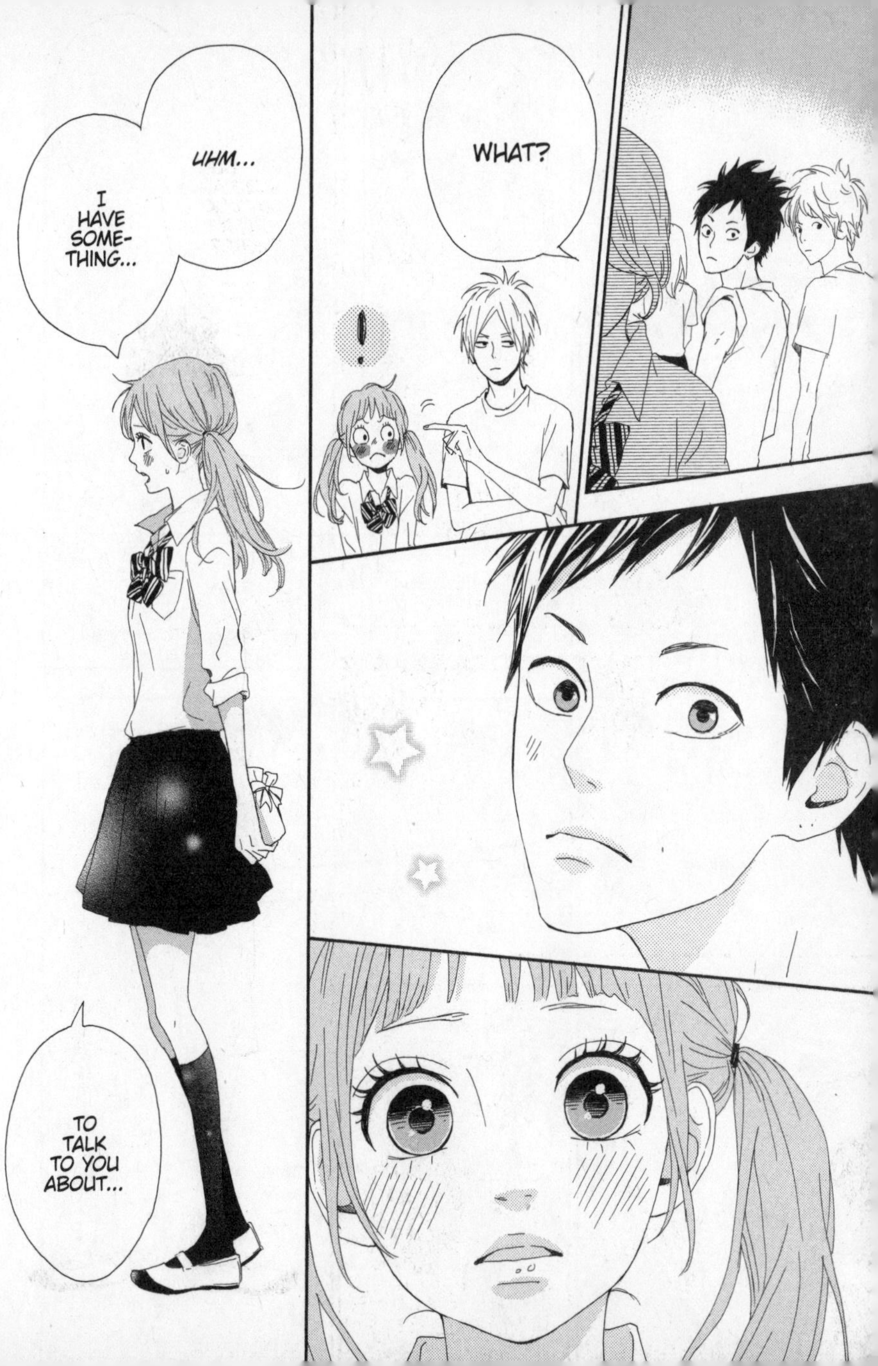
WHAT?
!
UHM...
I HAVE SOMETHING...
TO TALK TO YOU ABOUT...

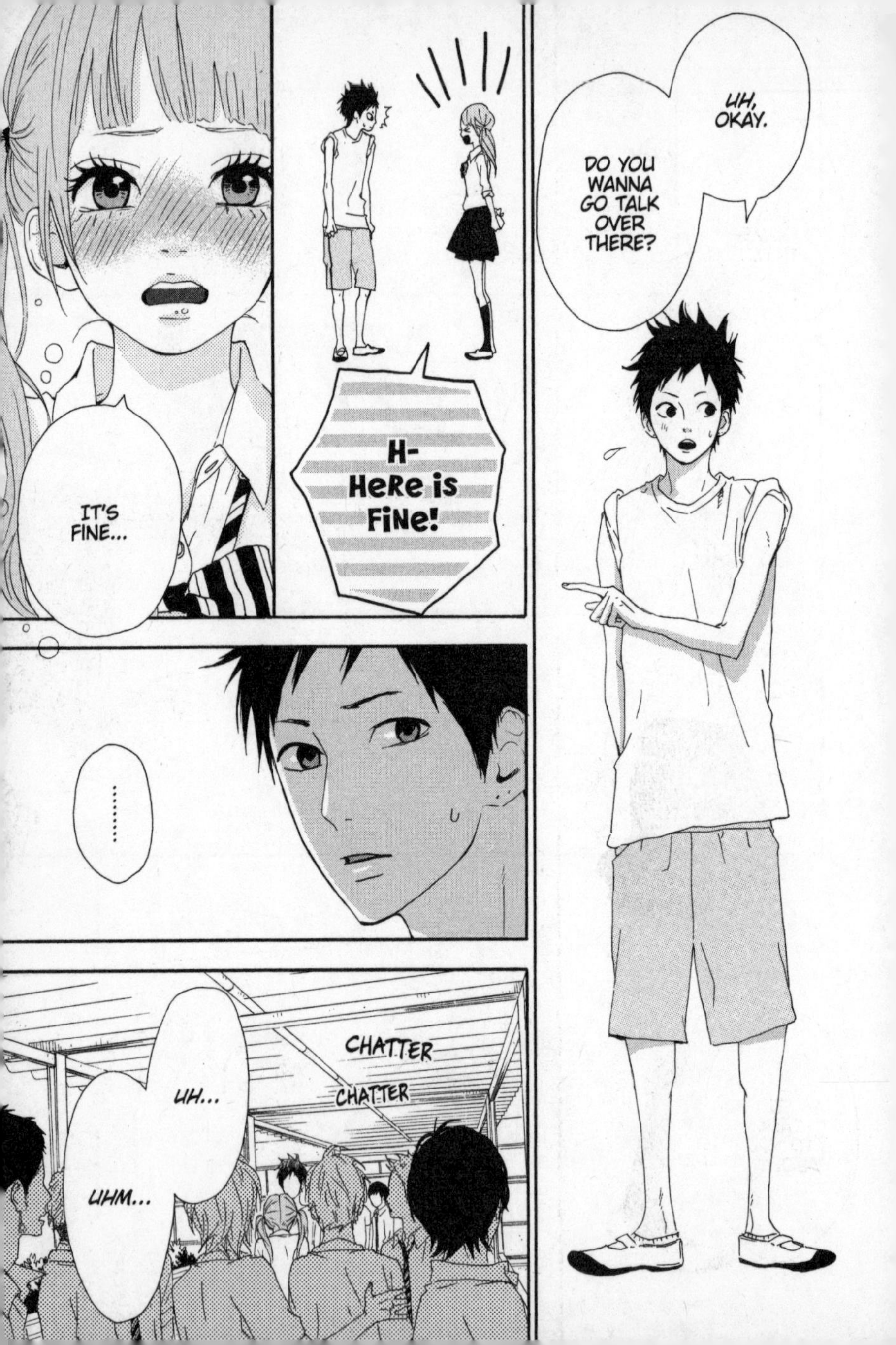
UH, OKAY.
DO YOU WANNA GO TALK OVER THERE?
H- HERE IS FINE!
IT'S FINE...
......
CHATTER
CHATTER
UH...
UHM...

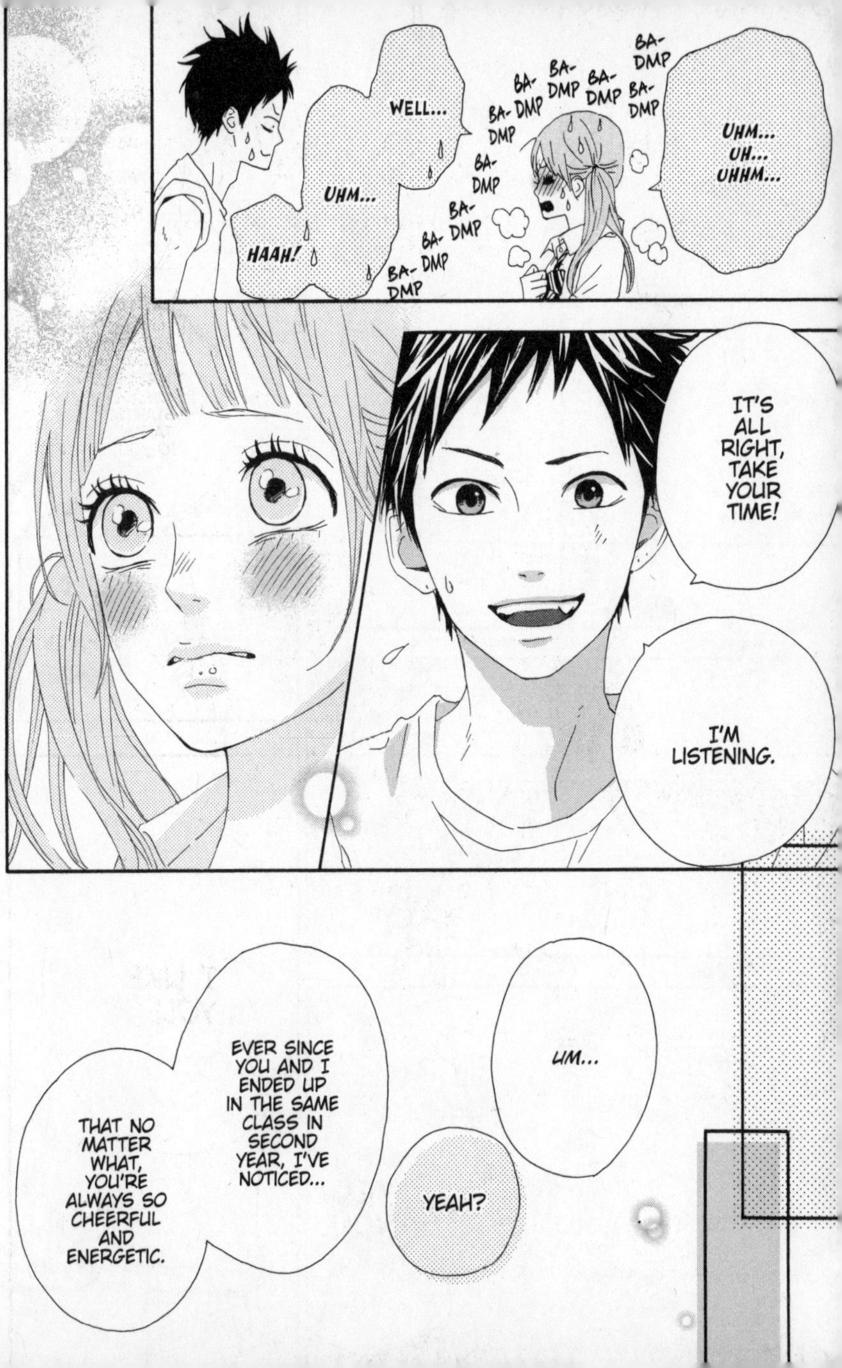
UHM... UH... UHHM...
BA-DMP BA-DMP BA-DMP BA-DMP BA-DMP BA-DMP BA-DMP BA-DMP BA-DMP BA-DMP
WELL...
UHM...
HAAH!
IT'S ALL RIGHT, TAKE YOUR TIME!
I'M LISTENING.
UM...
YEAH?
EVER SINCE YOU AND I ENDED UP IN THE SAME CLASS IN SECOND YEAR, I'VE NOTICED...
THAT NO MATTER WHAT, YOU'RE ALWAYS SO CHEERFUL AND ENERGETIC.

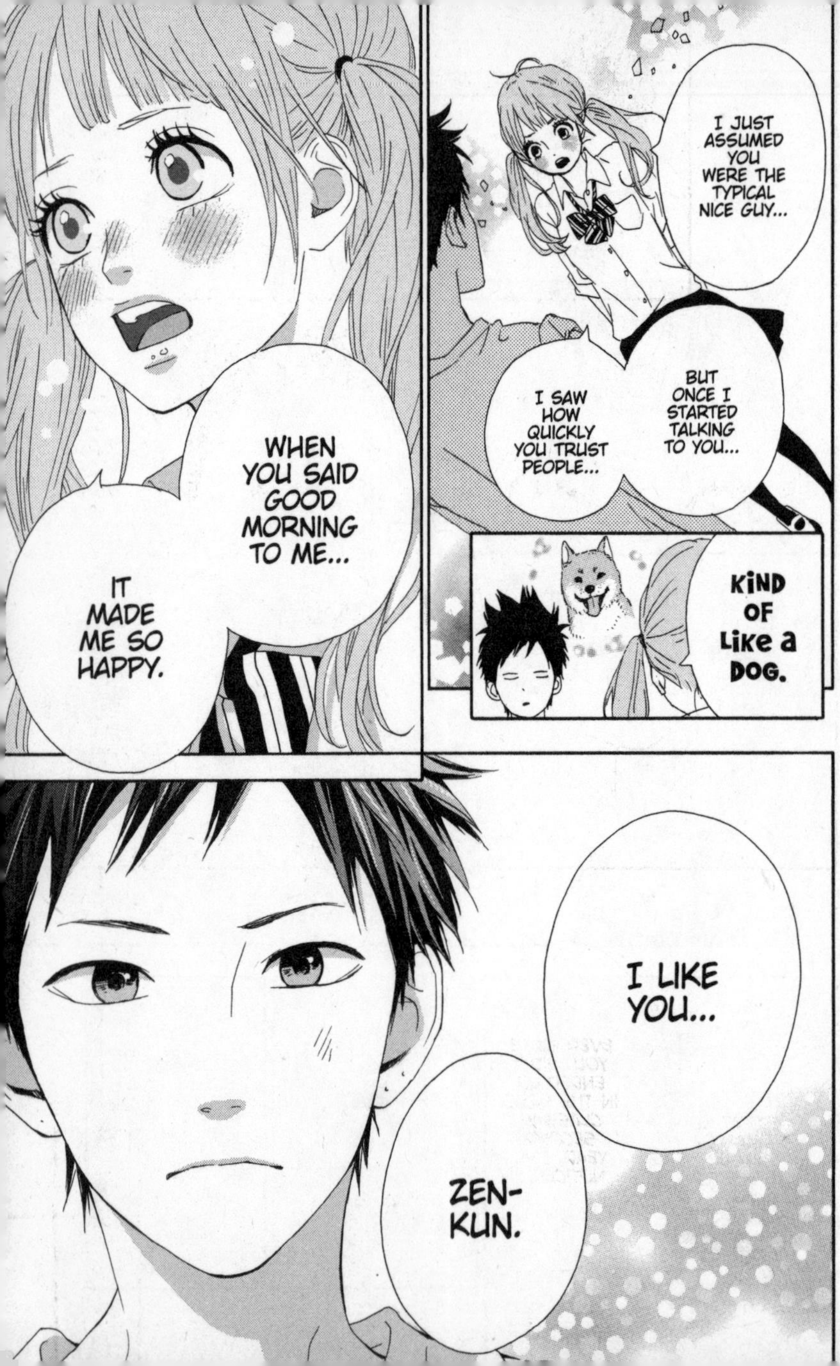
I JUST ASSUMED YOU WERE THE TYPICAL NICE GUY...
BUT ONCE I STARTED TALKING TO YOU...
I SAW HOW QUICKLY YOU TRUST PEOPLE...
KIND OF LIKE A DOG.
WHEN YOU SAID GOOD MORNING TO ME...
IT MADE ME SO HAPPY.
I LIKE YOU...
ZEN-KUN.

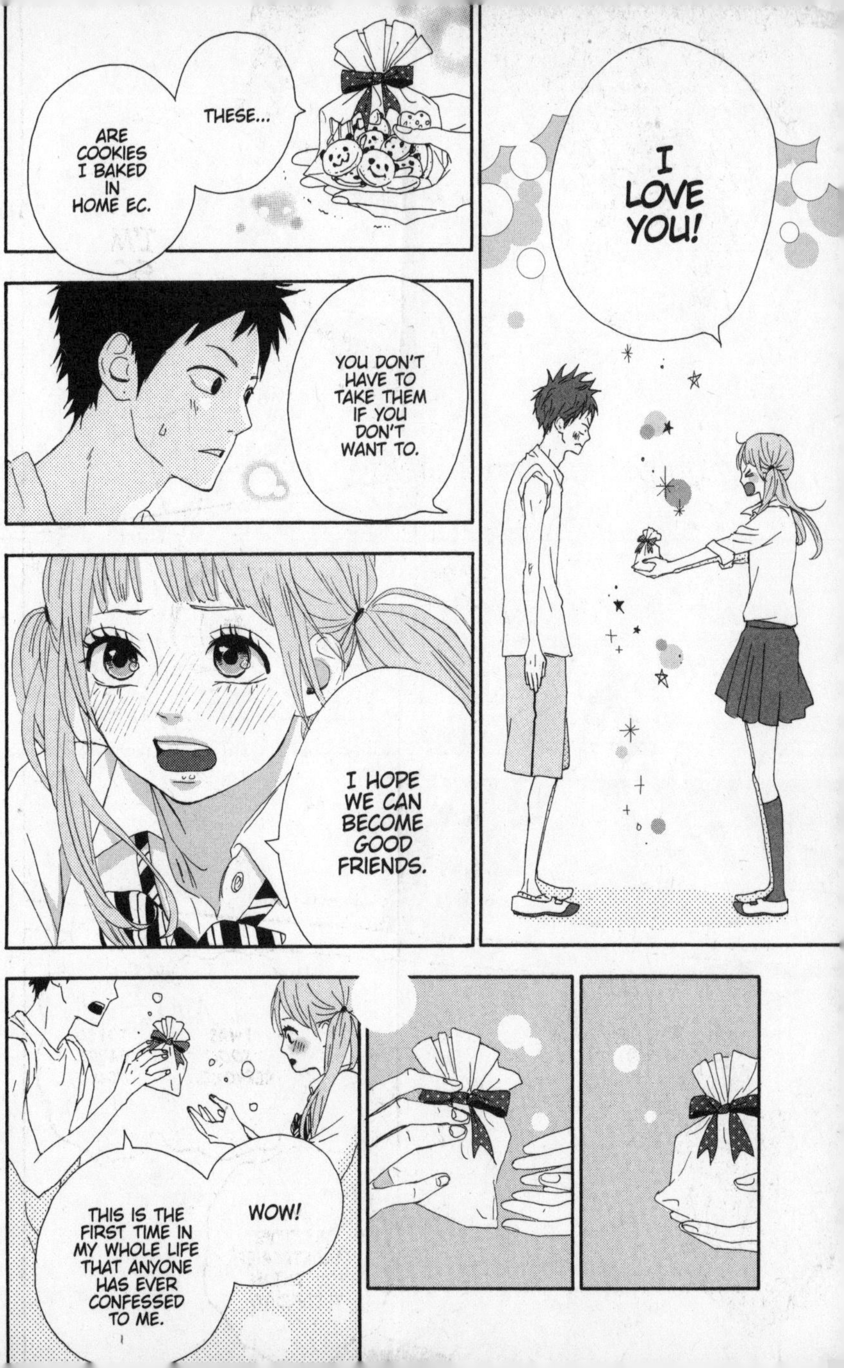
I LOVE YOU!
THESE...
ARE COOKIES I BAKED IN HOME EC.
YOU DON'T HAVE TO TAKE THEM IF YOU DON'T WANT TO.
I HOPE WE CAN BECOME GOOD FRIENDS.
WOW!
THIS IS THE FIRST TIME IN MY WHOLE LIFE THAT ANYONE HAS EVER CONFESSED TO ME.

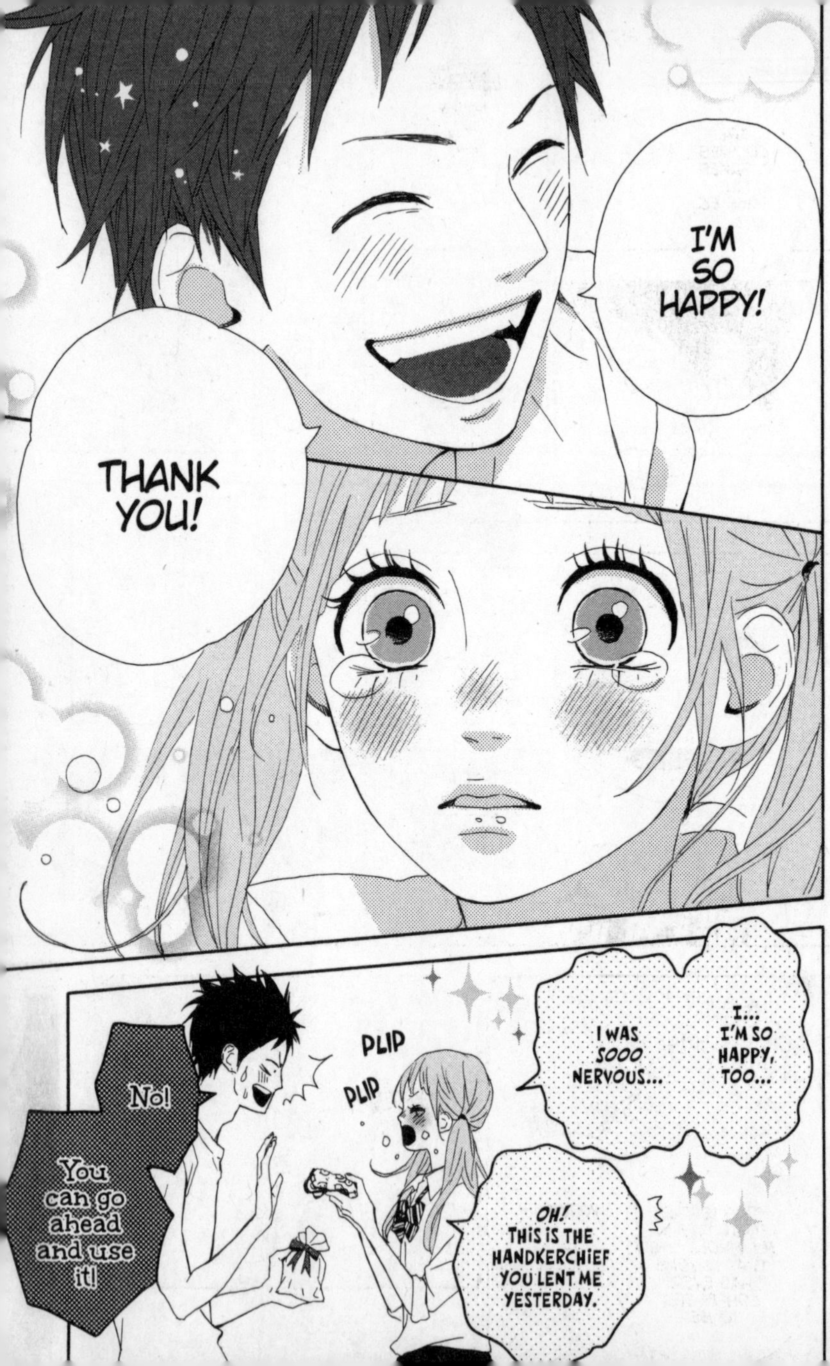
I'M SO HAPPY!
THANK YOU!
I... I'M SO HAPPY, TOO...
I WAS SOOO NERVOUS...
PLIP
PLIP
OH! THIS IS THE HANDKERCHIEF YOU LENT ME YESTERDAY.
No!
You can go ahead and use it!

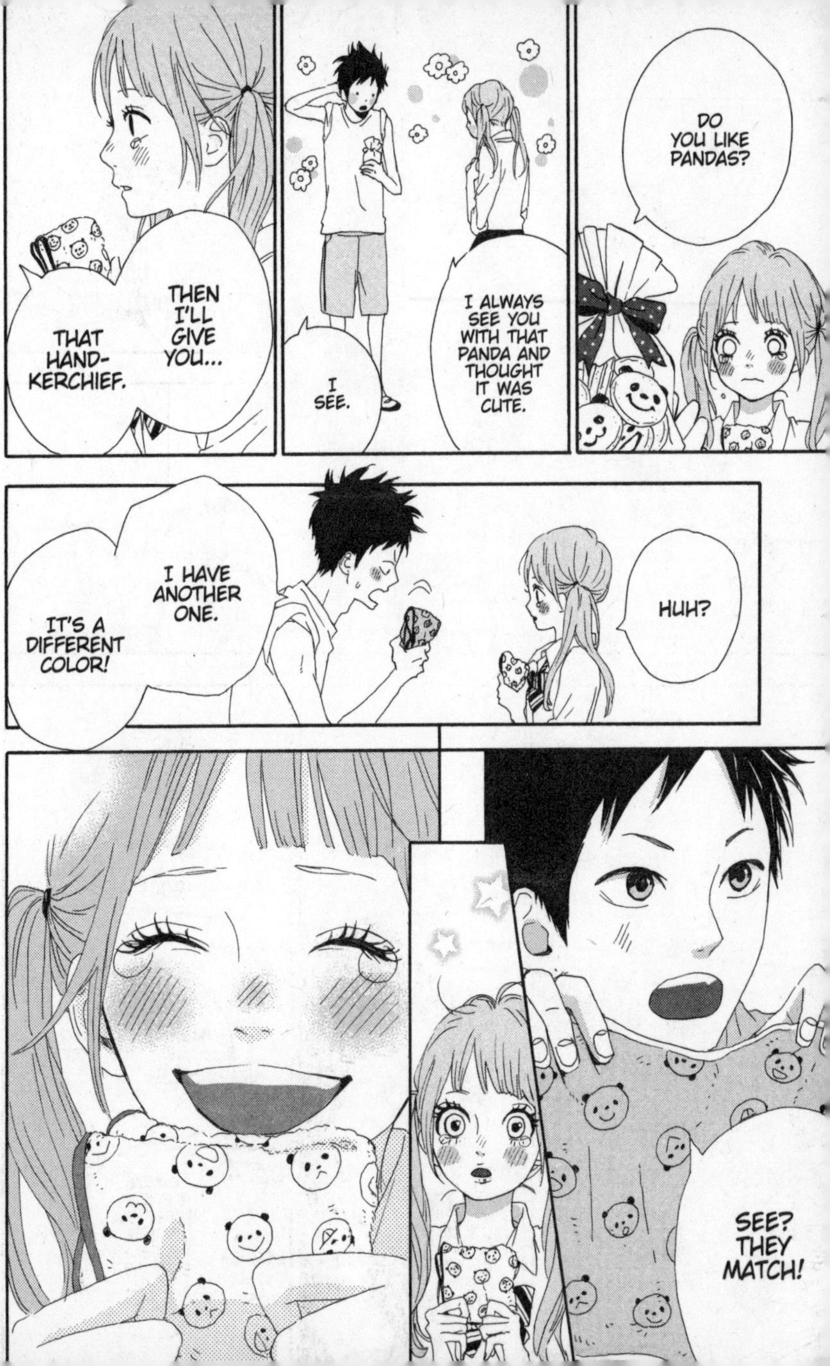
DO YOU LIKE PANDAS?
I ALWAYS SEE YOU WITH THAT PANDA AND THOUGHT IT WAS CUTE.
I SEE.
THEN I'LL GIVE YOU...
THAT HAND-KERCHIEF.
HUH?
I HAVE ANOTHER ONE.
IT'S A DIFFERENT COLOR!
SEE? THEY MATCH!

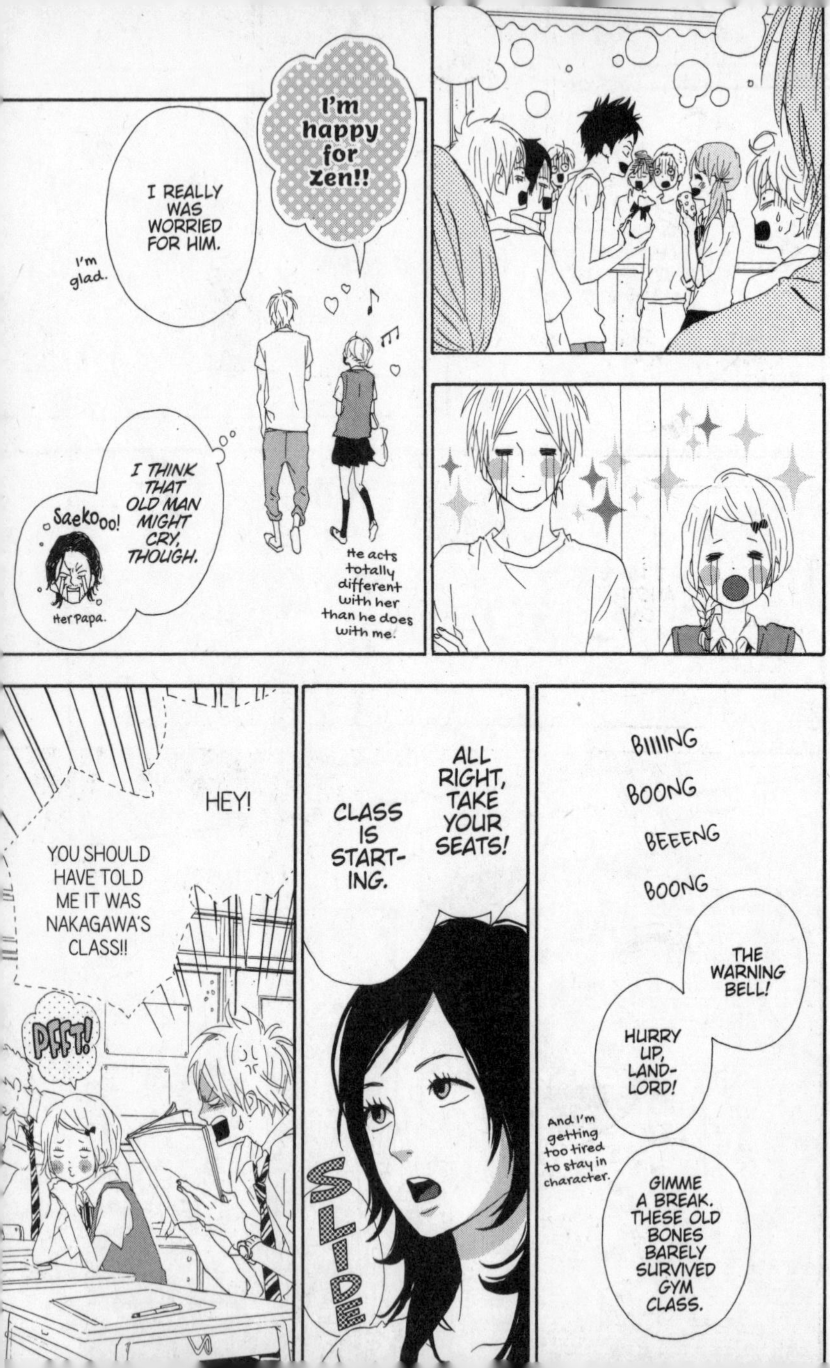
I'm happy for zen!!
I REALLY WAS WORRIED FOR HIM.
I'm glad.
He acts totally different with her than he does with me.
I THINK THAT OLD MAN MIGHT CRY, THOUGH.
Saekooo!
Her Papa.
BIIIING
BOONG
BEEENG
BOONG
THE WARNING BELL!
HURRY UP, LANDLORD!
And I'm getting too tired to stay in character.
GIMME A BREAK. THESE OLD BONES BARELY SURVIVED GYM CLASS.
ALL RIGHT, TAKE YOUR SEATS!
CLASS IS STARTING.
SLIDE
HEY!
YOU SHOULD HAVE TOLD ME IT WAS NAKAGAWA'S CLASS!!
PFFT!

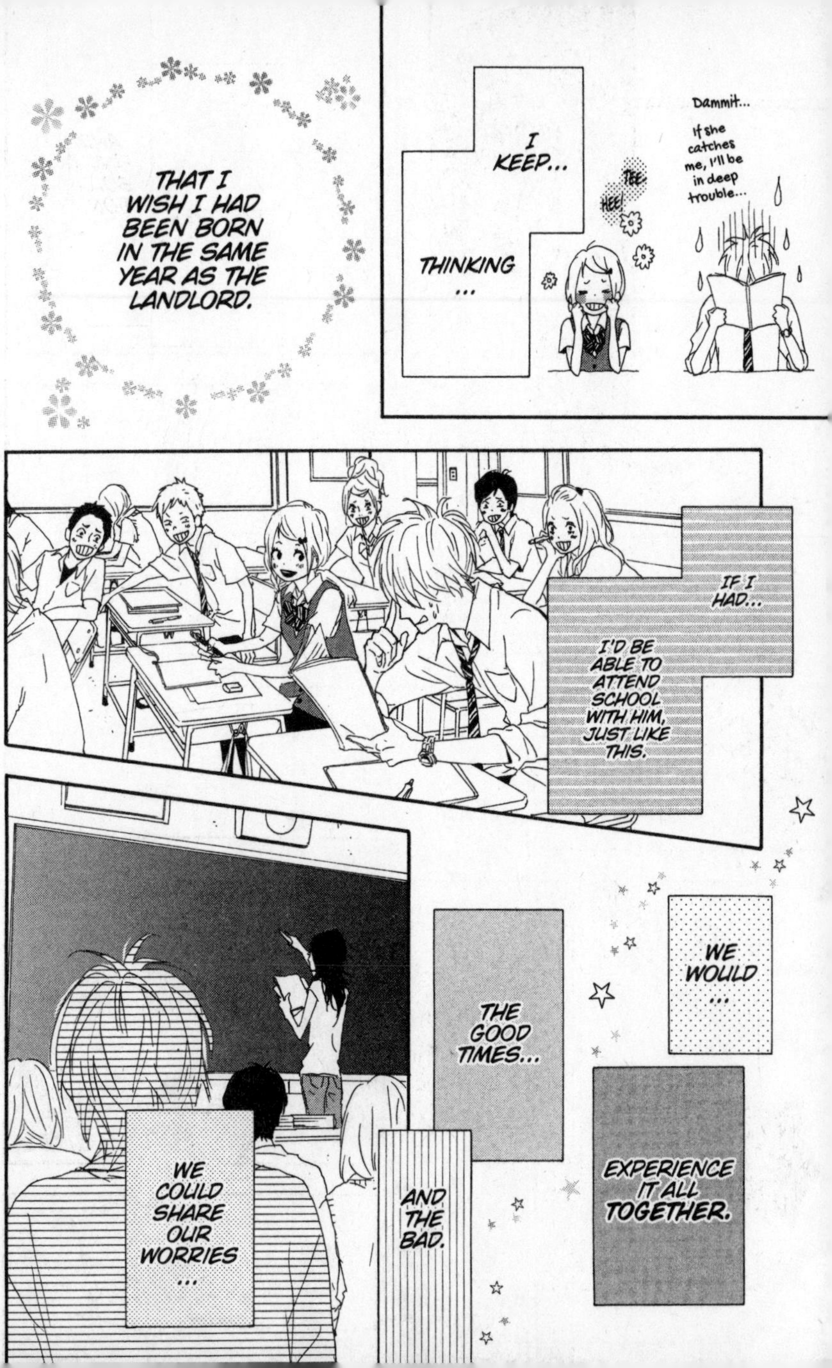
I KEEP...
THINKING...
TEE HEE!
Dammit... If she catches me, I'll be in deep trouble...
THAT I WISH I HAD BEEN BORN IN THE SAME YEAR AS THE LANDLORD.
IF I HAD...
I'D BE ABLE TO ATTEND SCHOOL WITH HIM, JUST LIKE THIS.
WE WOULD...
EXPERIENCE IT ALL TOGETHER.
THE GOOD TIMES...
AND THE BAD.
WE COULD SHARE OUR WORRIES...

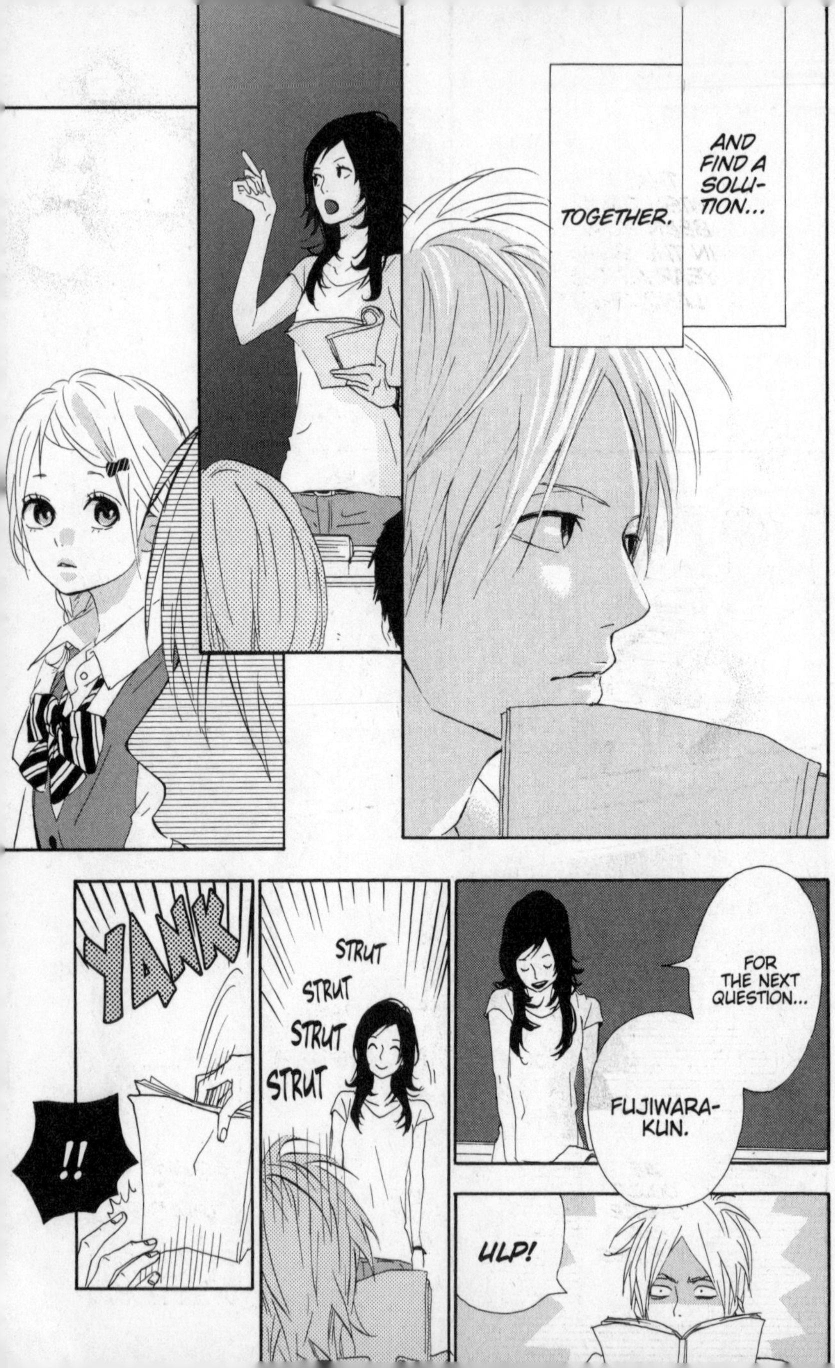
AND FIND A SOLU-TION...
TOGETHER.
FOR THE NEXT QUESTION...
FUJIWARA-KUN.
ULP!
STRUT
STRUT
STRUT
STRUT
YANK
!!

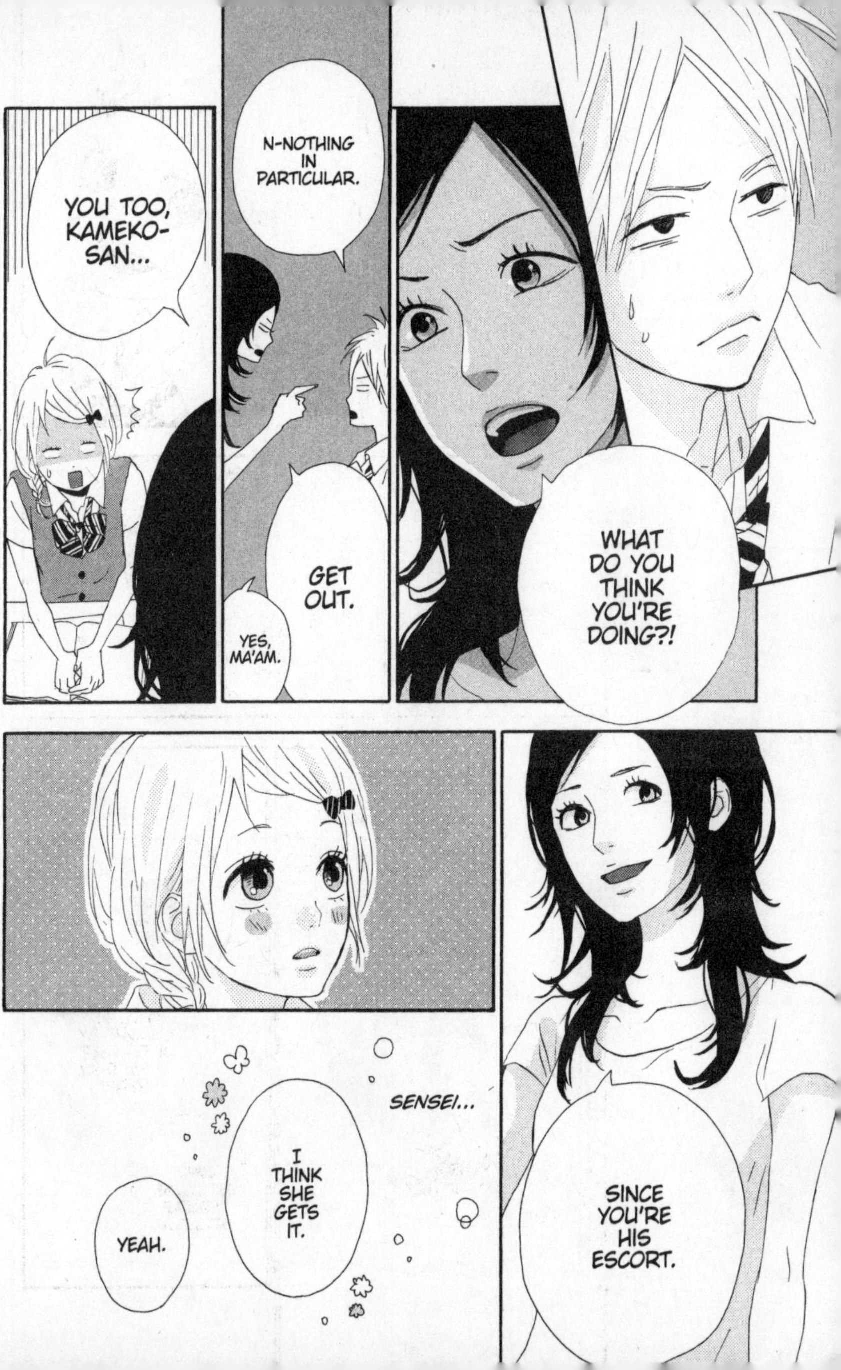
WHAT DO YOU THINK YOU'RE DOING?!
N-NOTHING IN PARTICULAR.
GET OUT.
YES, MA'AM.
YOU TOO, KAMEKO-SAN...
SINCE YOU'RE HIS ESCORT.
SENSEI...
I THINK SHE GETS IT.
YEAH.

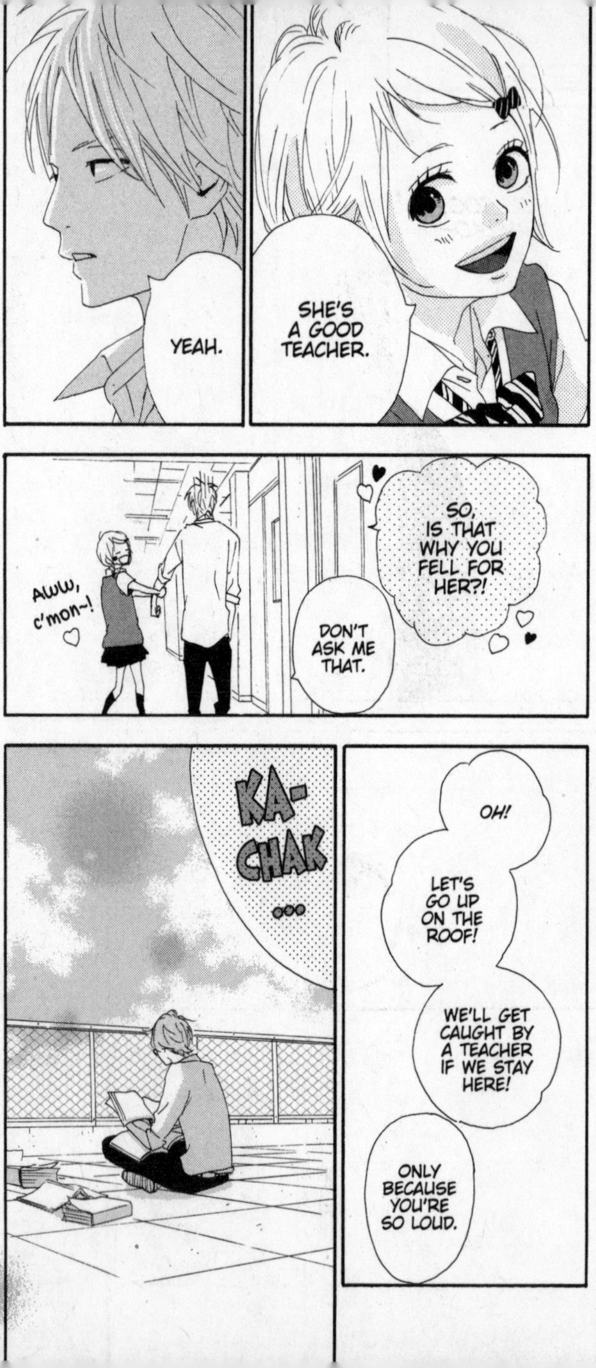
SHE'S A GOOD TEACHER.
YEAH.
SO, IS THAT WHY YOU FELL FOR HER?!
DON'T ASK ME THAT.
AWW, C'MON~!
OH!
LET'S GO UP ON THE ROOF!
WE'LL GET CAUGHT BY A TEACHER IF WE STAY HERE!
ONLY BECAUSE YOU'RE SO LOUD.
KA-CHAK...

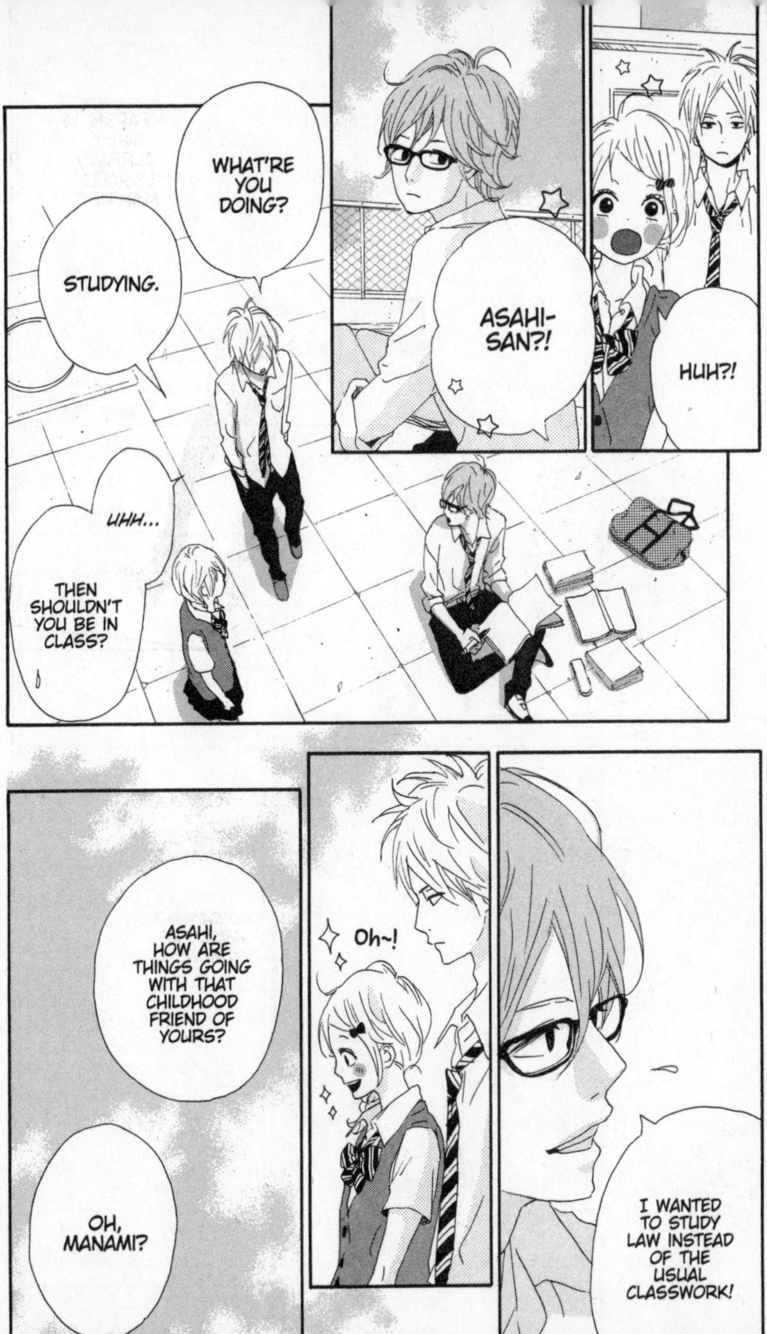
HUH?!
ASAHI-SAN?!
WHAT'RE YOU DOING?
STUDYING.
UHH...
THEN SHOULDN'T YOU BE IN CLASS?
I WANTED TO STUDY LAW INSTEAD OF THE USUAL CLASSWORK!
Oh~!
ASAHI, HOW ARE THINGS GOING WITH THAT CHILDHOOD FRIEND OF YOURS?
OH, MANAMI?

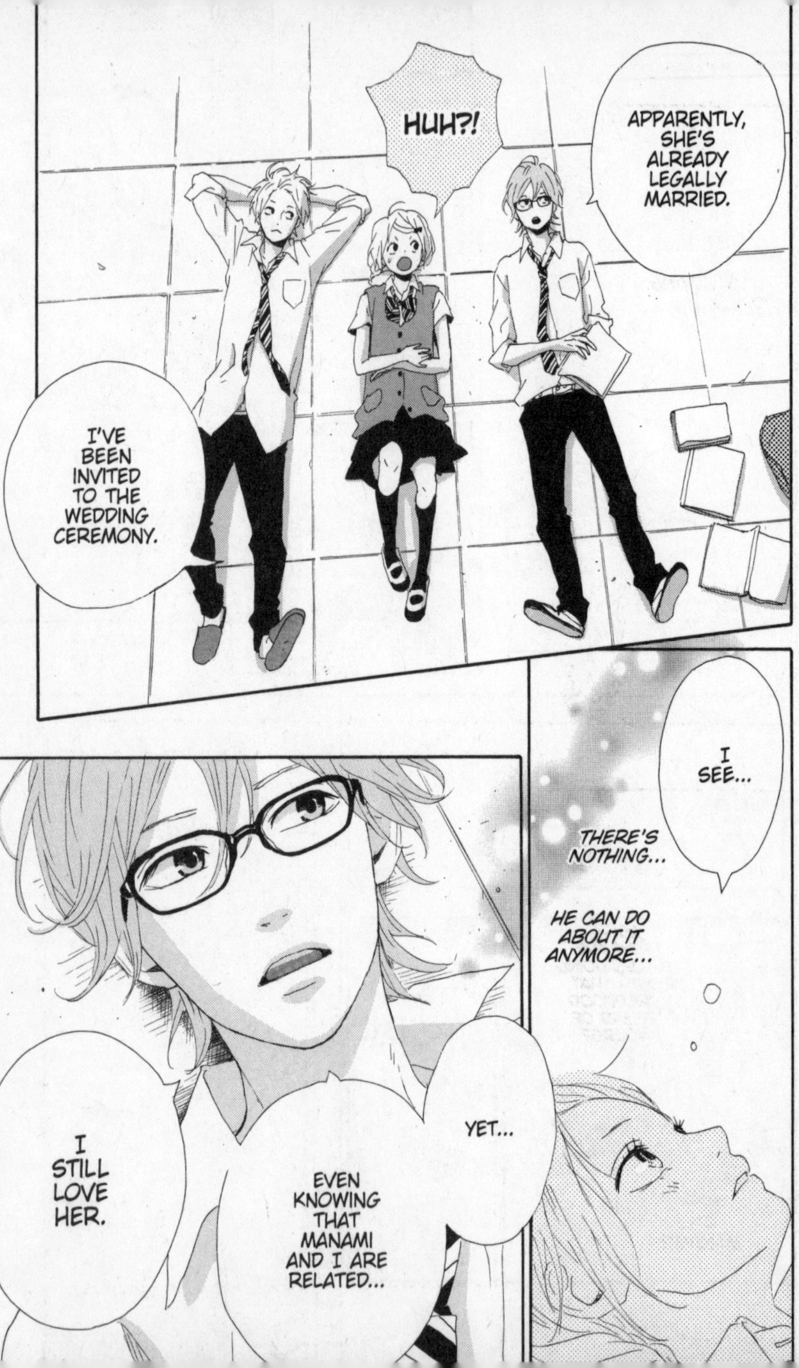
APPARENTLY, SHE'S ALREADY LEGALLY MARRIED.
HUH?!
I'VE BEEN INVITED TO THE WEDDING CEREMONY.
I SEE...
THERE'S NOTHING...
HE CAN DO ABOUT IT ANYMORE...
YET...
EVEN KNOWING THAT MANAMI AND I ARE RELATED...
I STILL LOVE HER.

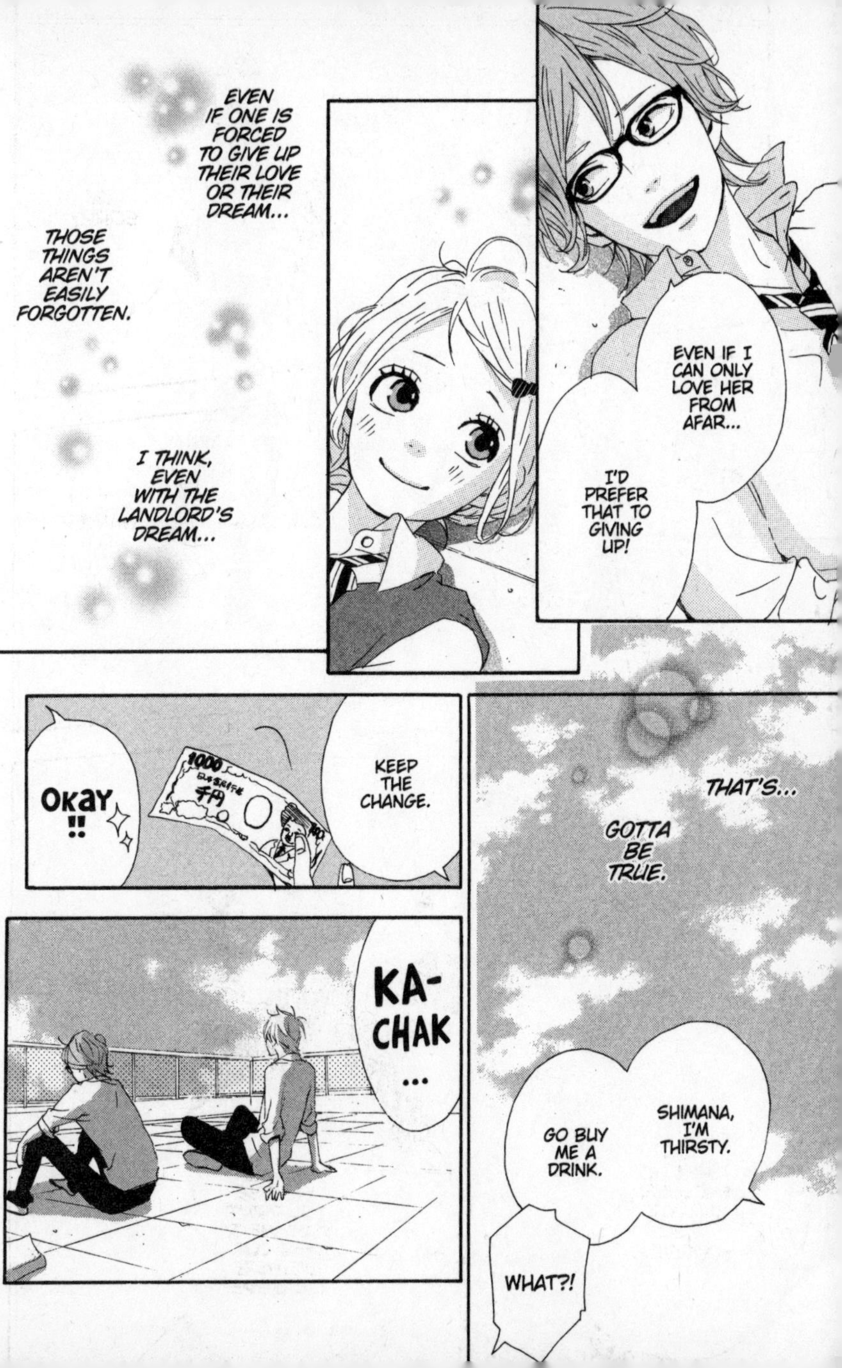
EVEN IF I CAN ONLY LOVE HER FROM AFAR...
I'D PREFER THAT TO GIVING UP!
EVEN IF ONE IS FORCED TO GIVE UP THEIR LOVE OR THEIR DREAM...
THOSE THINGS AREN'T EASILY FORGOTTEN.
I THINK, EVEN WITH THE LANDLORD'S DREAM...
THAT'S...
GOTTA BE TRUE.
SHIMANA, I'M THIRSTY.
GO BUY ME A DRINK.
WHAT?!
KEEP THE CHANGE.
OKAY!!
KA-CHAK...

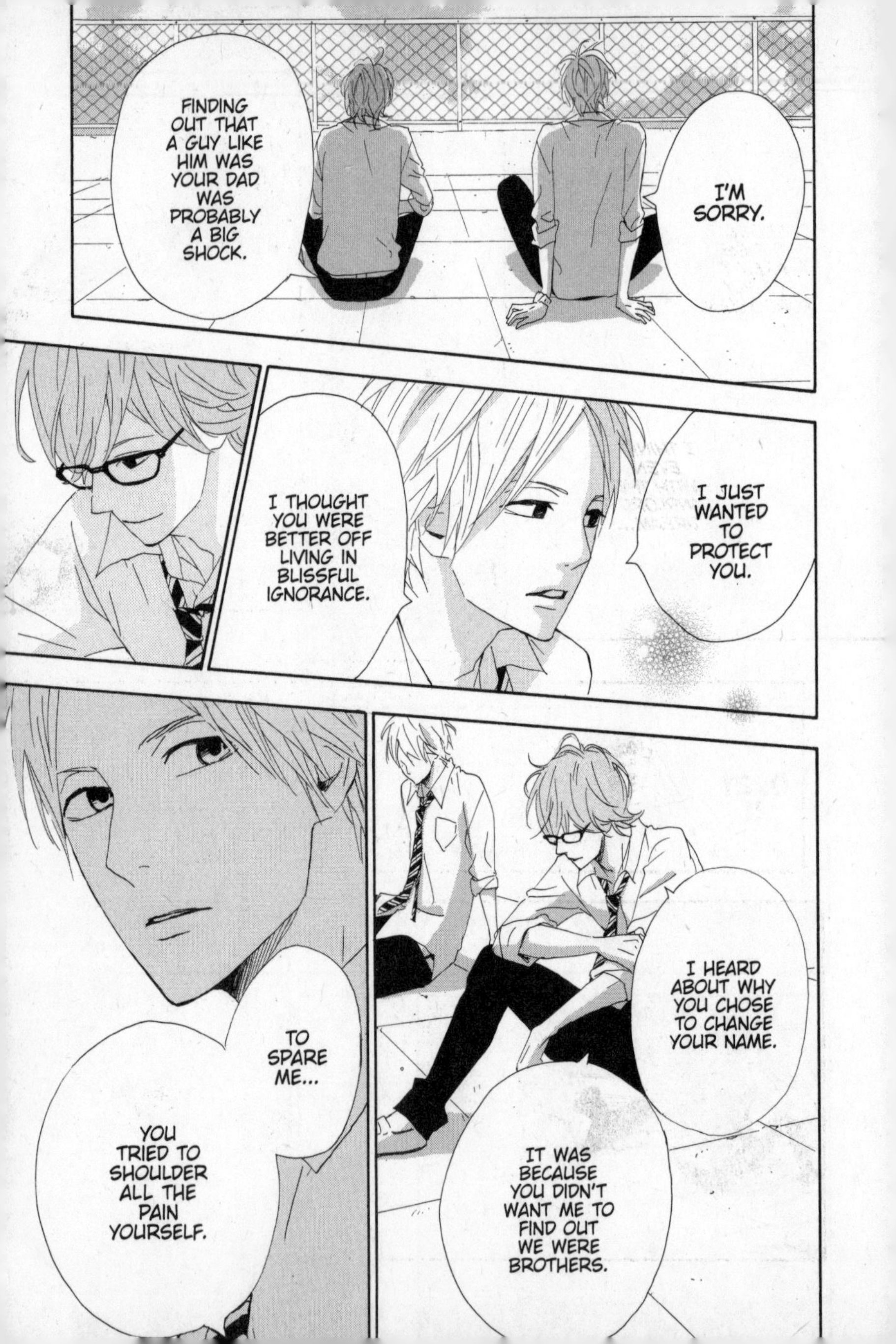
I'M SORRY.
FINDING OUT THAT A GUY LIKE HIM WAS YOUR DAD WAS PROBABLY A BIG SHOCK.
I JUST WANTED TO PROTECT YOU.
I THOUGHT YOU WERE BETTER OFF LIVING IN BLISSFUL IGNORANCE.
I HEARD ABOUT WHY YOU CHOSE TO CHANGE YOUR NAME.
IT WAS BECAUSE YOU DIDN'T WANT ME TO FIND OUT WE WERE BROTHERS.
TO SPARE ME...
YOU TRIED TO SHOULDER ALL THE PAIN YOURSELF.

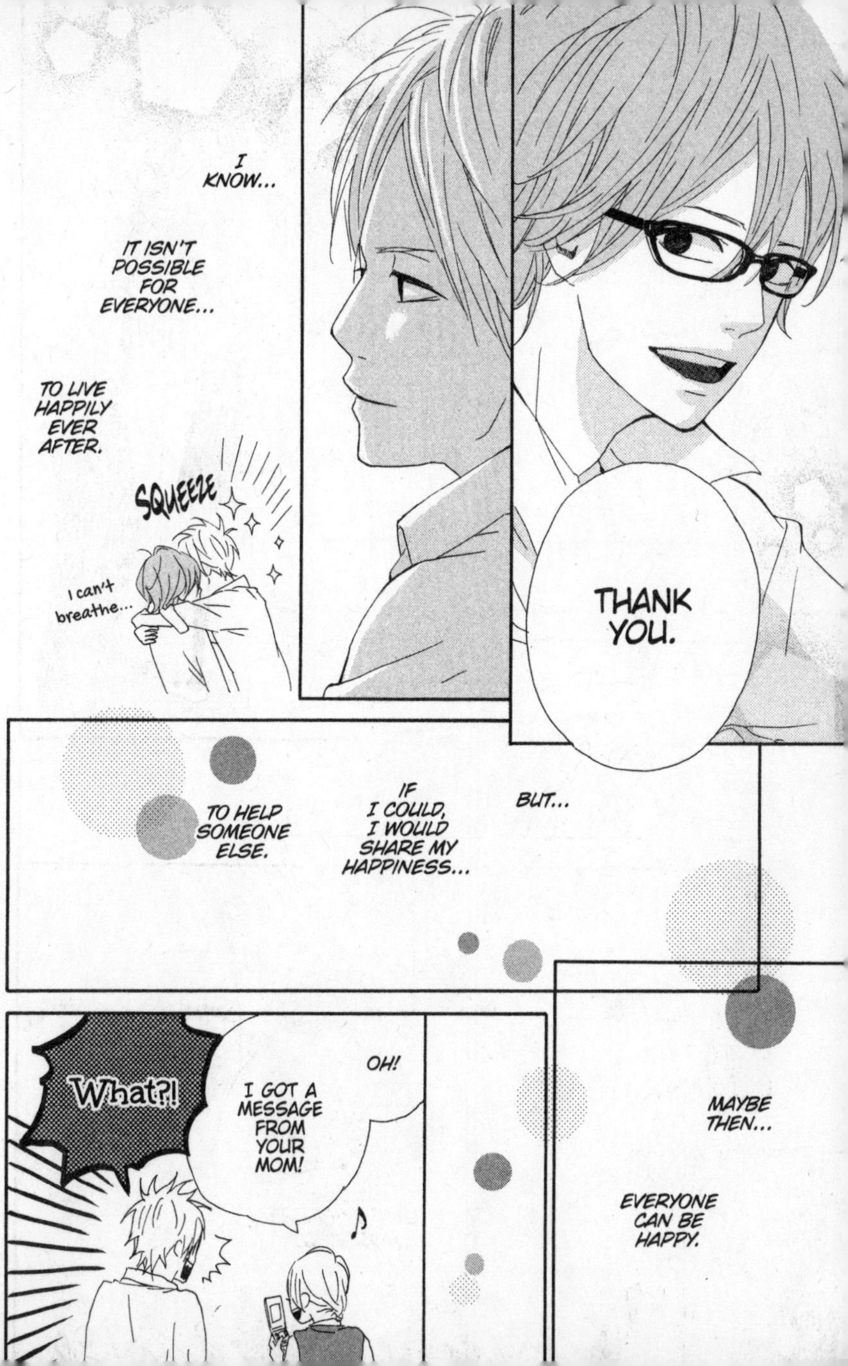
THANK YOU.
I KNOW...
IT ISN'T POSSIBLE FOR EVERYONE...
TO LIVE HAPPILY EVER AFTER.
SQUEEZE
I can't breathe...
BUT...
IF I COULD, I WOULD SHARE MY HAPPINESS...
TO HELP SOMEONE ELSE.
MAYBE THEN...
EVERYONE CAN BE HAPPY.
OH!
I GOT A MESSAGE FROM YOUR MOM!
What?!

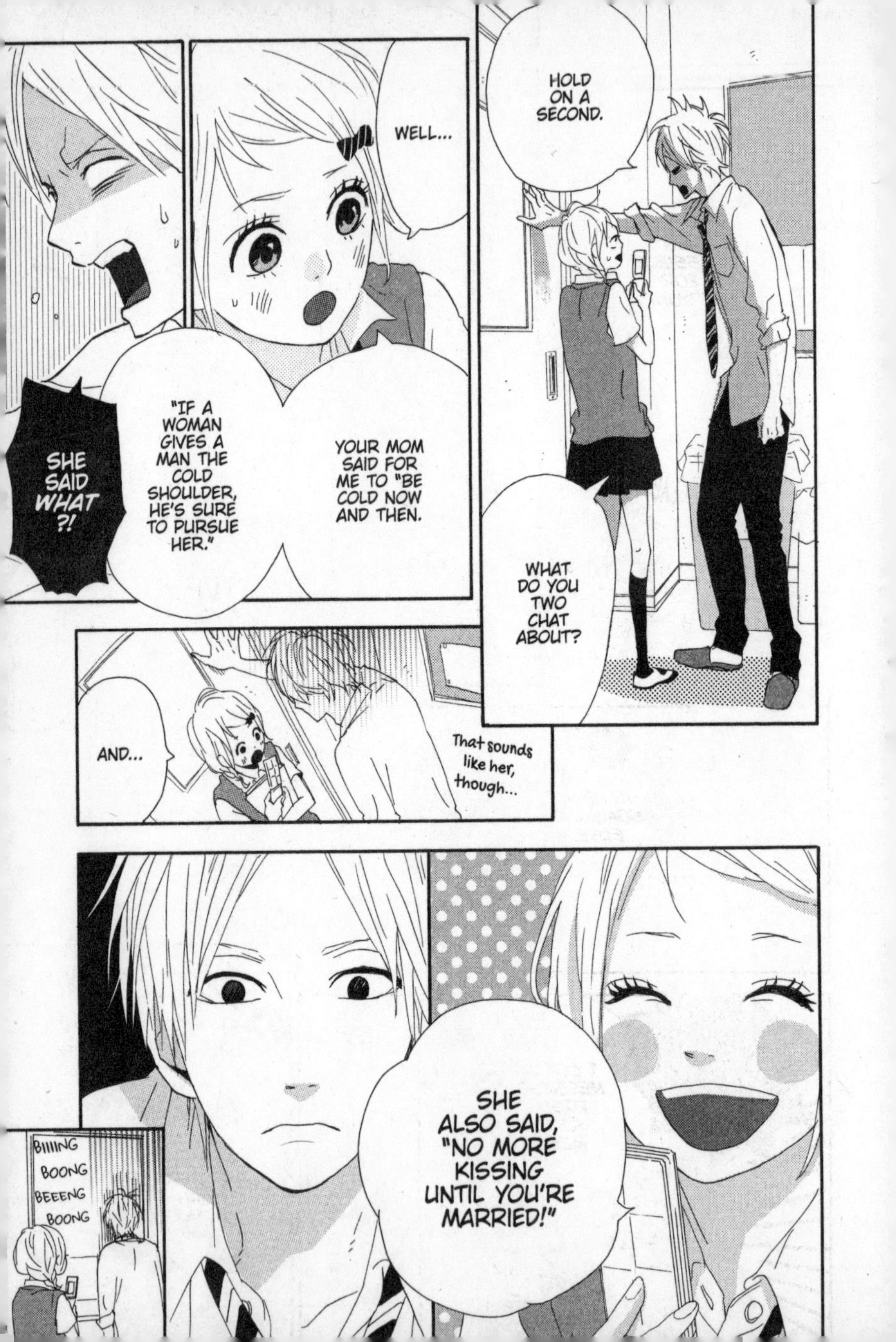
HOLD ON A SECOND.
WHAT DO YOU TWO CHAT ABOUT?
WELL...
YOUR MOM SAID FOR ME TO "BE COLD NOW AND THEN.
"IF A WOMAN GIVES A MAN THE COLD SHOULDER, HE'S SURE TO PURSUE HER."
SHE SAID *WHAT* ?!
That sounds like her, though...
AND...
SHE ALSO SAID, "NO MORE KISSING UNTIL YOU'RE MARRIED!"
BIIING
BOONG
BEEENG
BOONG

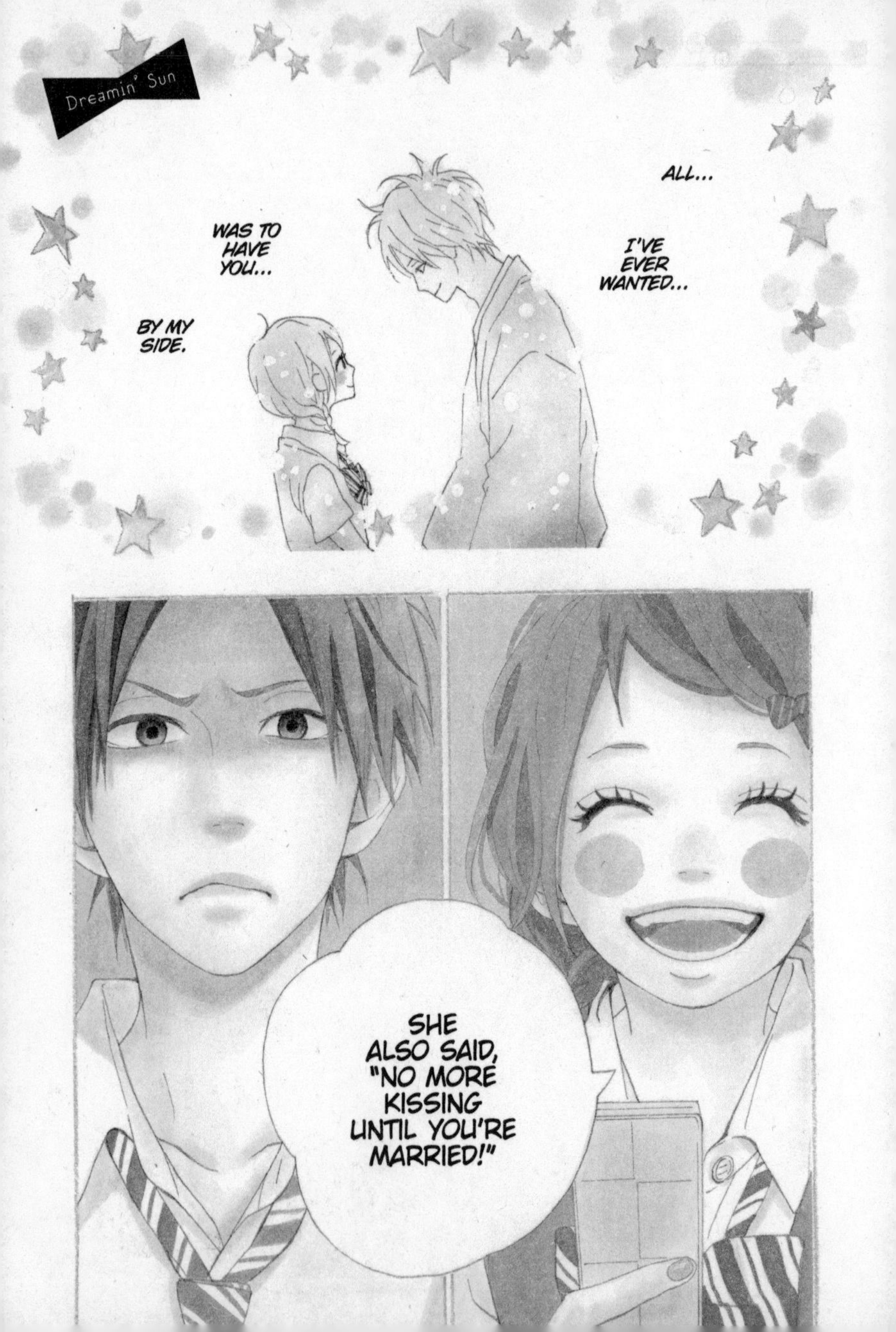
Dreamin' Sun
ALL...
I'VE EVER WANTED...
WAS TO HAVE YOU...
BY MY SIDE.
SHE ALSO SAID, "NO MORE KISSING UNTIL YOU'RE MARRIED!"

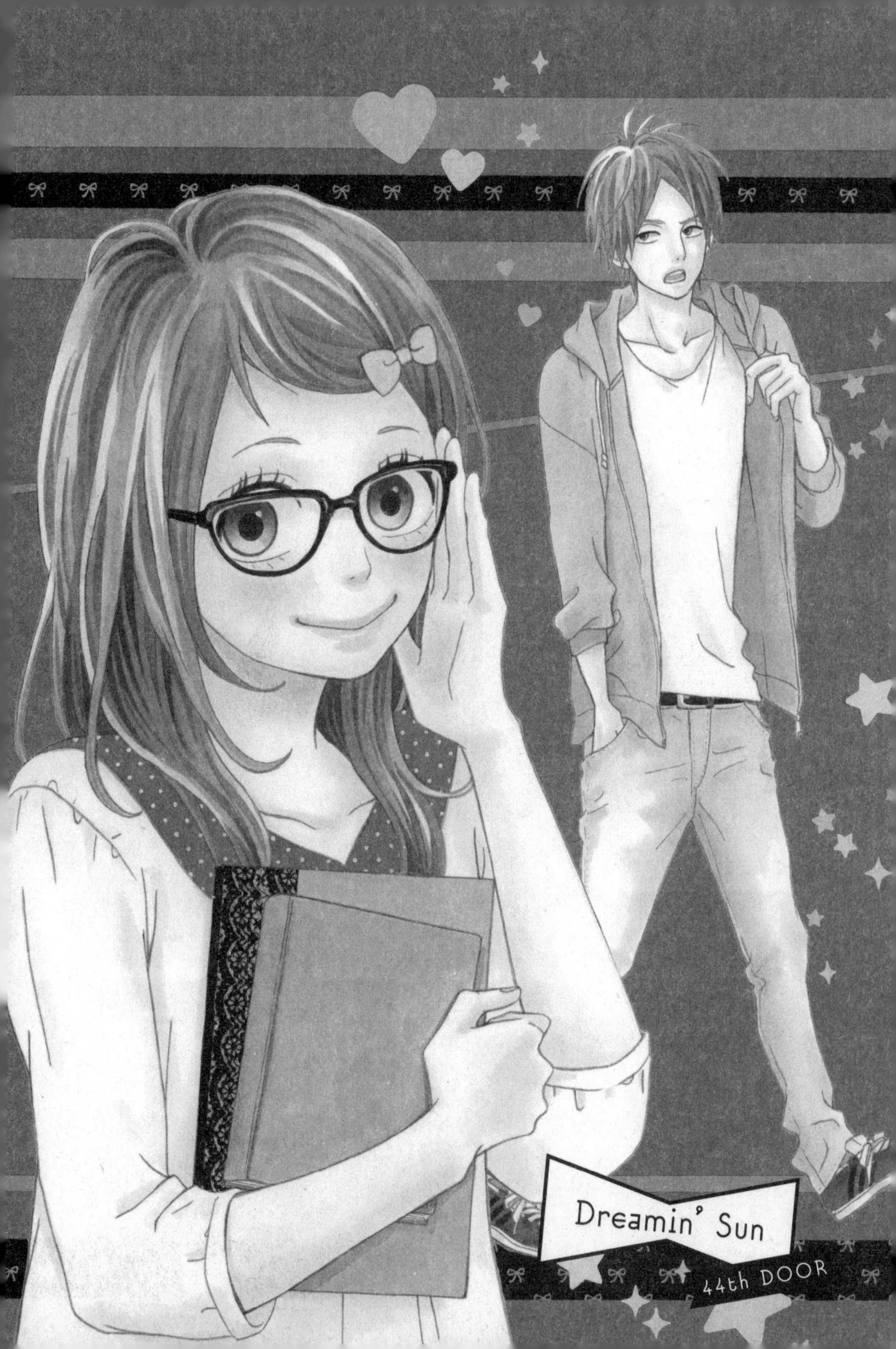
Dreamin' Sun
44th DOOR

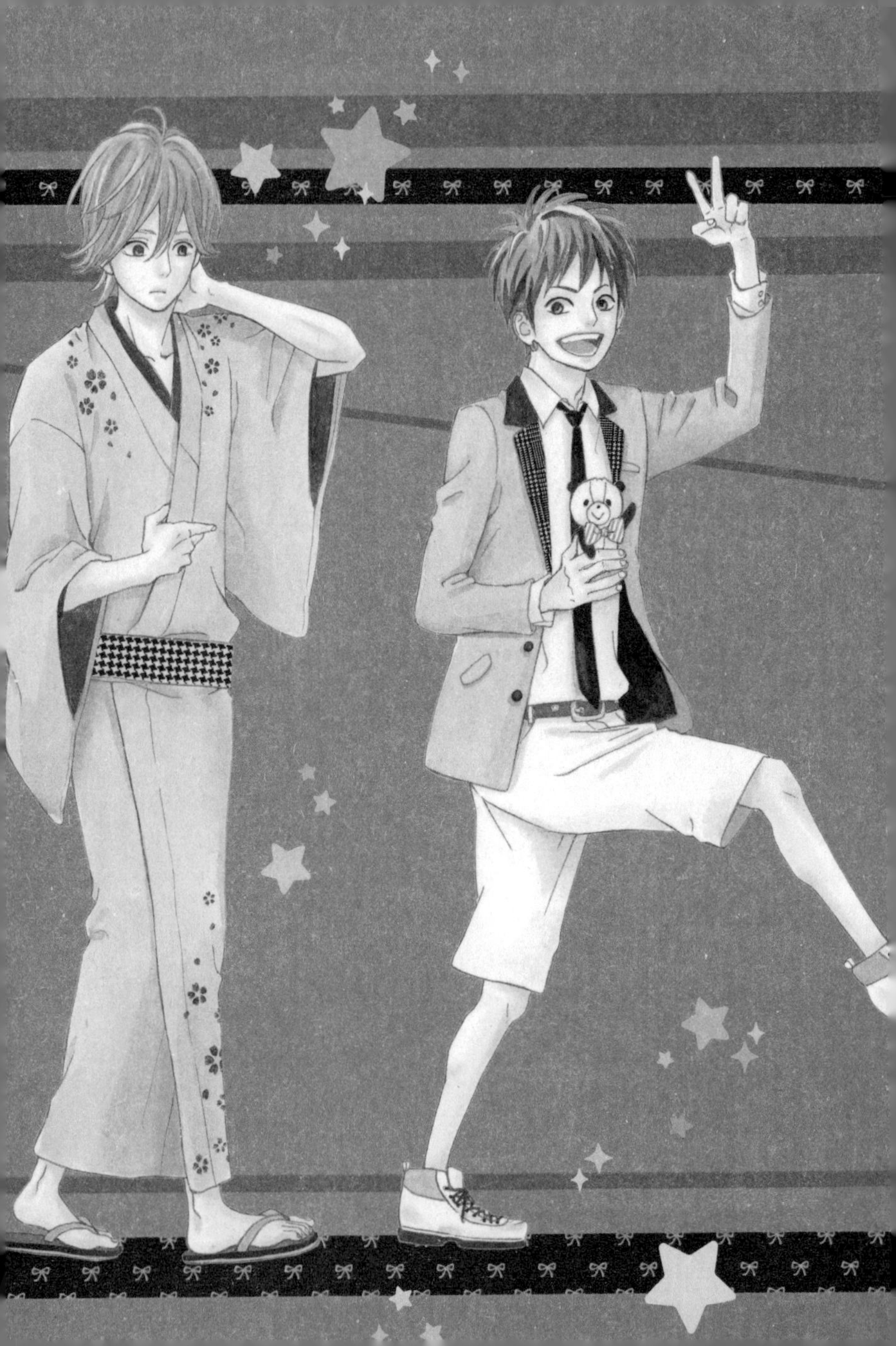

Dreamin'
Sun

BIIIING
BOONG
BEEENG
BOONG
AH! WE'RE IN A DIFFERENT CLASSROOM NEXT PERIOD!
HURRY, MR. LANDLORD!
THWUD
CLATTER
SLIIIDE
WHAT WAS THAT ABOUT?

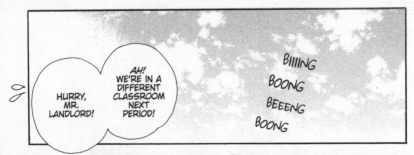

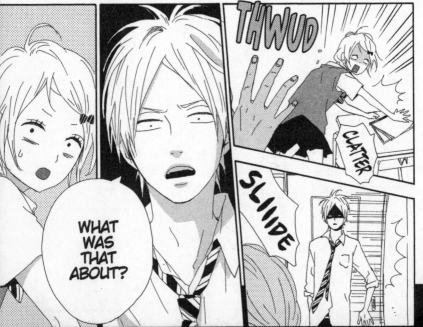

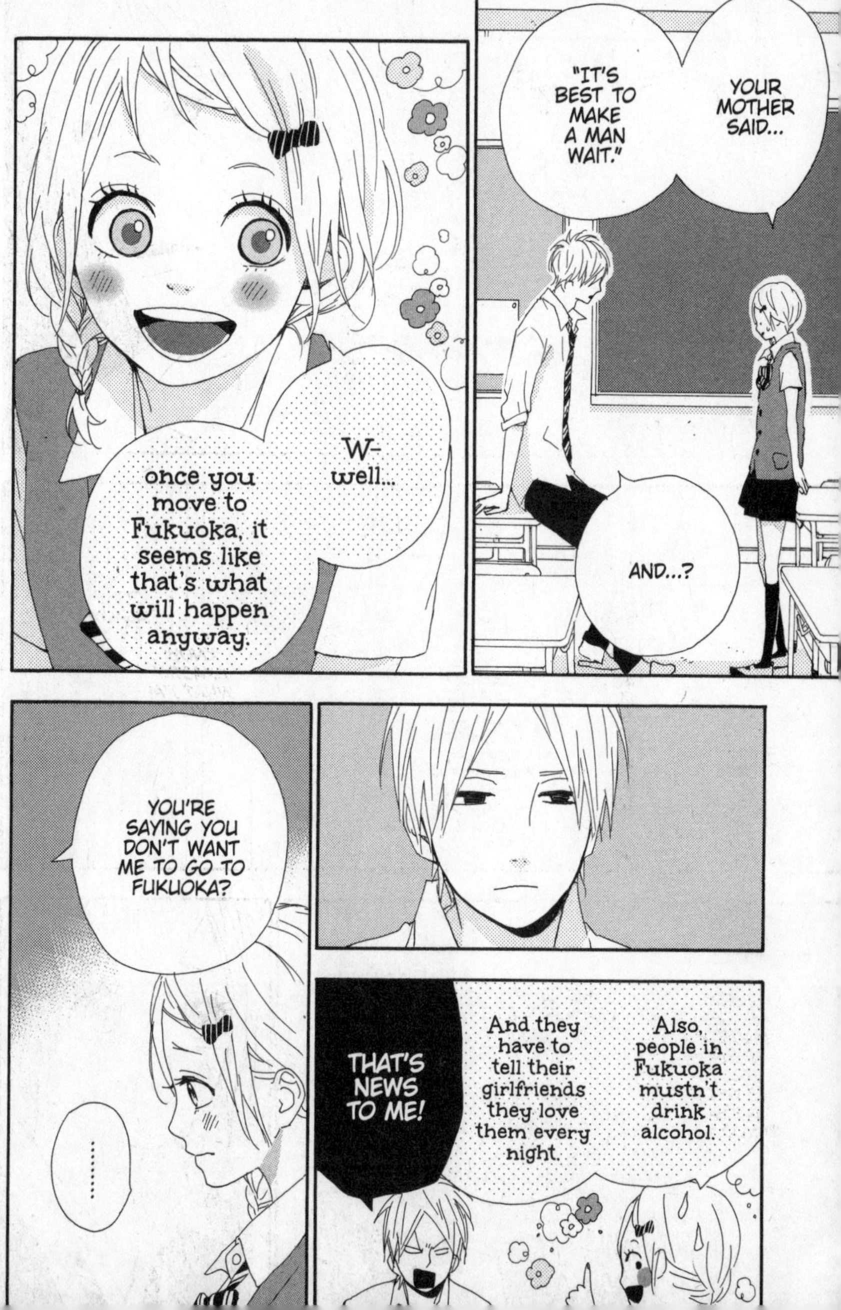

YOUR MOTHER SAID...
"IT'S BEST TO MAKE A MAN WAIT."
AND...?
W-well...
once you move to Fukuoka, it seems like that's what will happen anyway.
Also, people in Fukuoka mustn't drink alcohol.
And they have to tell their girlfriends they love them every night.
THAT'S NEWS TO ME!
YOU'RE SAYING YOU DON'T WANT ME TO GO TO FUKUOKA?
......

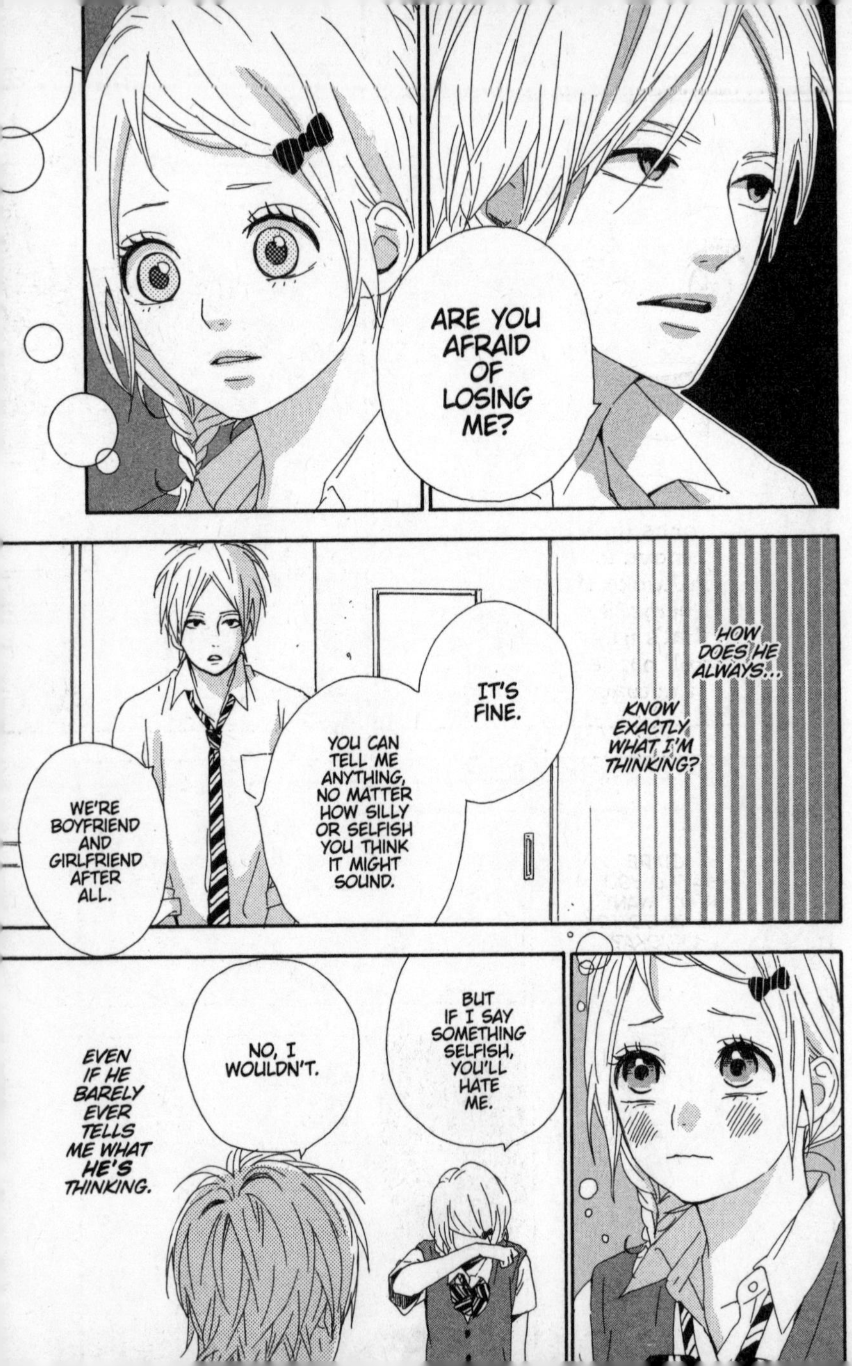
ARE YOU AFRAID OF LOSING ME?
HOW DOES HE ALWAYS...
KNOW EXACTLY WHAT I'M THINKING?
IT'S FINE.
YOU CAN TELL ME ANYTHING, NO MATTER HOW SILLY OR SELFISH YOU THINK IT MIGHT SOUND.
WE'RE BOYFRIEND AND GIRLFRIEND AFTER ALL.
BUT IF I SAY SOMETHING SELFISH, YOU'LL HATE ME.
NO, I WOULDN'T.
EVEN IF HE BARELY EVER TELLS ME WHAT HE'S THINKING.

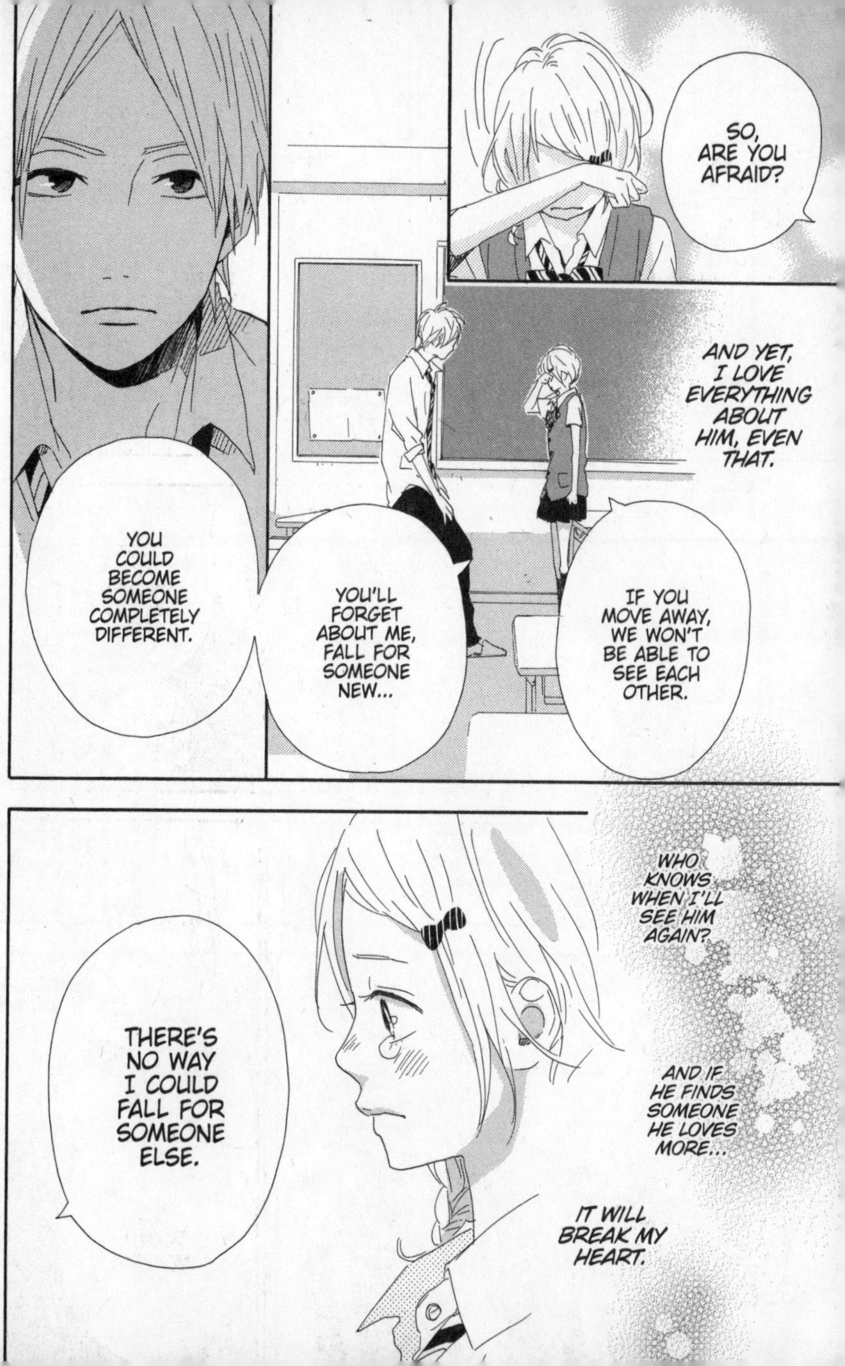
SO, ARE YOU AFRAID?
AND YET, I LOVE EVERYTHING ABOUT HIM, EVEN THAT.
IF YOU MOVE AWAY, WE WON'T BE ABLE TO SEE EACH OTHER.
YOU'LL FORGET ABOUT ME, FALL FOR SOMEONE NEW...
YOU COULD BECOME SOMEONE COMPLETELY DIFFERENT.
WHO KNOWS WHEN I'LL SEE HIM AGAIN?
AND IF HE FINDS SOMEONE HE LOVES MORE...
IT WILL BREAK MY HEART.
THERE'S NO WAY I COULD FALL FOR SOMEONE ELSE.

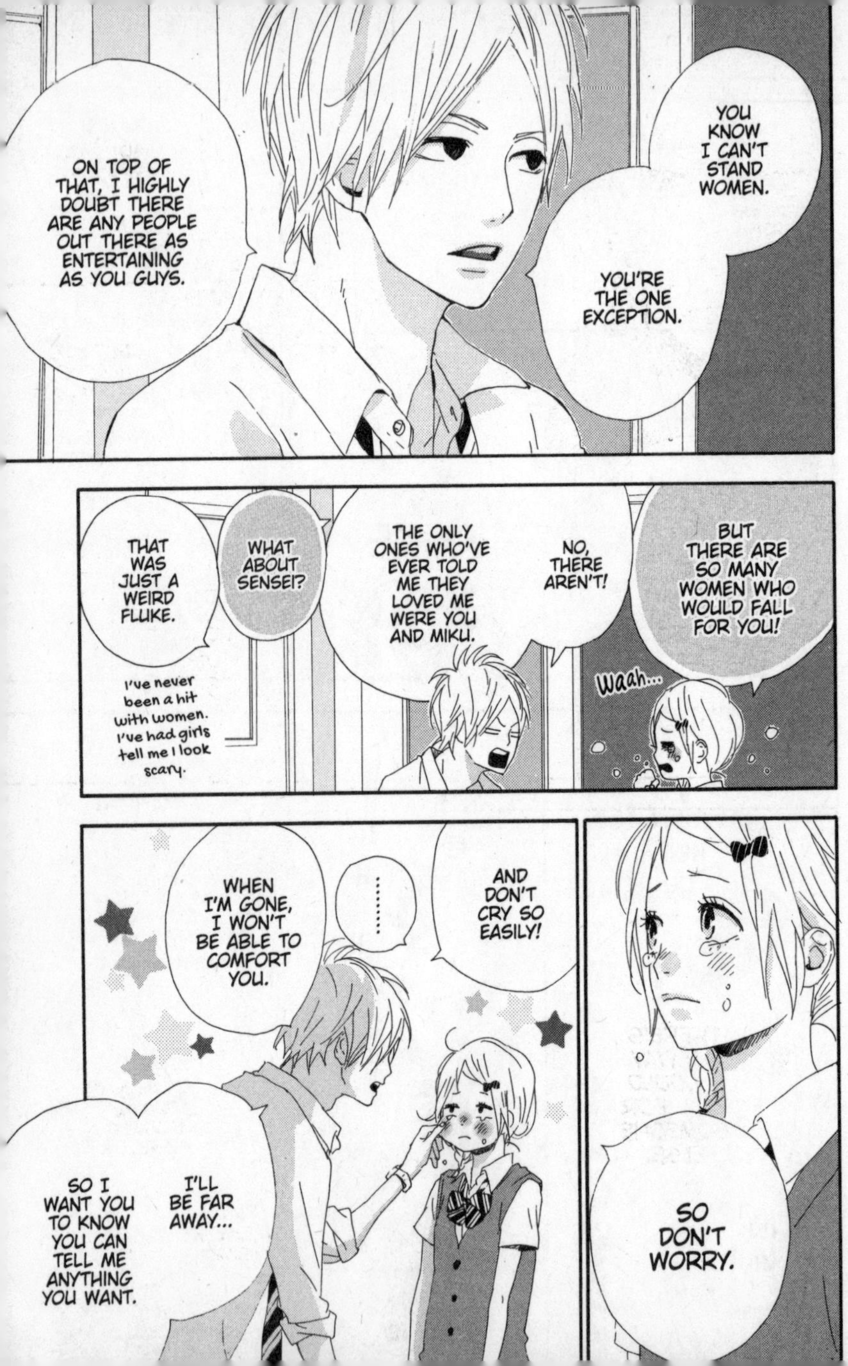
YOU KNOW I CAN'T STAND WOMEN.
YOU'RE THE ONE EXCEPTION.
ON TOP OF THAT, I HIGHLY DOUBT THERE ARE ANY PEOPLE OUT THERE AS ENTERTAINING AS YOU GUYS.
BUT THERE ARE SO MANY WOMEN WHO WOULD FALL FOR YOU!
Waah...
NO, THERE AREN'T!
THE ONLY ONES WHO'VE EVER TOLD ME THEY LOVED ME WERE YOU AND MIKU.
WHAT ABOUT SENSEI?
THAT WAS JUST A WEIRD FLUKE.
I've never been a hit with women. I've had girls tell me I look scary.
SO DON'T WORRY.
AND DON'T CRY SO EASILY!
......
WHEN I'M GONE, I WON'T BE ABLE TO COMFORT YOU.
I'LL BE FAR AWAY...
SO I WANT YOU TO KNOW YOU CAN TELL ME ANYTHING YOU WANT.

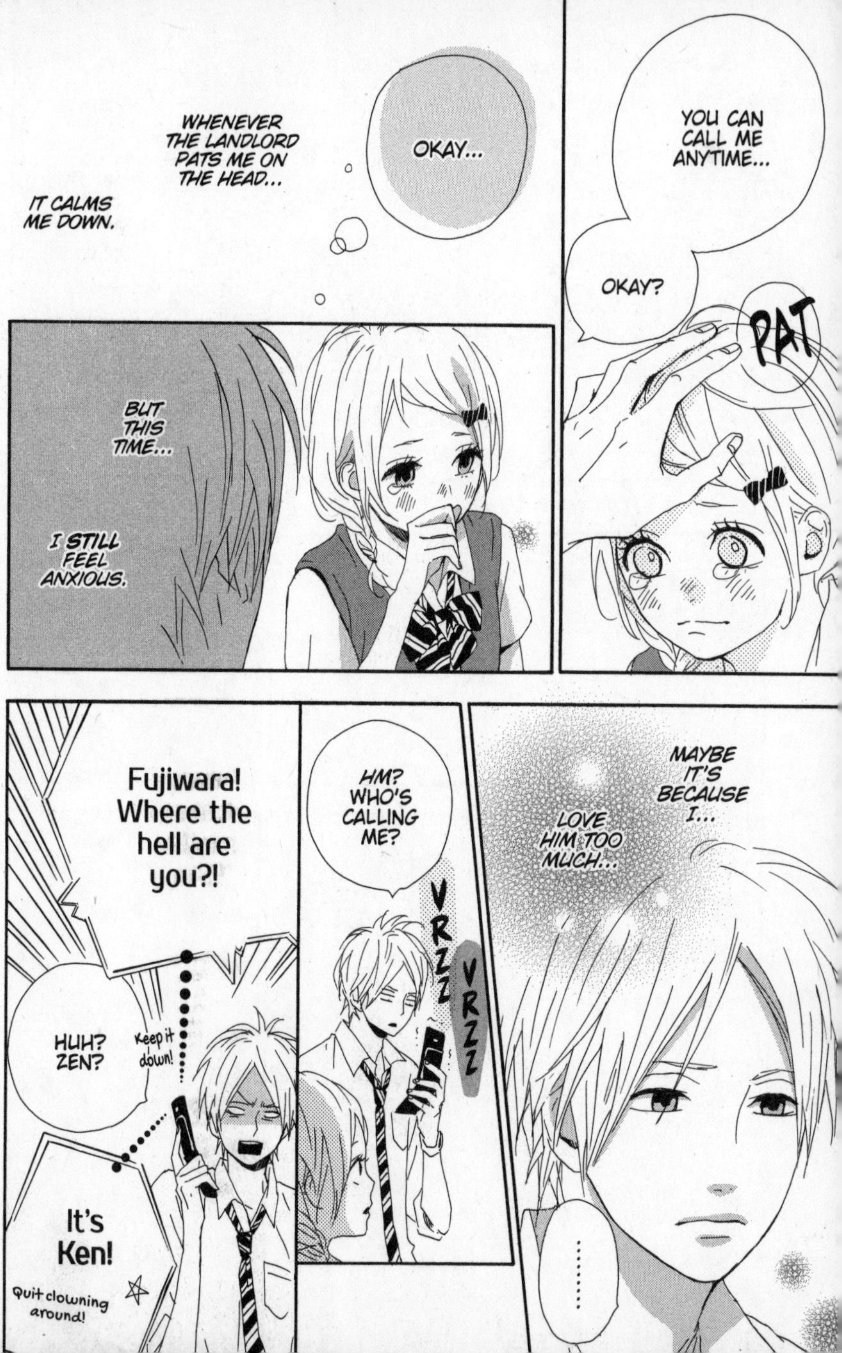
YOU CAN CALL ME ANYTIME...
OKAY?
PAT
OKAY...
WHENEVER THE LANDLORD PATS ME ON THE HEAD...
IT CALMS ME DOWN.
BUT THIS TIME...
I STILL FEEL ANXIOUS.
MAYBE IT'S BECAUSE I...
LOVE HIM TOO MUCH...
......
HM? WHO'S CALLING ME?
VRZZ
VRZZ
Fujiwara! Where the hell are you?!
HUH? ZEN?
Keep it down!
It's Ken!
Quit clowning around!

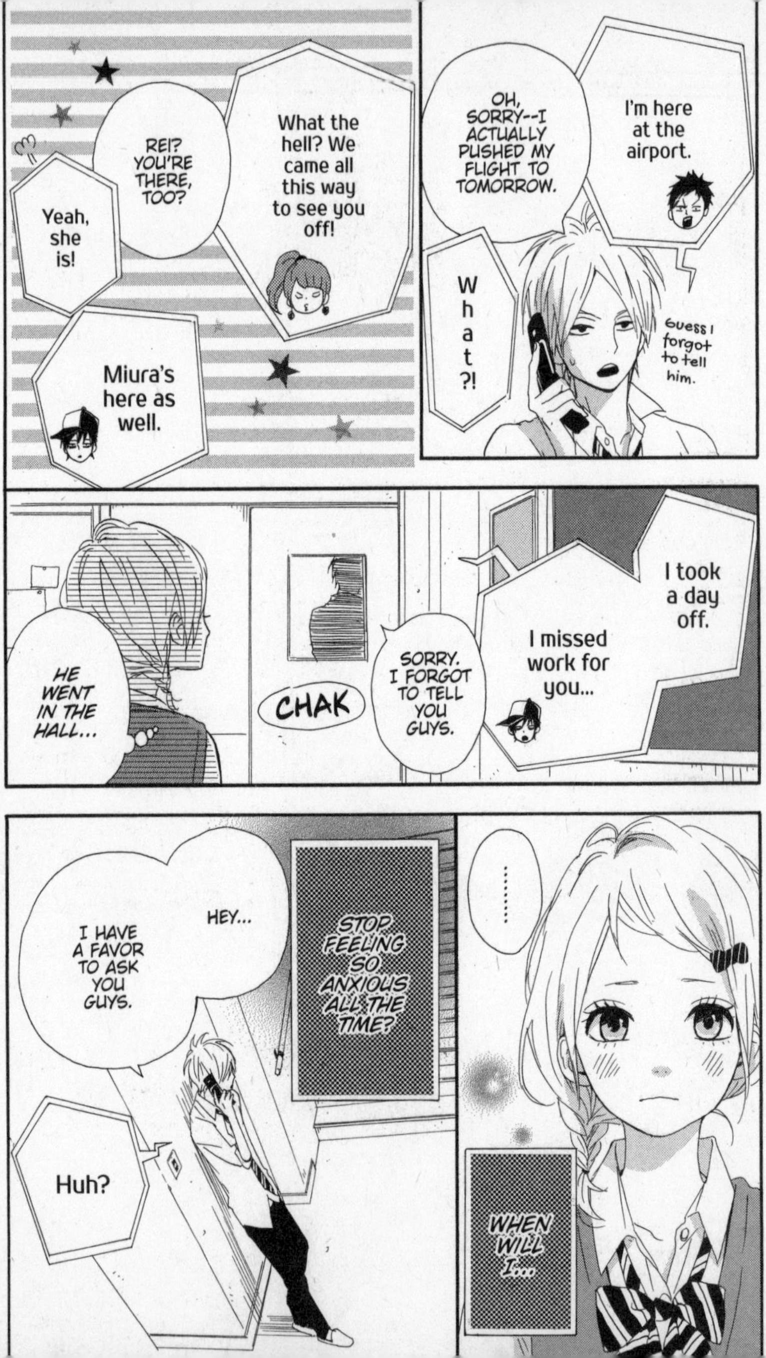
I'm here at the airport.
OH, SORRY--I ACTUALLY PUSHED MY FLIGHT TO TOMORROW.
What?!
Guess I forgot to tell him.
What the hell? We came all this way to see you off!
REI? YOU'RE THERE, TOO?
Yeah, she is!
Miura's here as well.
I took a day off.
I missed work for you...
SORRY. I FORGOT TO TELL YOU GUYS.
CHAK
HE WENT IN THE HALL...
......
WHEN WILL I...
STOP FEELING SO ANXIOUS ALL THE TIME?
HEY...
I HAVE A FAVOR TO ASK YOU GUYS.
Huh?

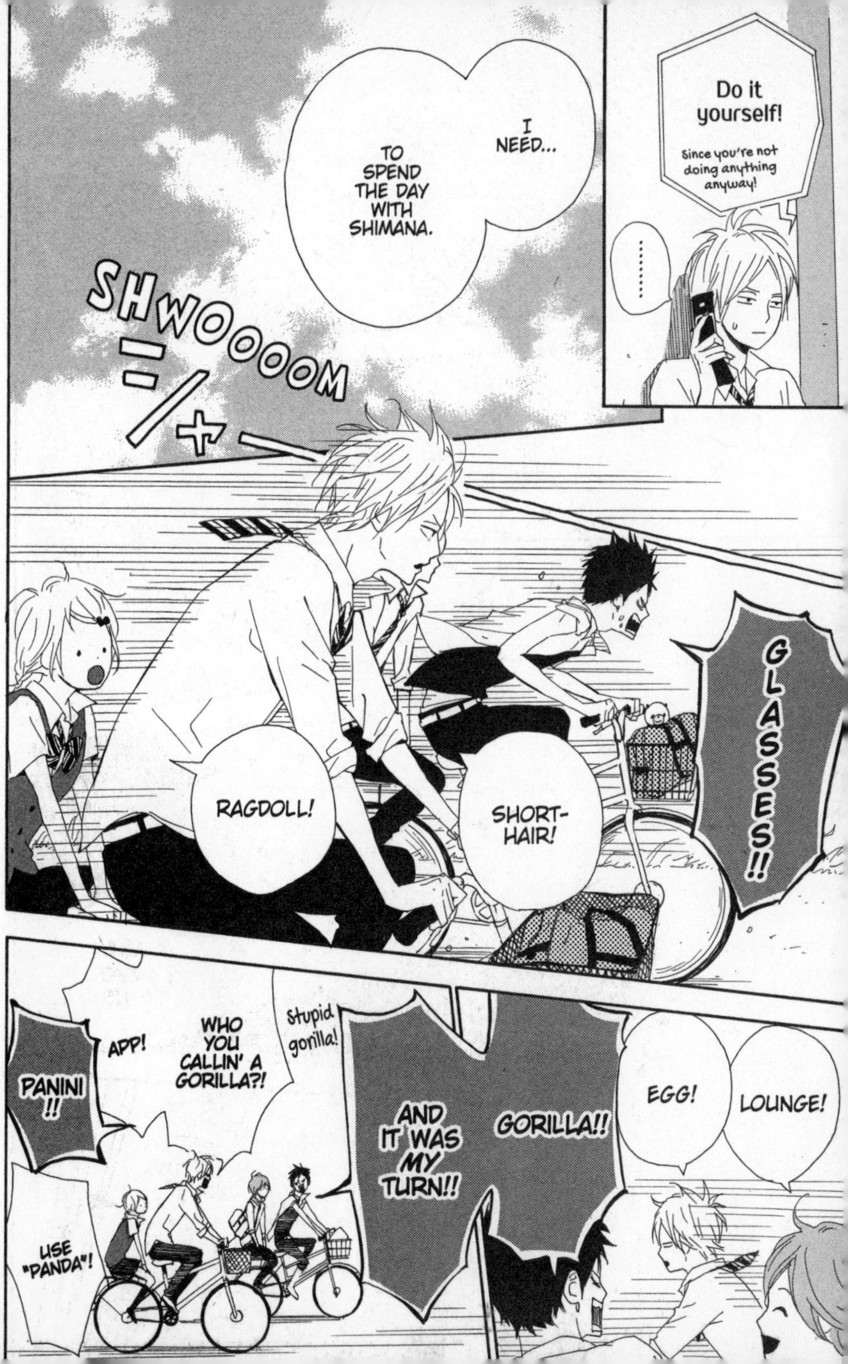
Do it yourself!
Since you're not doing anything anyway!
......
I NEED...
TO SPEND THE DAY WITH SHIMANA.
SHWOOOOOM
GLASSES!!
SHORT-HAIR!
RAGDOLL!
LOUNGE!
EGG!
GORILLA!!
AND IT WAS MY TURN!!
Stupid gorilla!
WHO YOU CALLIN' A GORILLA?!
APP!
PANINI!!
USE "PANDA"!

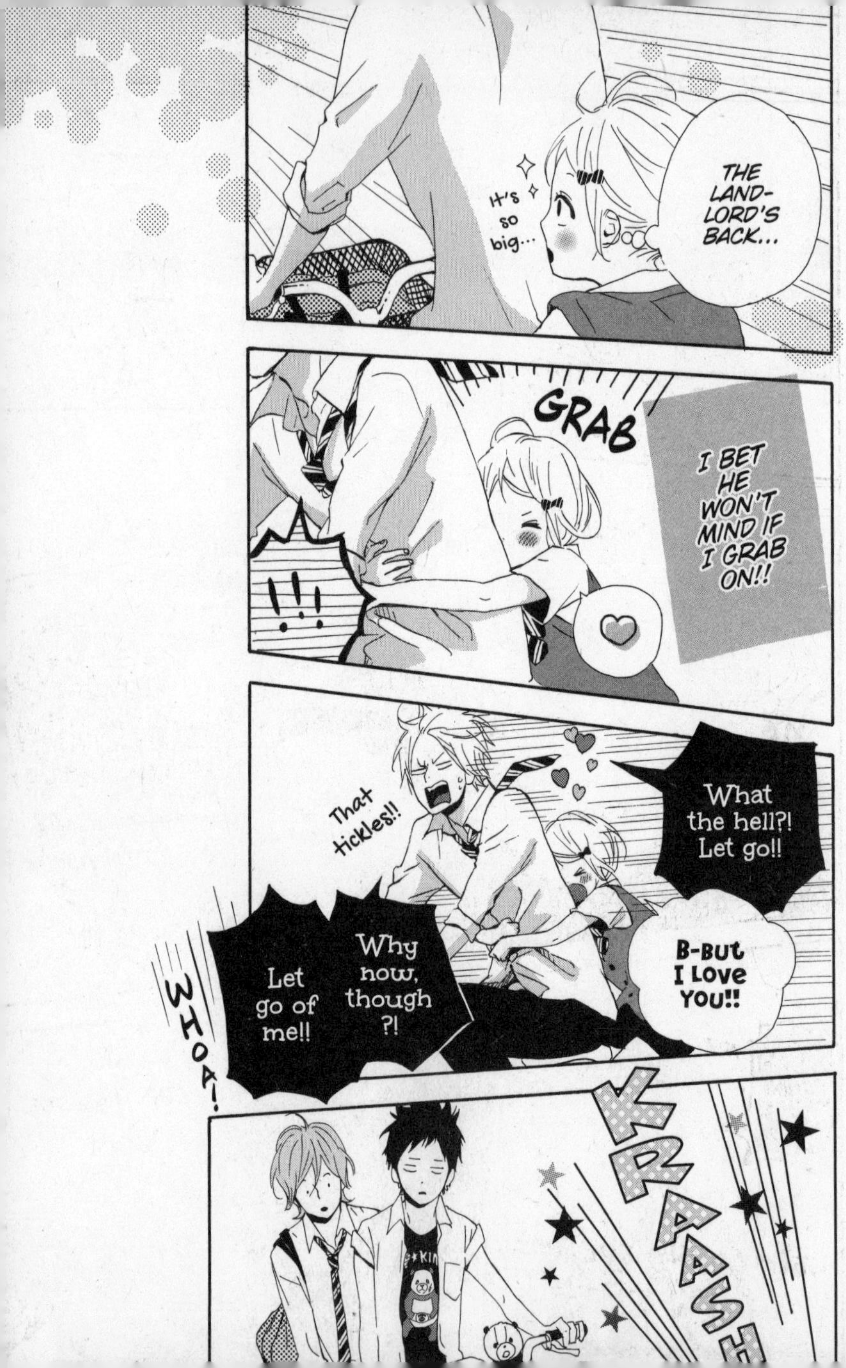
THE LAND-LORD'S BACK...
It's so big...
I BET HE WON'T MIND IF I GRAB ON!!
GRAB
What the hell?! Let go!!
That tickles!!
B-But I Love YOU!!
Why now, though ?!
Let go of me!!
WHOA!
KRASH

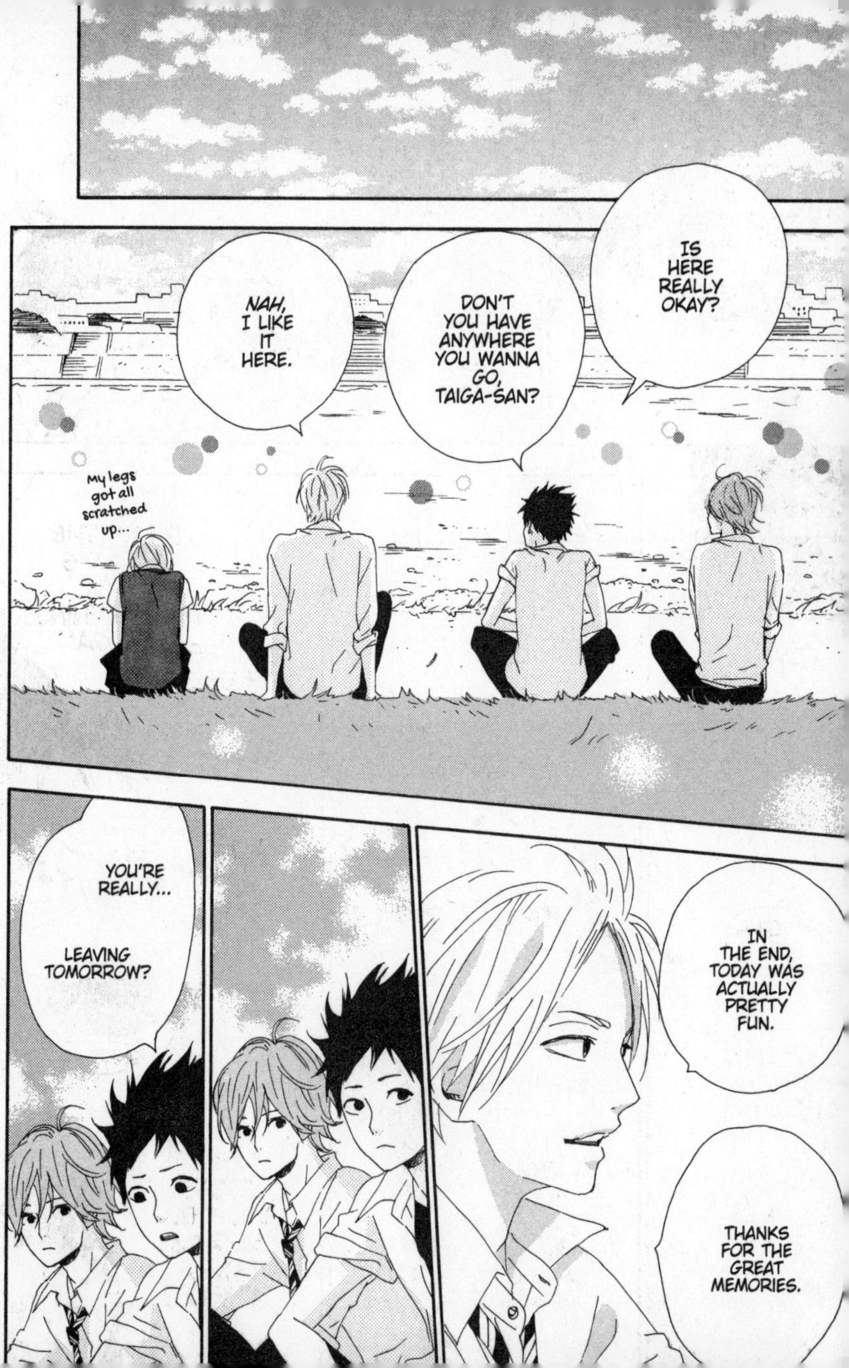
IS HERE REALLY OKAY?
DON'T YOU HAVE ANYWHERE YOU WANNA GO, TAIGA-SAN?
NAH, I LIKE IT HERE.
My legs got all scratched up...
IN THE END, TODAY WAS ACTUALLY PRETTY FUN.
THANKS FOR THE GREAT MEMORIES.
YOU'RE REALLY... LEAVING TOMORROW?

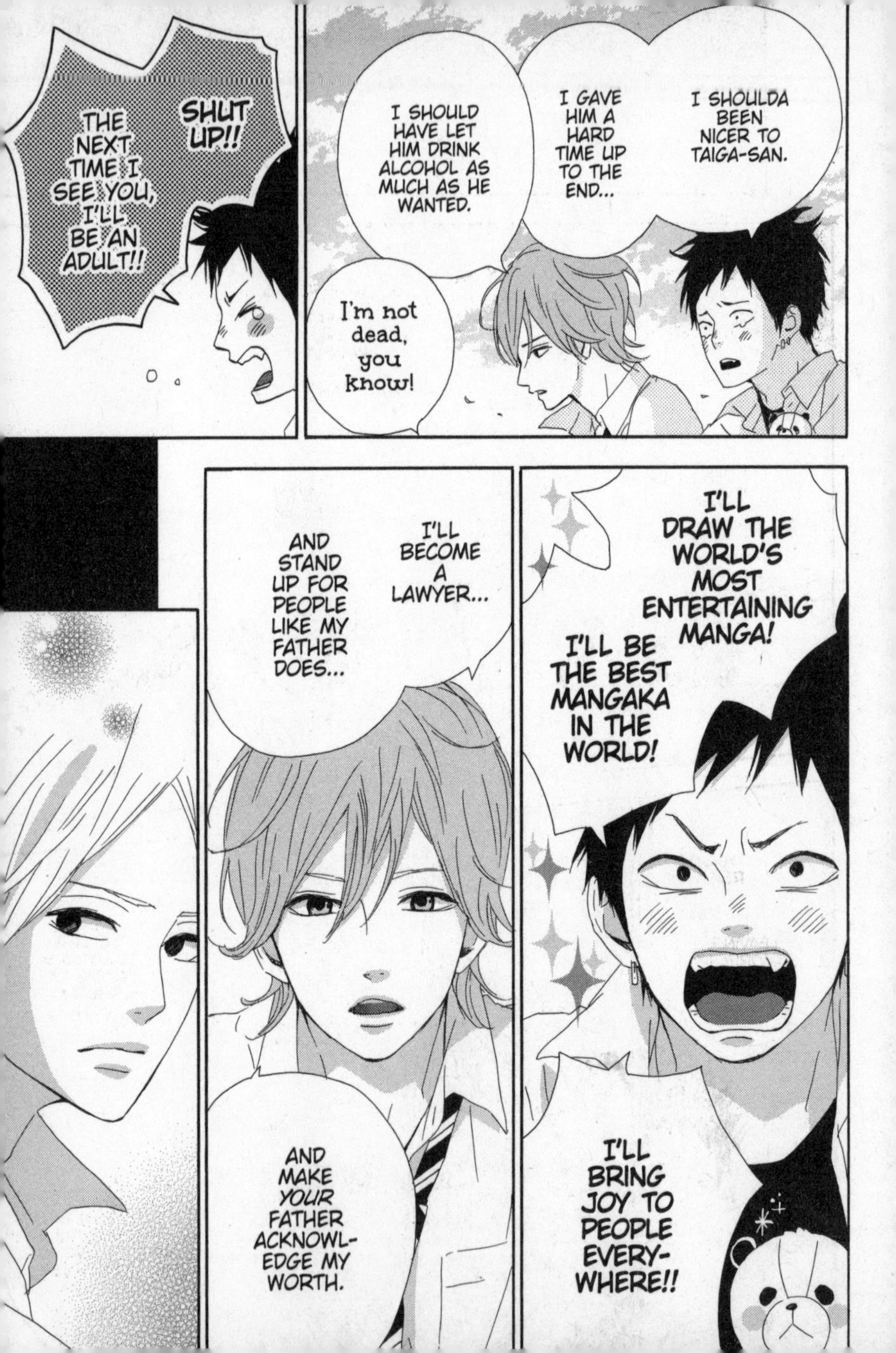
I SHOULDA BEEN NICER TO TAIGA-SAN.
I GAVE HIM A HARD TIME UP TO THE END...
I SHOULD HAVE LET HIM DRINK ALCOHOL AS MUCH AS HE WANTED.
I'm not dead, you know!
SHUT UP!!
THE NEXT TIME I SEE YOU, I'LL BE AN ADULT!!
I'LL DRAW THE WORLD'S MOST ENTERTAINING MANGA!
I'LL BE THE BEST MANGAKA IN THE WORLD!
I'LL BRING JOY TO PEOPLE EVERY-WHERE!!
I'LL BECOME A LAWYER...
AND STAND UP FOR PEOPLE LIKE MY FATHER DOES...
AND MAKE *YOUR* FATHER ACKNOWL-EDGE MY WORTH.

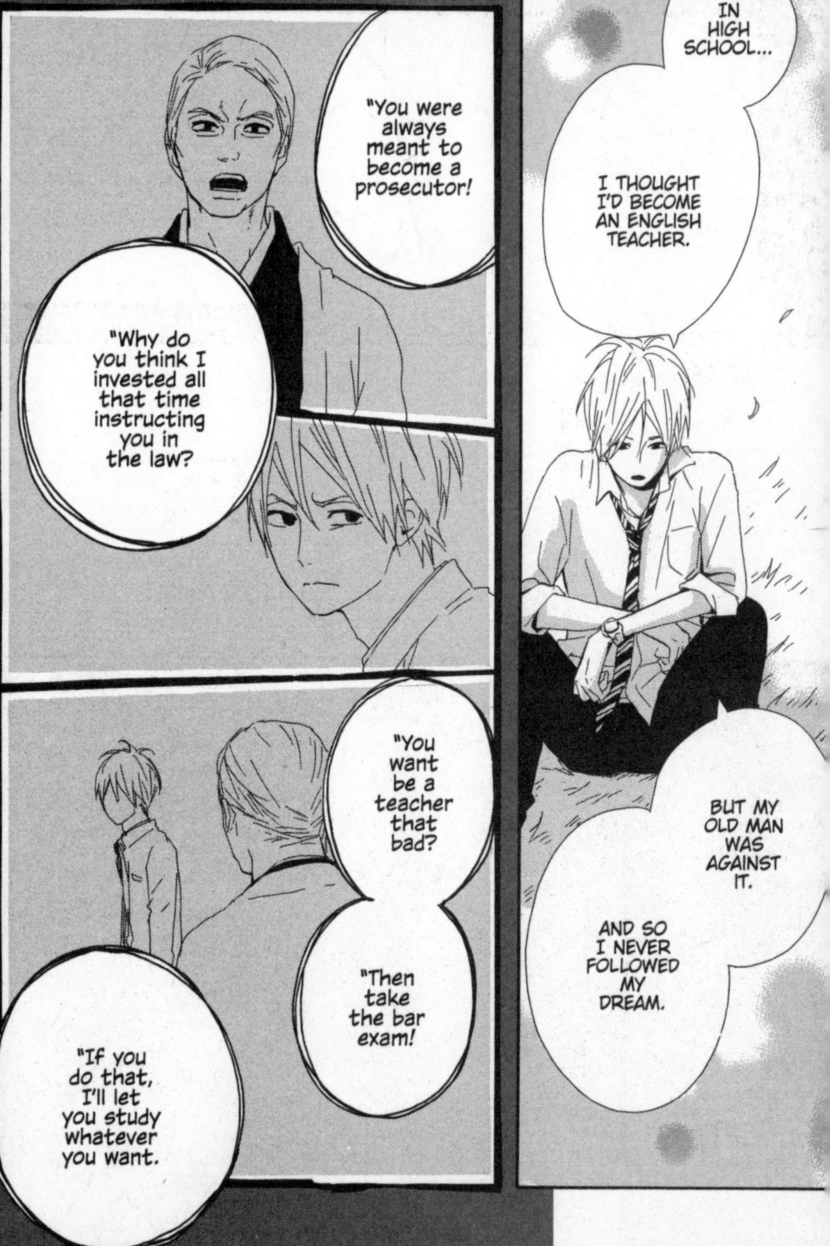
IN HIGH SCHOOL...
I THOUGHT I'D BECOME AN ENGLISH TEACHER.
BUT MY OLD MAN WAS AGAINST IT.
AND SO I NEVER FOLLOWED MY DREAM.
"You were always meant to become a prosecutor!
"Why do you think I invested all that time instructing you in the law?
"You want be a teacher that bad?
"Then take the bar exam!
"If you do that, I'll let you study whatever you want.

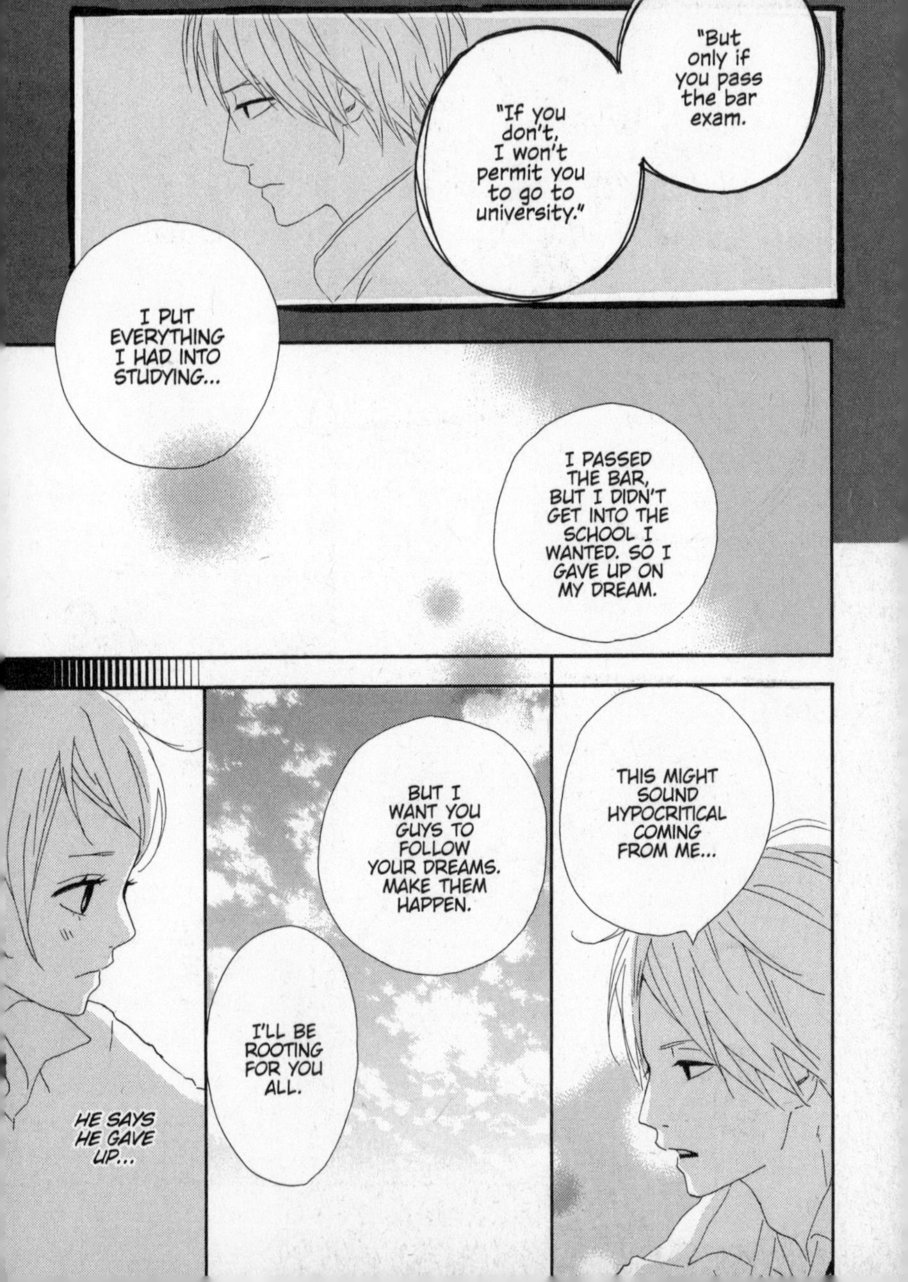
"But only if you pass the bar exam.
"If you don't, I won't permit you to go to university."
I PUT EVERYTHING I HAD INTO STUDYING...
I PASSED THE BAR, BUT I DIDN'T GET INTO THE SCHOOL I WANTED. SO I GAVE UP ON MY DREAM.
THIS MIGHT SOUND HYPOCRITICAL COMING FROM ME...
BUT I WANT YOU GUYS TO FOLLOW YOUR DREAMS. MAKE THEM HAPPEN.
I'LL BE ROOTING FOR YOU ALL.
HE SAYS HE GAVE UP...

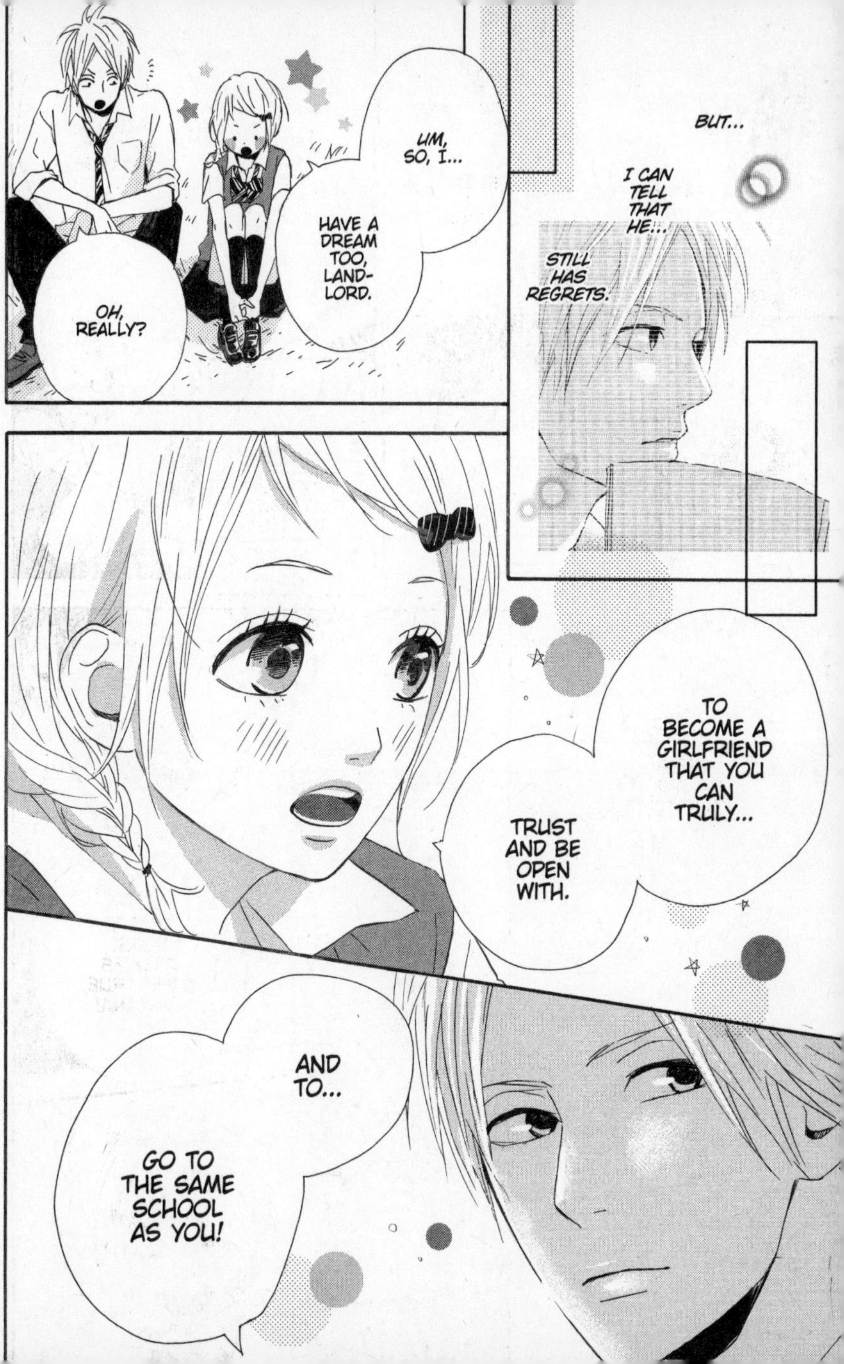
BUT...
I CAN TELL THAT HE...
STILL HAS REGRETS.
UM, SO, I...
HAVE A DREAM TOO, LANDLORD.
OH, REALLY?
TO BECOME A GIRLFRIEND THAT YOU CAN TRULY...
TRUST AND BE OPEN WITH.
AND TO...
GO TO THE SAME SCHOOL AS YOU!

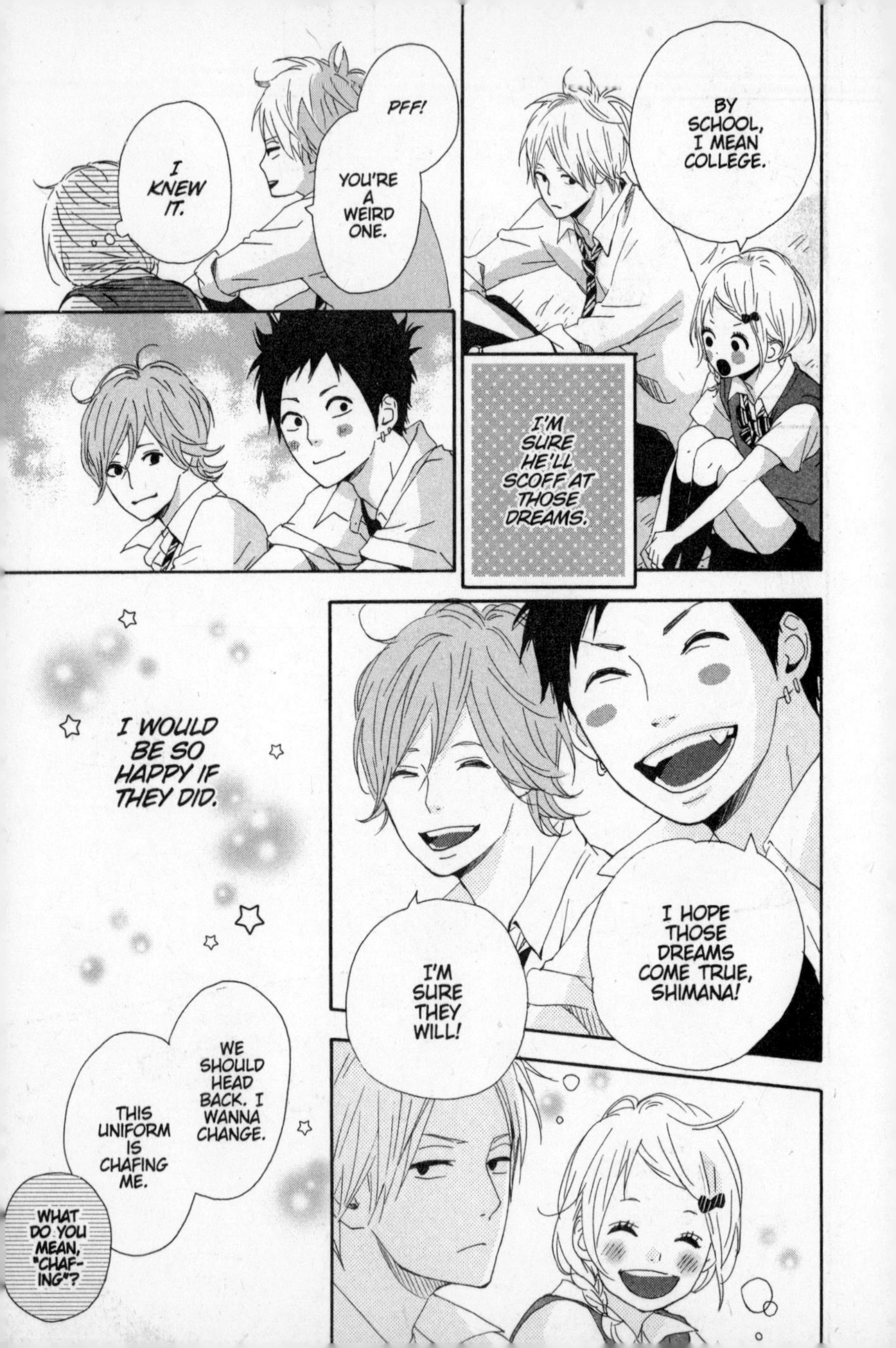
BY SCHOOL, I MEAN COLLEGE.
I'M SURE HE'LL SCOFF AT THOSE DREAMS.
PFF!
YOU'RE A WEIRD ONE.
I KNEW IT.
I HOPE THOSE DREAMS COME TRUE, SHIMANA!
I'M SURE THEY WILL!
I WOULD BE SO HAPPY IF THEY DID.
WE SHOULD HEAD BACK. I WANNA CHANGE.
THIS UNIFORM IS CHAFING ME.
WHAT DO YOU MEAN, "CHAF-ING"?

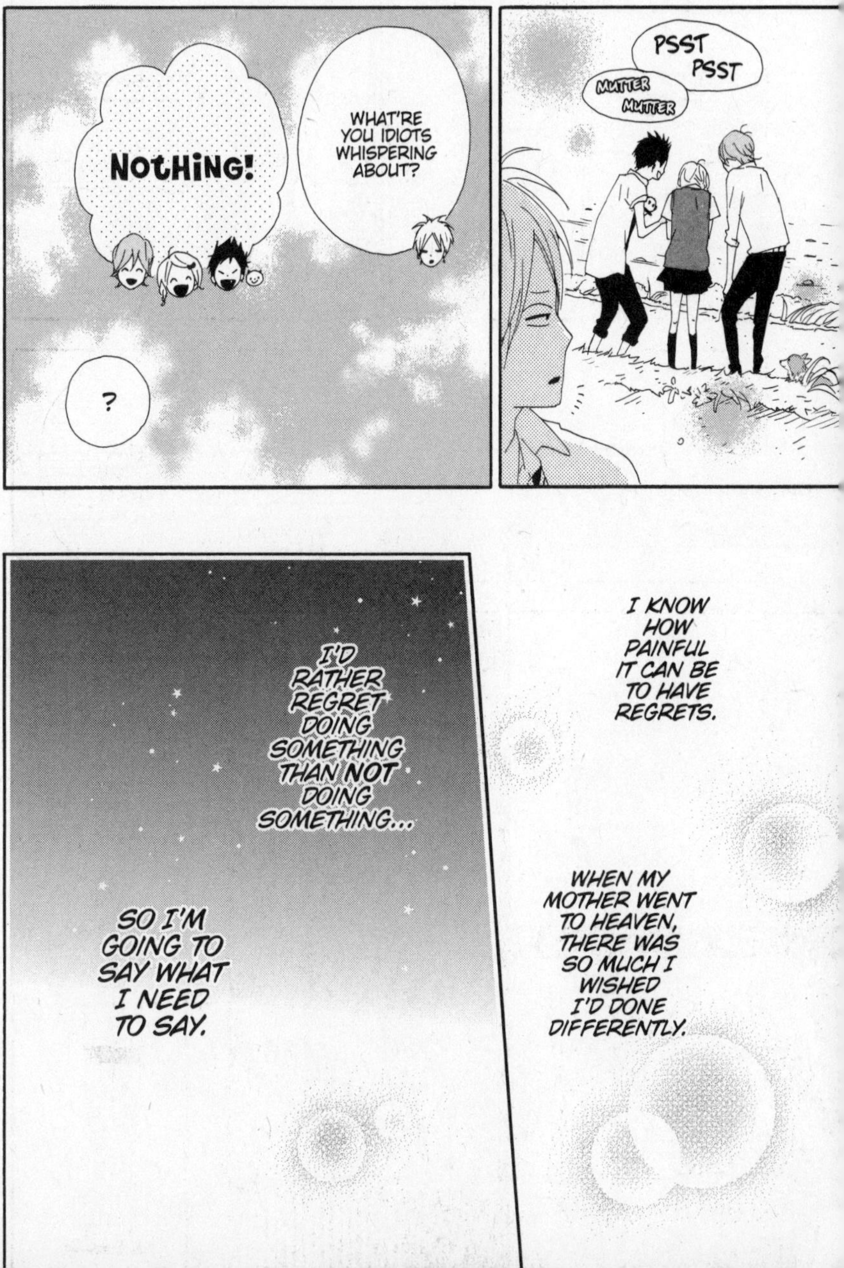
PSST PSST
MUTTER MUTTER
WHAT'RE YOU IDIOTS WHISPERING ABOUT?
NOTHING!
?
I KNOW HOW PAINFUL IT CAN BE TO HAVE REGRETS.
WHEN MY MOTHER WENT TO HEAVEN, THERE WAS SO MUCH I WISHED I'D DONE DIFFERENTLY.
I'D RATHER REGRET DOING SOMETHING THAN NOT DOING SOMETHING...
SO I'M GOING TO SAY WHAT I NEED TO SAY.

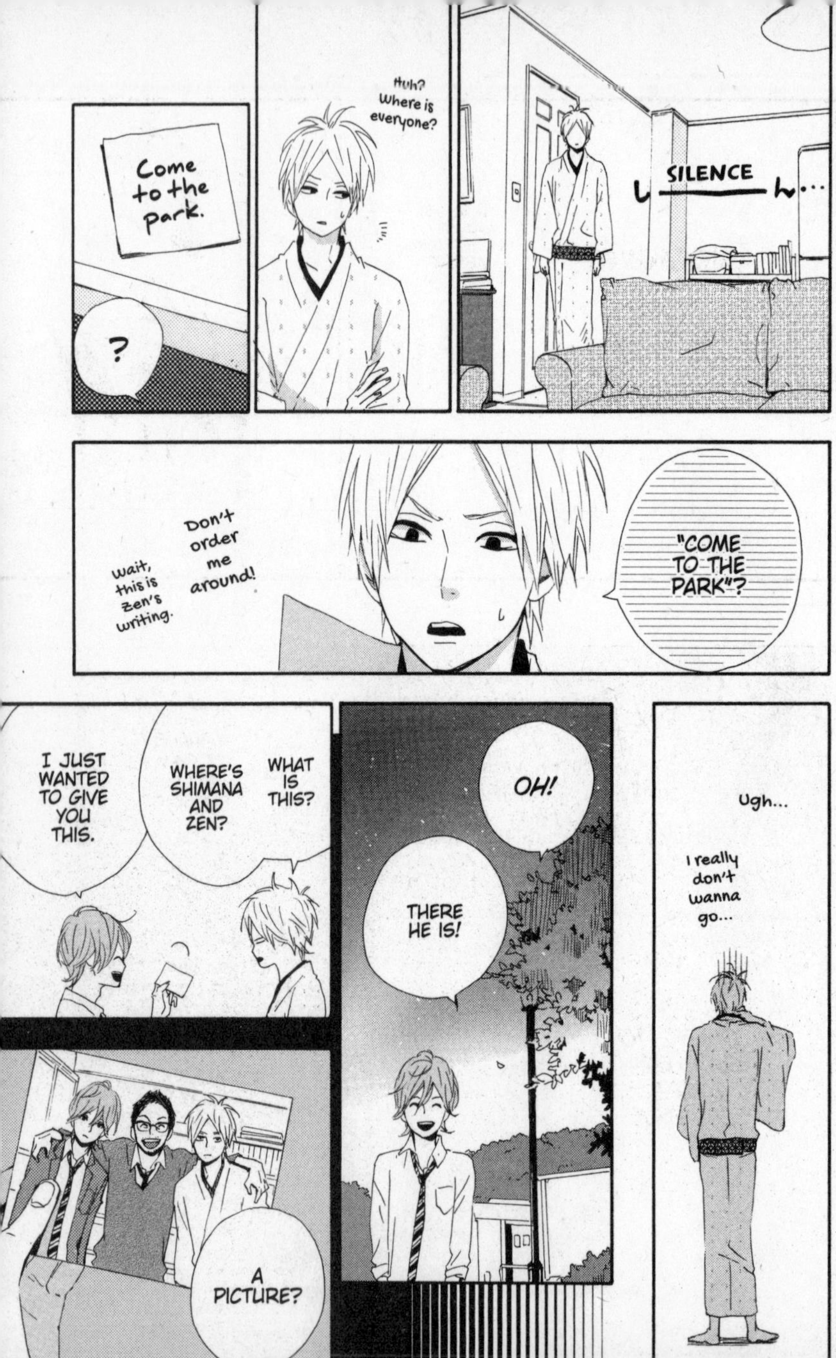
SILENCE
Huh? Where is everyone?
Come to the park.
?
"COME TO THE PARK"?
Don't order me around!
Wait, this is Zen's writing.
Ugh...
I really don't wanna go...
OH!
THERE HE IS!
WHAT IS THIS?
WHERE'S SHIMANA AND ZEN?
I JUST WANTED TO GIVE YOU THIS.
A PICTURE?

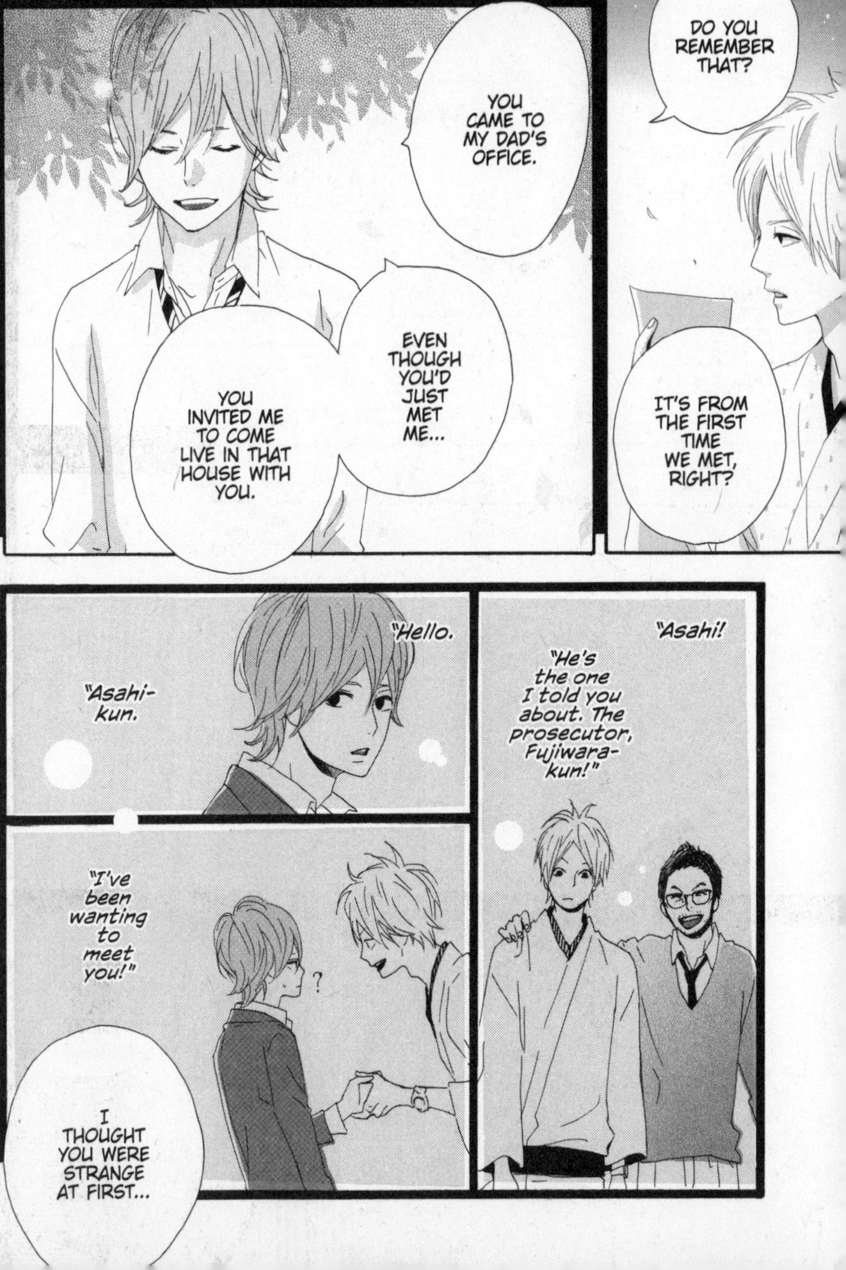
DO YOU REMEMBER THAT?
IT'S FROM THE FIRST TIME WE MET, RIGHT?
YOU CAME TO MY DAD'S OFFICE.
EVEN THOUGH YOU'D JUST MET ME...
YOU INVITED ME TO COME LIVE IN THAT HOUSE WITH YOU.
"Asahi!
"He's the one I told you about. The prosecutor, Fujiwara-kun!"
"Hello.
"Asahi-kun.
"I've been wanting to meet you!"
I THOUGHT YOU WERE STRANGE AT FIRST...

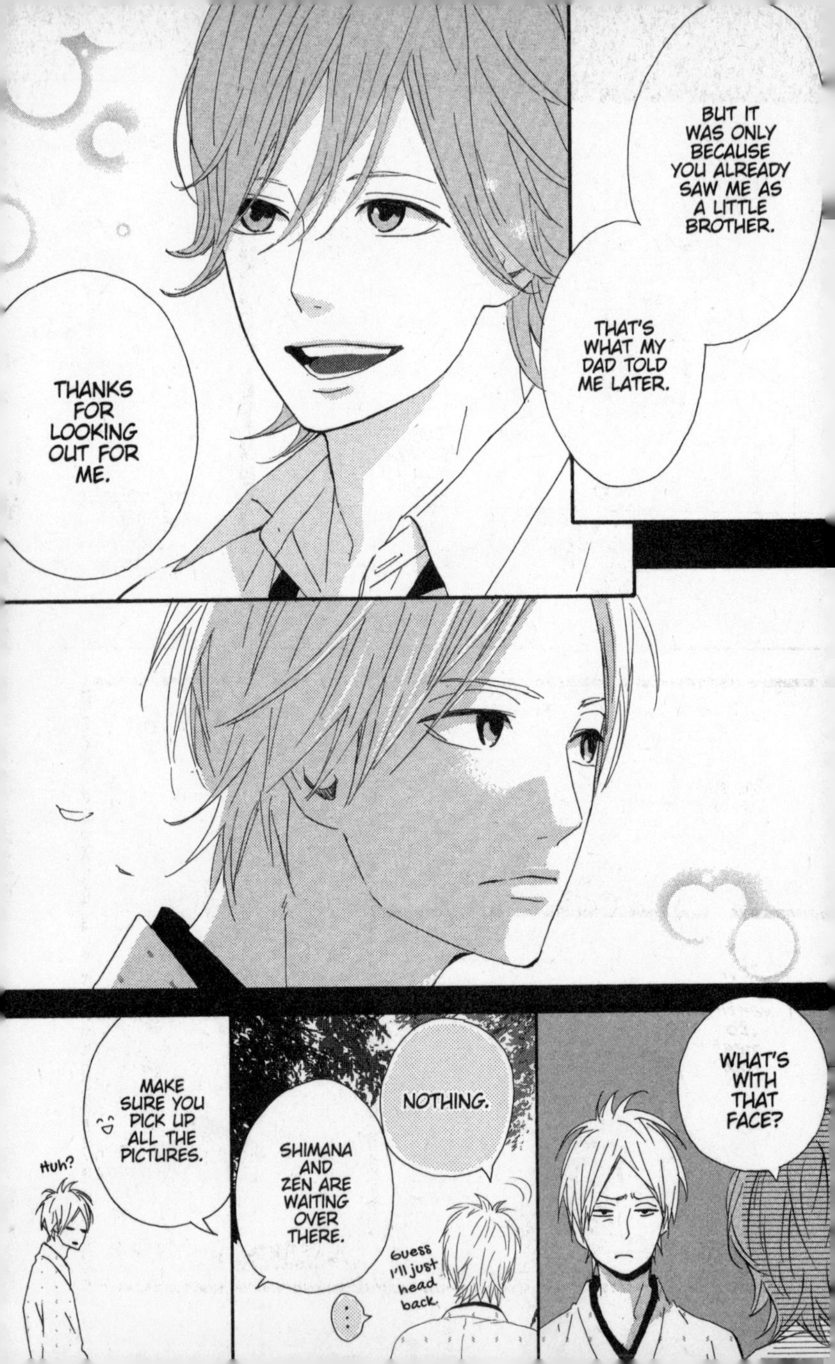
BUT IT WAS ONLY BECAUSE YOU ALREADY SAW ME AS A LITTLE BROTHER.
THAT'S WHAT MY DAD TOLD ME LATER.
THANKS FOR LOOKING OUT FOR ME.
WHAT'S WITH THAT FACE?
NOTHING.
SHIMANA AND ZEN ARE WAITING OVER THERE.
Guess I'll just head back.
...
MAKE SURE YOU PICK UP ALL THE PICTURES.
Huh?

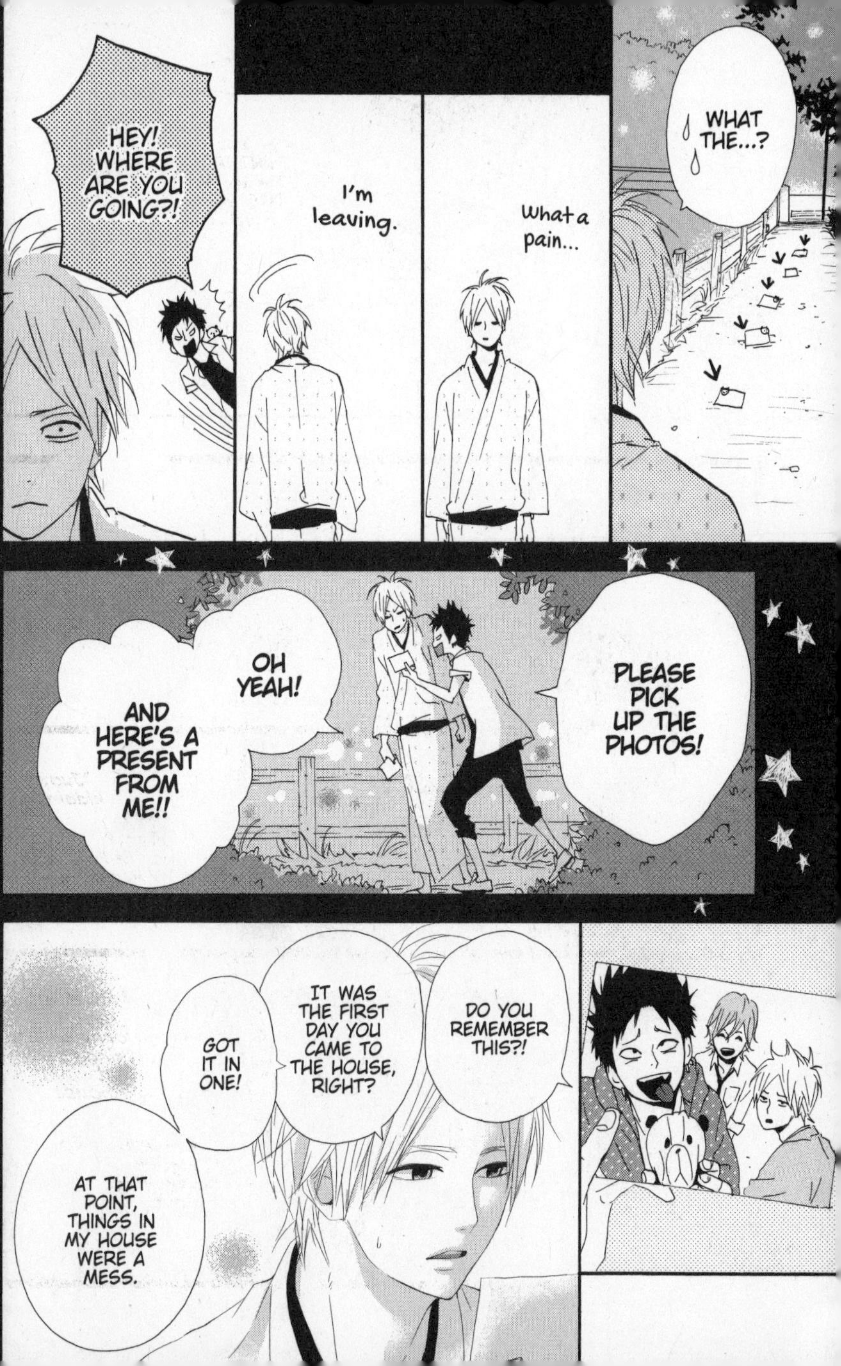
WHAT THE...?
What a pain...
I'm leaving.
HEY! WHERE ARE YOU GOING?!
PLEASE PICK UP THE PHOTOS!
OH YEAH!
AND HERE'S A PRESENT FROM ME!!
DO YOU REMEMBER THIS?!
IT WAS THE FIRST DAY YOU CAME TO THE HOUSE, RIGHT?
GOT IT IN ONE!
AT THAT POINT, THINGS IN MY HOUSE WERE A MESS.

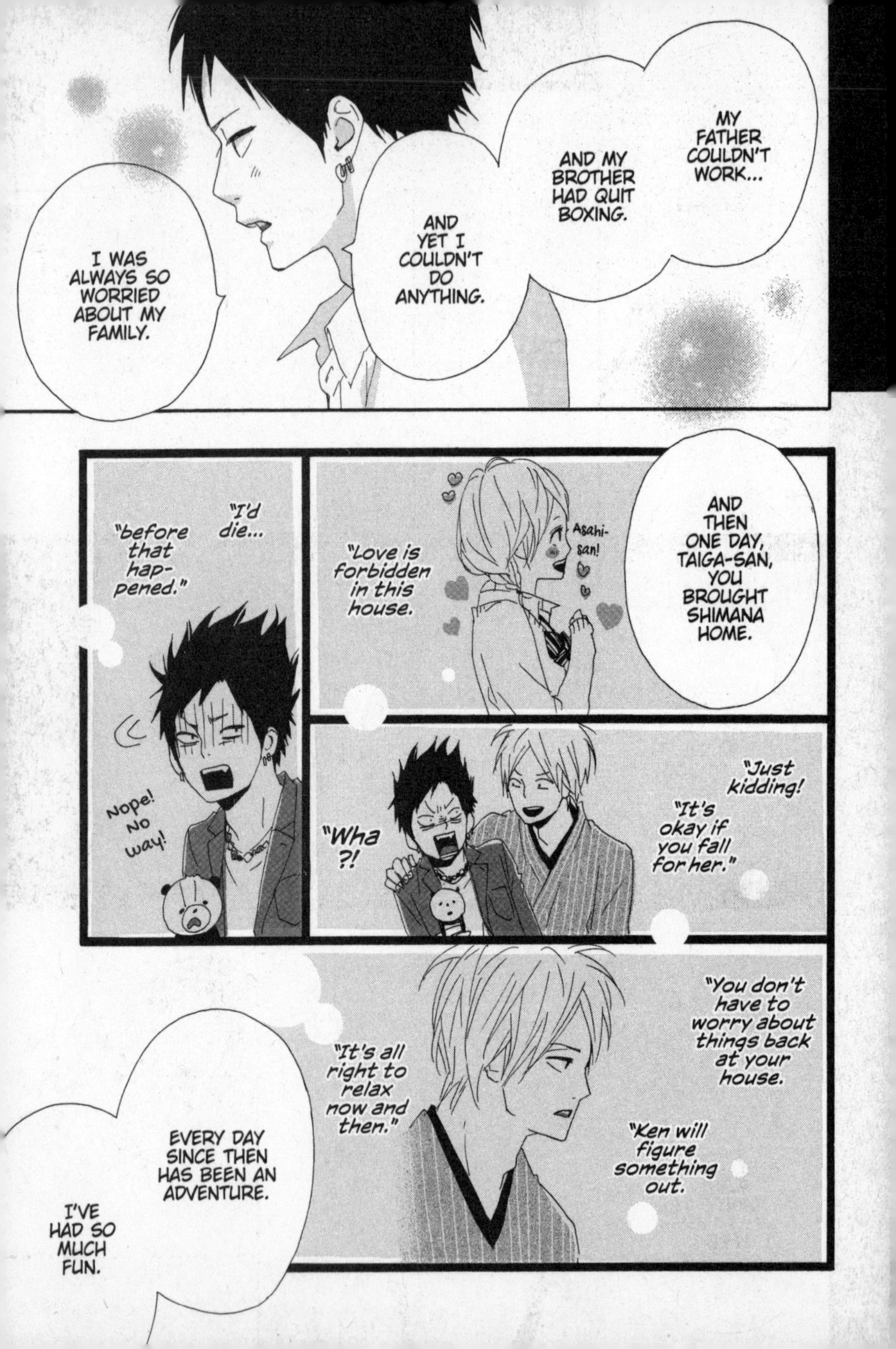
MY FATHER COULDN'T WORK...
AND MY BROTHER HAD QUIT BOXING.
AND YET I COULDN'T DO ANYTHING.
I WAS ALWAYS SO WORRIED ABOUT MY FAMILY.
AND THEN ONE DAY, TAIGA-SAN, YOU BROUGHT SHIMANA HOME.
Asahi-san!
"Love is forbidden in this house.
"Just kidding!
"It's okay if you fall for her."
"Wha?!
"I'd die...
"before that hap-pened."
Nope! No way!
"You don't have to worry about things back at your house.
"Ken will figure something out.
"It's all right to relax now and then."
EVERY DAY SINCE THEN HAS BEEN AN ADVENTURE.
I'VE HAD SO MUCH FUN.

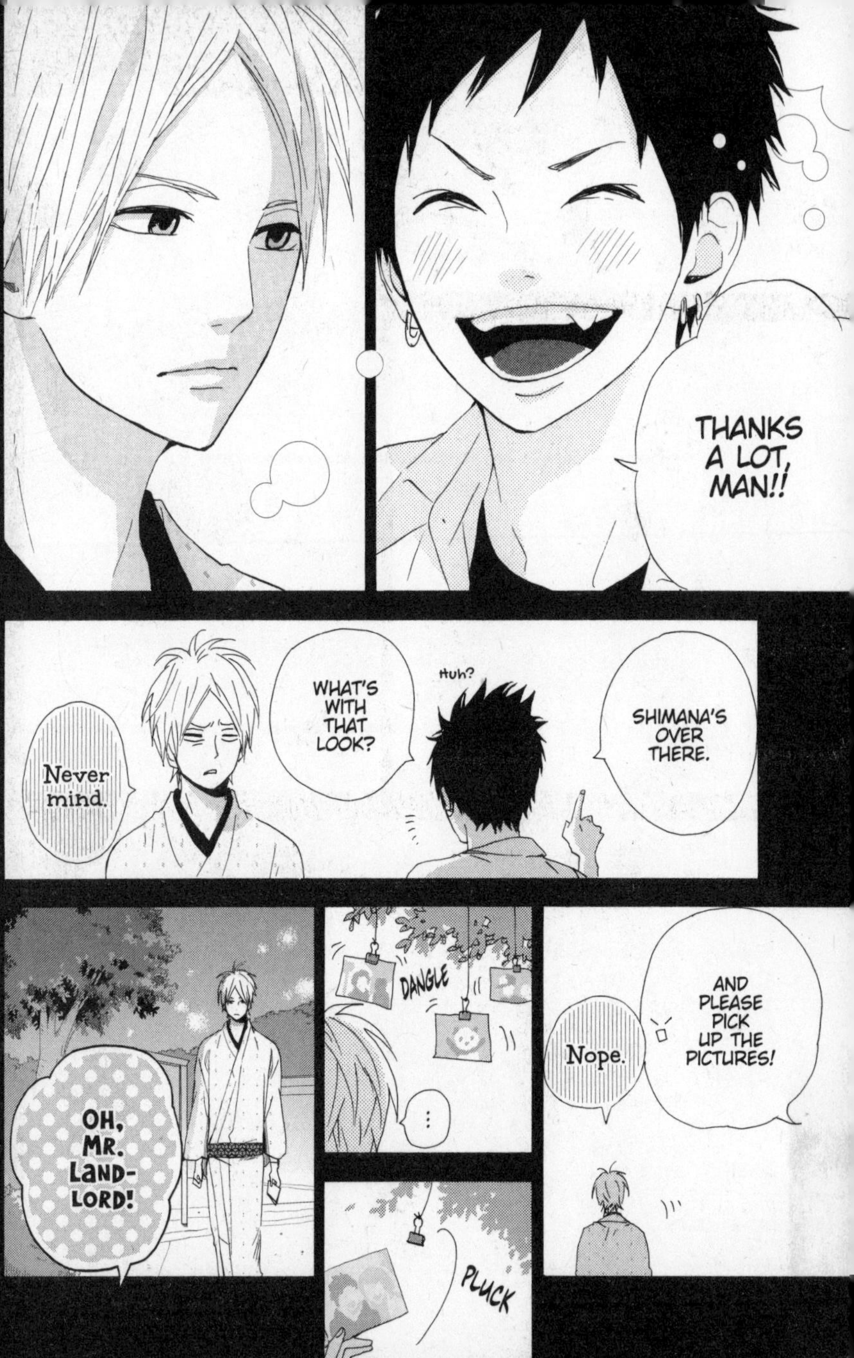
THANKS A LOT, MAN!!
SHIMANA'S OVER THERE.
Huh?
WHAT'S WITH THAT LOOK?
Never mind.
AND PLEASE PICK UP THE PICTURES!
Nope.
DANGLE
...
PLUCK
OH, MR. LAND-LORD!

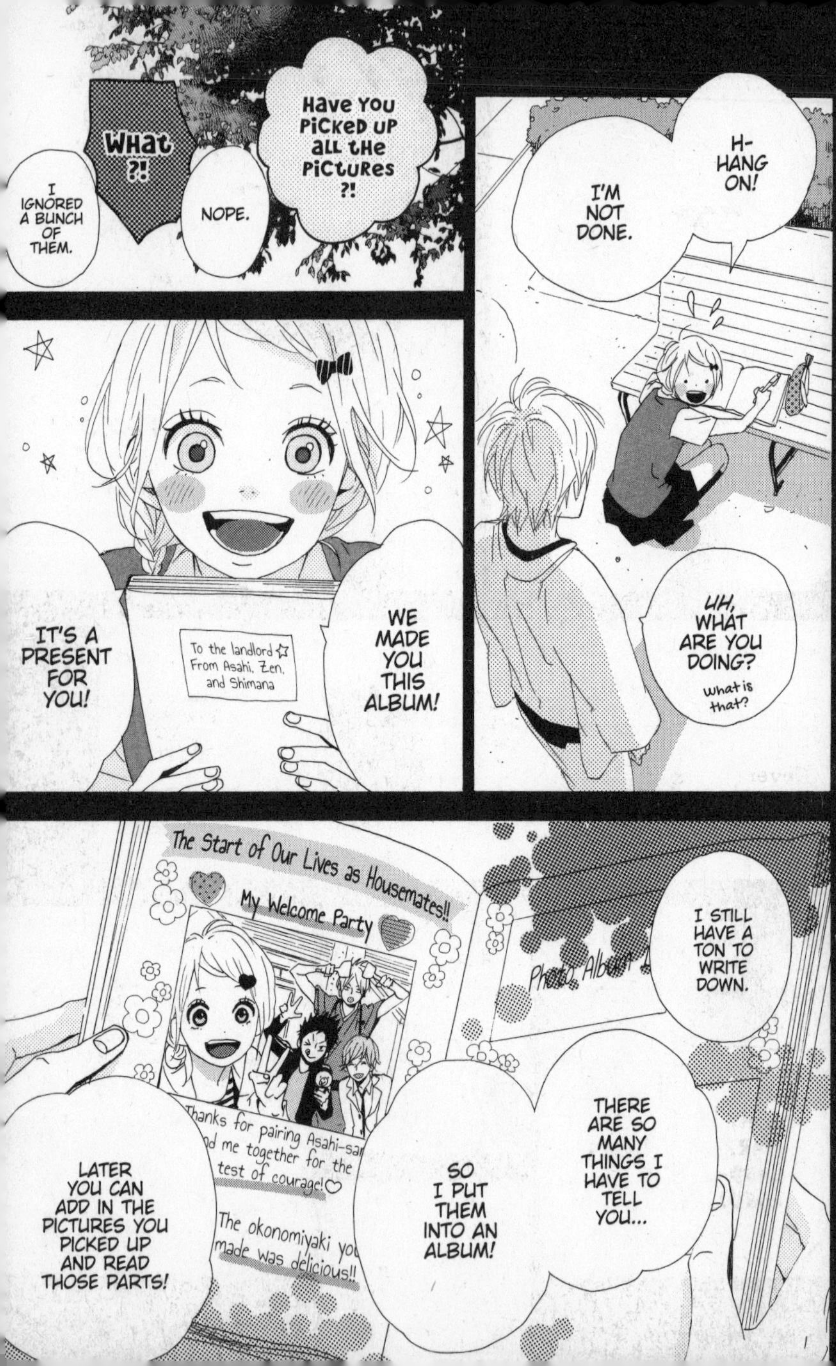
H-HANG ON!
I'M NOT DONE.
UH, WHAT ARE YOU DOING?
what is that?
Have you picked up all the pictures?!
NOPE.
WHAT?!
I IGNORED A BUNCH OF THEM.
WE MADE YOU THIS ALBUM!
To the landlord☆ From Asahi, Zen, and Shimana
IT'S A PRESENT FOR YOU!
I STILL HAVE A TON TO WRITE DOWN.
Photo Album
The Start of Our Lives as Housemates!!
My Welcome Party
hanks for pairing Asahi-sa
nd me together for the
test of courage!♡
The okonomiyaki you
made was delicious!!
THERE ARE SO MANY THINGS I HAVE TO TELL YOU...
SO I PUT THEM INTO AN ALBUM!
LATER YOU CAN ADD IN THE PICTURES YOU PICKED UP AND READ THOSE PARTS!

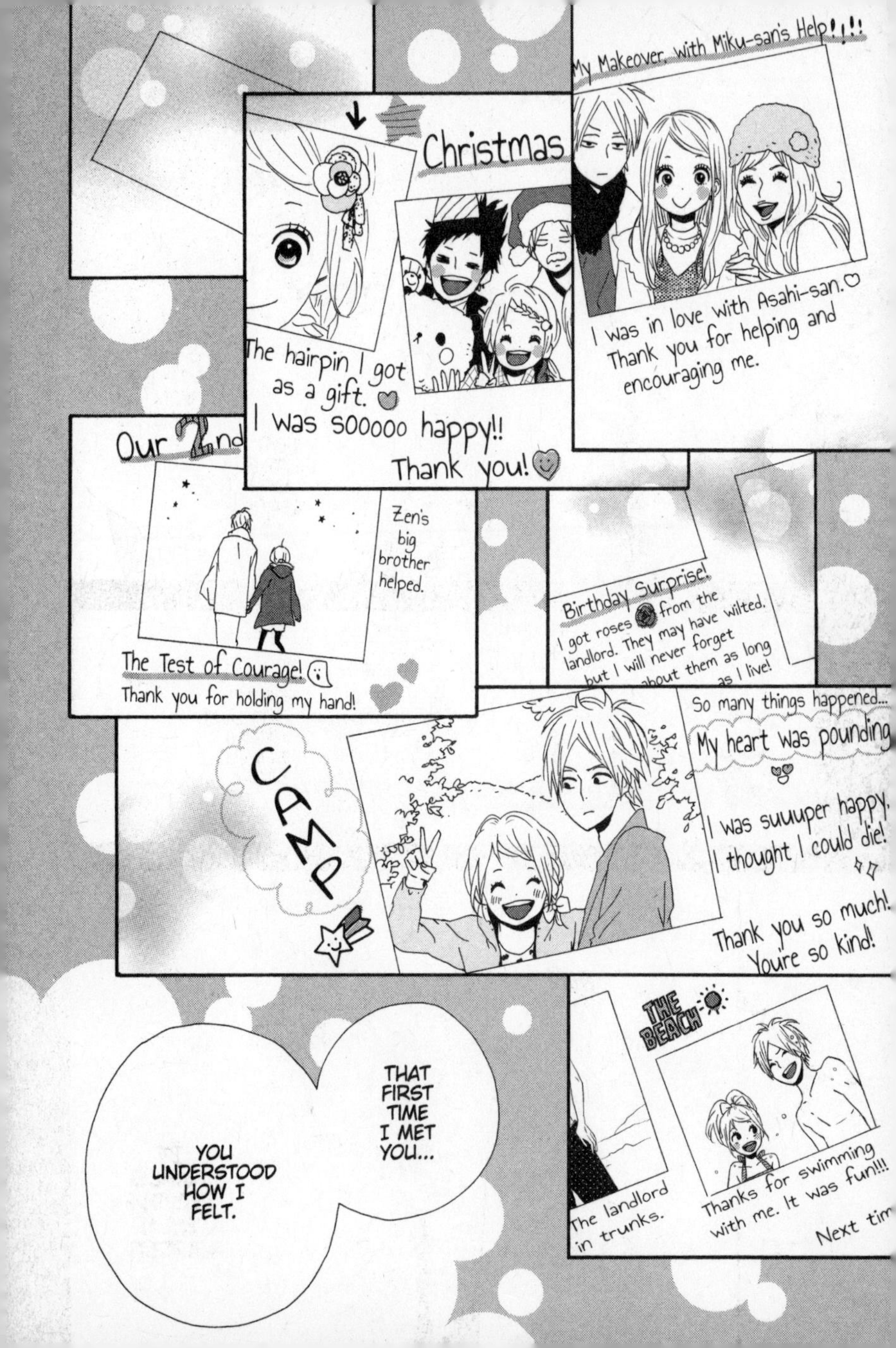

My Makeover, with Miku-san's Help!!!!
I was in love with Asahi-san. Thank you for helping and encouraging me.
Christmas
The hairpin I got as a gift. I was sooooo happy!! Thank you!
Birthday Surprise!
I got roses from the landlord. They may have wilted, but I will never forget about them as long as I live!
Our 2nd
Zen's big brother helped.
The Test of Courage!
Thank you for holding my hand!
So many things happened... My heart was pounding
I was suuuper happy, I thought I could die!
Thank you so much! You're so kind!
CAMP
THE BEACH
Thanks for swimming with me. It was fun!!!
Next tim
The landlord in trunks.
THAT FIRST TIME I MET YOU...
YOU UNDERSTOOD HOW I FELT.

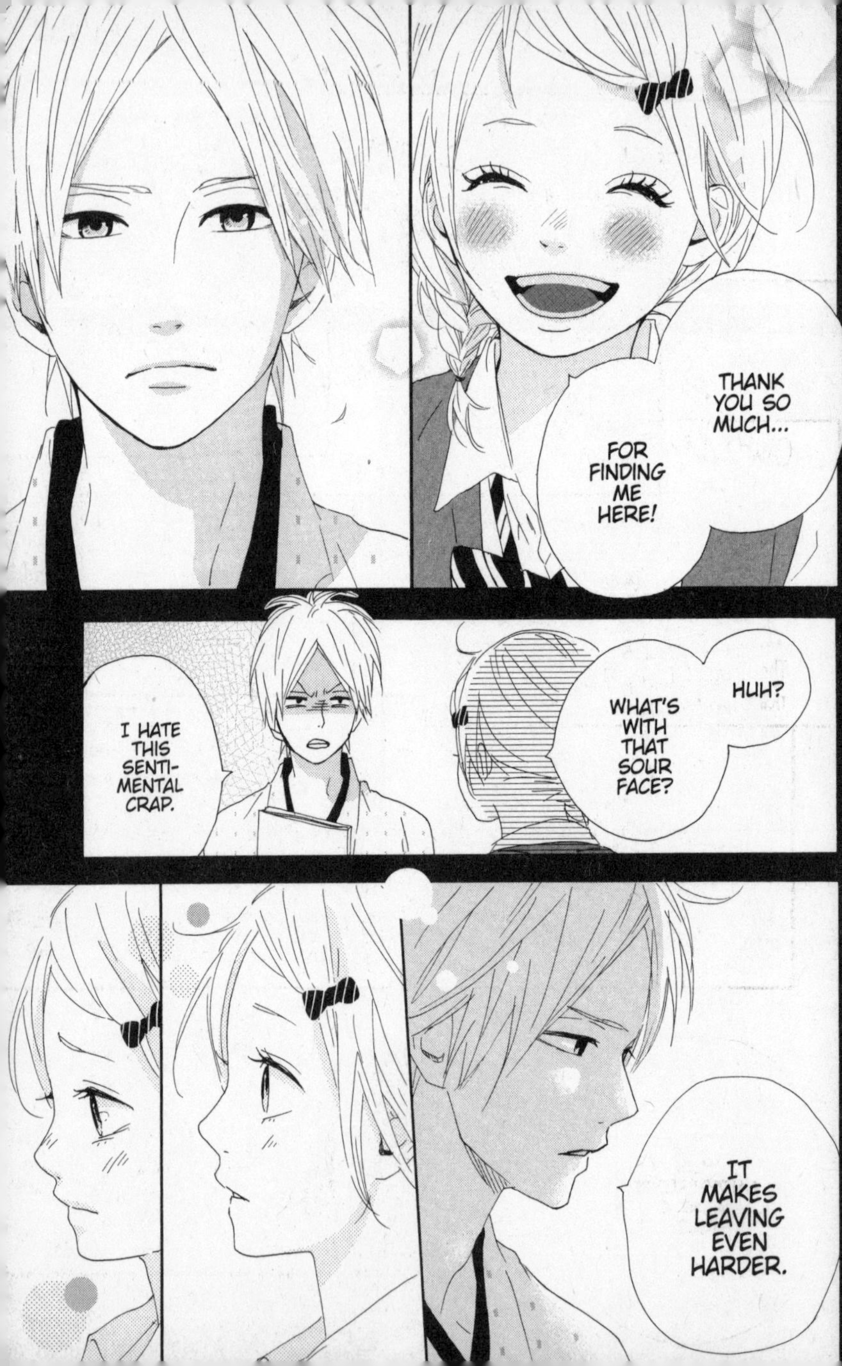
THANK YOU SO MUCH...
FOR FINDING ME HERE!
HUH?
WHAT'S WITH THAT SOUR FACE?
I HATE THIS SENTI-MENTAL CRAP.
IT MAKES LEAVING EVEN HARDER.

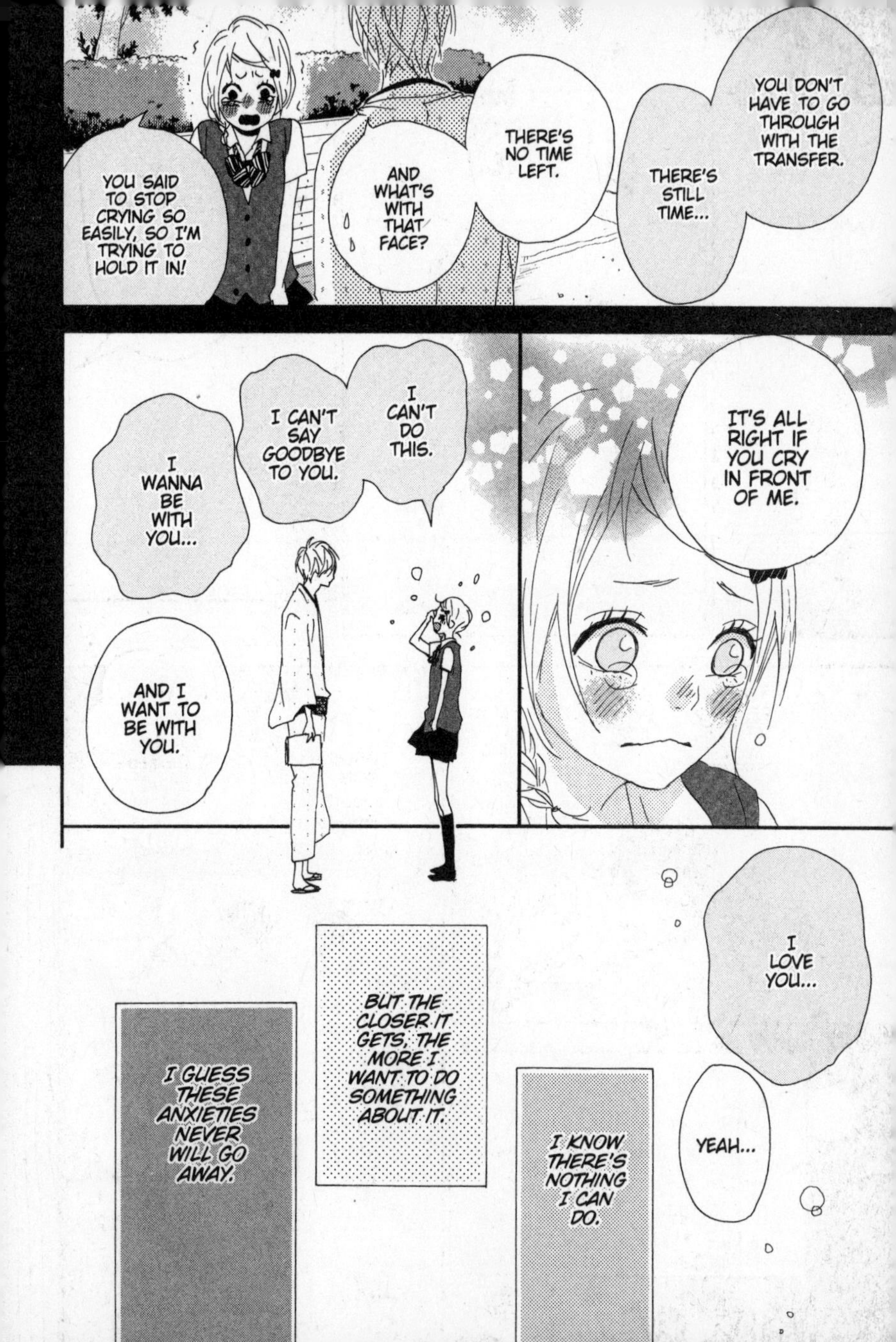
YOU DON'T HAVE TO GO THROUGH WITH THE TRANSFER.
THERE'S STILL TIME...
THERE'S NO TIME LEFT.
AND WHAT'S WITH THAT FACE?
YOU SAID TO STOP CRYING SO EASILY, SO I'M TRYING TO HOLD IT IN!
IT'S ALL RIGHT IF YOU CRY IN FRONT OF ME.
I CAN'T DO THIS.
I CAN'T SAY GOODBYE TO YOU.
I WANNA BE WITH YOU...
AND I WANT TO BE WITH YOU.
I LOVE YOU...
YEAH...
I KNOW THERE'S NOTHING I CAN DO.
BUT THE CLOSER IT GETS, THE MORE I WANT TO DO SOMETHING ABOUT IT.
I GUESS THESE ANXIETIES NEVER WILL GO AWAY.

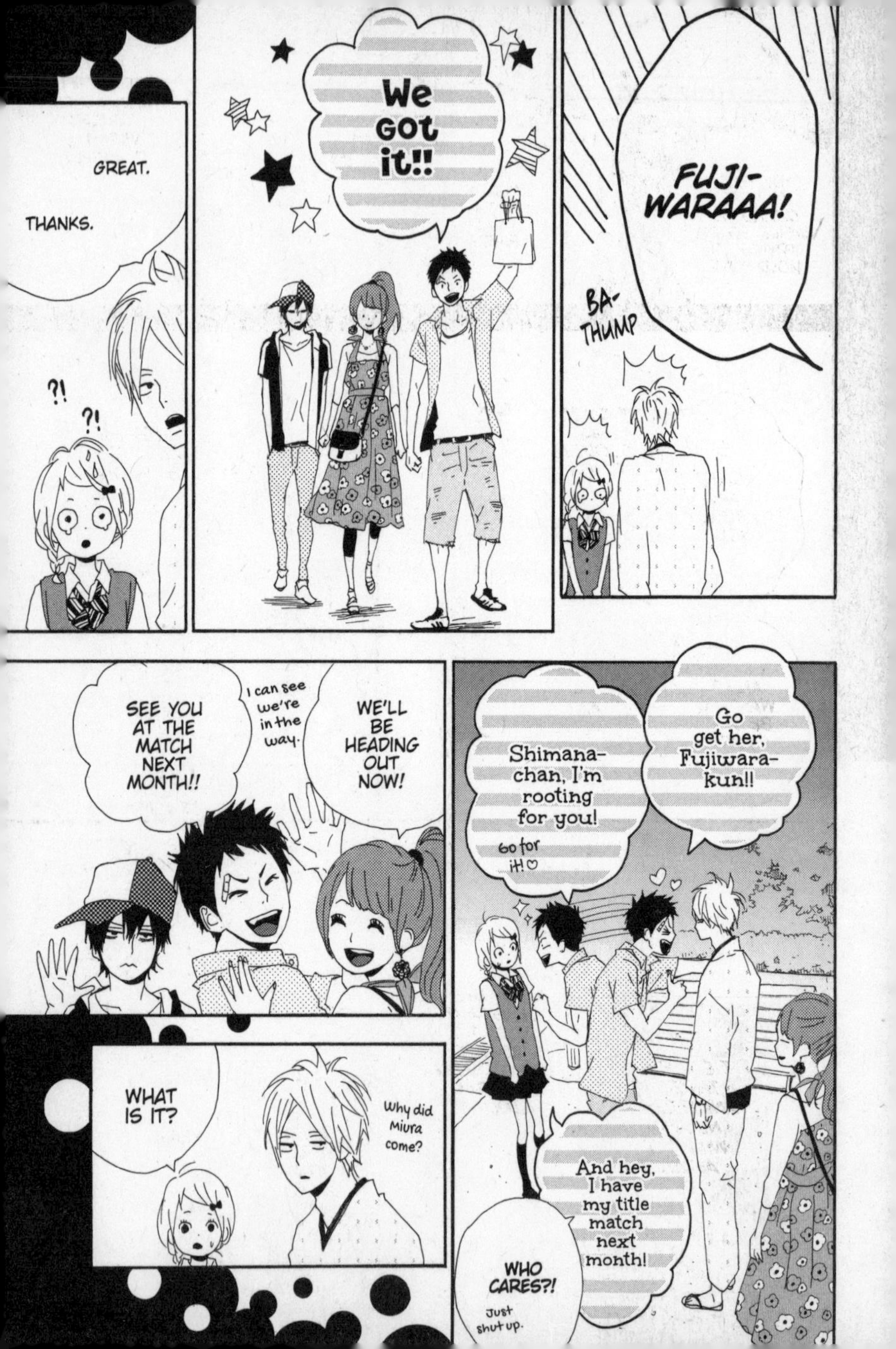
FUJI-WARAAA!
BA-THUMP
We got it!!
GREAT.
THANKS.
?!
?!
Go get her, Fujiwara-kun!!
Shimana-chan, I'm rooting for you!
Go for it!♡
And hey, I have my title match next month!
WHO CARES?!
Just shut up.
WE'LL BE HEADING OUT NOW!
I can see we're in the way.
SEE YOU AT THE MATCH NEXT MONTH!!
WHAT IS IT?
Why did Miura come?

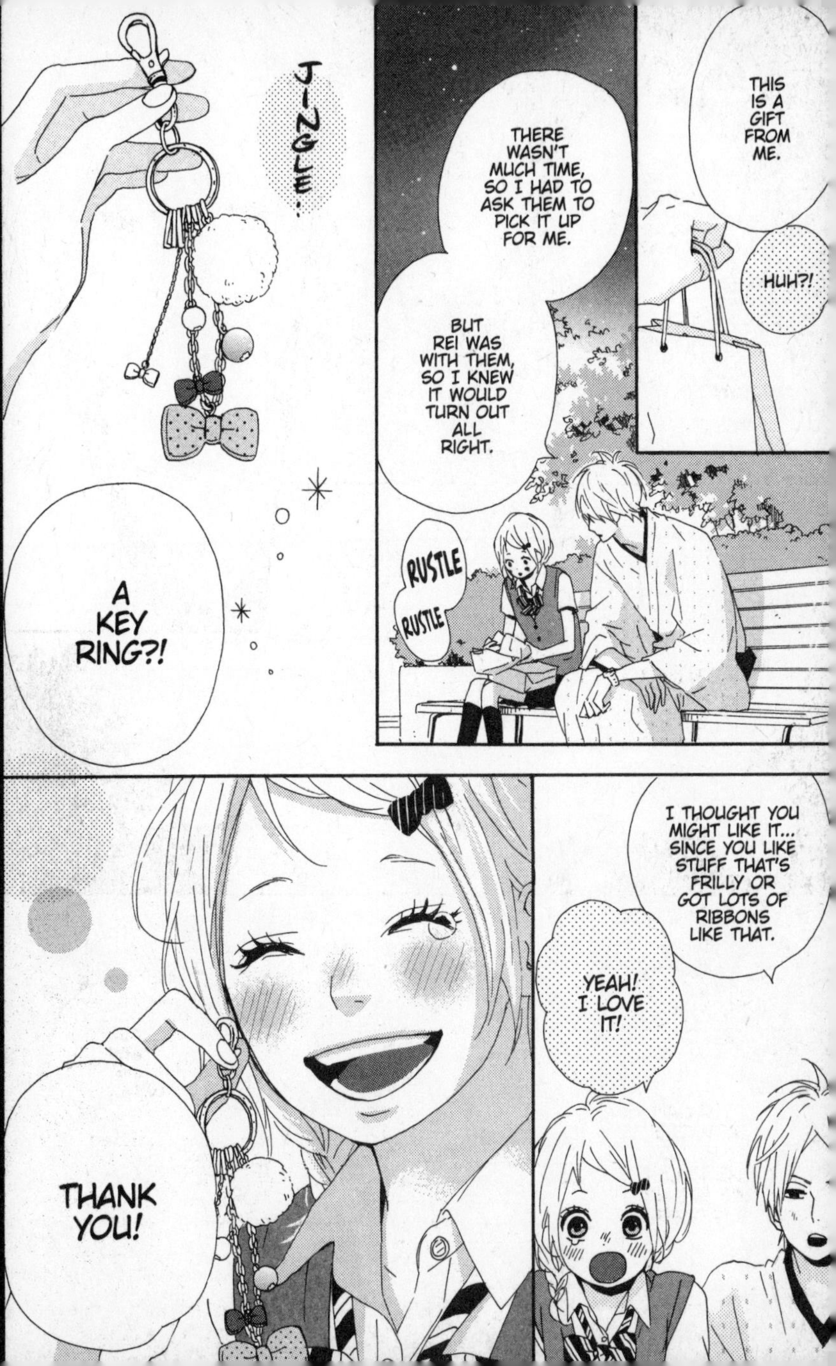
THIS IS A GIFT FROM ME.
HUH?!
THERE WASN'T MUCH TIME, SO I HAD TO ASK THEM TO PICK IT UP FOR ME.
BUT REI WAS WITH THEM, SO I KNEW IT WOULD TURN OUT ALL RIGHT.
RUSTLE
RUSTLE
JINGLE..
A KEY RING?!
I THOUGHT YOU MIGHT LIKE IT... SINCE YOU LIKE STUFF THAT'S FRILLY OR GOT LOTS OF RIBBONS LIKE THAT.
YEAH! I LOVE IT!
THANK YOU!

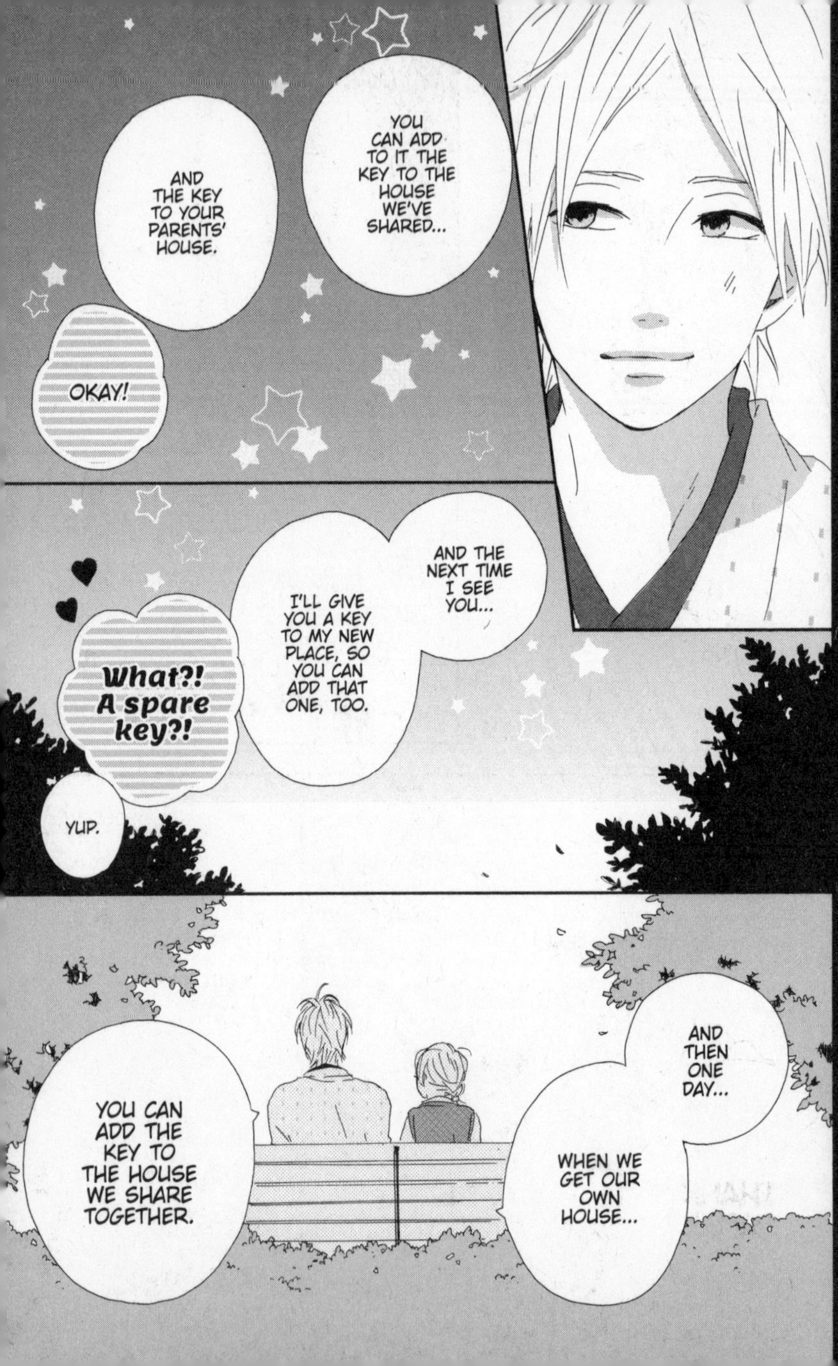

YOU CAN ADD TO IT THE KEY TO THE HOUSE WE'VE SHARED...
AND THE KEY TO YOUR PARENTS' HOUSE.
OKAY!
AND THE NEXT TIME I SEE YOU...
I'LL GIVE YOU A KEY TO MY NEW PLACE, SO YOU CAN ADD THAT ONE, TOO.
What?! A spare key?!
YUP.
AND THEN ONE DAY...
WHEN WE GET OUR OWN HOUSE...
YOU CAN ADD THE KEY TO THE HOUSE WE SHARE TOGETHER.

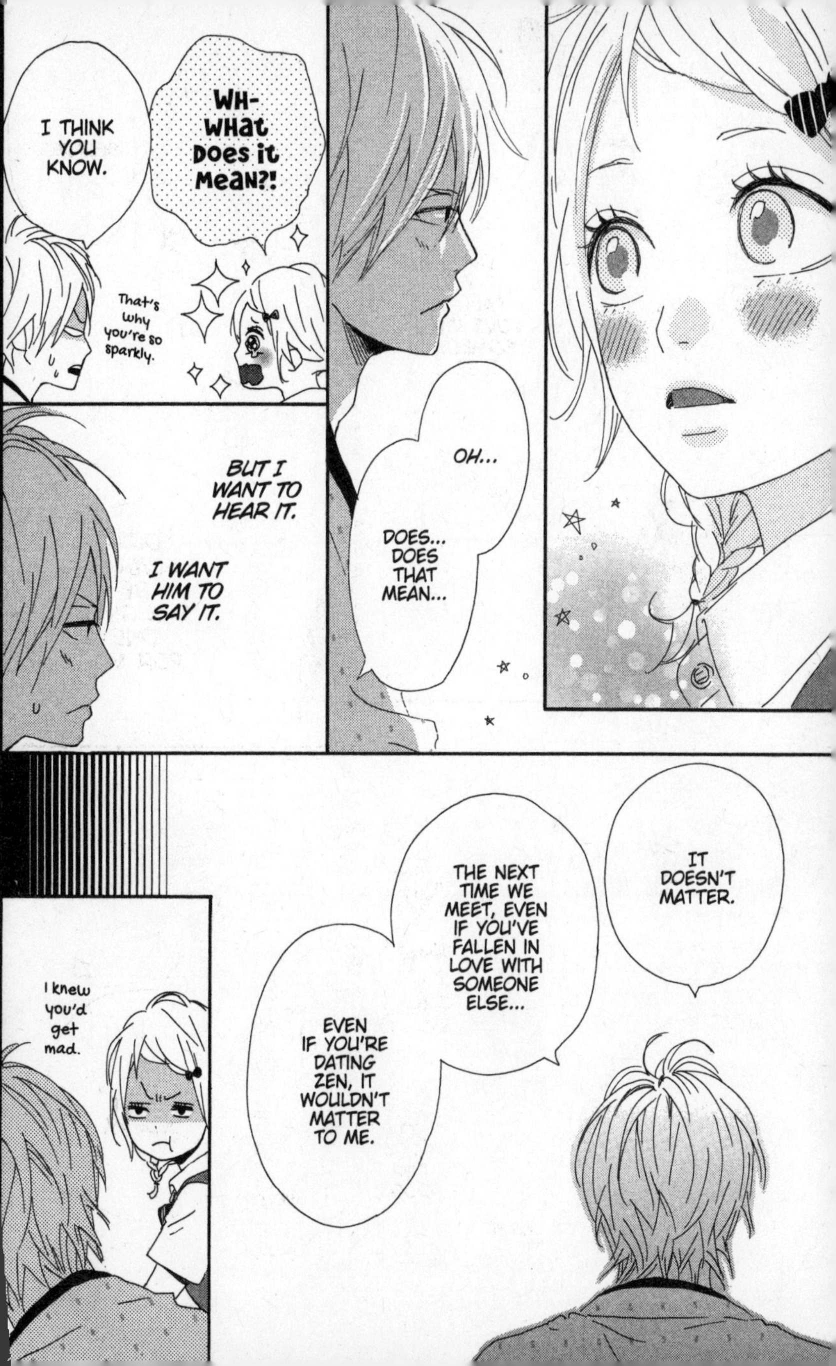
OH...
DOES... DOES THAT MEAN...
I THINK YOU KNOW.
WH-WHAT DOES IT MEAN?!
That's why you're so sparkly.
BUT I WANT TO HEAR IT.
I WANT HIM TO SAY IT.
IT DOESN'T MATTER.
THE NEXT TIME WE MEET, EVEN IF YOU'VE FALLEN IN LOVE WITH SOMEONE ELSE...
EVEN IF YOU'RE DATING ZEN, IT WOULDN'T MATTER TO ME.
I knew you'd get mad.

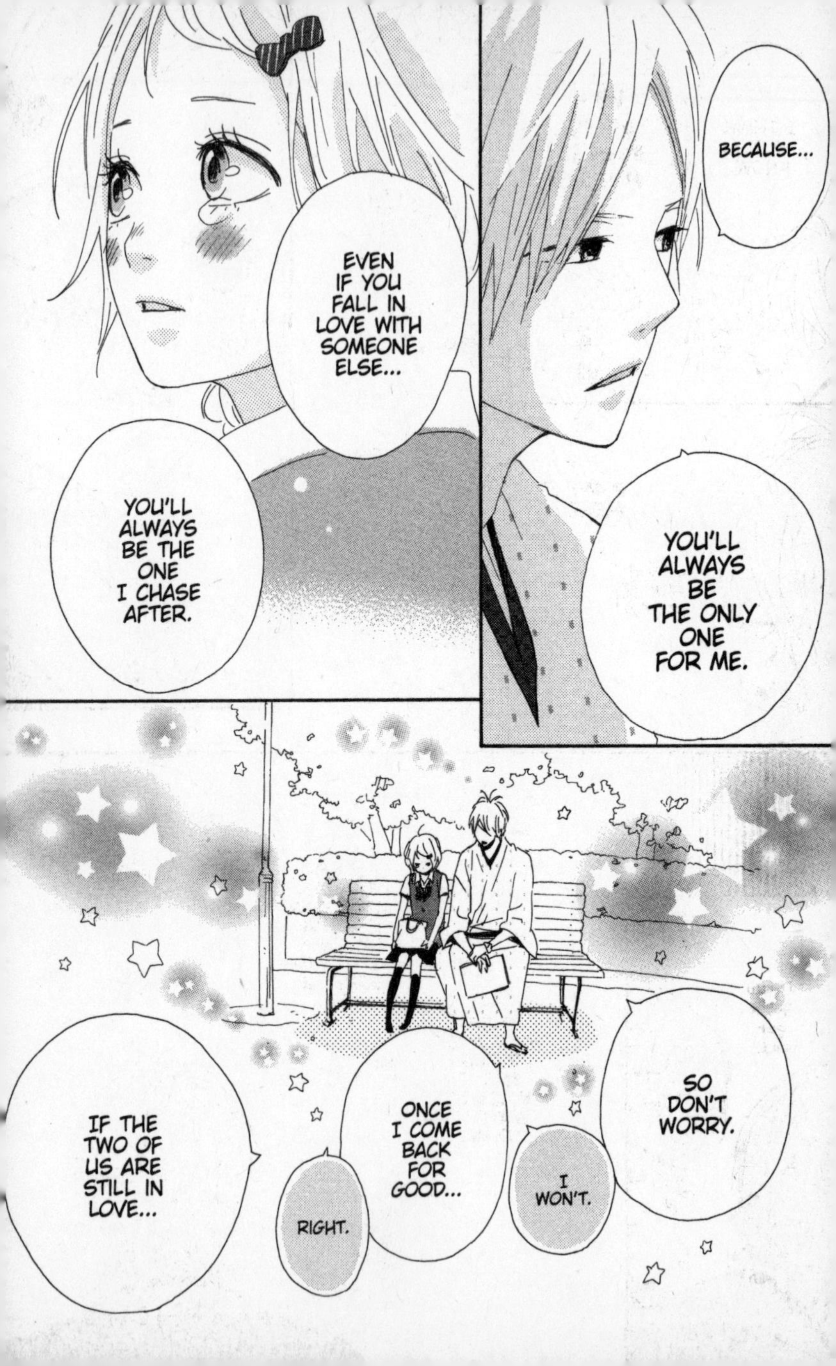
BECAUSE...
YOU'LL ALWAYS BE THE ONLY ONE FOR ME.
EVEN IF YOU FALL IN LOVE WITH SOMEONE ELSE...
YOU'LL ALWAYS BE THE ONE I CHASE AFTER.
SO DON'T WORRY.
I WON'T.
ONCE I COME BACK FOR GOOD...
RIGHT.
IF THE TWO OF US ARE STILL IN LOVE...

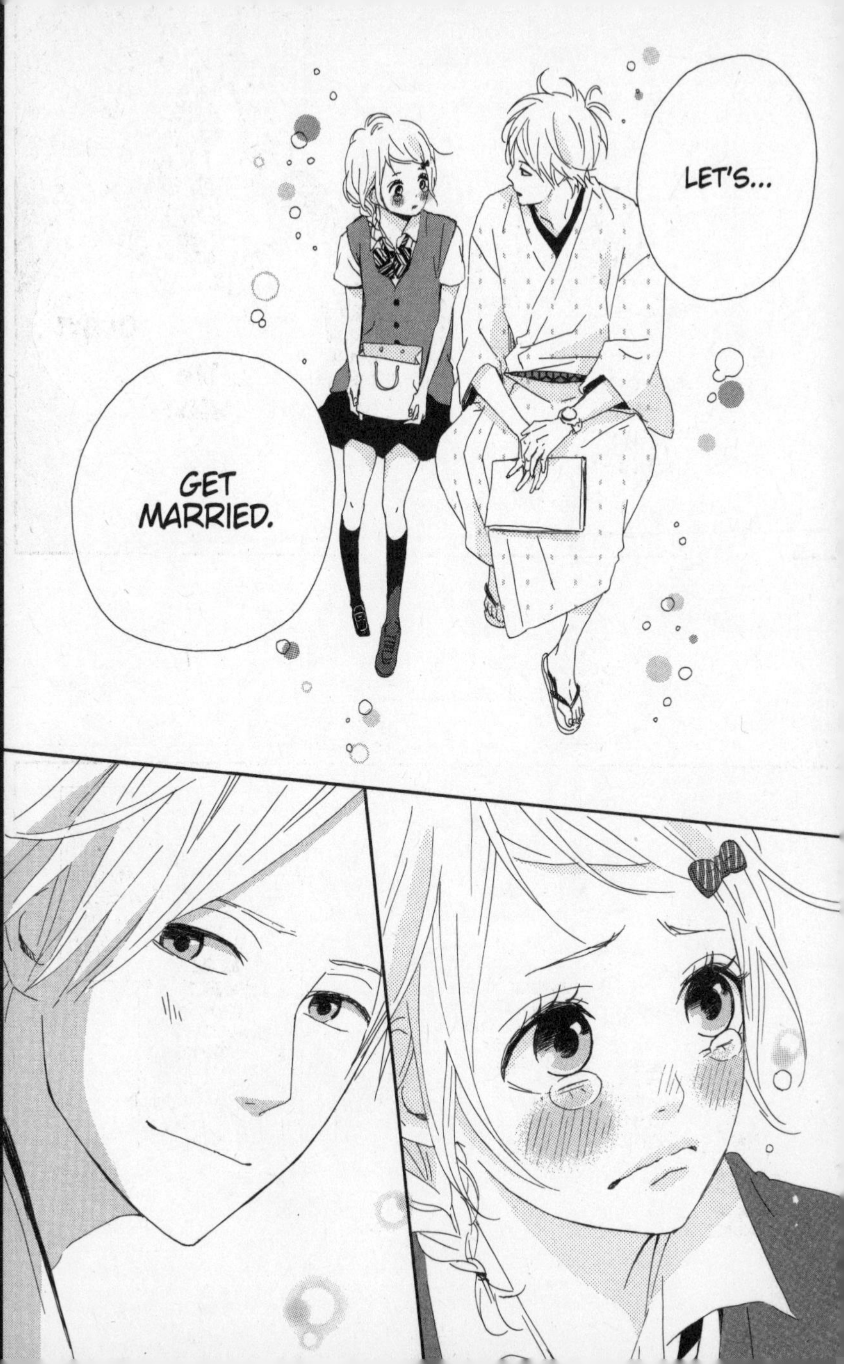
LET'S...
GET MARRIED.

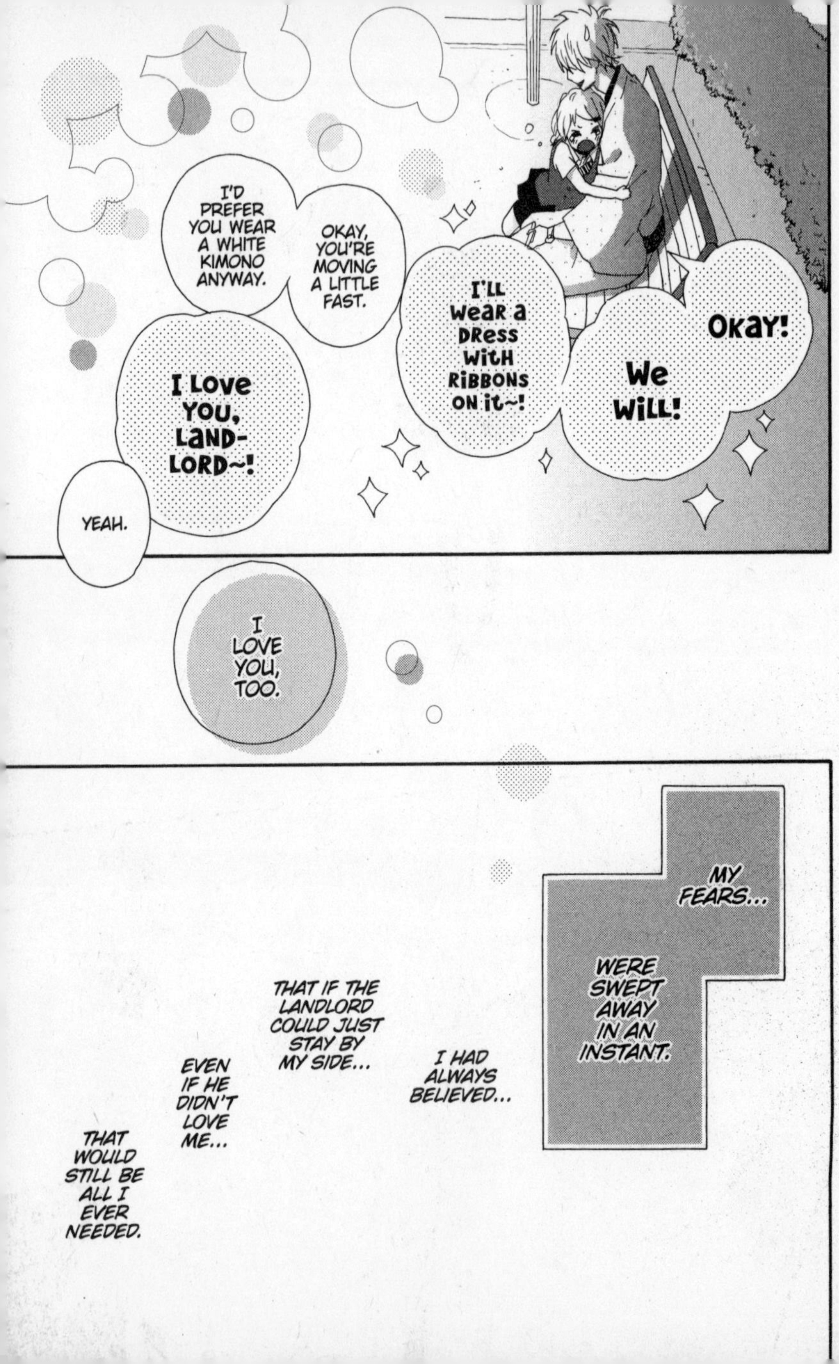
OKAY! We WILL!
I'LL WEAR A DRESS WITH RIBBONS ON IT~!
OKAY, YOU'RE MOVING A LITTLE FAST.
I'D PREFER YOU WEAR A WHITE KIMONO ANYWAY.
I LOVE YOU, LAND-LORD~!
YEAH.
I LOVE YOU, TOO.
MY FEARS...
WERE SWEPT AWAY IN AN INSTANT.
I HAD ALWAYS BELIEVED...
THAT IF THE LANDLORD COULD JUST STAY BY MY SIDE...
EVEN IF HE DIDN'T LOVE ME...
THAT WOULD STILL BE ALL I EVER NEEDED.

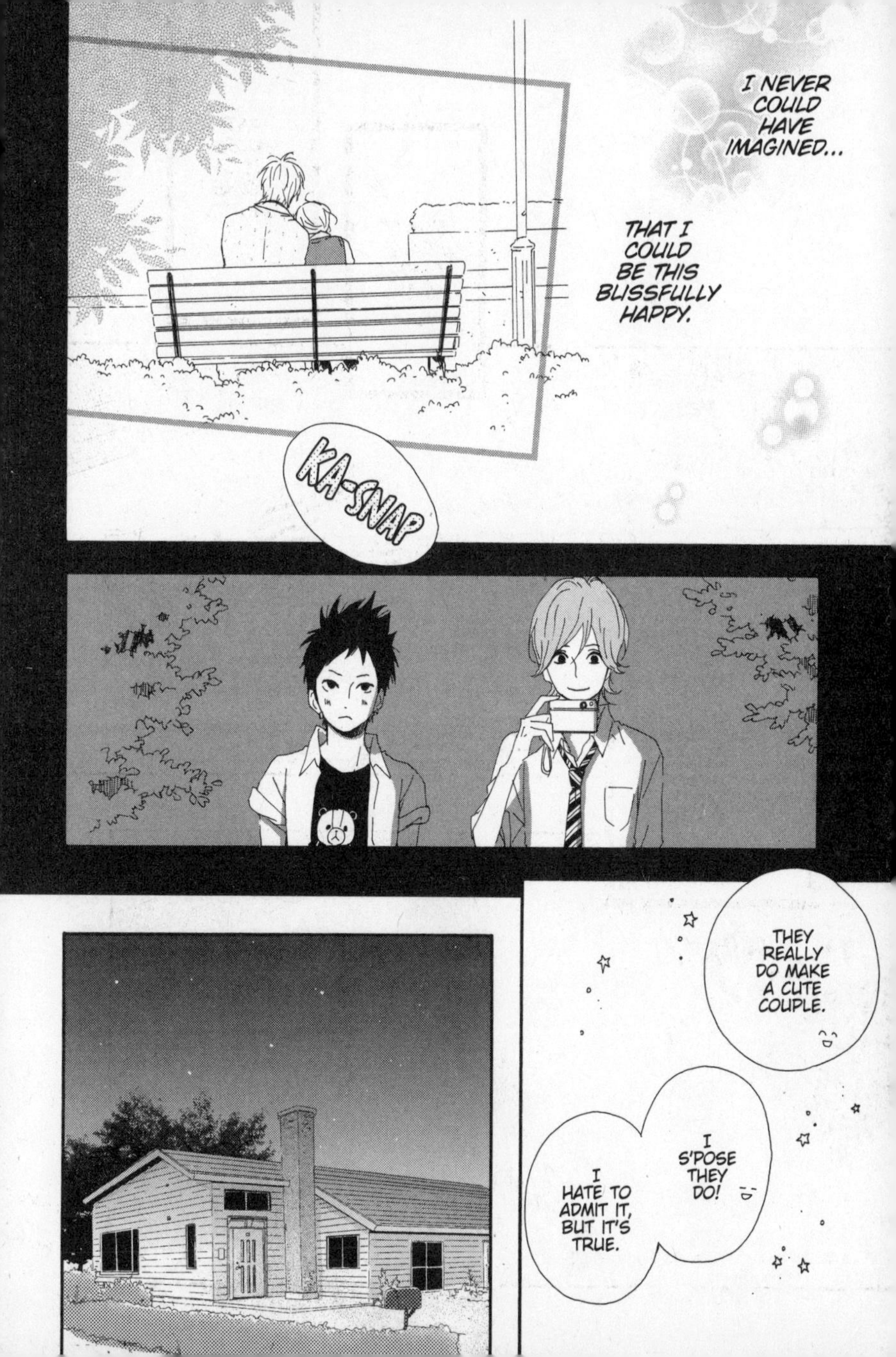
I NEVER COULD HAVE IMAGINED...
THAT I COULD BE THIS BLISSFULLY HAPPY.
KA-SNAP
THEY REALLY DO MAKE A CUTE COUPLE.
I S'POSE THEY DO!
I HATE TO ADMIT IT, BUT IT'S TRUE.

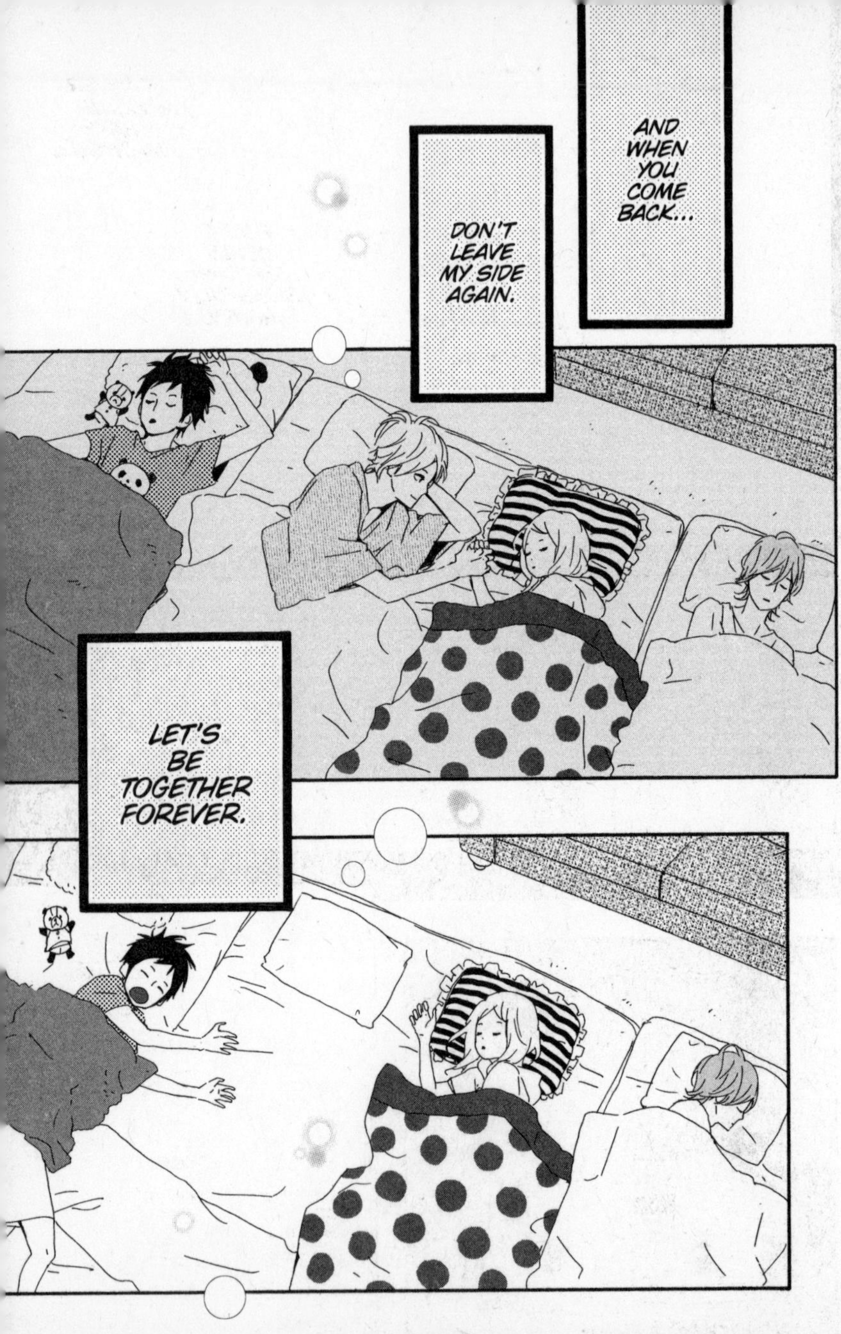
AND WHEN YOU COME BACK...
DON'T LEAVE MY SIDE AGAIN.
LET'S BE TOGETHER FOREVER.

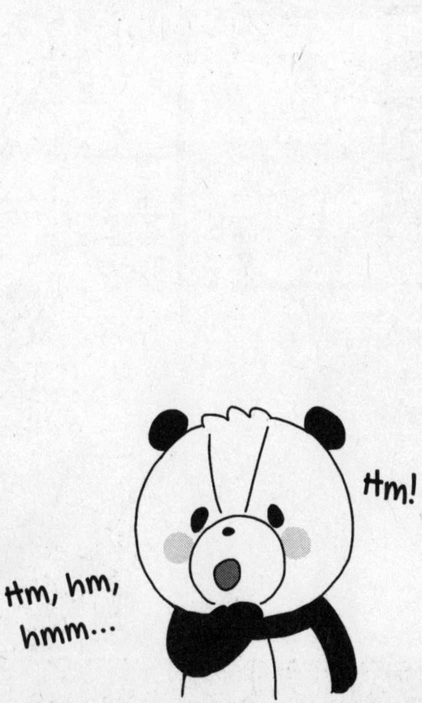
Hm!
Hm, hm, hmm...

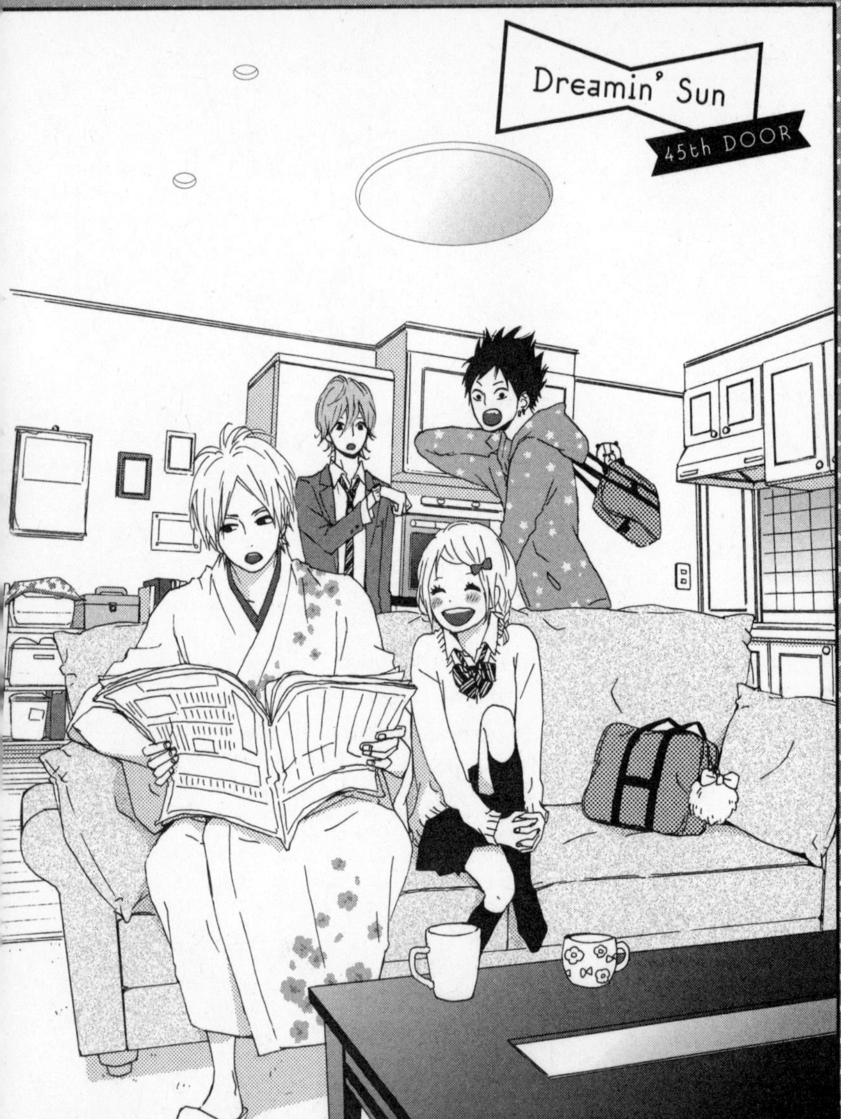
Dreamin' Sun
45th DOOR

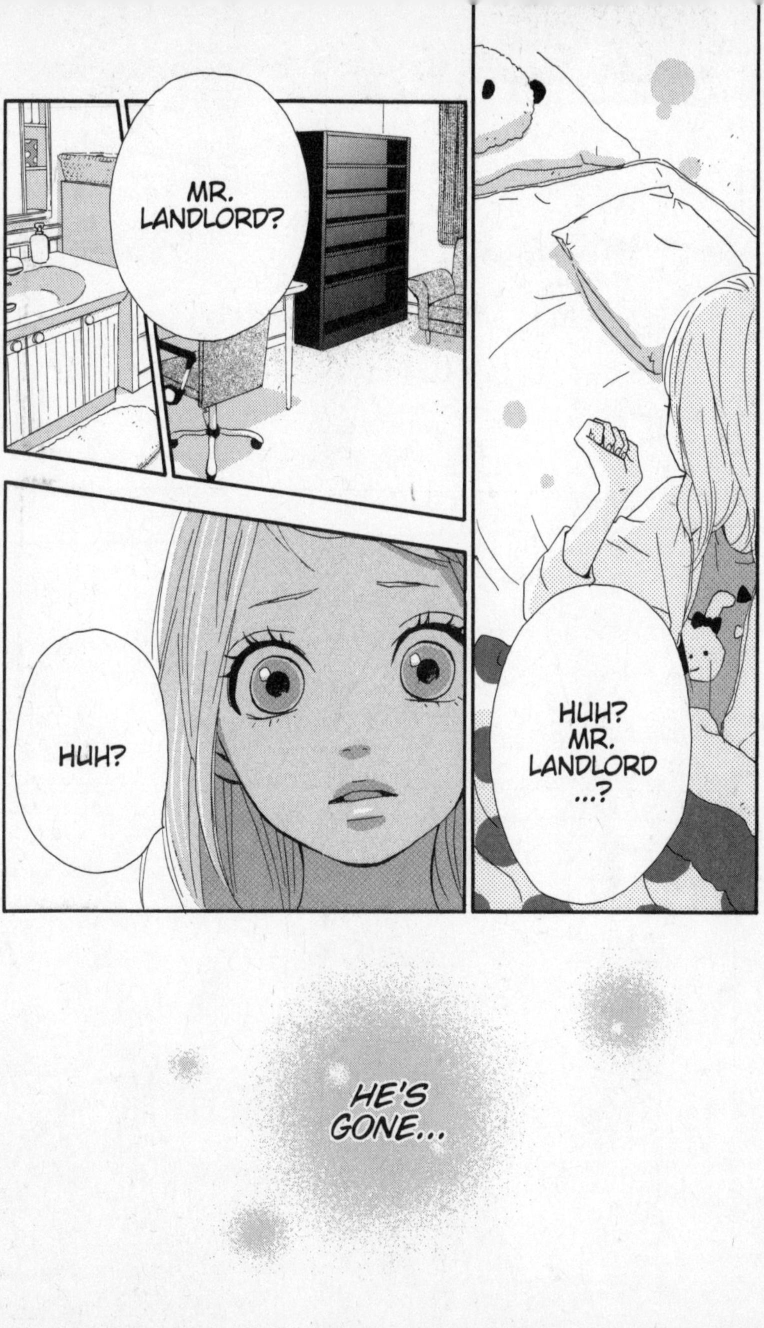
HUH? MR. LANDLORD ...?
MR. LANDLORD?
HUH?
HE'S GONE...

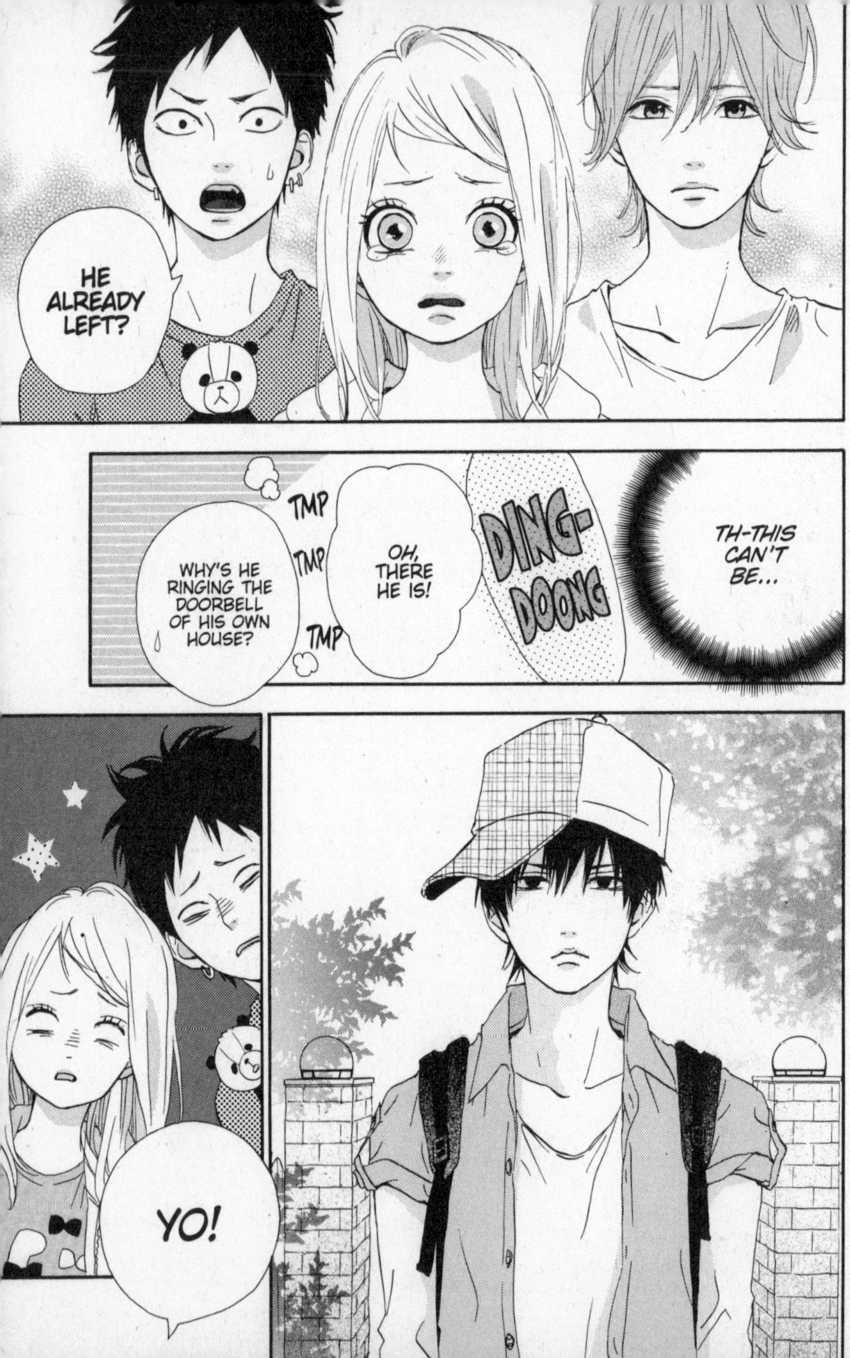
HE ALREADY LEFT?
TH-THIS CAN'T BE...
DING-DOONG
OH, THERE HE IS!
TMP
TMP
TMP
WHY'S HE RINGING THE DOORBELL OF HIS OWN HOUSE?
YO!

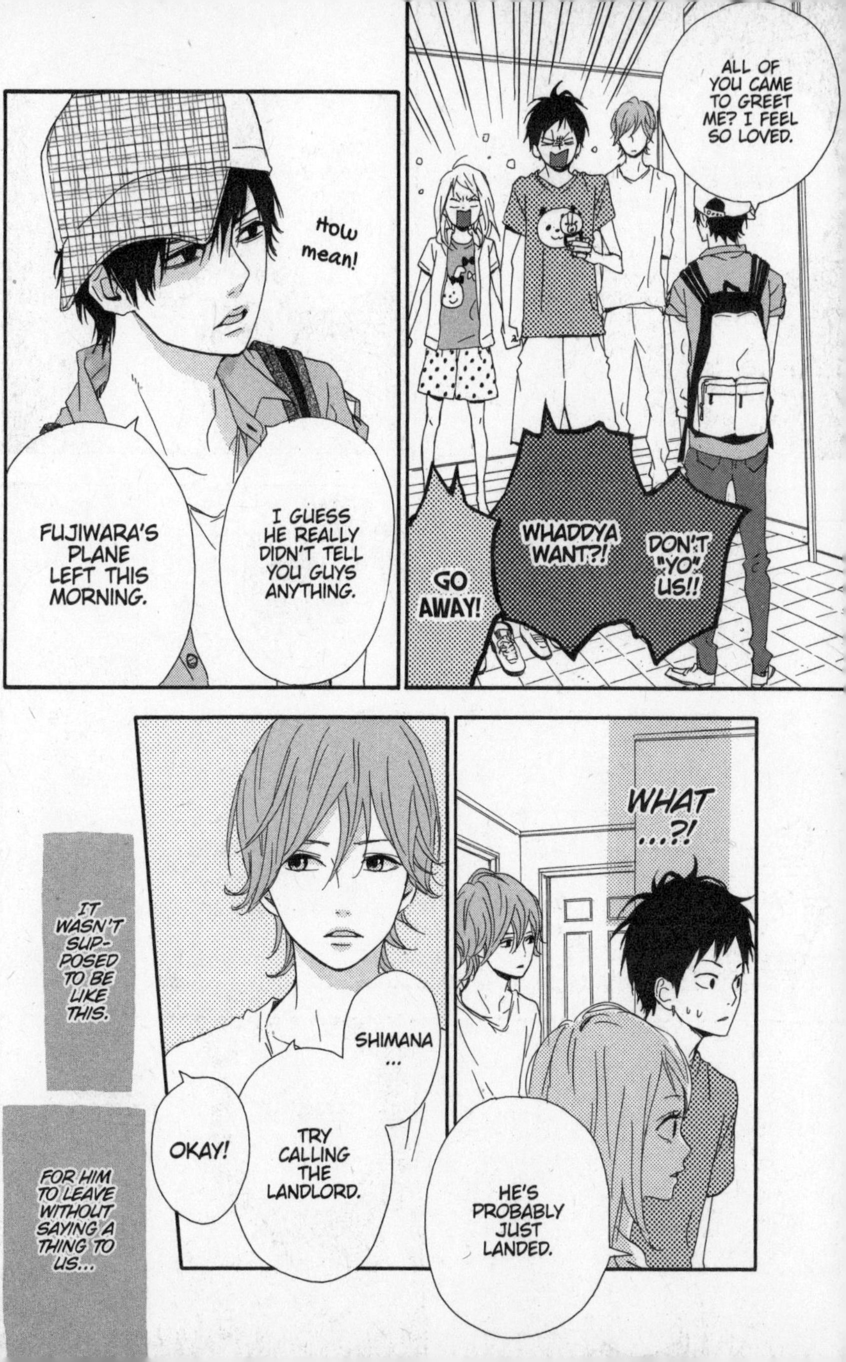
ALL OF YOU CAME TO GREET ME? I FEEL SO LOVED.
DON'T "YO" US!!
WHADDYA WANT?!
GO AWAY!
How mean!
I GUESS HE REALLY DIDN'T TELL YOU GUYS ANYTHING.
FUJIWARA'S PLANE LEFT THIS MORNING.
WHAT ...?!
HE'S PROBABLY JUST LANDED.
SHIMANA ...
TRY CALLING THE LANDLORD.
OKAY!
IT WASN'T SUP-POSED TO BE LIKE THIS.
FOR HIM TO LEAVE WITHOUT SAYING A THING TO US...

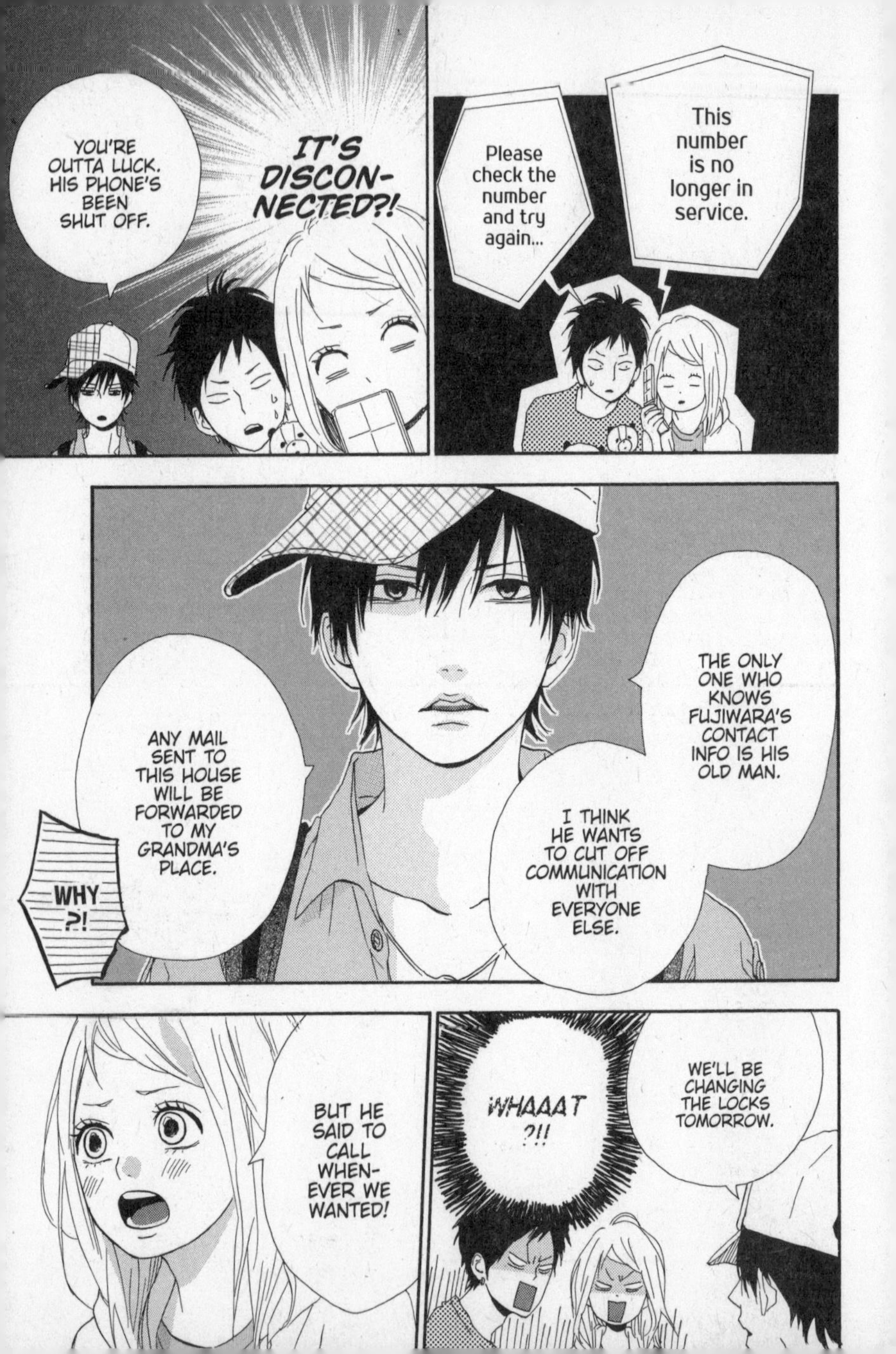
This number is no longer in service.
Please check the number and try again...
IT'S DISCONNECTED?!
YOU'RE OUTTA LUCK. HIS PHONE'S BEEN SHUT OFF.
THE ONLY ONE WHO KNOWS FUJIWARA'S CONTACT INFO IS HIS OLD MAN.
I THINK HE WANTS TO CUT OFF COMMUNICATION WITH EVERYONE ELSE.
ANY MAIL SENT TO THIS HOUSE WILL BE FORWARDED TO MY GRANDMA'S PLACE.
WHY?!
WE'LL BE CHANGING THE LOCKS TOMORROW.
WHAAAT?!!
BUT HE SAID TO CALL WHENEVER WE WANTED!

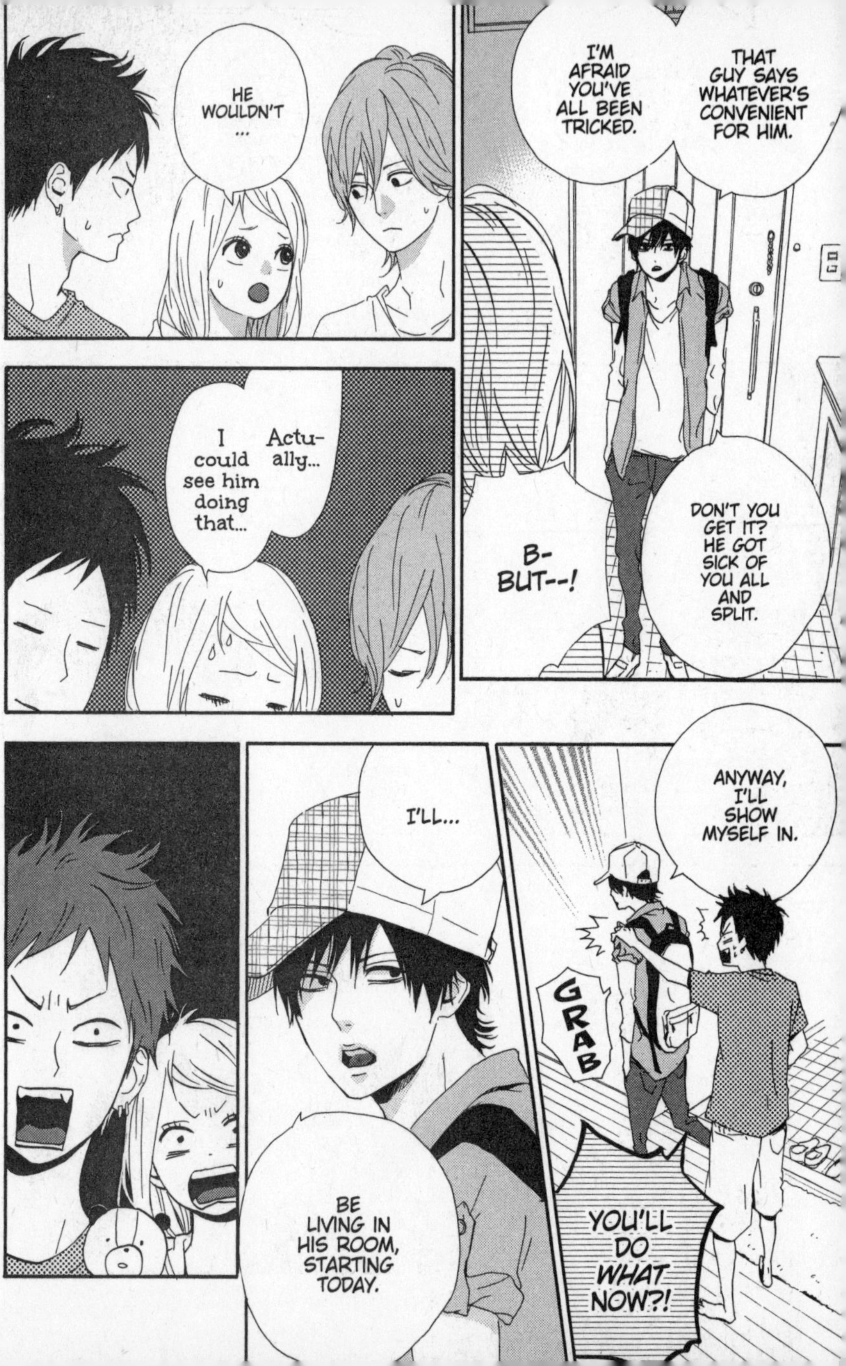
THAT GUY SAYS WHATEVER'S CONVENIENT FOR HIM.
I'M AFRAID YOU'VE ALL BEEN TRICKED.
DON'T YOU GET IT? HE GOT SICK OF YOU ALL AND SPLIT.
B-BUT--!
HE WOULDN'T ...
Actually... I could see him doing that...
ANYWAY, I'LL SHOW MYSELF IN.
GRAB
I'LL...
BE LIVING IN HIS ROOM, STARTING TODAY.
YOU'LL DO WHAT NOW?!

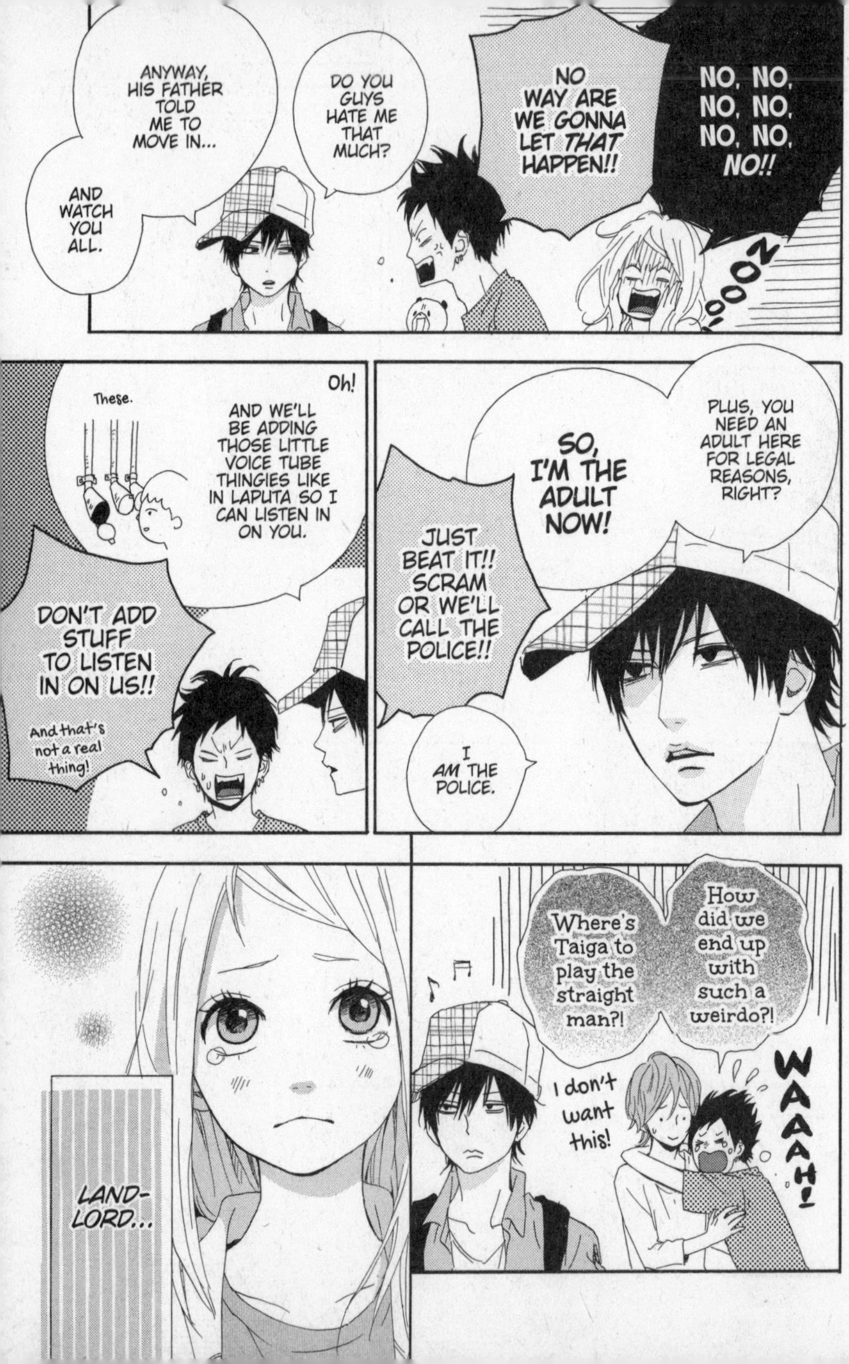
NO, NO, NO, NO, NO, NO, NO!!
NOOOOO
NO WAY ARE WE GONNA LET THAT HAPPEN!!
DO YOU GUYS HATE ME THAT MUCH?
ANYWAY, HIS FATHER TOLD ME TO MOVE IN...
AND WATCH YOU ALL.
PLUS, YOU NEED AN ADULT HERE FOR LEGAL REASONS, RIGHT?
SO, I'M THE ADULT NOW!
JUST BEAT IT!! SCRAM OR WE'LL CALL THE POLICE!!
I AM THE POLICE.
Oh!
AND WE'LL BE ADDING THOSE LITTLE VOICE TUBE THINGIES LIKE IN LAPUTA SO I CAN LISTEN IN ON YOU.
These.
DON'T ADD STUFF TO LISTEN IN ON US!!
And that's not a real thing!
How did we end up with such a weirdo?!
Where's Taiga to play the straight man?!
WAAAH!
I don't want this!
LAND-LORD...

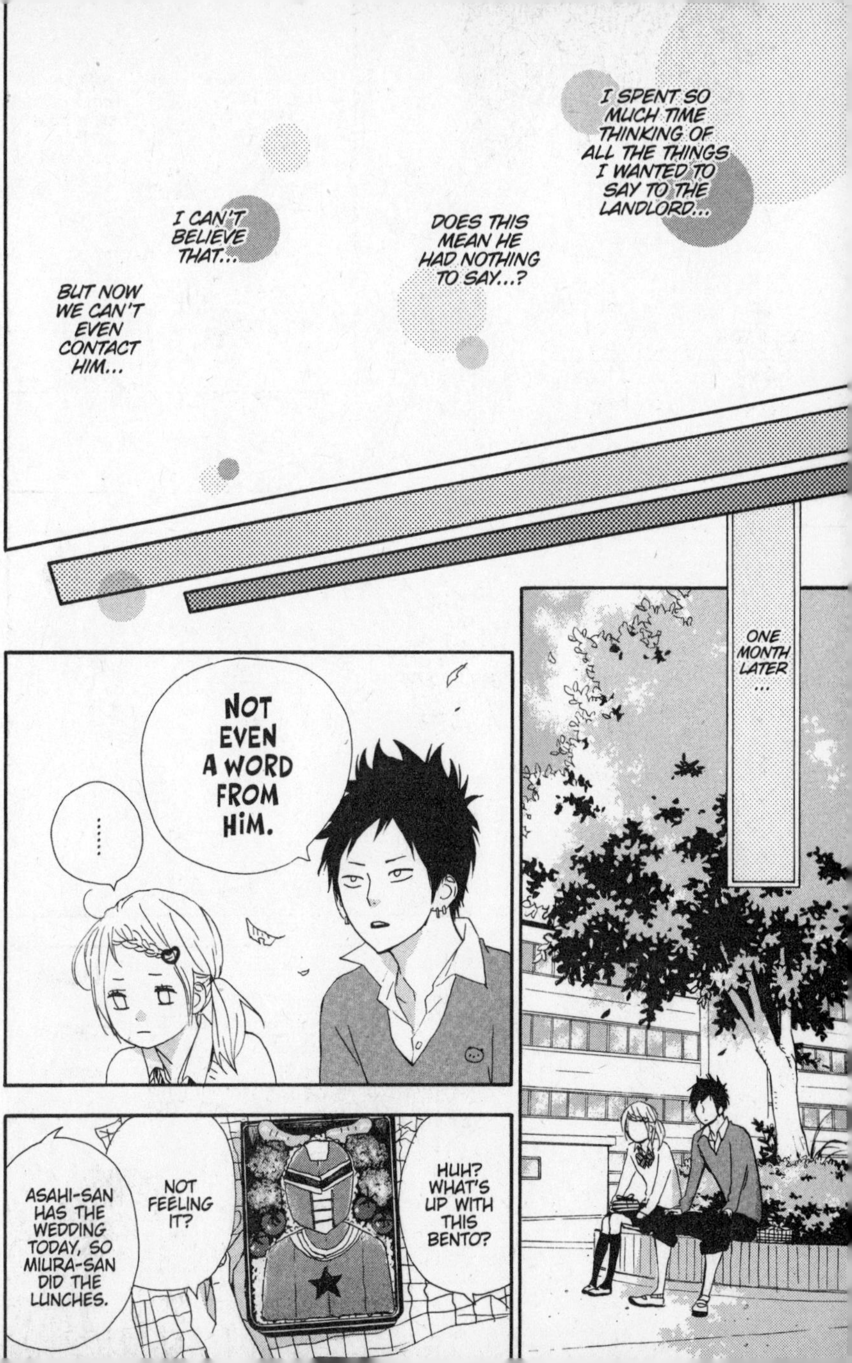
I SPENT SO MUCH TIME THINKING OF ALL THE THINGS I WANTED TO SAY TO THE LANDLORD...
DOES THIS MEAN HE HAD NOTHING TO SAY...?
I CAN'T BELIEVE THAT...
BUT NOW WE CAN'T EVEN CONTACT HIM...
ONE MONTH LATER...
NOT EVEN A WORD FROM HIM.
......
HUH? WHAT'S UP WITH THIS BENTO?
NOT FEELING IT?
ASAHI-SAN HAS THE WEDDING TODAY, SO MIURA-SAN DID THE LUNCHES.

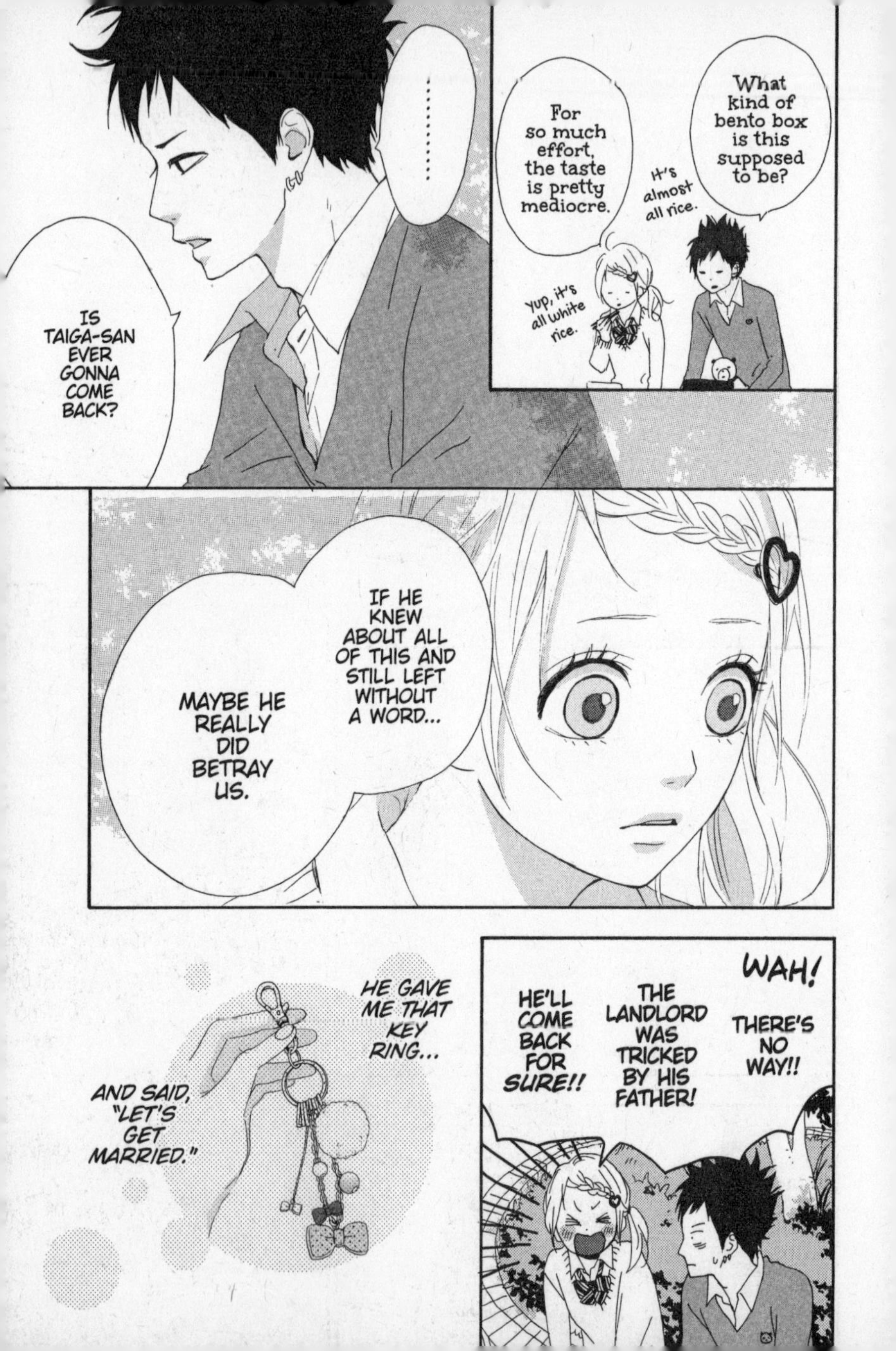
What kind of bento box is this supposed to be?
It's almost all rice.
For so much effort, the taste is pretty mediocre.
Yup, it's all white rice.
......
IS TAIGA-SAN EVER GONNA COME BACK?
IF HE KNEW ABOUT ALL OF THIS AND STILL LEFT WITHOUT A WORD...
MAYBE HE REALLY DID BETRAY US.
WAH!
THERE'S NO WAY!!
THE LANDLORD WAS TRICKED BY HIS FATHER!
HE'LL COME BACK FOR SURE!!
HE GAVE ME THAT KEY RING...
AND SAID, "LET'S GET MARRIED."

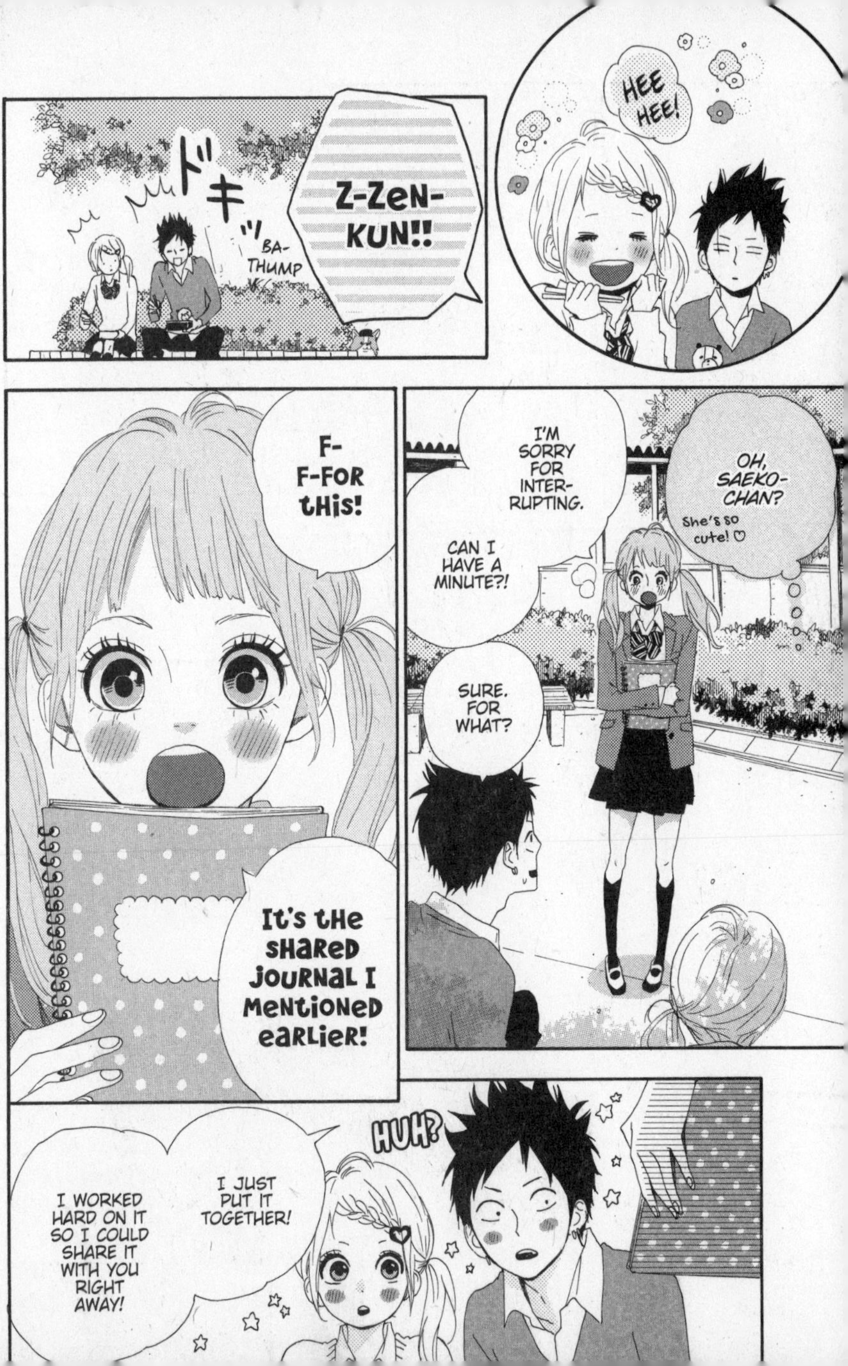

HEE HEE!
ドキッ
BA-THUMP
Z-ZEN-KUN!!
OH, SAEKO-CHAN?
She's so cute! ♡
I'M SORRY FOR INTER-RUPTING.
CAN I HAVE A MINUTE?!
SURE. FOR WHAT?
F-F-FOR THIS!
IT'S THE SHARED JOURNAL I MENTIONED EARLIER!
HUH?
I JUST PUT IT TOGETHER!
I WORKED HARD ON IT SO I COULD SHARE IT WITH YOU RIGHT AWAY!

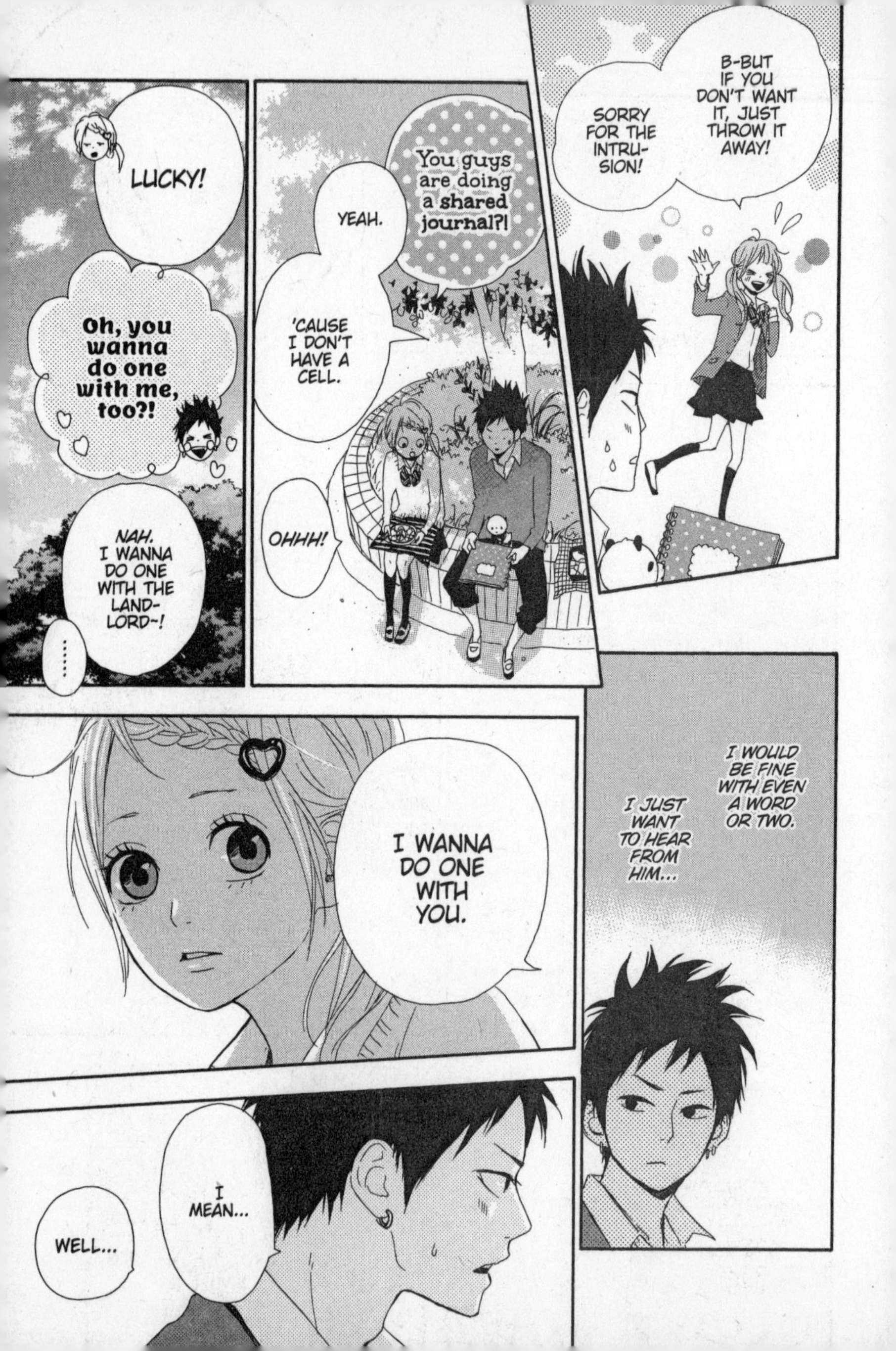
B-BUT IF YOU DON'T WANT IT, JUST THROW IT AWAY!
SORRY FOR THE INTRU-SION!
You guys are doing a shared journal?!
YEAH.
'CAUSE I DON'T HAVE A CELL.
OHHH!
LUCKY!
Oh, you wanna do one with me, too?!
NAH. I WANNA DO ONE WITH THE LAND-LORD~!
......
I WOULD BE FINE WITH EVEN A WORD OR TWO.
I JUST WANT TO HEAR FROM HIM...
I WANNA DO ONE WITH YOU.
I MEAN...
WELL...

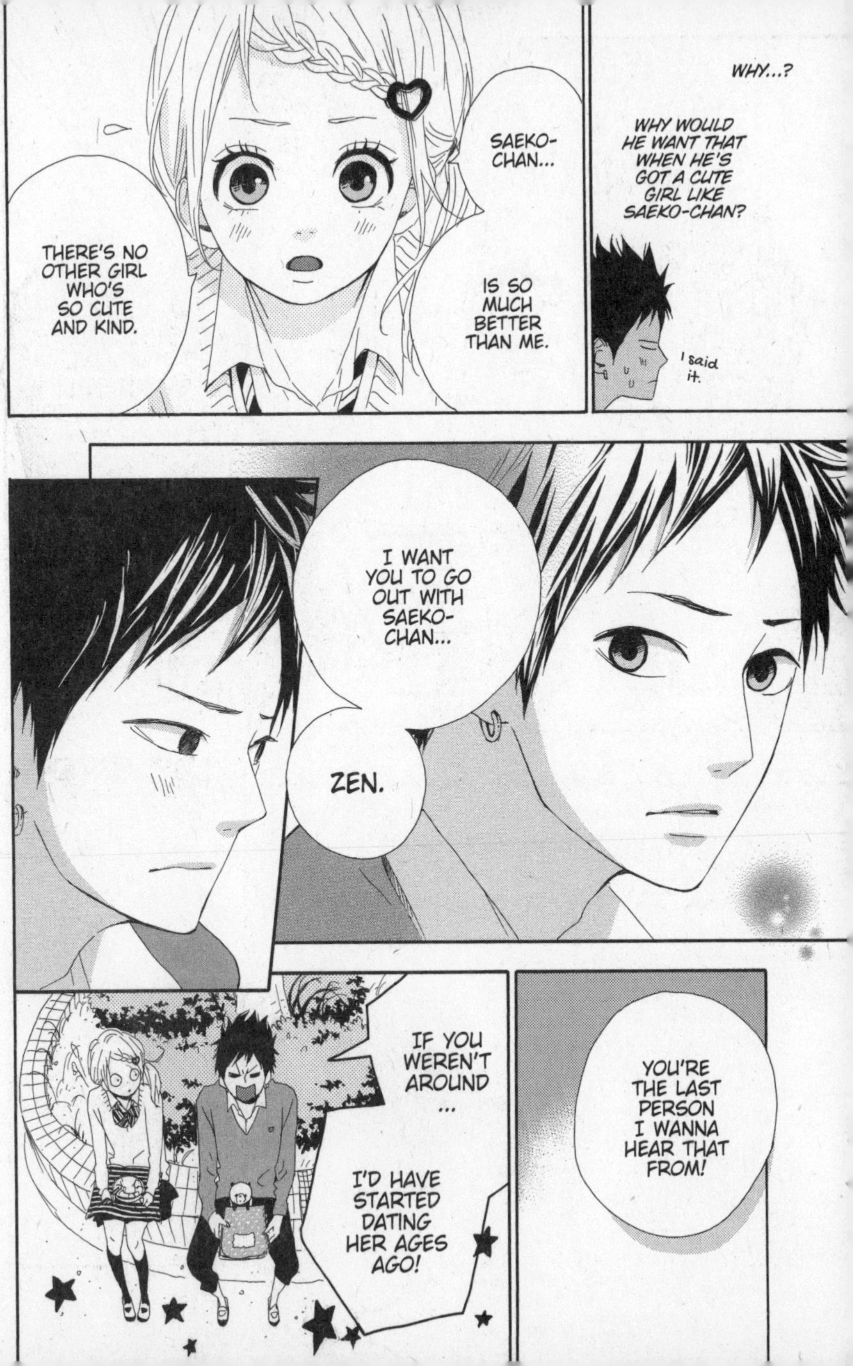
WHY...?
WHY WOULD HE WANT THAT WHEN HE'S GOT A CUTE GIRL LIKE SAEKO-CHAN?
I said it.
SAEKO-CHAN...
IS SO MUCH BETTER THAN ME.
THERE'S NO OTHER GIRL WHO'S SO CUTE AND KIND.
I WANT YOU TO GO OUT WITH SAEKO-CHAN...
ZEN.
YOU'RE THE LAST PERSON I WANNA HEAR THAT FROM!
IF YOU WEREN'T AROUND...
I'D HAVE STARTED DATING HER AGES AGO!

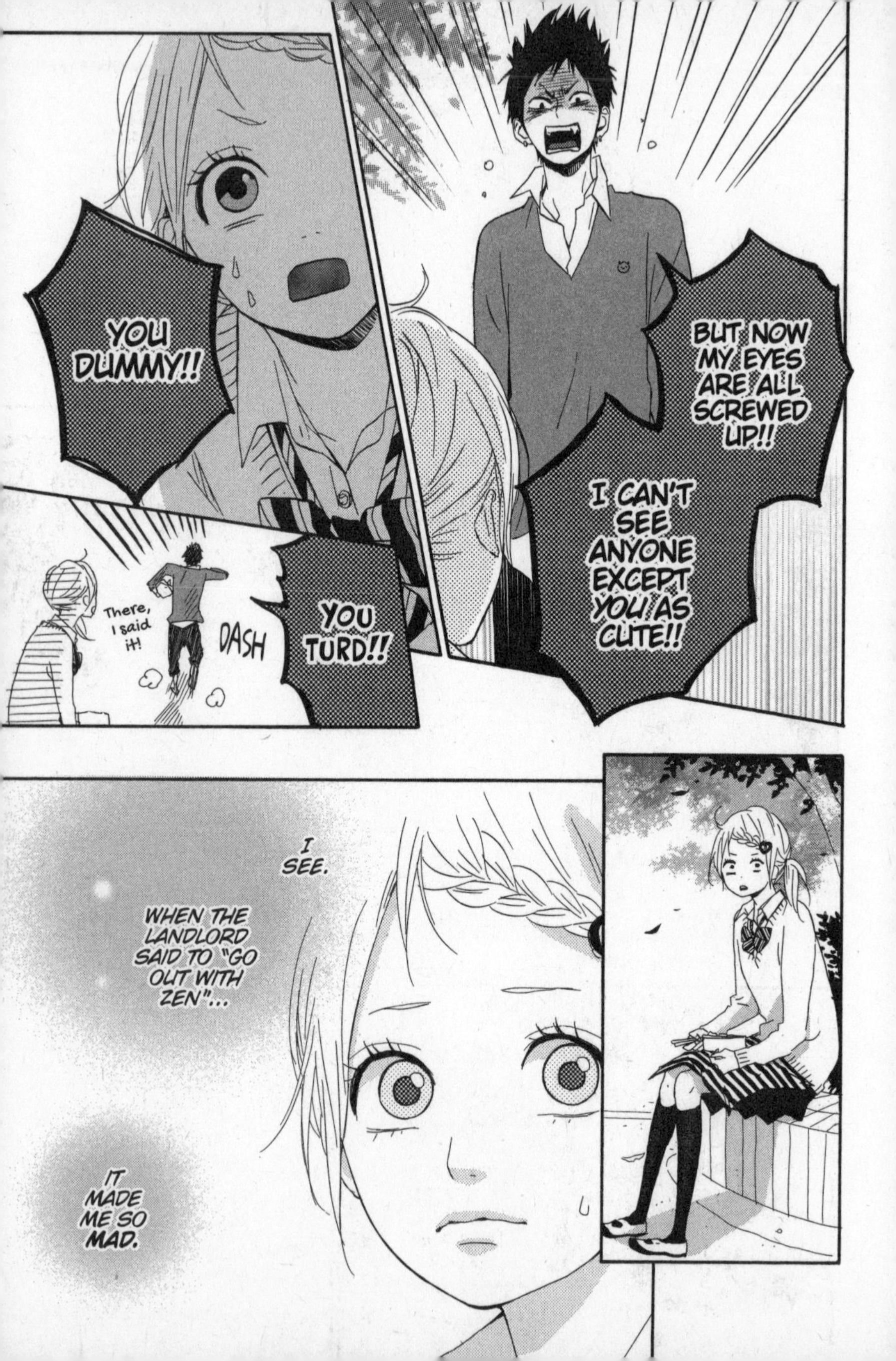
BUT NOW MY EYES ARE ALL SCREWED UP!!
I CAN'T SEE ANYONE EXCEPT YOU AS CUTE!!
YOU DUMMY!!
YOU TURD!!
DASH
There, I said it!
I SEE.
WHEN THE LANDLORD SAID TO "GO OUT WITH ZEN"...
IT MADE ME SO MAD.

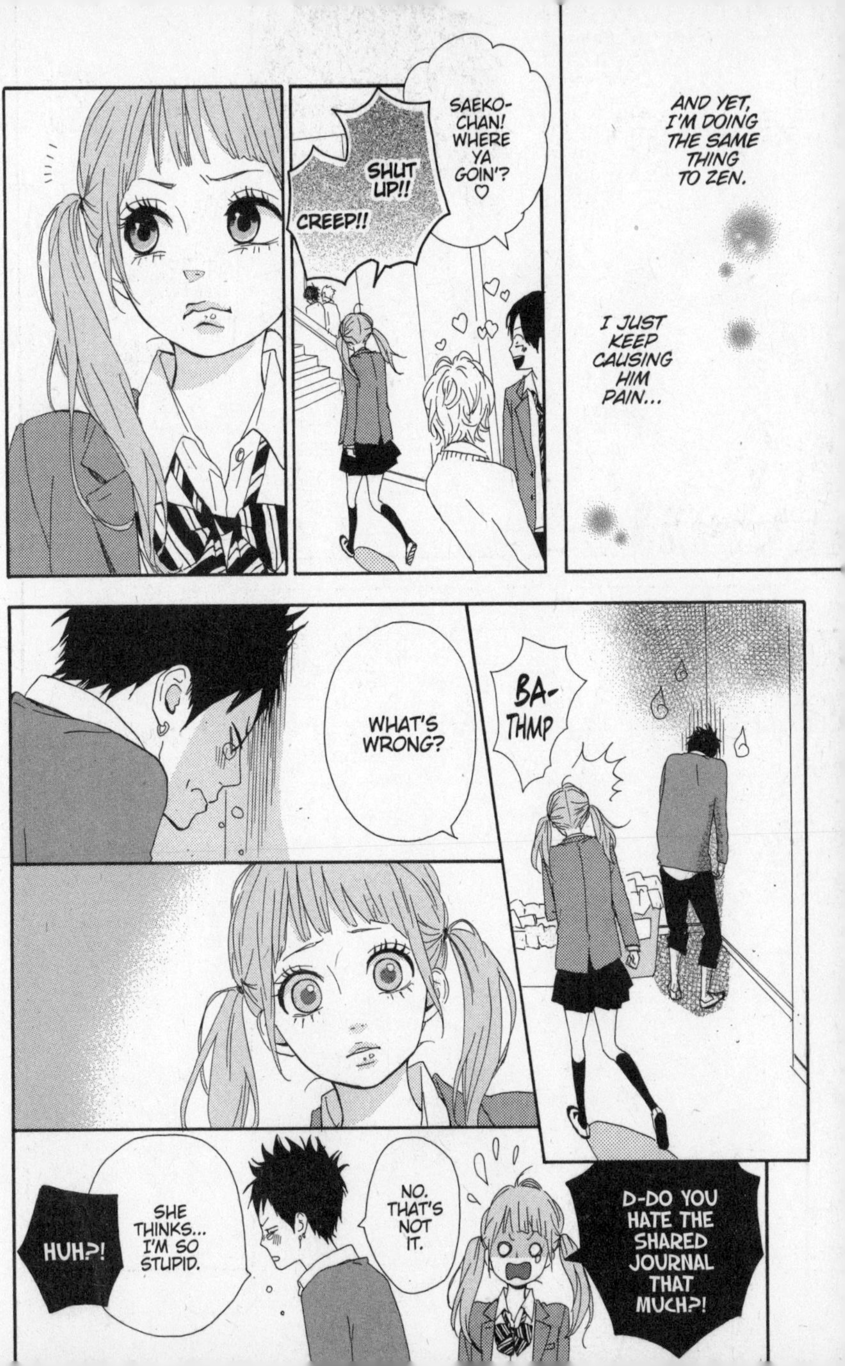
AND YET, I'M DOING THE SAME THING TO ZEN.
I JUST KEEP CAUSING HIM PAIN...
SAEKO-CHAN! WHERE YA GOIN'? ♡
SHUT UP!!
CREEP!!
BA-THMP
WHAT'S WRONG?
D-DO YOU HATE THE SHARED JOURNAL THAT MUCH?!
NO. THAT'S NOT IT.
SHE THINKS... I'M SO STUPID.
HUH?!

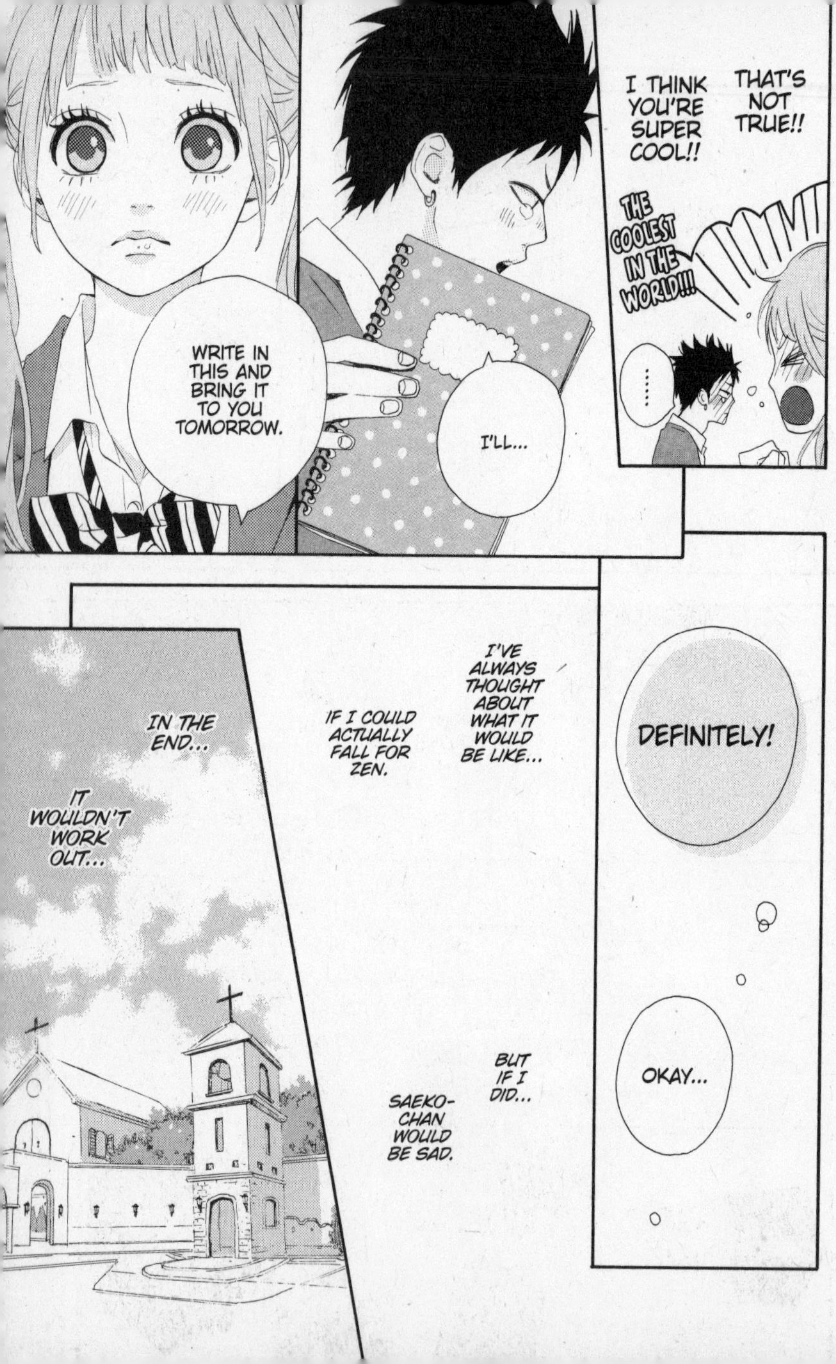
THAT'S NOT TRUE!!
I THINK YOU'RE SUPER COOL!!
THE COOLEST IN THE WORLD!!!
……
I'LL...
WRITE IN THIS AND BRING IT TO YOU TOMORROW.
DEFINITELY!
OKAY...
I'VE ALWAYS THOUGHT ABOUT WHAT IT WOULD BE LIKE...
IF I COULD ACTUALLY FALL FOR ZEN.
BUT IF I DID...
SAEKO-CHAN WOULD BE SAD.
IN THE END...
IT WOULDN'T WORK OUT...

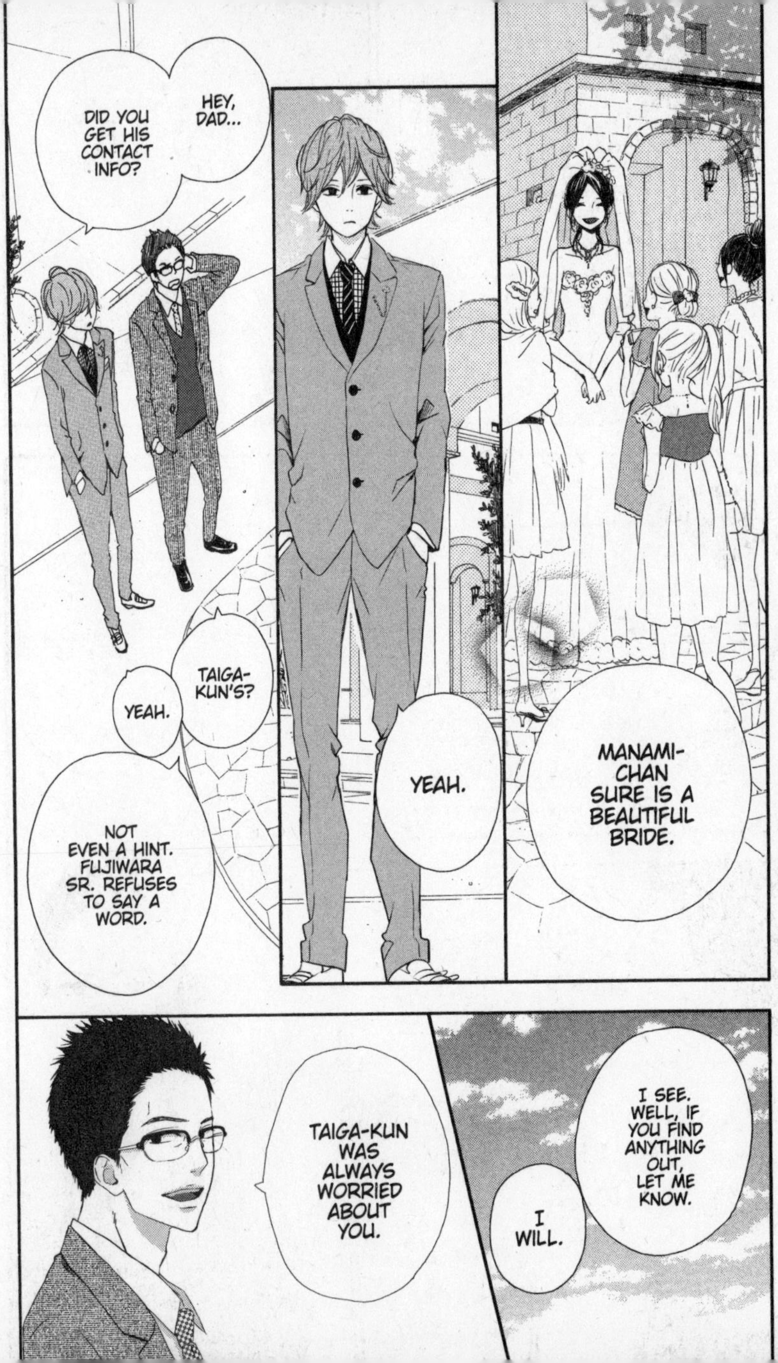
MANAMI-CHAN SURE IS A BEAUTIFUL BRIDE.
YEAH.
HEY, DAD...
DID YOU GET HIS CONTACT INFO?
TAIGA-KUN'S?
YEAH.
NOT EVEN A HINT. FUJIWARA SR. REFUSES TO SAY A WORD.
I SEE. WELL, IF YOU FIND ANYTHING OUT, LET ME KNOW.
I WILL.
TAIGA-KUN WAS ALWAYS WORRIED ABOUT YOU.

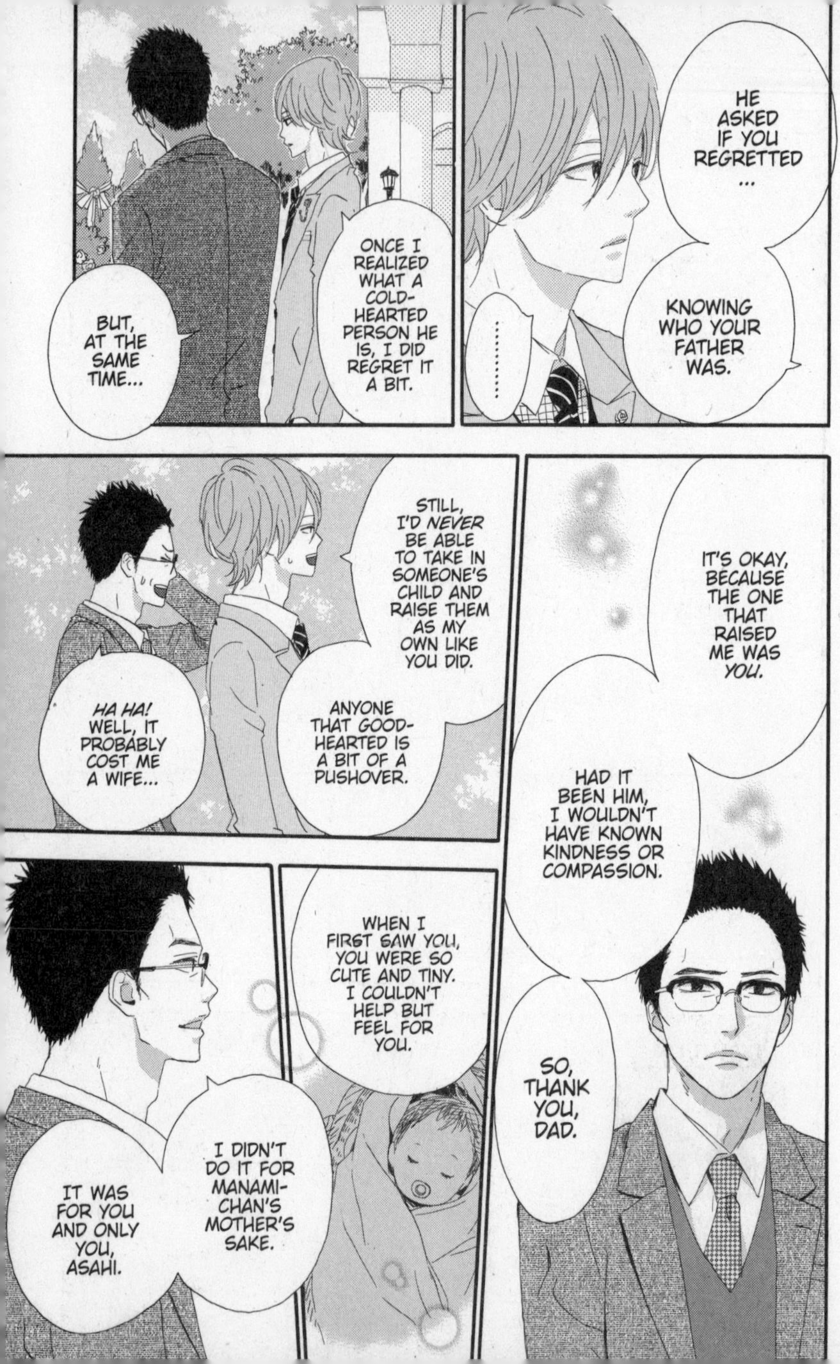
HE ASKED IF YOU REGRETTED ...
KNOWING WHO YOUR FATHER WAS.
......
ONCE I REALIZED WHAT A COLD-HEARTED PERSON HE IS, I DID REGRET IT A BIT.
BUT, AT THE SAME TIME...
IT'S OKAY, BECAUSE THE ONE THAT RAISED ME WAS *YOU.*
HAD IT BEEN HIM, I WOULDN'T HAVE KNOWN KINDNESS OR COMPASSION.
SO, THANK YOU, DAD.
STILL, I'D *NEVER* BE ABLE TO TAKE IN SOMEONE'S CHILD AND RAISE THEM AS MY OWN LIKE YOU DID.
ANYONE THAT GOOD-HEARTED IS A BIT OF A PUSHOVER.
HA HA! WELL, IT PROBABLY COST ME A WIFE...
WHEN I FIRST SAW YOU, YOU WERE SO CUTE AND TINY. I COULDN'T HELP BUT FEEL FOR YOU.
I DIDN'T DO IT FOR MANAMI-CHAN'S MOTHER'S SAKE.
IT WAS FOR YOU AND ONLY YOU, ASAHI.

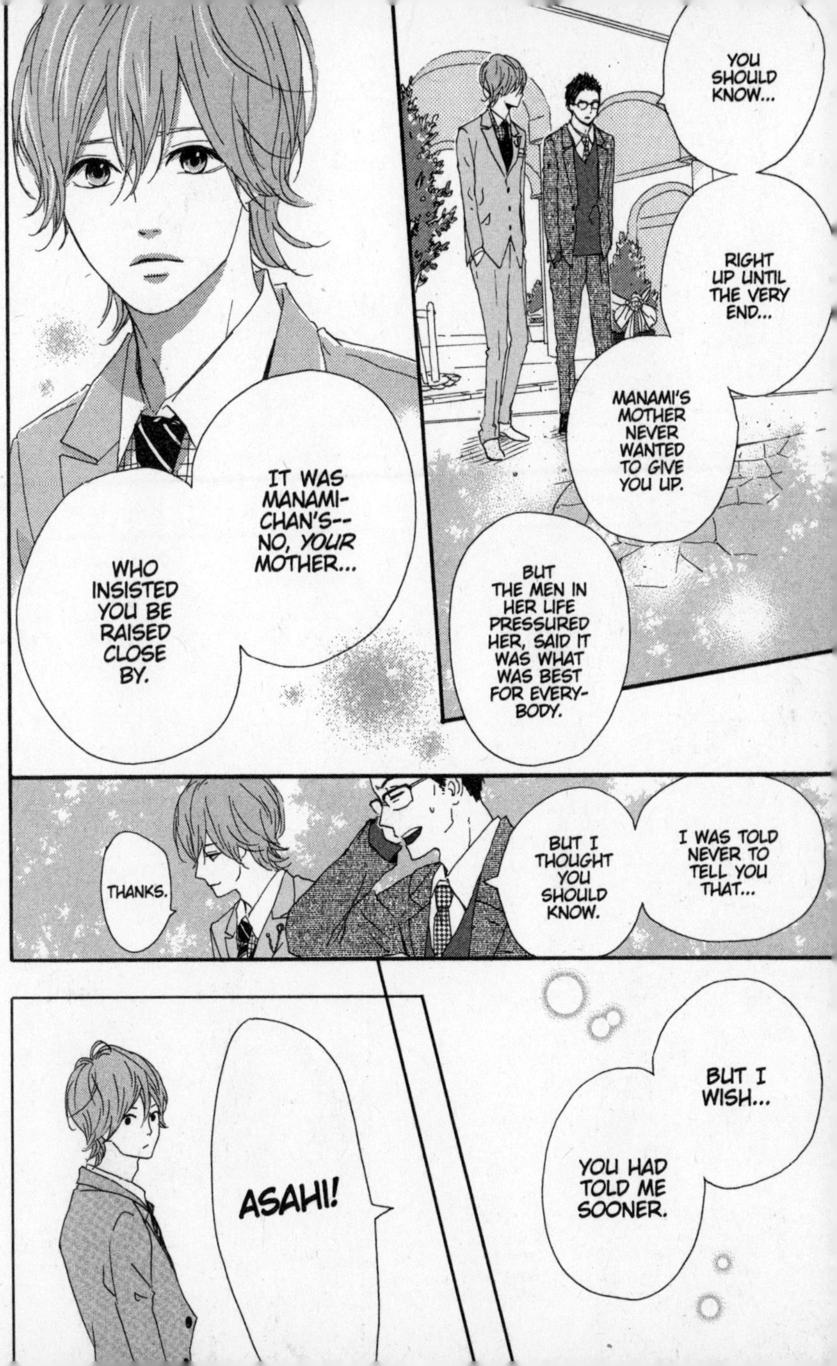
YOU SHOULD KNOW...
RIGHT UP UNTIL THE VERY END...
MANAMI'S MOTHER NEVER WANTED TO GIVE YOU UP.
BUT THE MEN IN HER LIFE PRESSURED HER, SAID IT WAS WHAT WAS BEST FOR EVERYBODY.
IT WAS MANAMI-CHAN'S-- NO, *YOUR* MOTHER...
WHO INSISTED YOU BE RAISED CLOSE BY.
I WAS TOLD NEVER TO TELL YOU THAT...
BUT I THOUGHT YOU SHOULD KNOW.
THANKS.
BUT I WISH...
YOU HAD TOLD ME SOONER.
ASAHI!

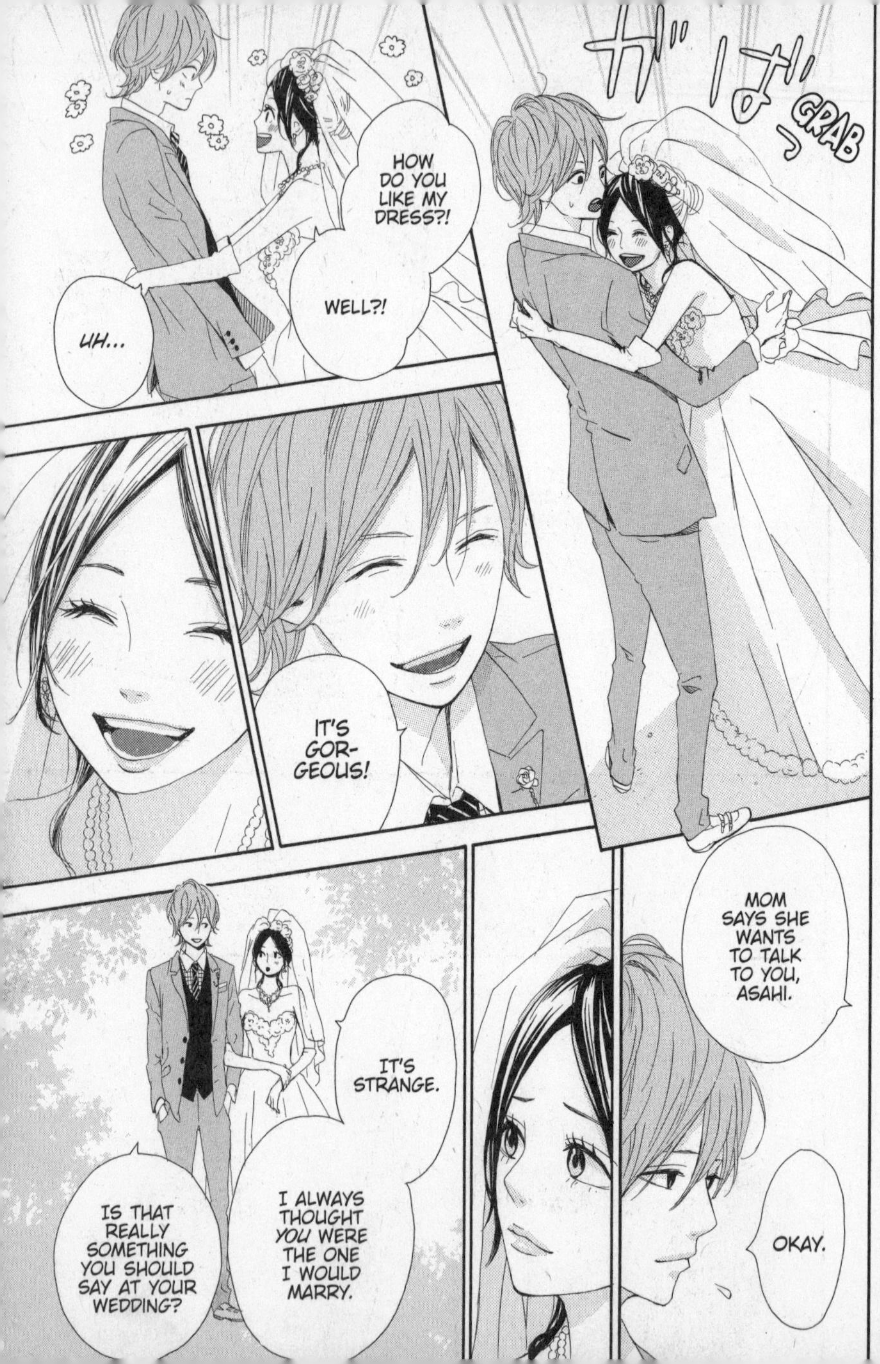
がばっ
GRAB
HOW DO YOU LIKE MY DRESS?!
WELL?!
UH...
IT'S GORGEOUS!
MOM SAYS SHE WANTS TO TALK TO YOU, ASAHI.
OKAY.
IT'S STRANGE.
I ALWAYS THOUGHT *YOU* WERE THE ONE I WOULD MARRY.
IS THAT REALLY SOMETHING YOU SHOULD SAY AT YOUR WEDDING?

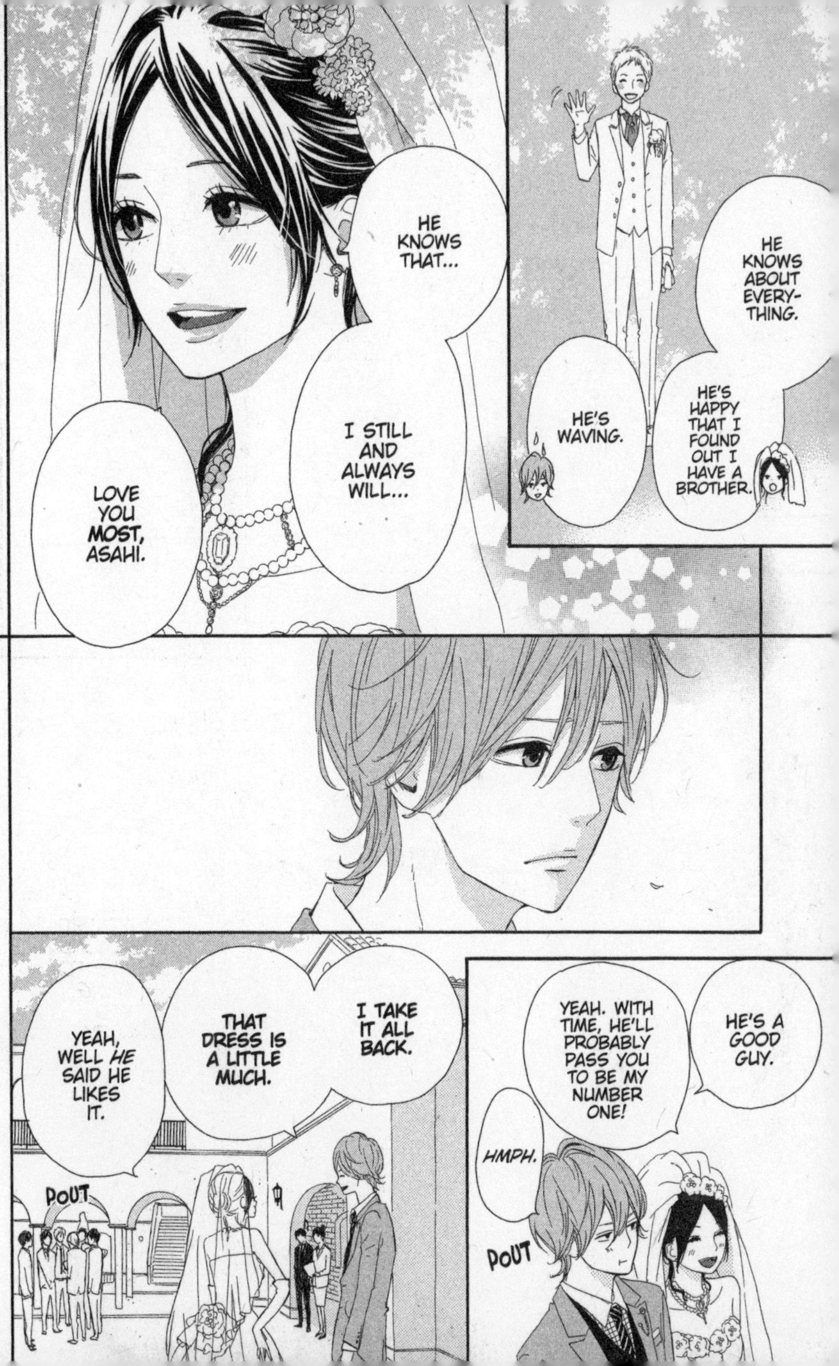
HE KNOWS ABOUT EVERY-THING.
HE'S HAPPY THAT I FOUND OUT I HAVE A BROTHER.
HE'S WAVING.
HE KNOWS THAT...
I STILL AND ALWAYS WILL...
LOVE YOU MOST, ASAHI.
HE'S A GOOD GUY.
YEAH. WITH TIME, HE'LL PROBABLY PASS YOU TO BE MY NUMBER ONE!
HMPH.
POUT
I TAKE IT ALL BACK.
THAT DRESS IS A LITTLE MUCH.
YEAH, WELL *HE* SAID HE LIKES IT.
POUT

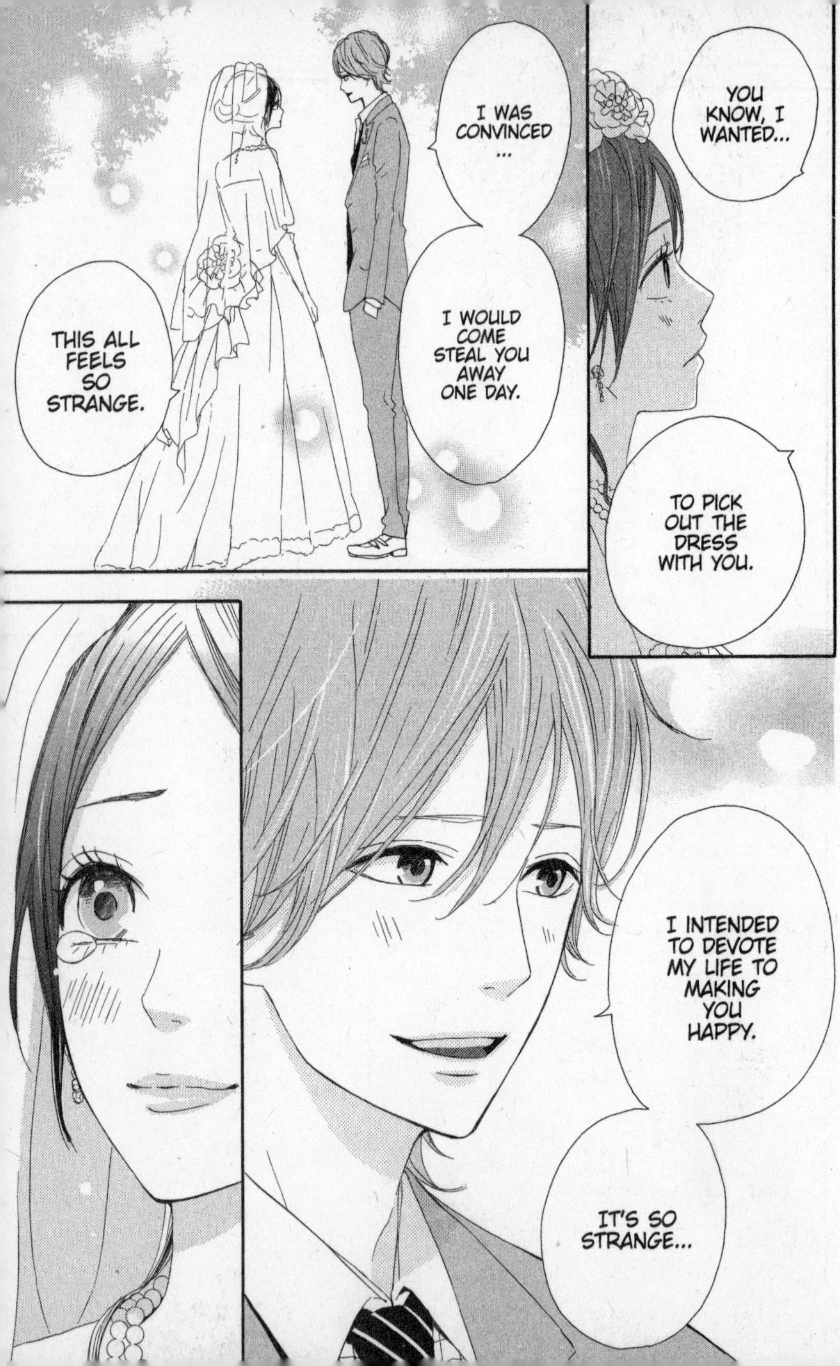
YOU KNOW, I WANTED...
TO PICK OUT THE DRESS WITH YOU.
I WAS CONVINCED...
I WOULD COME STEAL YOU AWAY ONE DAY.
THIS ALL FEELS SO STRANGE.
I INTENDED TO DEVOTE MY LIFE TO MAKING YOU HAPPY.
IT'S SO STRANGE...

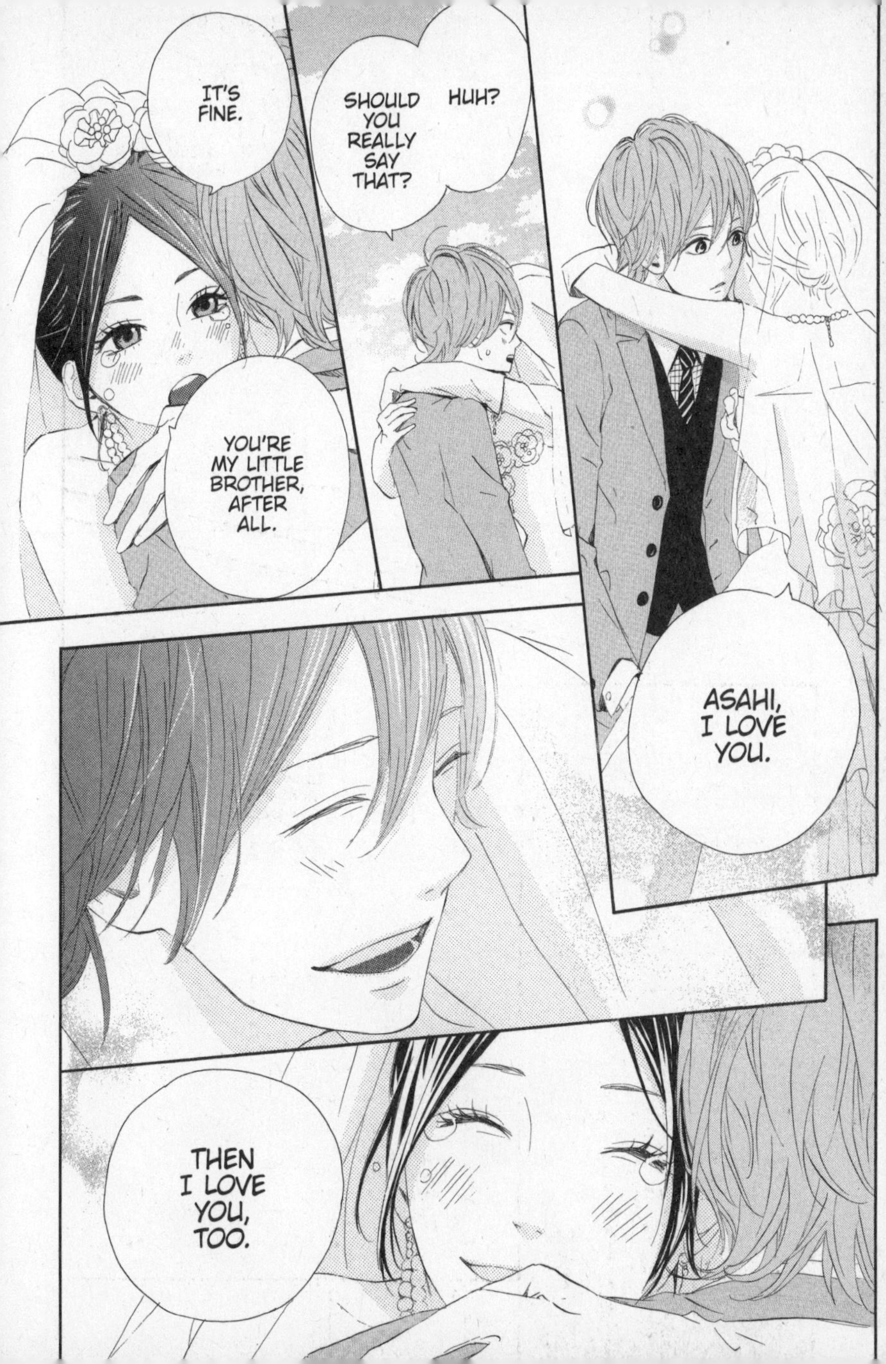
ASAHI, I LOVE YOU.
HUH?
SHOULD YOU REALLY SAY THAT?
IT'S FINE.
YOU'RE MY LITTLE BROTHER, AFTER ALL.
THEN I LOVE YOU, TOO.

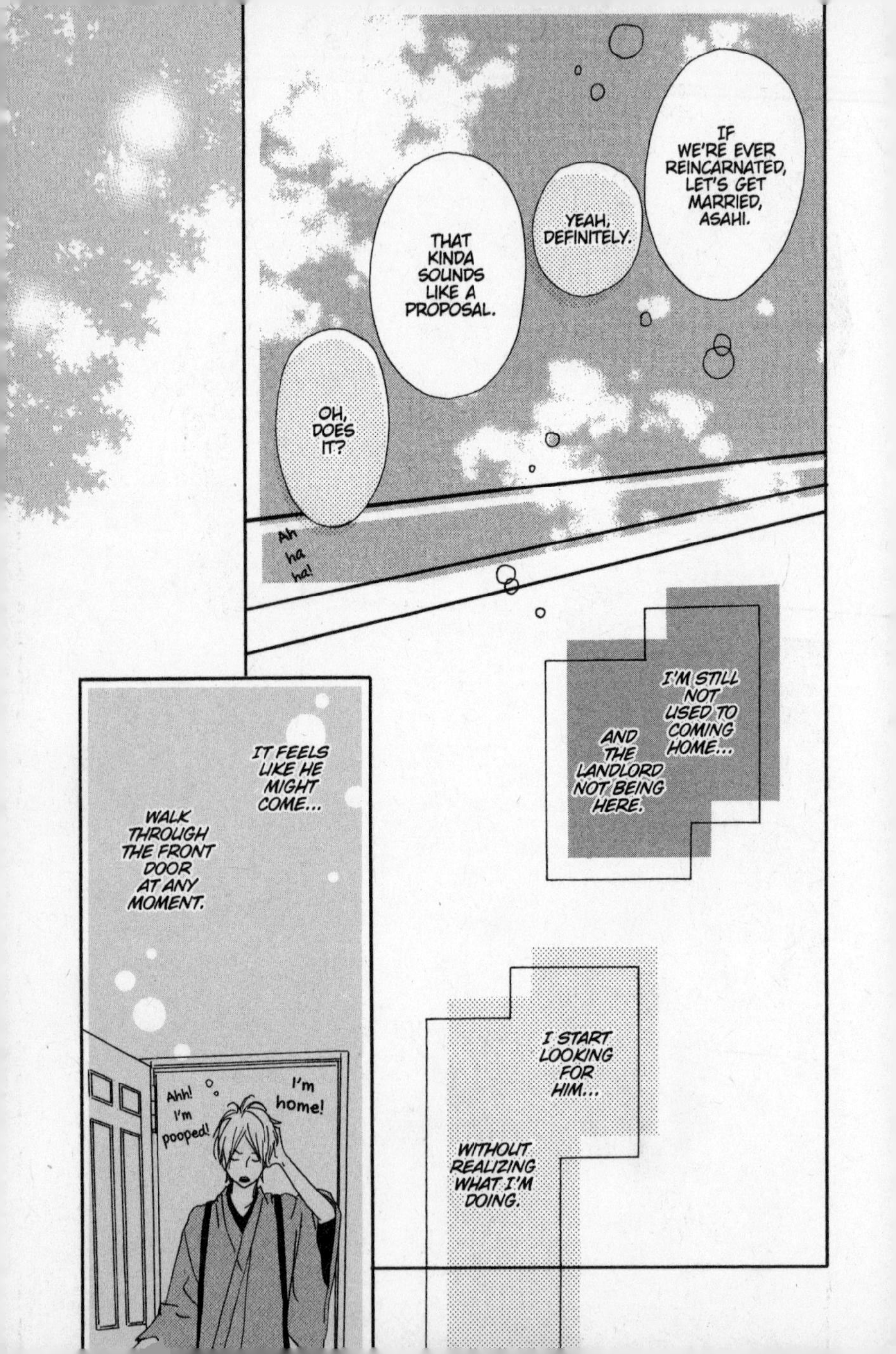
IF WE'RE EVER REINCARNATED, LET'S GET MARRIED, ASAHI.
YEAH, DEFINITELY.
THAT KINDA SOUNDS LIKE A PROPOSAL.
OH, DOES IT?
Ah ha ha!
I'M STILL NOT USED TO COMING HOME...
AND THE LANDLORD NOT BEING HERE.
I START LOOKING FOR HIM...
WITHOUT REALIZING WHAT I'M DOING.
IT FEELS LIKE HE MIGHT COME...
WALK THROUGH THE FRONT DOOR AT ANY MOMENT.
I'm home!
Ahh! I'm pooped!

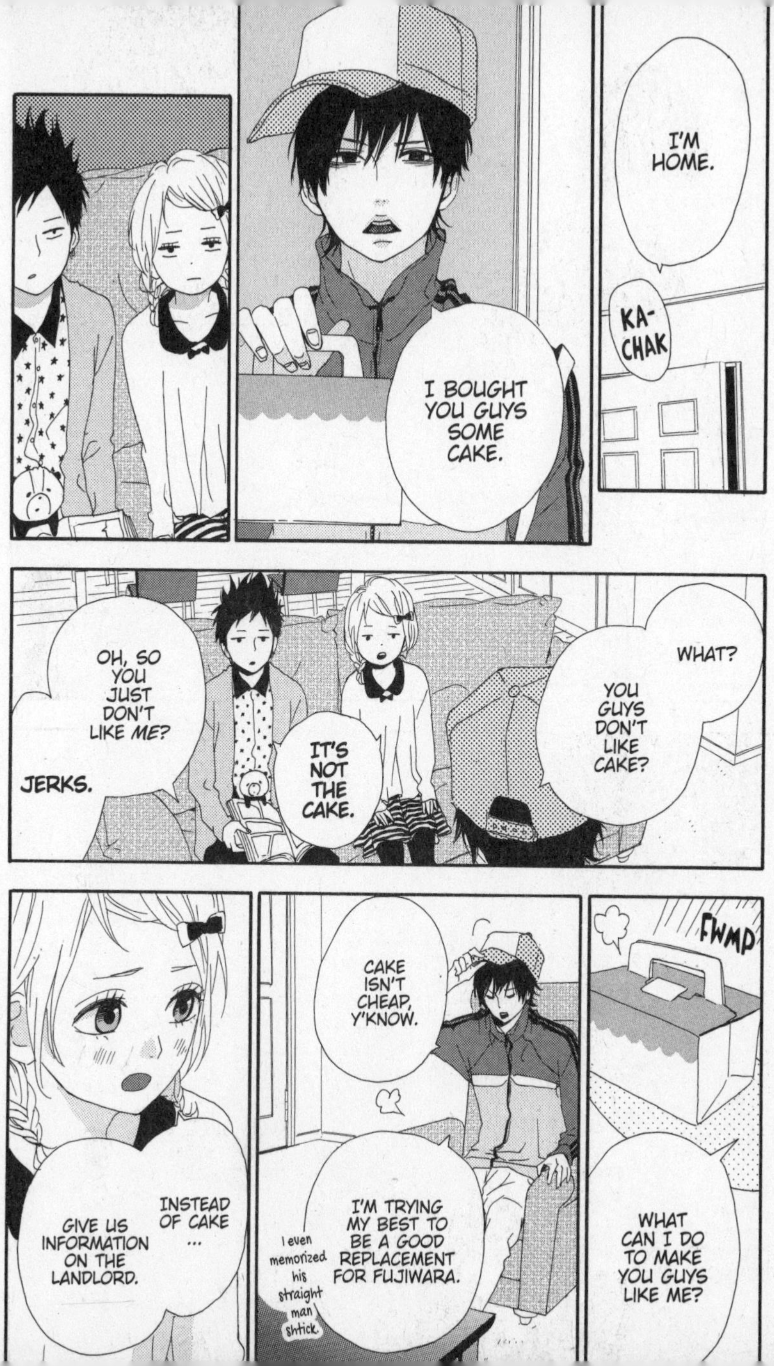
I'M HOME.
KA-CHAK
I BOUGHT YOU GUYS SOME CAKE.
WHAT?
YOU GUYS DON'T LIKE CAKE?
IT'S NOT THE CAKE.
OH, SO YOU JUST DON'T LIKE ME?
JERKS.
FWMP
WHAT CAN I DO TO MAKE YOU GUYS LIKE ME?
CAKE ISN'T CHEAP, Y'KNOW.
I'M TRYING MY BEST TO BE A GOOD REPLACEMENT FOR FUJIWARA.
I even memorized his straight man shtick.
INSTEAD OF CAKE ...
GIVE US INFORMATION ON THE LANDLORD.

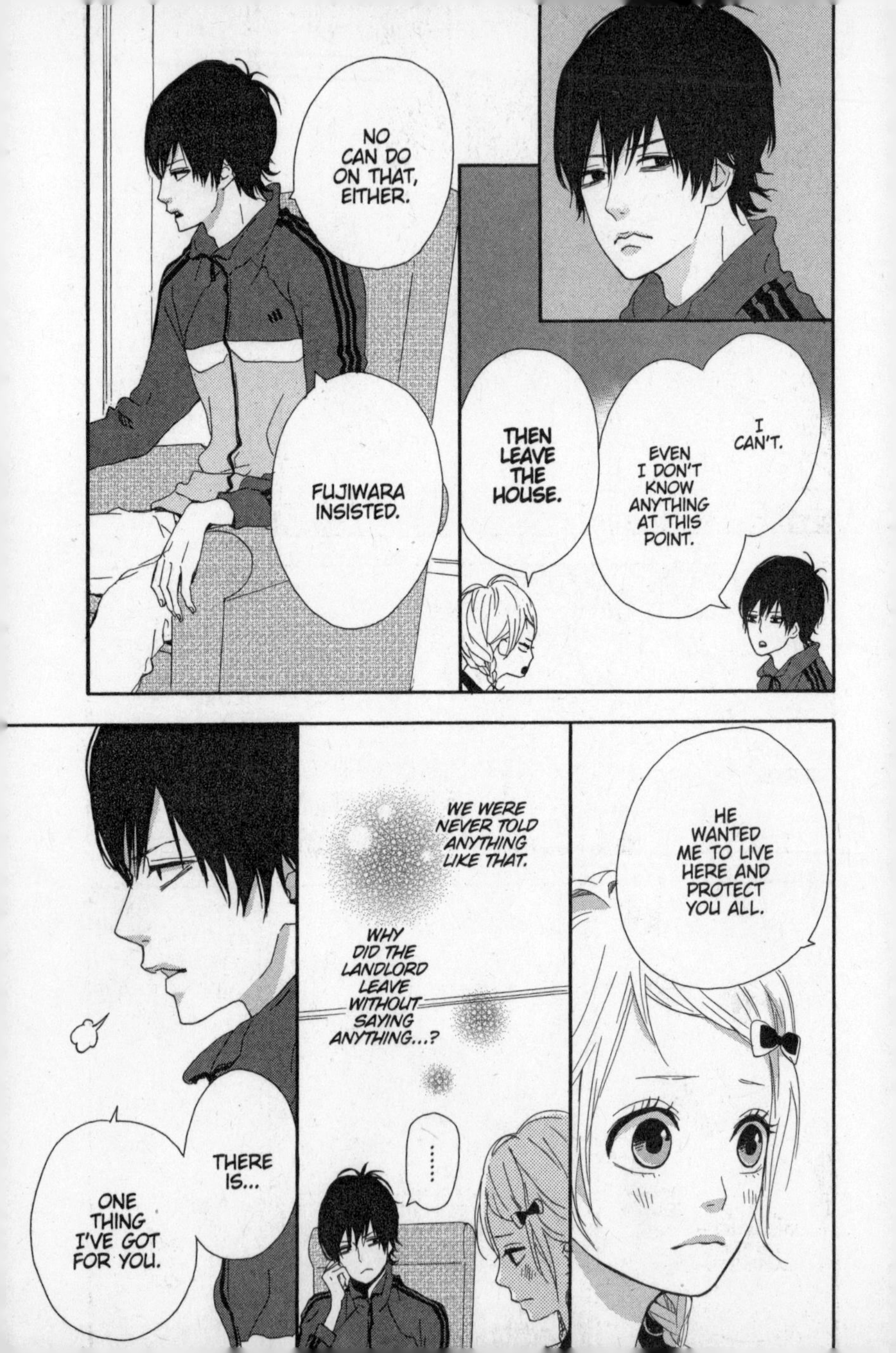
I CAN'T.
EVEN I DON'T KNOW ANYTHING AT THIS POINT.
THEN LEAVE THE HOUSE.
NO CAN DO ON THAT, EITHER.
FUJIWARA INSISTED.
HE WANTED ME TO LIVE HERE AND PROTECT YOU ALL.
WE WERE NEVER TOLD ANYTHING LIKE THAT.
WHY DID THE LANDLORD LEAVE WITHOUT SAYING ANYTHING...?
......
THERE IS...
ONE THING I'VE GOT FOR YOU.

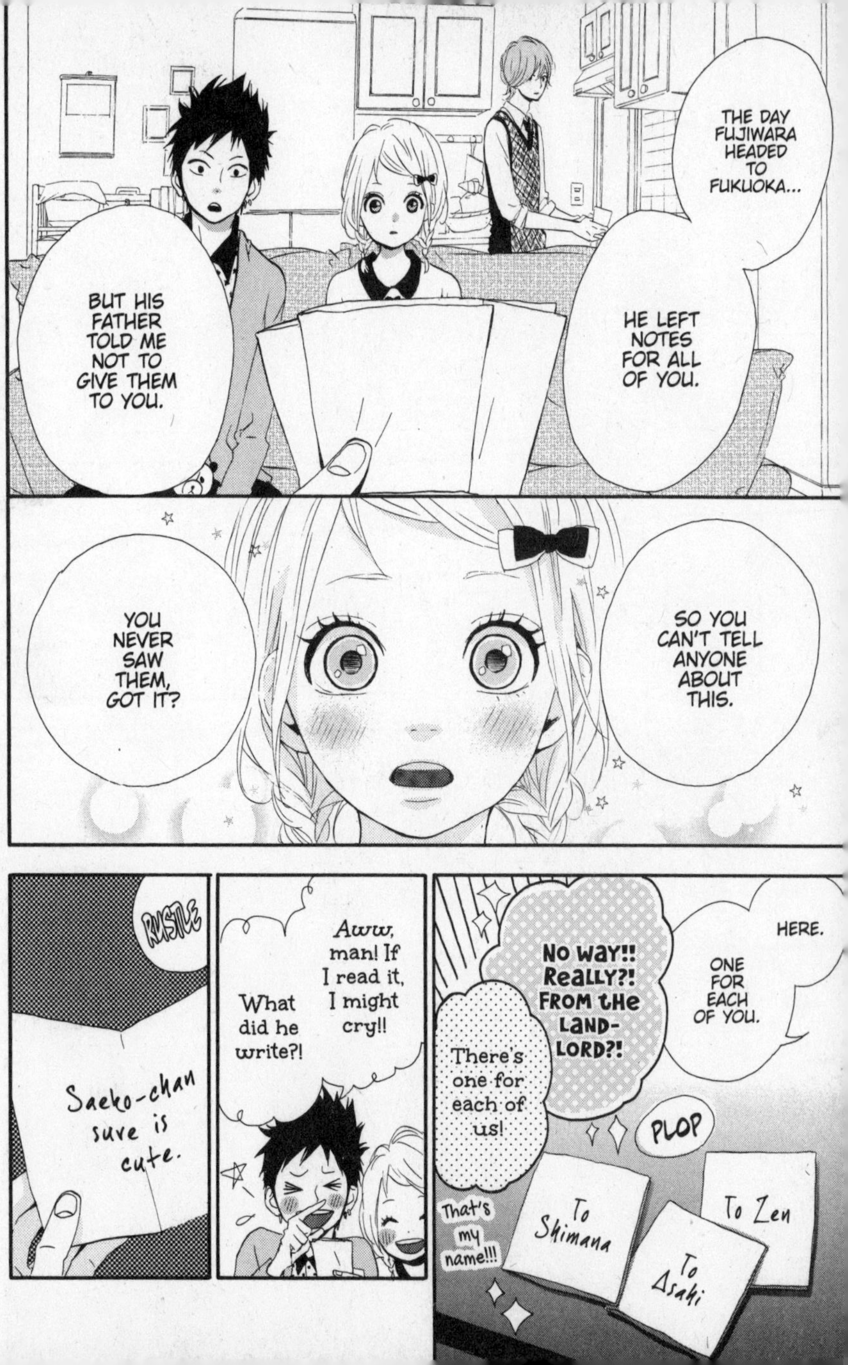
THE DAY FUJIWARA HEADED TO FUKUOKA...
HE LEFT NOTES FOR ALL OF YOU.
BUT HIS FATHER TOLD ME NOT TO GIVE THEM TO YOU.
SO YOU CAN'T TELL ANYONE ABOUT THIS.
YOU NEVER SAW THEM, GOT IT?
HERE.
ONE FOR EACH OF YOU.
NO WAY!! REALLY?! FROM THE LAND-LORD?!
There's one for each of us!
PLOP
To Zen
To Shimana
To Asahi
That's my name!!!
Aww, man! If I read it, I might cry!!
What did he write?!
RUSTLE
Saeko-chan sure is cute.

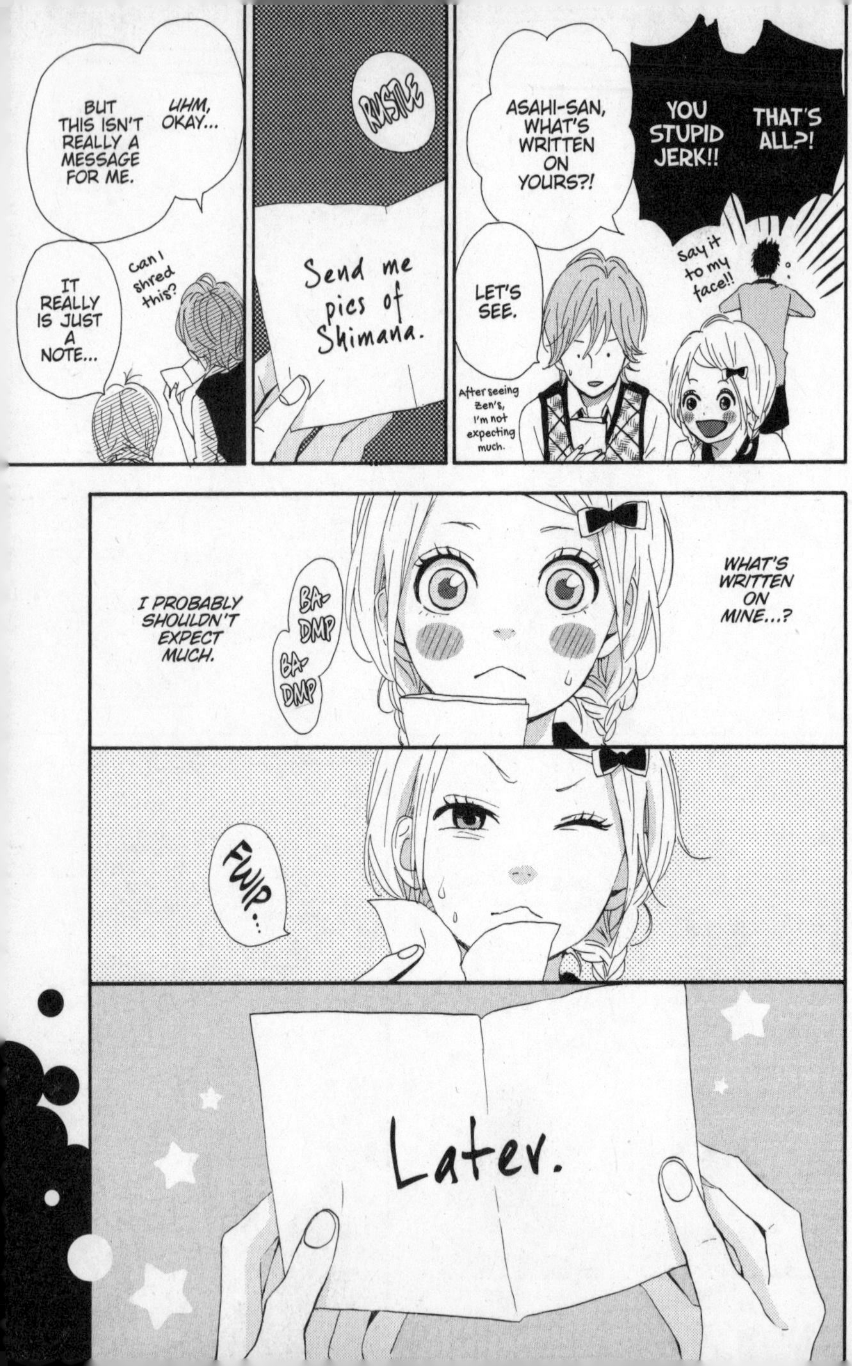
THAT'S ALL?!
YOU STUPID JERK!!
ASAHI-SAN, WHAT'S WRITTEN ON YOURS?!
Say it to my face!!
LET'S SEE.
After seeing Zen's, I'm not expecting much.
RUSTLE
Send me pics of Shimana.
UHM, OKAY...
BUT THIS ISN'T REALLY A MESSAGE FOR ME.
Can I shred this?
IT REALLY IS JUST A NOTE...
WHAT'S WRITTEN ON MINE...?
BA-DMP
BA-DMP
I PROBABLY SHOULDN'T EXPECT MUCH.
FWIP...
Later.

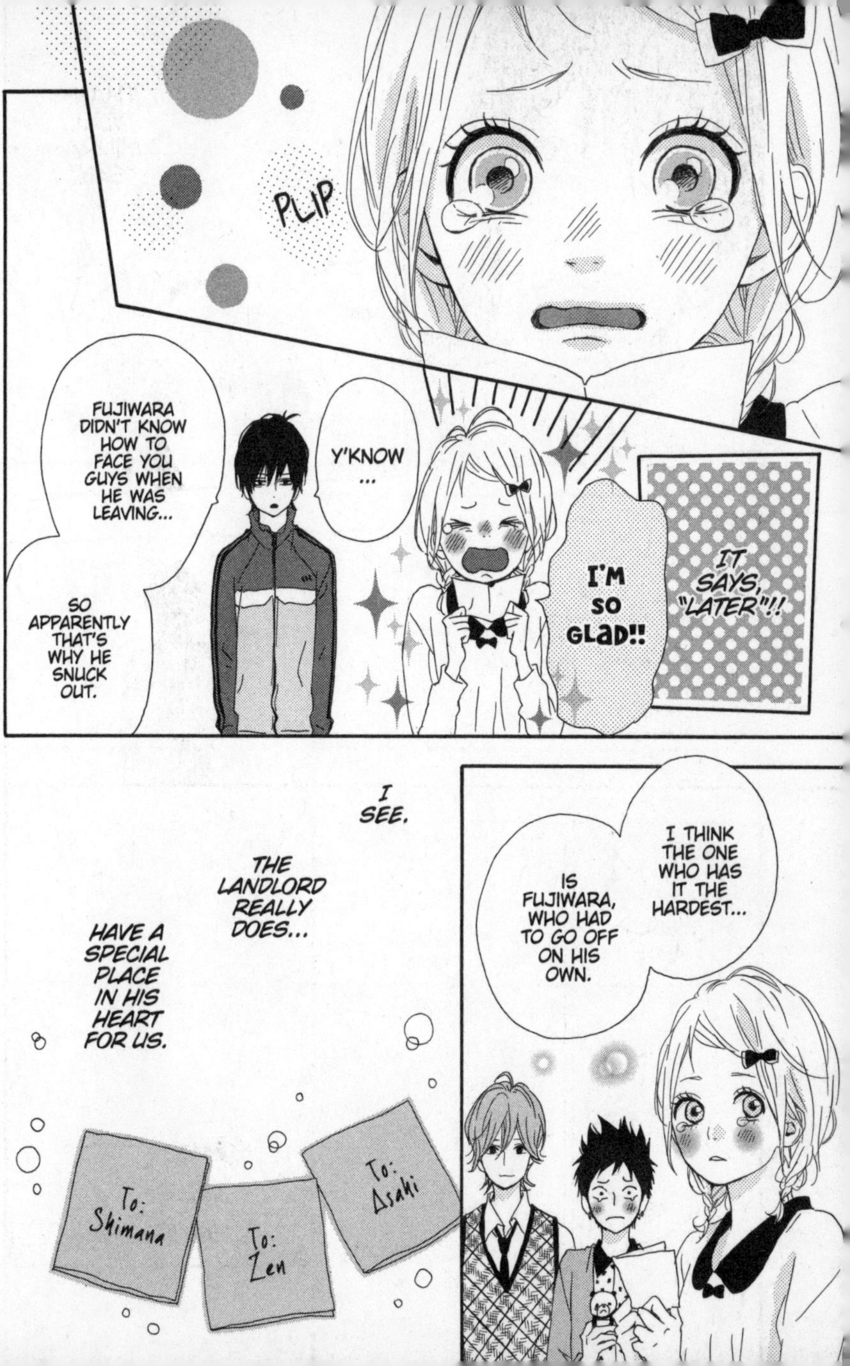
PLIP
IT SAYS, "LATER"!!
I'M SO GLAD!!
Y'KNOW ...
FUJIWARA DIDN'T KNOW HOW TO FACE YOU GUYS WHEN HE WAS LEAVING...
SO APPARENTLY THAT'S WHY HE SNUCK OUT.
I THINK THE ONE WHO HAS IT THE HARDEST...
IS FUJIWARA, WHO HAD TO GO OFF ON HIS OWN.
I SEE.
THE LANDLORD REALLY DOES...
HAVE A SPECIAL PLACE IN HIS HEART FOR US.
To: Asahi
To: Zen
To: Shimana

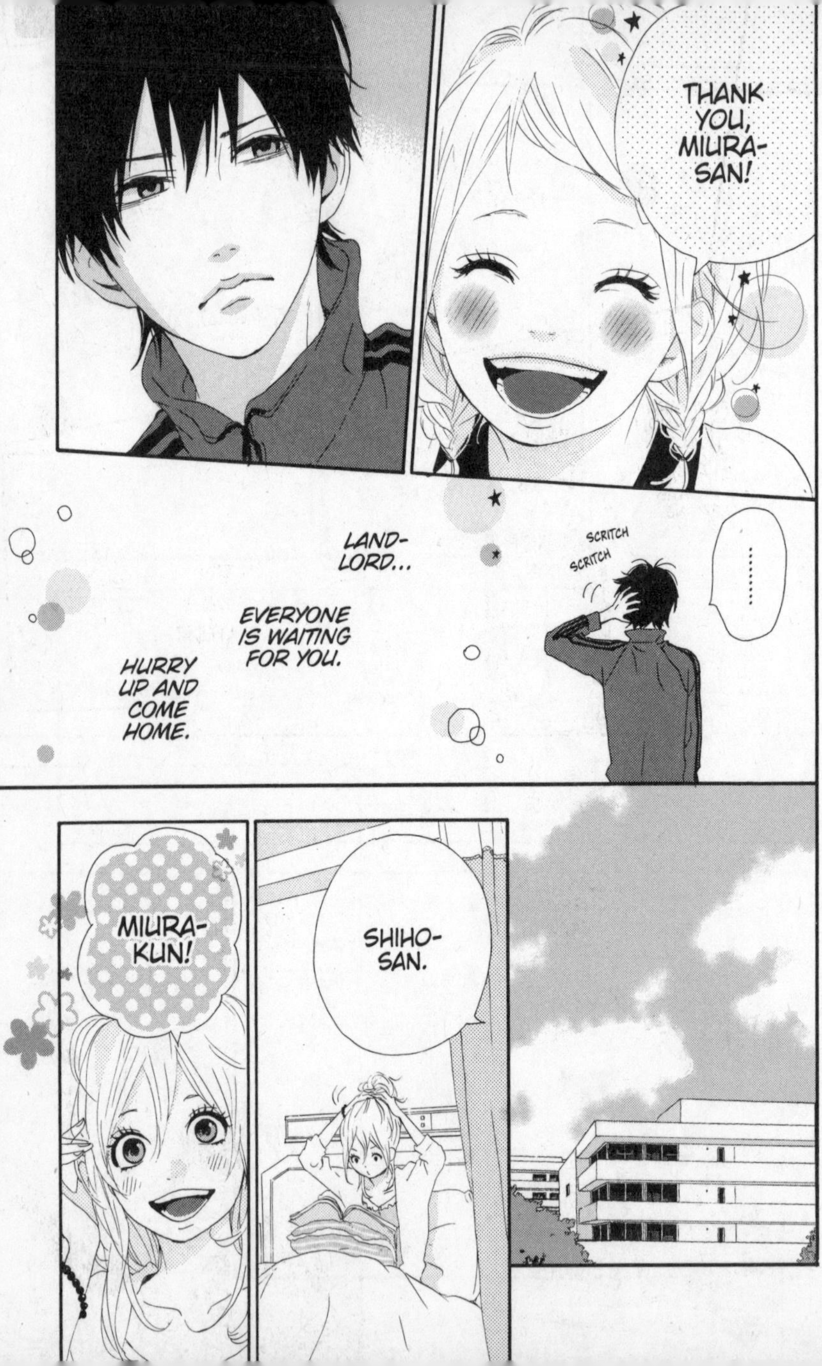
THANK YOU, MIURA-SAN!
......
SCRITCH SCRITCH
LAND-LORD...
EVERYONE IS WAITING FOR YOU.
HURRY UP AND COME HOME.
SHIHO-SAN.
MIURA-KUN!

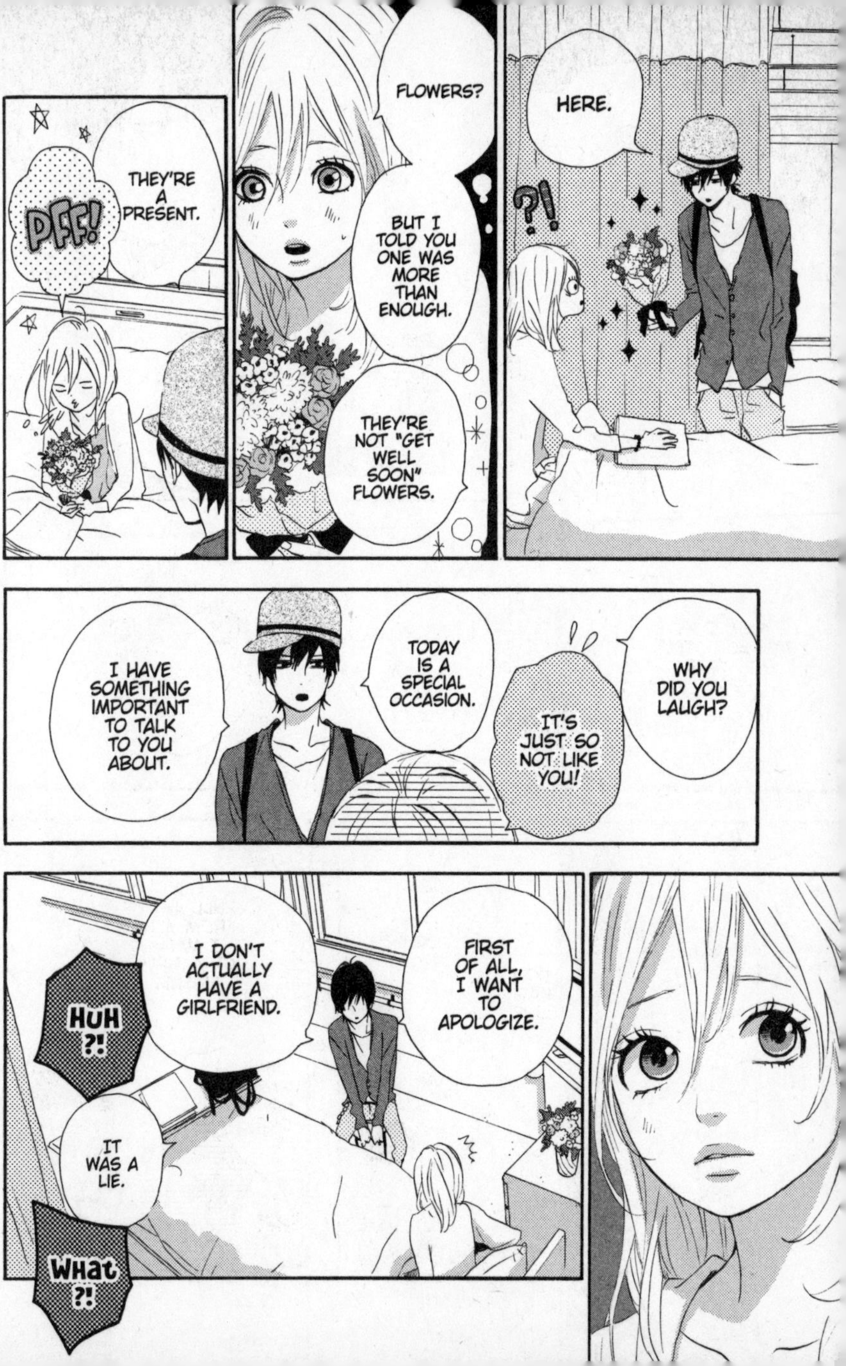
HERE.
?!
FLOWERS?
BUT I TOLD YOU ONE WAS MORE THAN ENOUGH.
THEY'RE NOT "GET WELL SOON" FLOWERS.
THEY'RE A PRESENT.
PFF!
WHY DID YOU LAUGH?
IT'S JUST SO NOT LIKE YOU!
TODAY IS A SPECIAL OCCASION.
I HAVE SOMETHING IMPORTANT TO TALK TO YOU ABOUT.
FIRST OF ALL, I WANT TO APOLOGIZE.
I DON'T ACTUALLY HAVE A GIRLFRIEND.
HUH?!
IT WAS A LIE.
WHAT?!

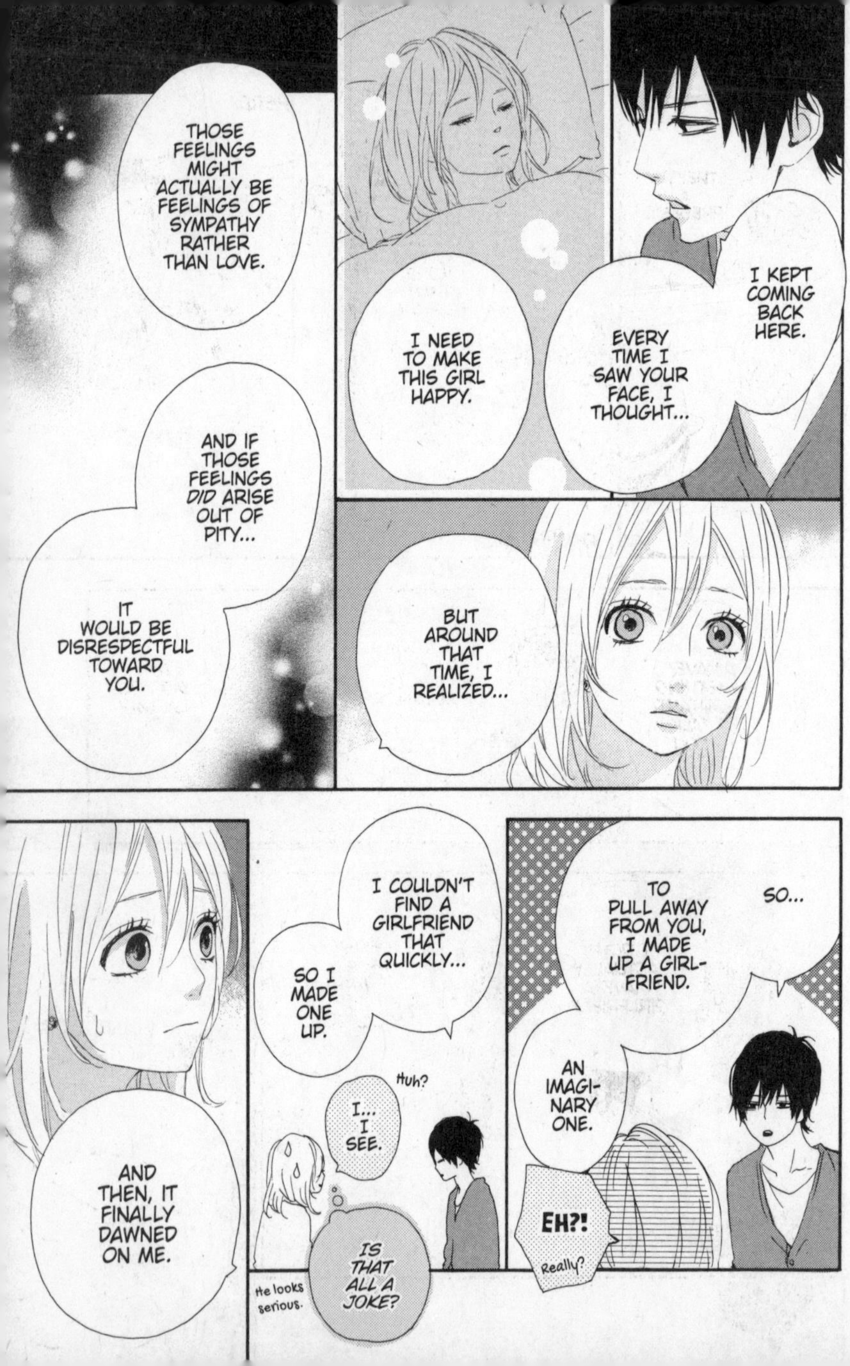
I KEPT COMING BACK HERE.
EVERY TIME I SAW YOUR FACE, I THOUGHT...
I NEED TO MAKE THIS GIRL HAPPY.
BUT AROUND THAT TIME, I REALIZED...
THOSE FEELINGS MIGHT ACTUALLY BE FEELINGS OF SYMPATHY RATHER THAN LOVE.
AND IF THOSE FEELINGS *DID* ARISE OUT OF PITY...
IT WOULD BE DISRESPECTFUL TOWARD YOU.
SO...
TO PULL AWAY FROM YOU, I MADE UP A GIRL-FRIEND.
AN IMAGINARY ONE.
EH?!
Really?
I COULDN'T FIND A GIRLFRIEND THAT QUICKLY...
SO I MADE ONE UP.
Huh?
I... I SEE.
IS THAT ALL A JOKE?
He looks serious.
AND THEN, IT FINALLY DAWNED ON ME.

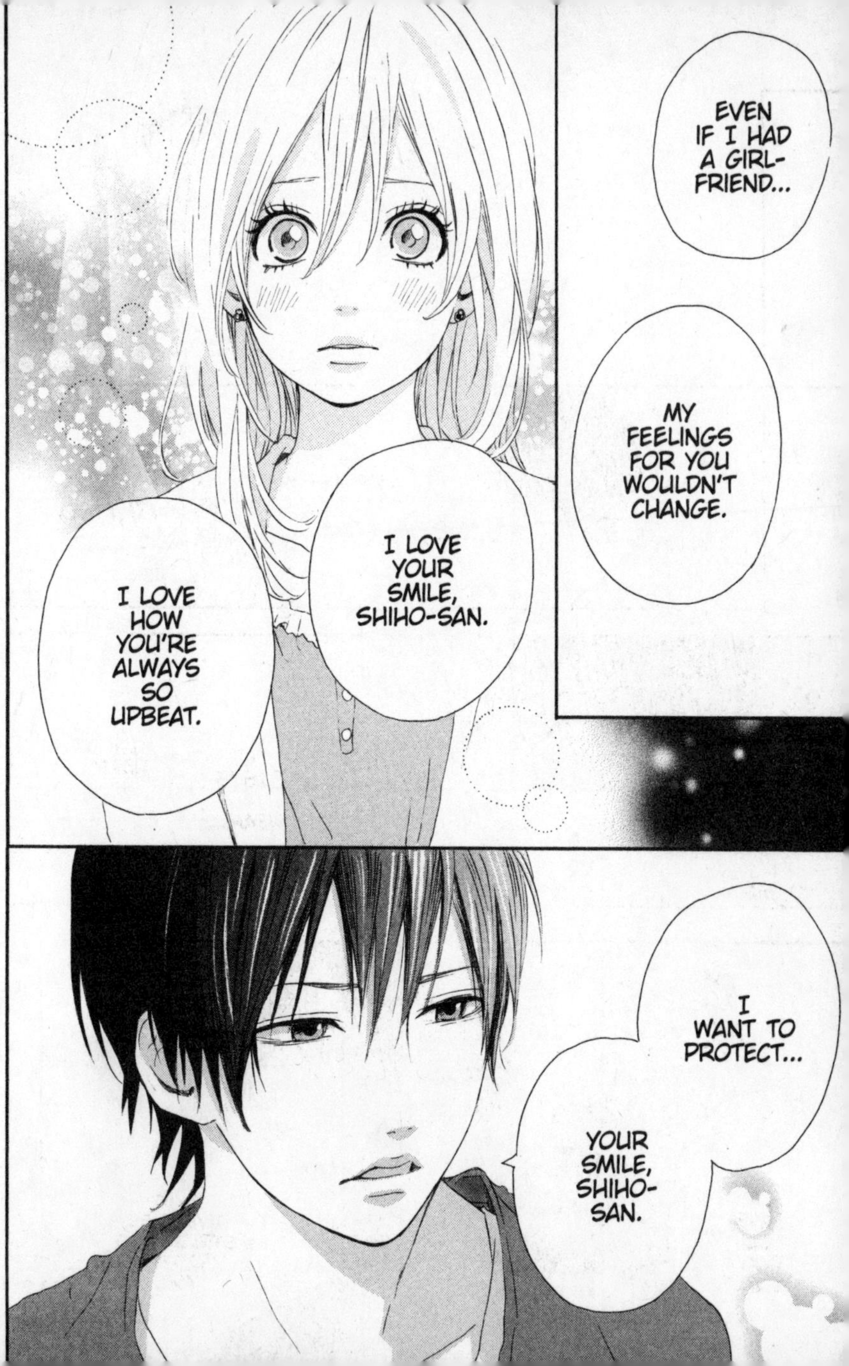
EVEN IF I HAD A GIRL-FRIEND...
MY FEELINGS FOR YOU WOULDN'T CHANGE.
I LOVE YOUR SMILE, SHIHO-SAN.
I LOVE HOW YOU'RE ALWAYS SO UPBEAT.
I WANT TO PROTECT...
YOUR SMILE, SHIHO-SAN.

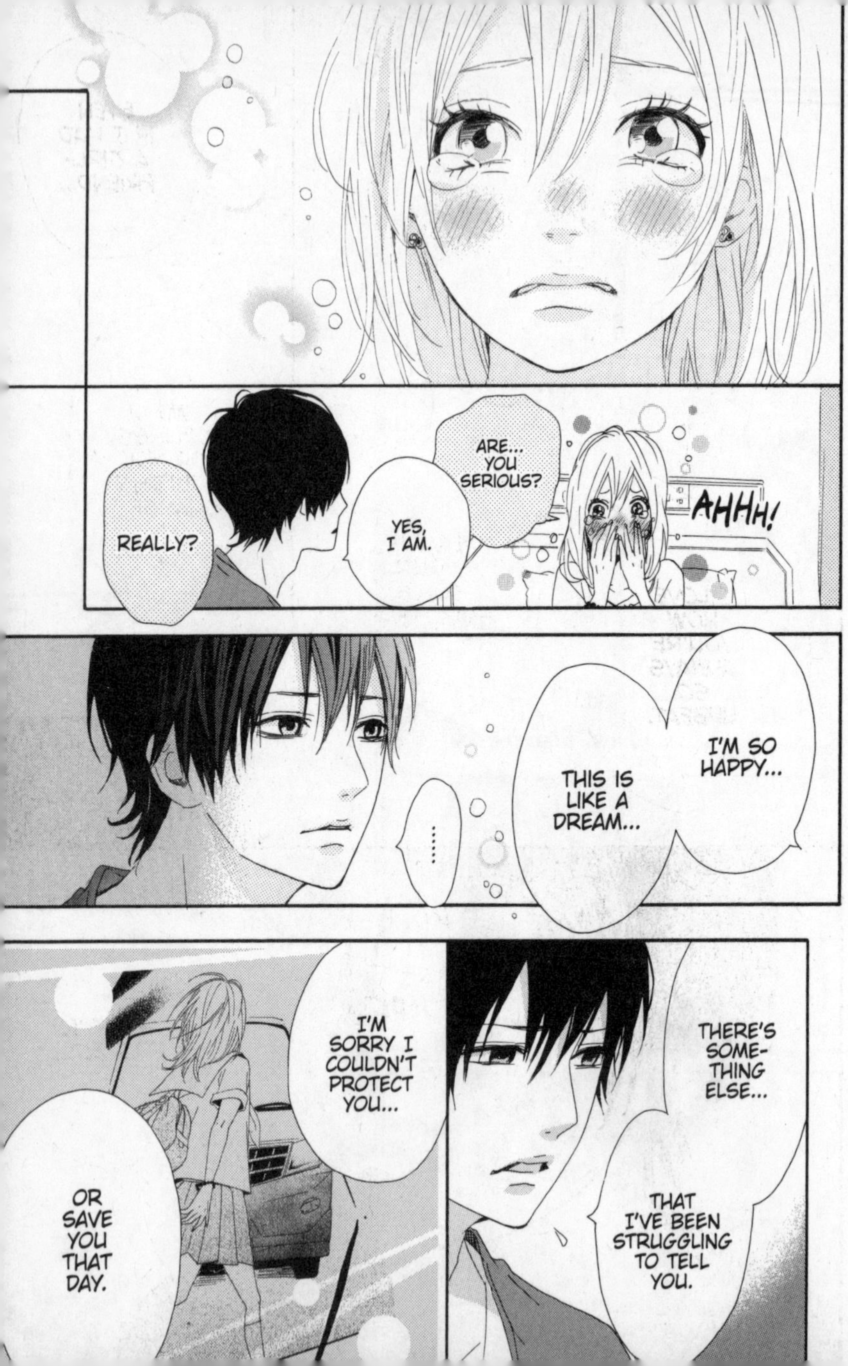
AHHH!
ARE... YOU SERIOUS?
YES, I AM.
REALLY?
I'M SO HAPPY...
THIS IS LIKE A DREAM...
......
THERE'S SOME-THING ELSE...
THAT I'VE BEEN STRUGGLING TO TELL YOU.
I'M SORRY I COULDN'T PROTECT YOU...
OR SAVE YOU THAT DAY.

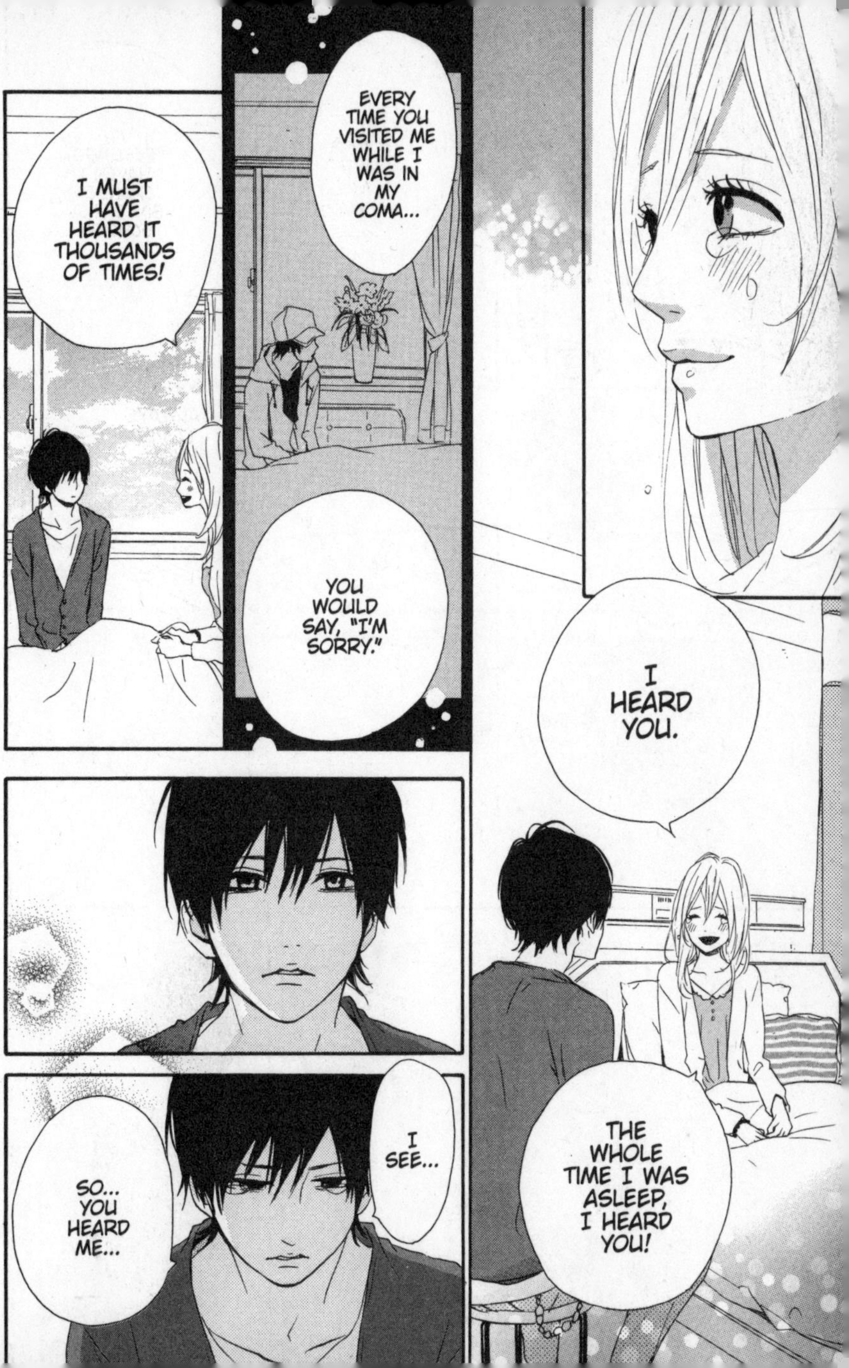
EVERY TIME YOU VISITED ME WHILE I WAS IN MY COMA...
YOU WOULD SAY, "I'M SORRY."
I MUST HAVE HEARD IT THOUSANDS OF TIMES!
I HEARD YOU.
THE WHOLE TIME I WAS ASLEEP, I HEARD YOU!
I SEE...
SO... YOU HEARD ME...

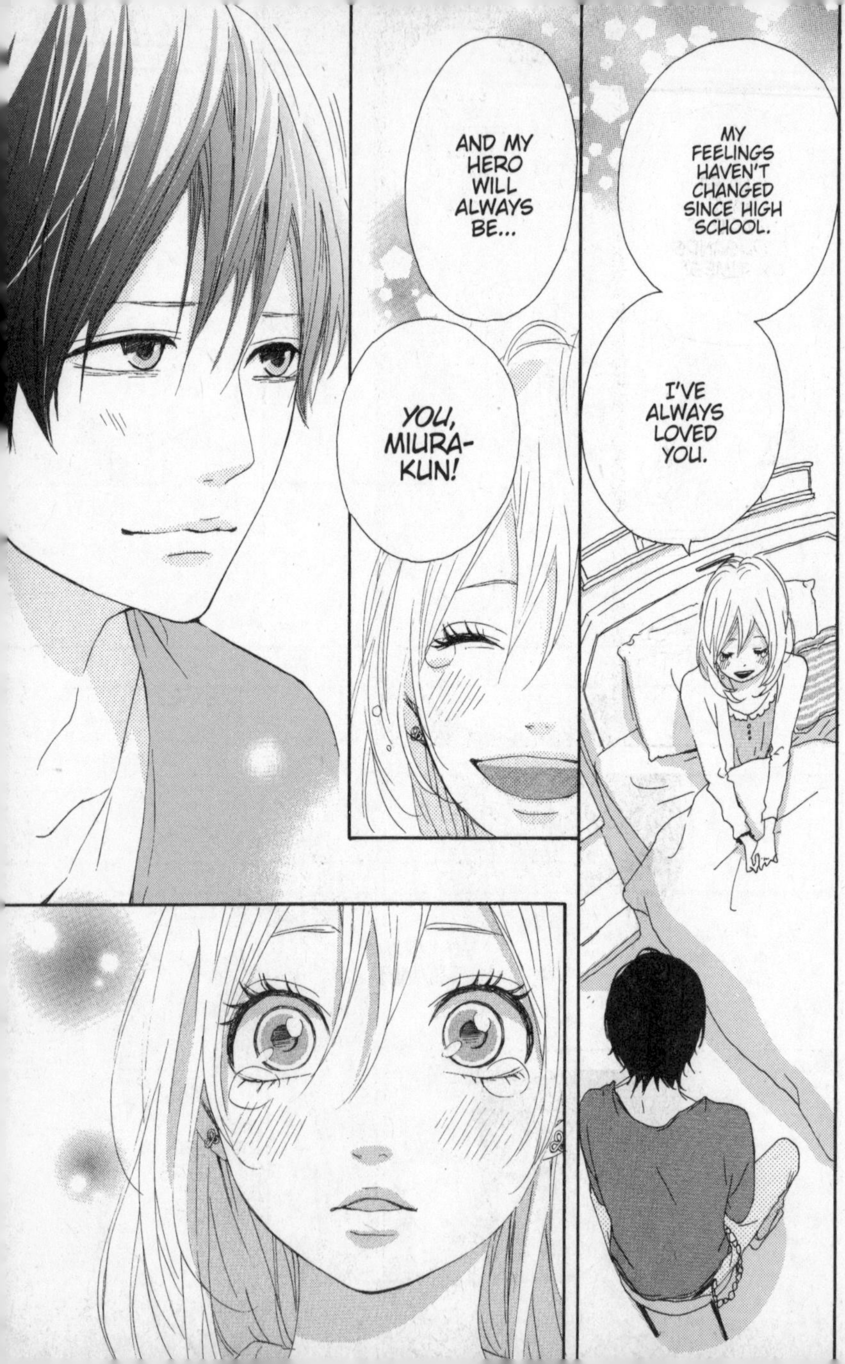
MY FEELINGS HAVEN'T CHANGED SINCE HIGH SCHOOL.
I'VE ALWAYS LOVED YOU.
AND MY HERO WILL ALWAYS BE...
YOU, MIURA-KUN!

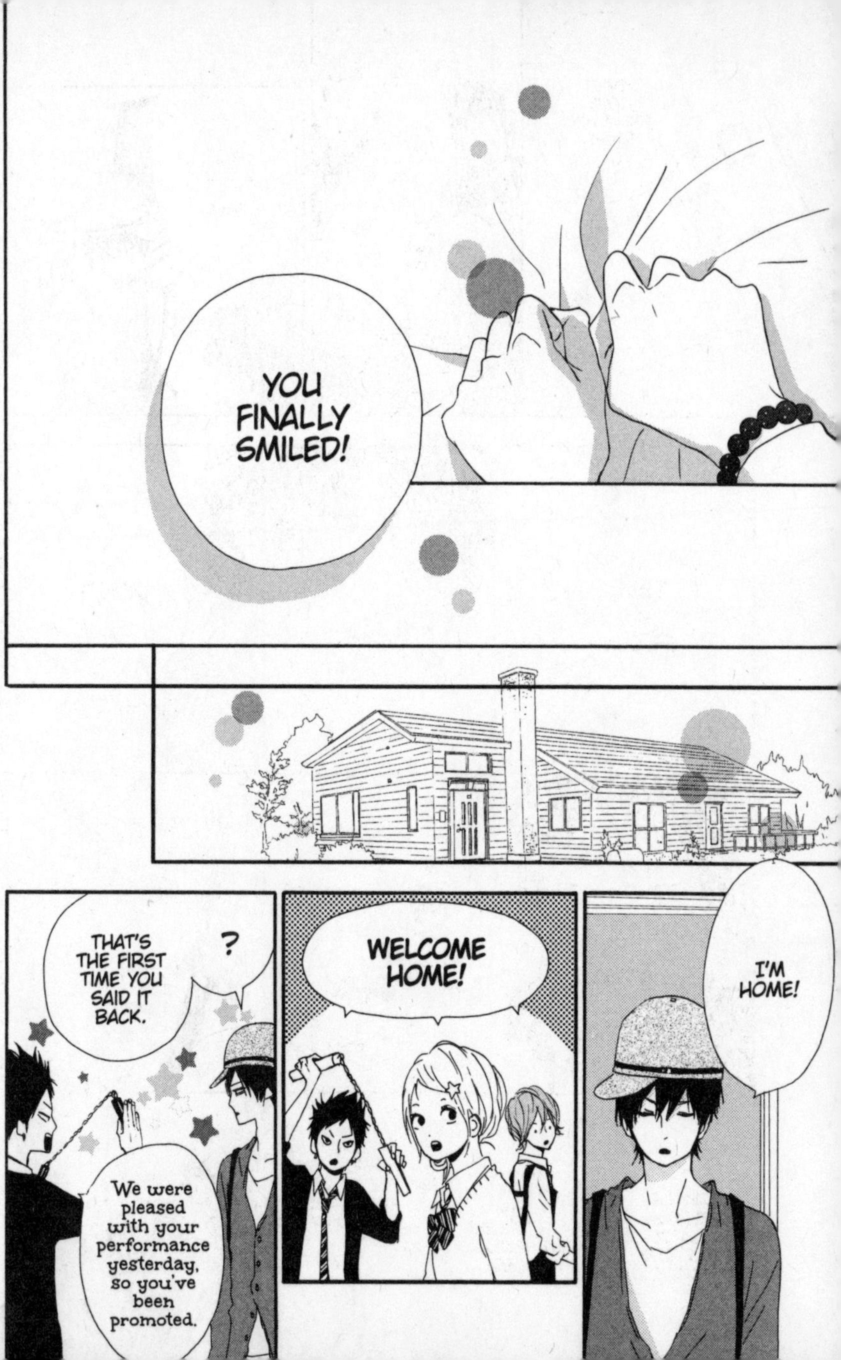
YOU FINALLY SMILED!
I'M HOME!
WELCOME HOME!
?
THAT'S THE FIRST TIME YOU SAID IT BACK.
We were pleased with your performance yesterday, so you've been promoted.

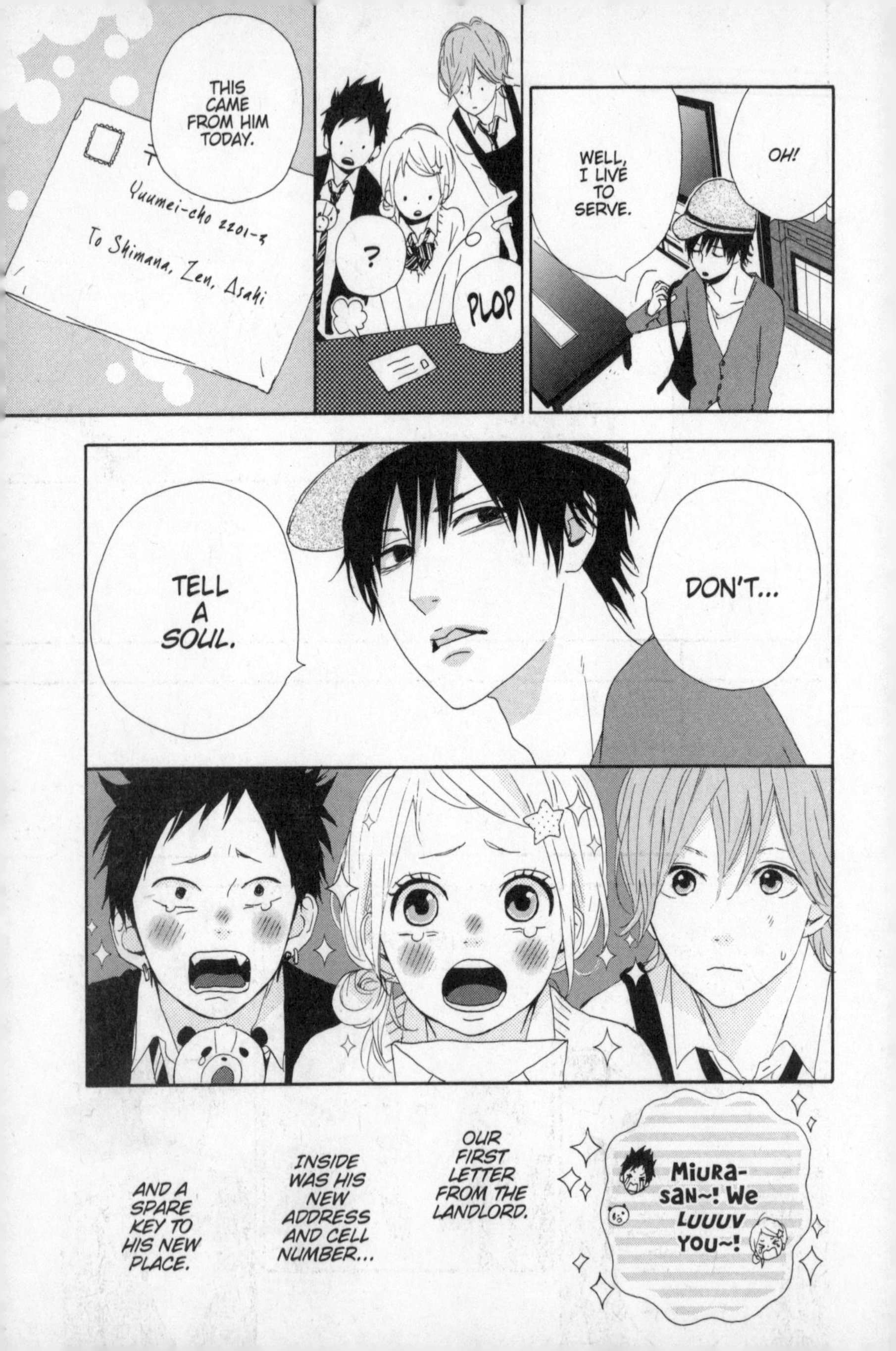
OH!
WELL, I LIVE TO SERVE.
?
PLOP
THIS CAME FROM HIM TODAY.
Yuumei-cho 2201-3
To Shimana, Zen, Asahi
DON'T...
TELL A SOUL.
Miura-san~! We Luuuv you~!
OUR FIRST LETTER FROM THE LANDLORD.
INSIDE WAS HIS NEW ADDRESS AND CELL NUMBER...
AND A SPARE KEY TO HIS NEW PLACE.

Picture by: Zen

Subject: Panda

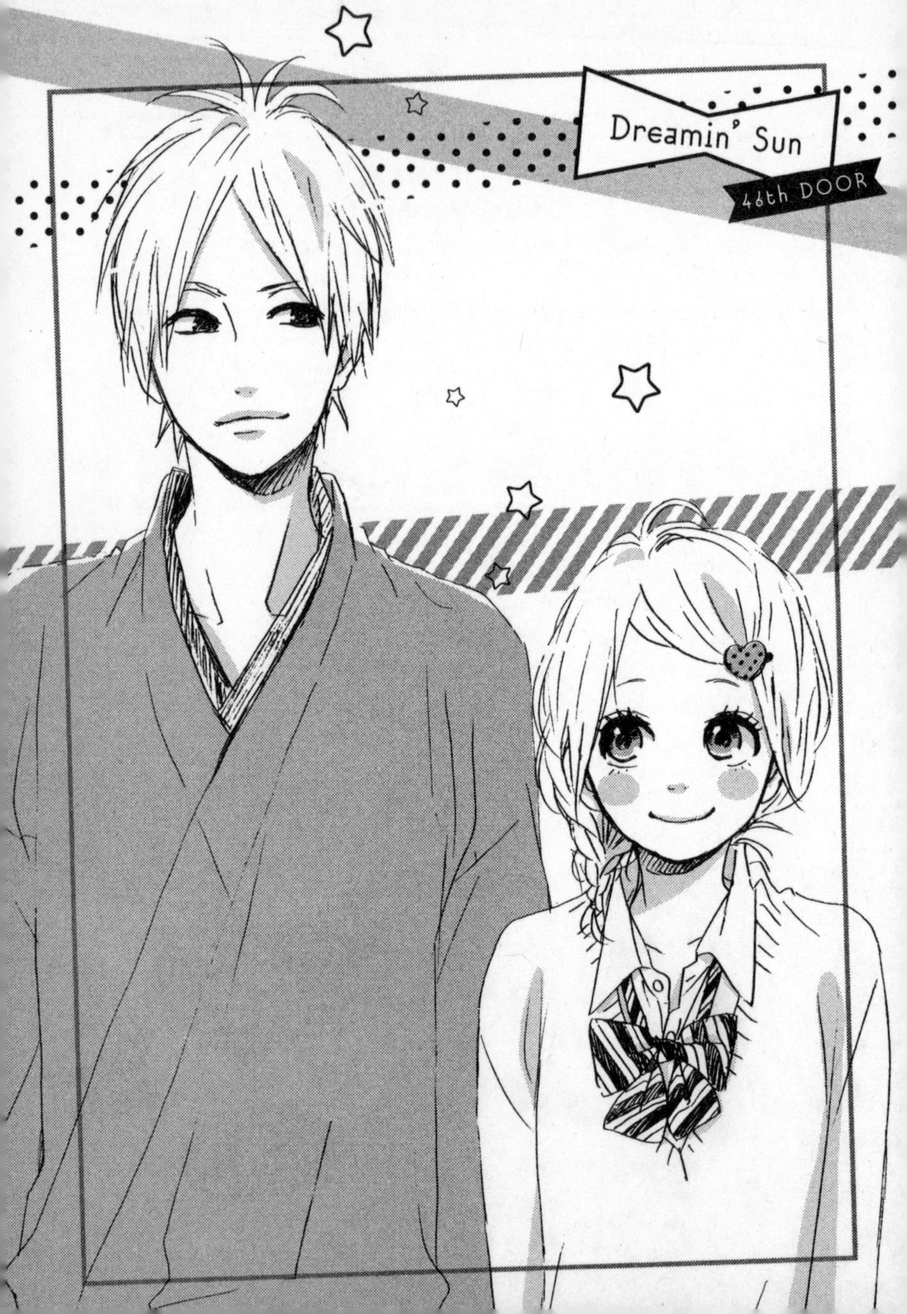
Dreamin' Sun
46th DOOR

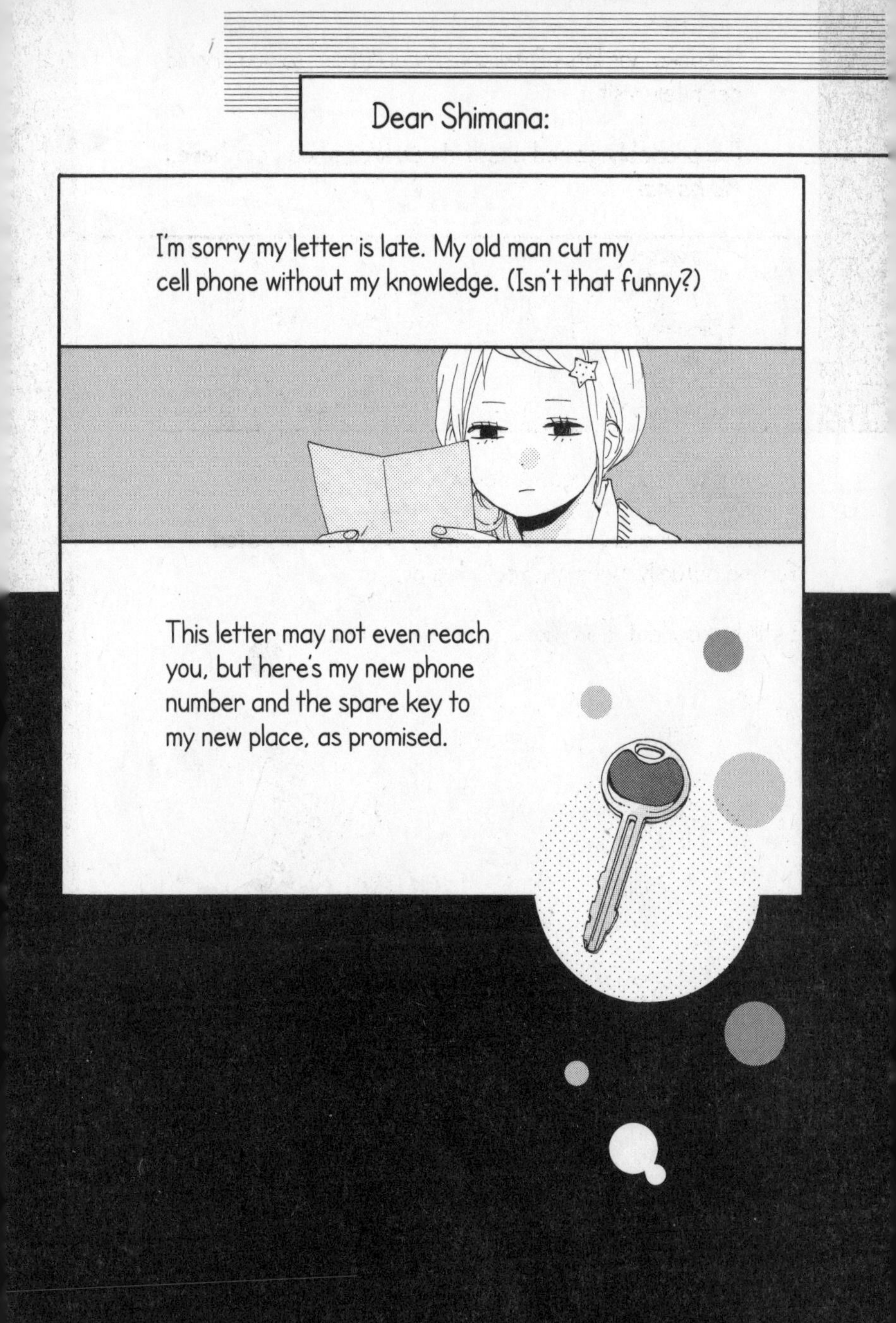
Dear Shimana:
I'm sorry my letter is late. My old man cut my cell phone without my knowledge. (Isn't that funny?)
This letter may not even reach you, but here's my new phone number and the spare key to my new place, as promised.

Fukuoka has lots of delicious local dishes, so you should definitely visit.

I've probably gained about three kilos since I got here. *Ha ha ha!*

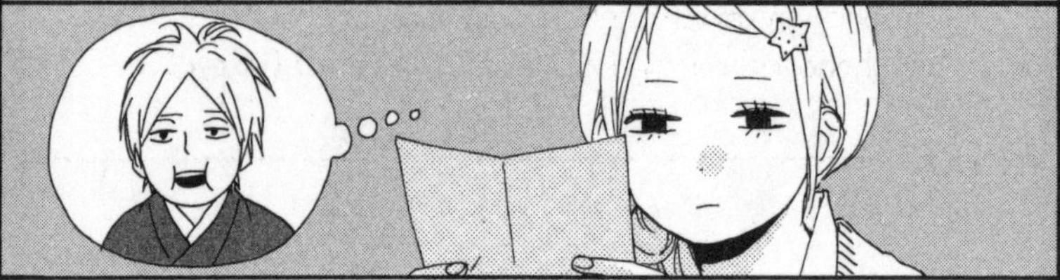

I have one thing I forgot to tell you.

That Entrance Exam Study Notebook you guys created for me actually made me really happy.

I still treasure it, even here, and look at it daily.

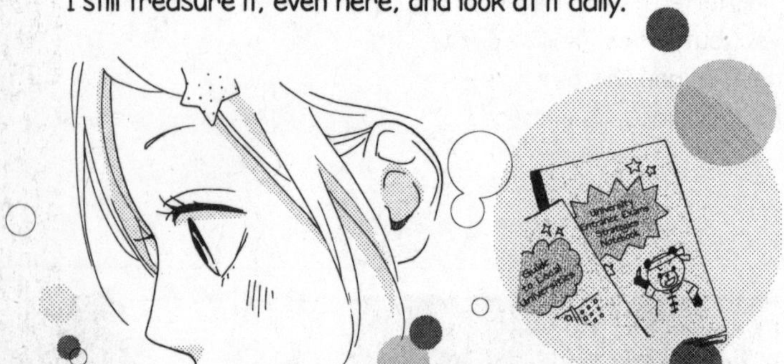
University Entrance Exams Strategies Notebook
Guide to Local Universities

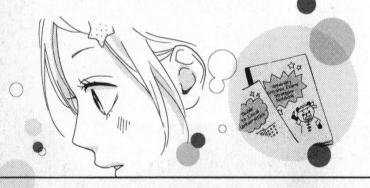

I thought I had completely given up on that dream, but seeing this notebook made me realize I really do want to be a teacher.

I mean, the notebooks are riddled with mistakes.

I doubt my old man would ever give me another shot, but if I only had one more chance...

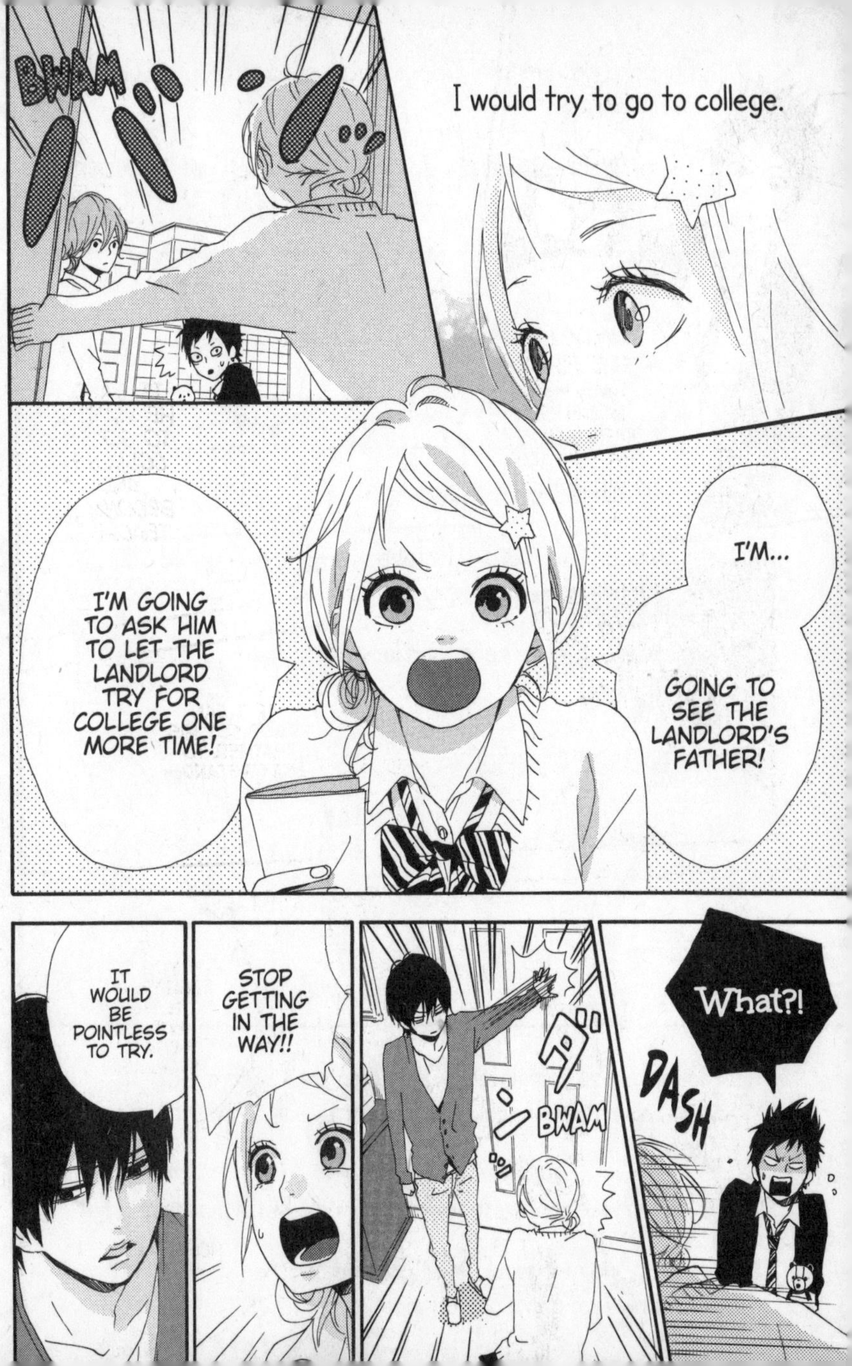

I would try to go to college.
BWAM
I'M...
GOING TO SEE THE LANDLORD'S FATHER!
I'M GOING TO ASK HIM TO LET THE LANDLORD TRY FOR COLLEGE ONE MORE TIME!
What?!
DASH
BWAM
STOP GETTING IN THE WAY!!
IT WOULD BE POINTLESS TO TRY.

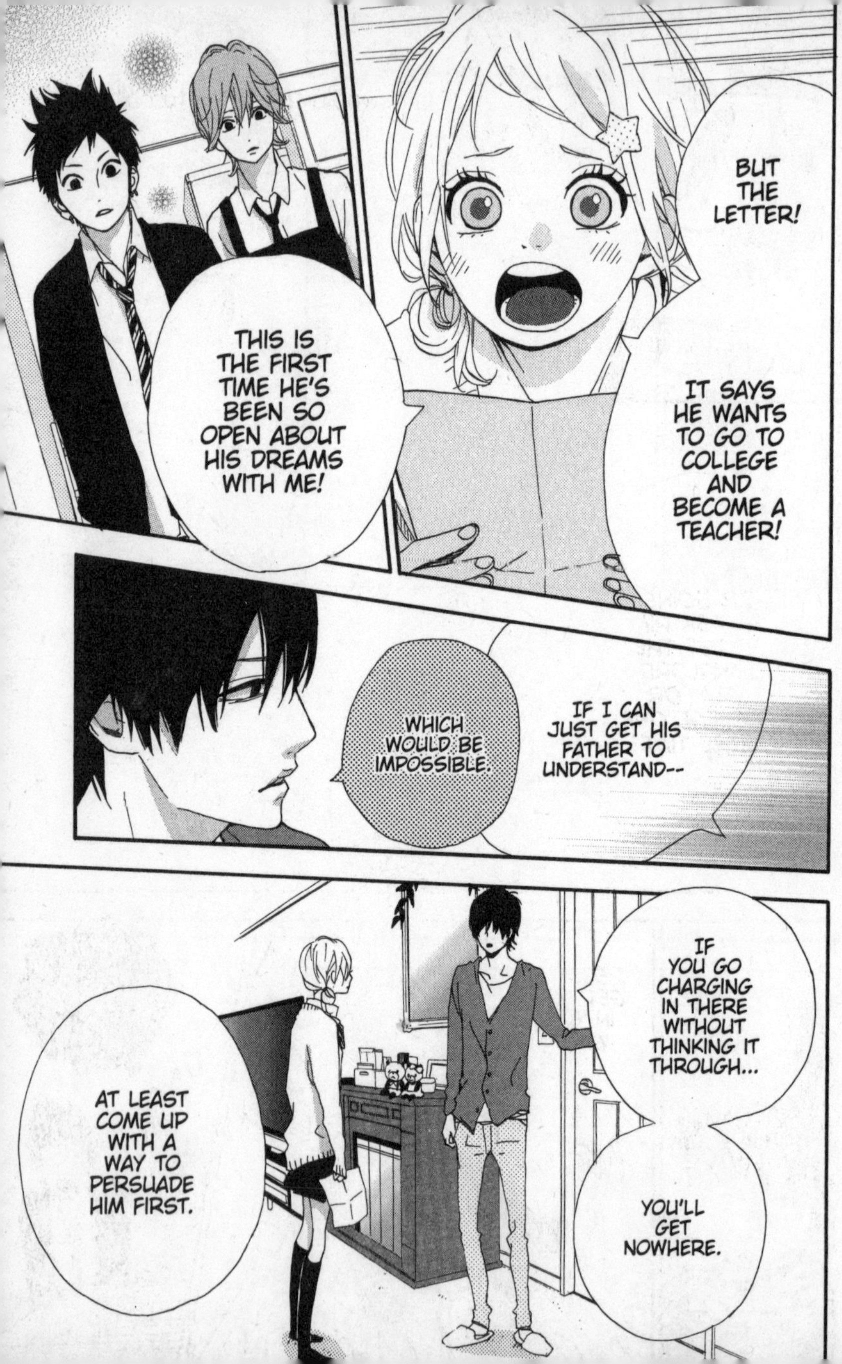
BUT THE LETTER!
IT SAYS HE WANTS TO GO TO COLLEGE AND BECOME A TEACHER!
THIS IS THE FIRST TIME HE'S BEEN SO OPEN ABOUT HIS DREAMS WITH ME!
IF I CAN JUST GET HIS FATHER TO UNDERSTAND--
WHICH WOULD BE IMPOSSIBLE.
IF YOU GO CHARGING IN THERE WITHOUT THINKING IT THROUGH...
YOU'LL GET NOWHERE.
AT LEAST COME UP WITH A WAY TO PERSUADE HIM FIRST.

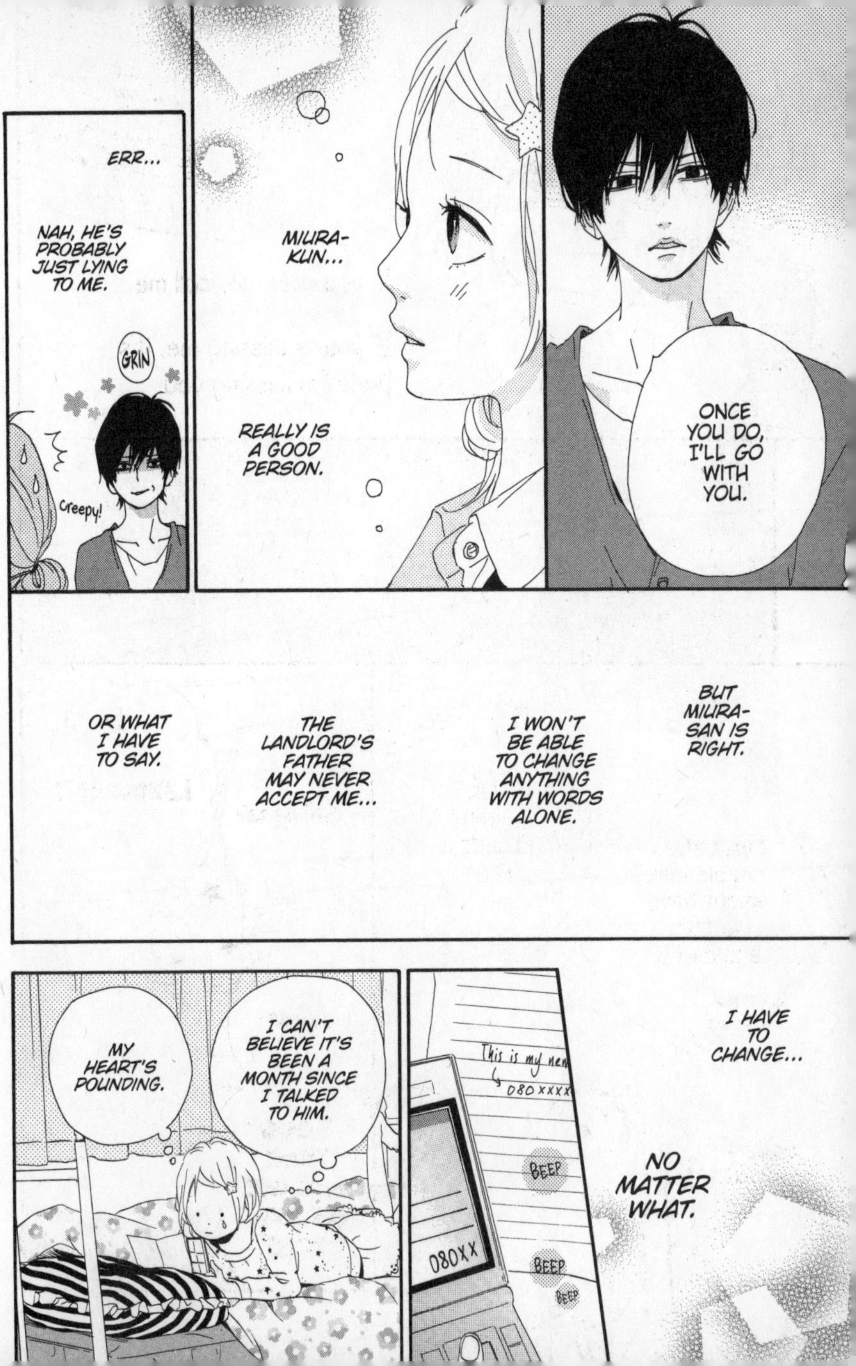
ONCE YOU DO, I'LL GO WITH YOU.
MIURA-KUN...
REALLY IS A GOOD PERSON.
ERR...
NAH, HE'S PROBABLY JUST LYING TO ME.
GRIN
Creepy!
BUT MIURA-SAN IS RIGHT.
I WON'T BE ABLE TO CHANGE ANYTHING WITH WORDS ALONE.
THE LANDLORD'S FATHER MAY NEVER ACCEPT ME...
OR WHAT I HAVE TO SAY.
I HAVE TO CHANGE...
This is my new
080 XXXX
BEEP
080XX
BEEP
BEEP
NO MATTER WHAT.
I CAN'T BELIEVE IT'S BEEN A MONTH SINCE I TALKED TO HIM.
MY HEART'S POUNDING.

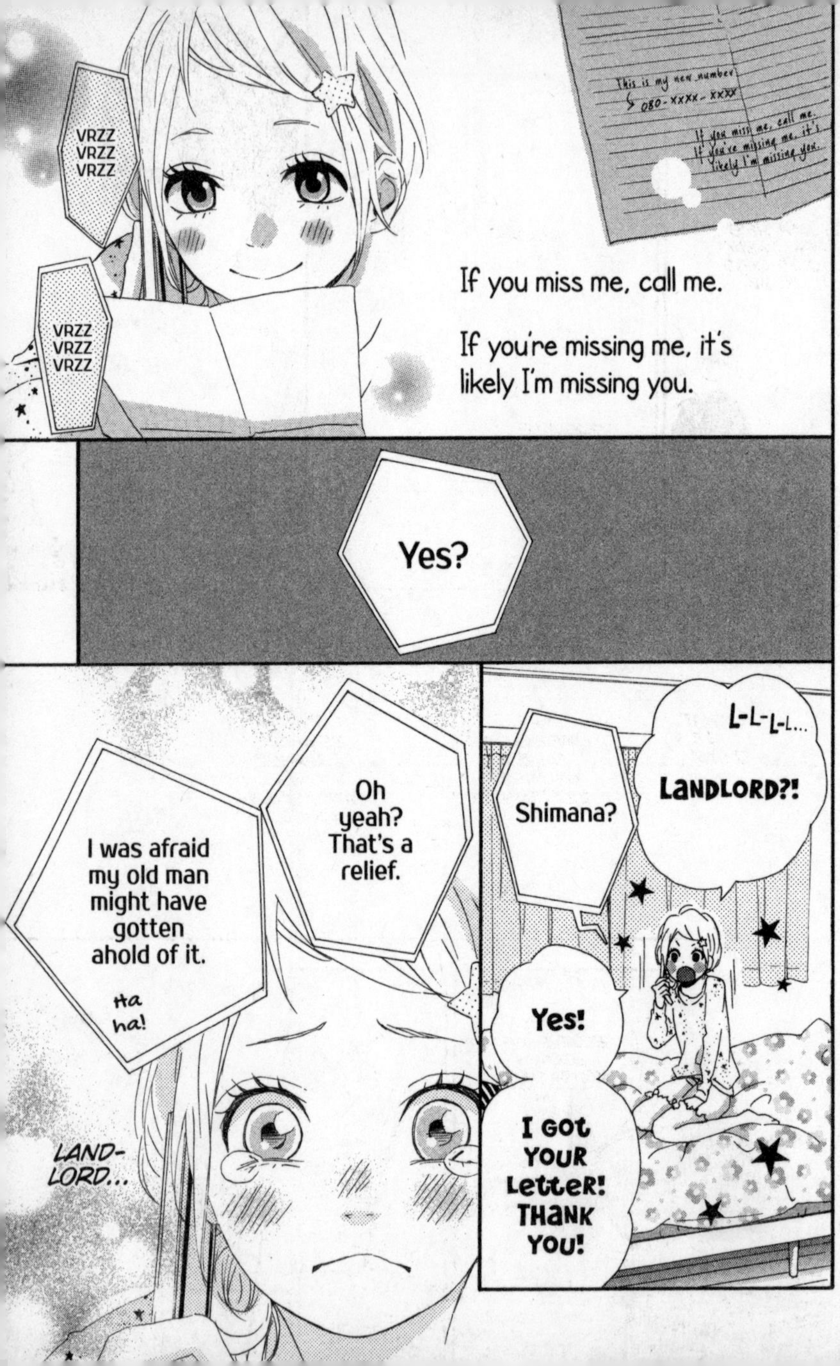
This is my new number.
→ 080-XXXX-XXXX
If you miss me, call me. If you're missing me, it's likely I'm missing you.
If you miss me, call me.
If you're missing me, it's likely I'm missing you.
VRZZ VRZZ VRZZ
VRZZ VRZZ VRZZ
Yes?
L-L-L-L... LANDLORD?!
Shimana?
Yes! I GOT YOUR LETTER! THANK YOU!
Oh yeah? That's a relief.
I was afraid my old man might have gotten ahold of it. Ha ha!
LAND-LORD...

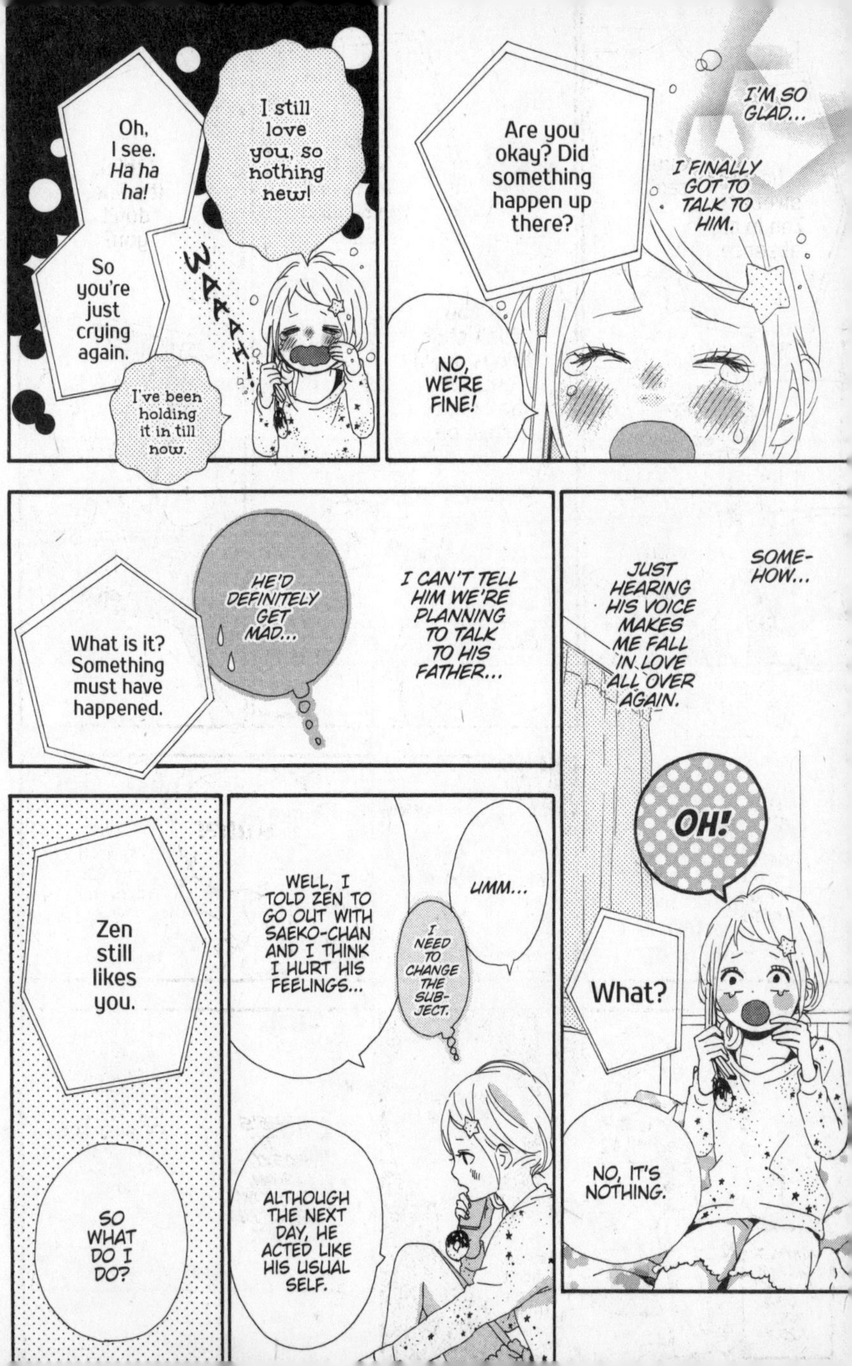
I'M SO GLAD...
I FINALLY GOT TO TALK TO HIM.
Are you okay? Did something happen up there?
NO, WE'RE FINE!
I still love you, so nothing new!
WAAAH!
Oh, I see. Ha ha ha!
So you're just crying again.
I've been holding it in till now.
SOME-HOW...
JUST HEARING HIS VOICE MAKES ME FALL IN LOVE ALL OVER AGAIN.
OH!
What?
NO, IT'S NOTHING.
I CAN'T TELL HIM WE'RE PLANNING TO TALK TO HIS FATHER...
HE'D DEFINITELY GET MAD...
What is it? Something must have happened.
UMM...
I NEED TO CHANGE THE SUB-JECT.
WELL, I TOLD ZEN TO GO OUT WITH SAEKO-CHAN AND I THINK I HURT HIS FEELINGS...
ALTHOUGH THE NEXT DAY, HE ACTED LIKE HIS USUAL SELF.
Zen still likes you.
SO WHAT DO I DO?

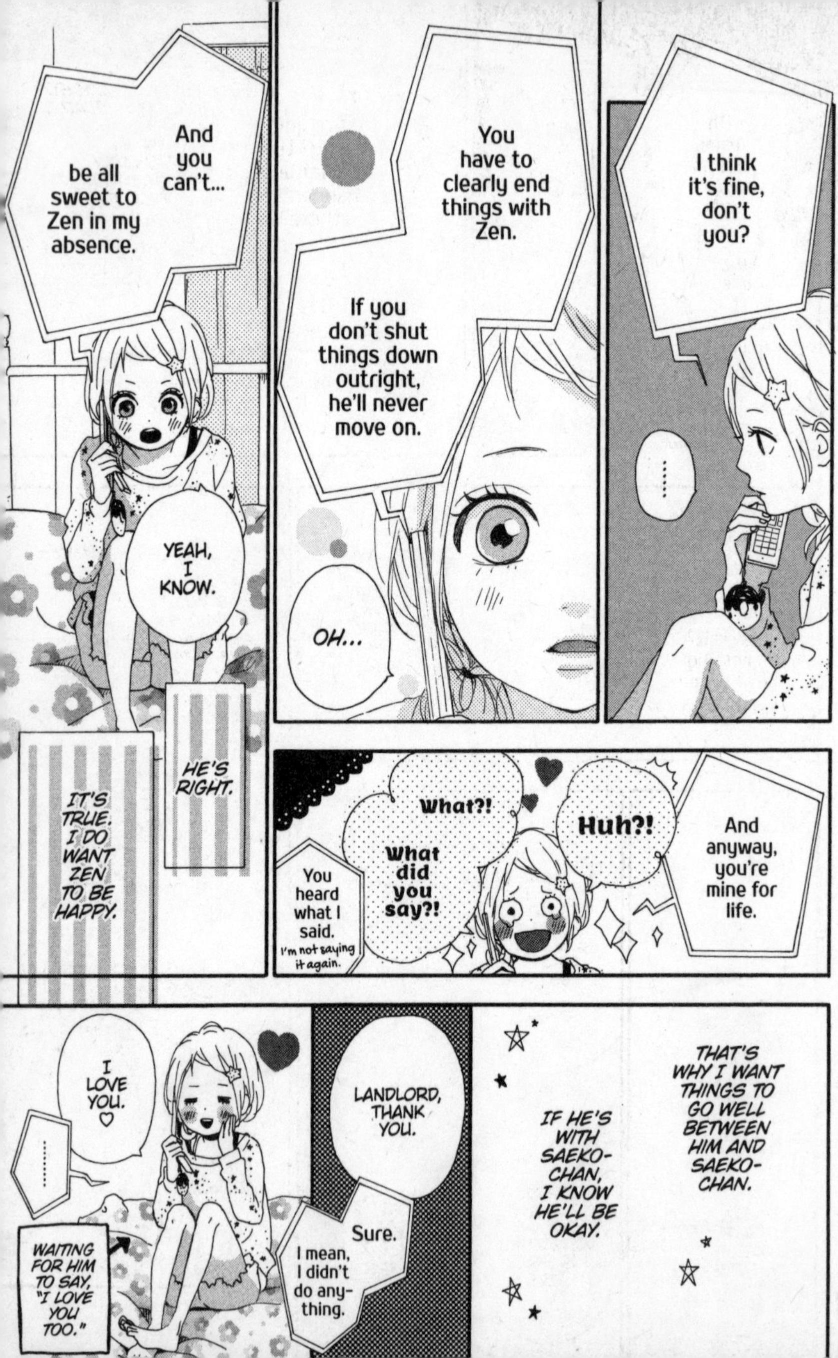
I think it's fine, don't you?
......
You have to clearly end things with Zen.
If you don't shut things down outright, he'll never move on.
OH...
And anyway, you're mine for life.
Huh?!
What?!
What did you say?!
You heard what I said.
I'm not saying it again.
And you can't...
be all sweet to Zen in my absence.
YEAH, I KNOW.
HE'S RIGHT.
IT'S TRUE. I DO WANT ZEN TO BE HAPPY.
THAT'S WHY I WANT THINGS TO GO WELL BETWEEN HIM AND SAEKO-CHAN.
IF HE'S WITH SAEKO-CHAN, I KNOW HE'LL BE OKAY.
LANDLORD, THANK YOU.
Sure.
I mean, I didn't do any-thing.
I LOVE YOU. ♡
......
WAITING FOR HIM TO SAY, "I LOVE YOU TOO."

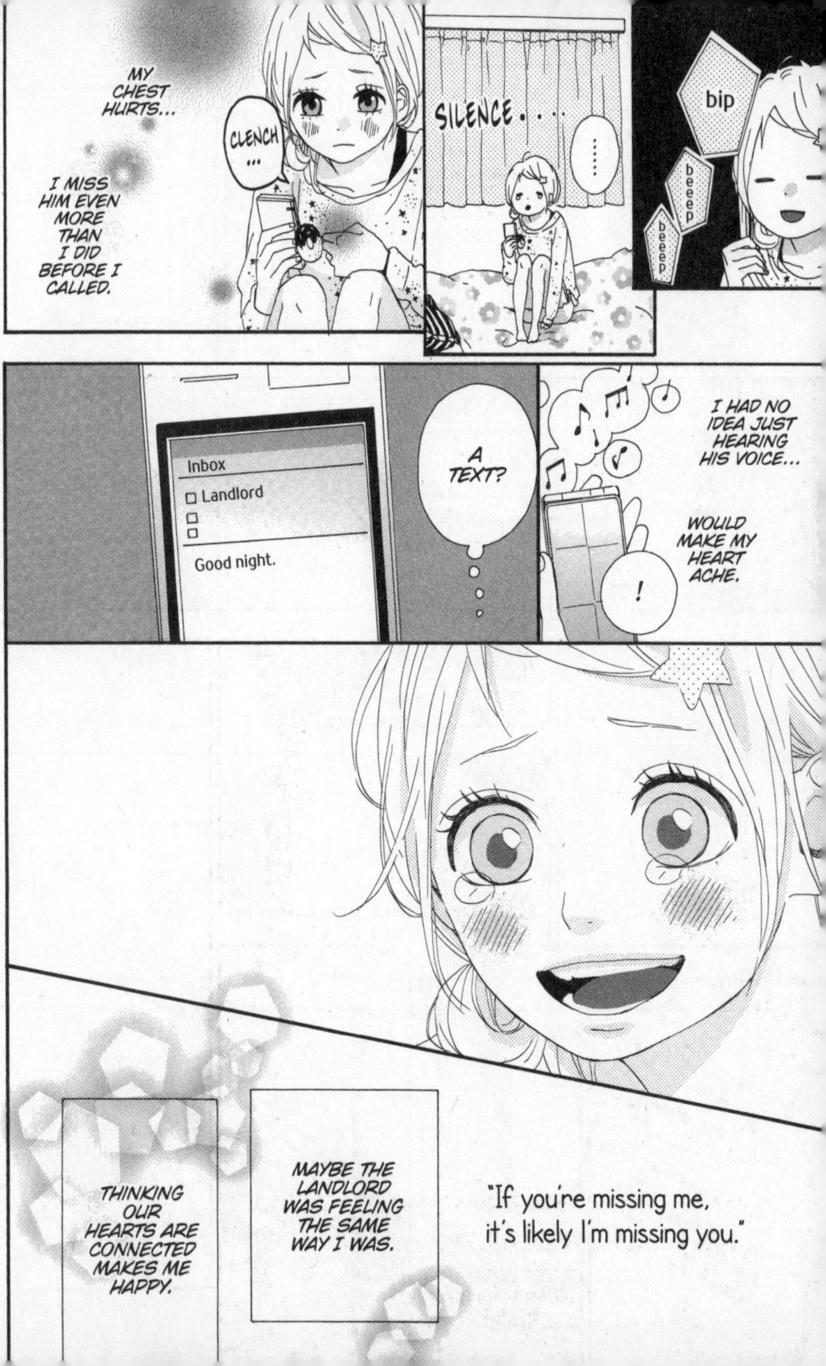
bip
beeep
beeep
SILENCE . . . .
......
CLENCH ...
MY CHEST HURTS...
I MISS HIM EVEN MORE THAN I DID BEFORE I CALLED.
I HAD NO IDEA JUST HEARING HIS VOICE...
WOULD MAKE MY HEART ACHE.
!
A TEXT?
Inbox
Landlord
Good night.
"If you're missing me, it's likely I'm missing you."
MAYBE THE LANDLORD WAS FEELING THE SAME WAY I WAS.
THINKING OUR HEARTS ARE CONNECTED MAKES ME HAPPY.

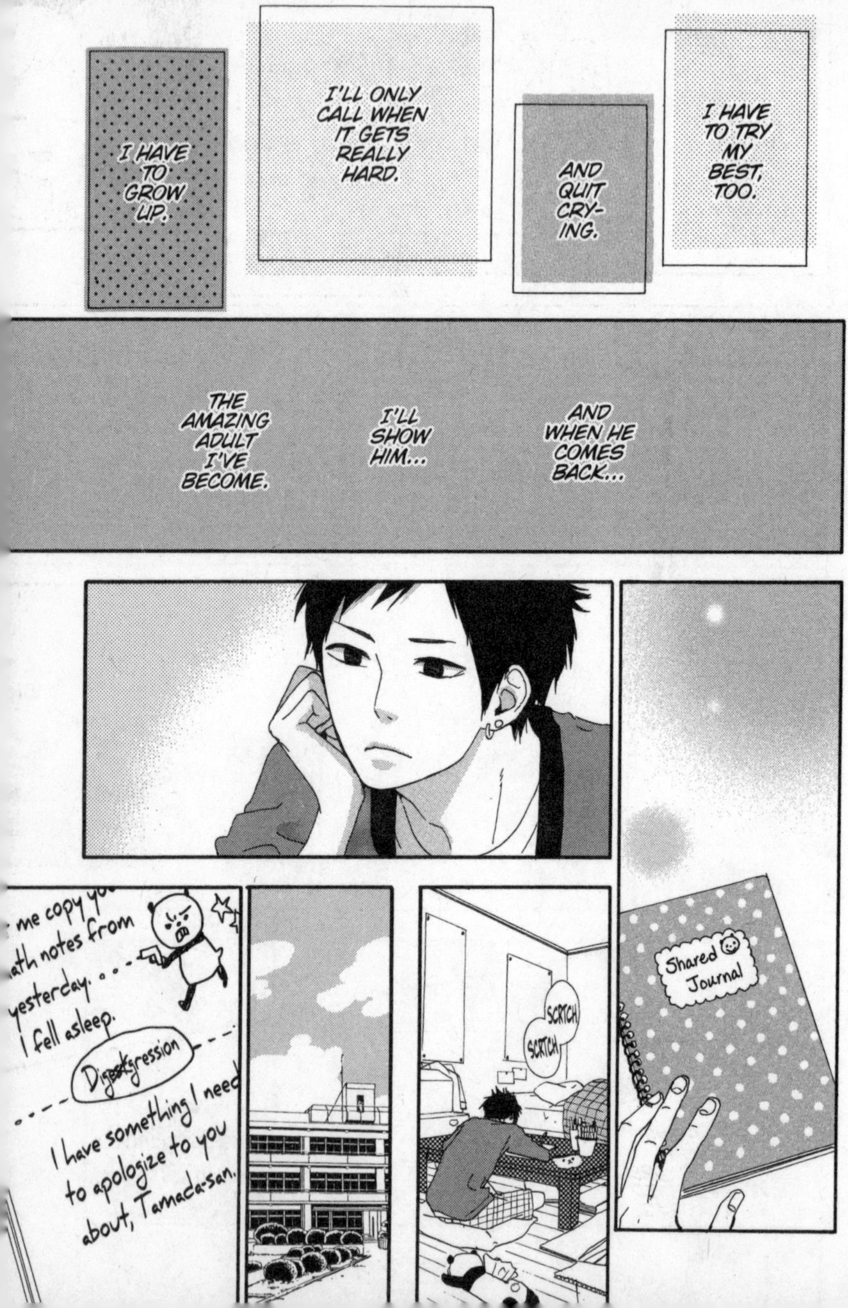
I HAVE TO TRY MY BEST, TOO.
AND QUIT CRY-ING.
I'LL ONLY CALL WHEN IT GETS REALLY HARD.
I HAVE TO GROW UP.
AND WHEN HE COMES BACK...
I'LL SHOW HIM...
THE AMAZING ADULT I'VE BECOME.
Shared Journal
SCRTCH
SCRTCH
me copy
ath notes from yesterday. . . .
I fell asleep.
Di~~gest~~gression
I have something I need to apologize to you about, Tamada-san.

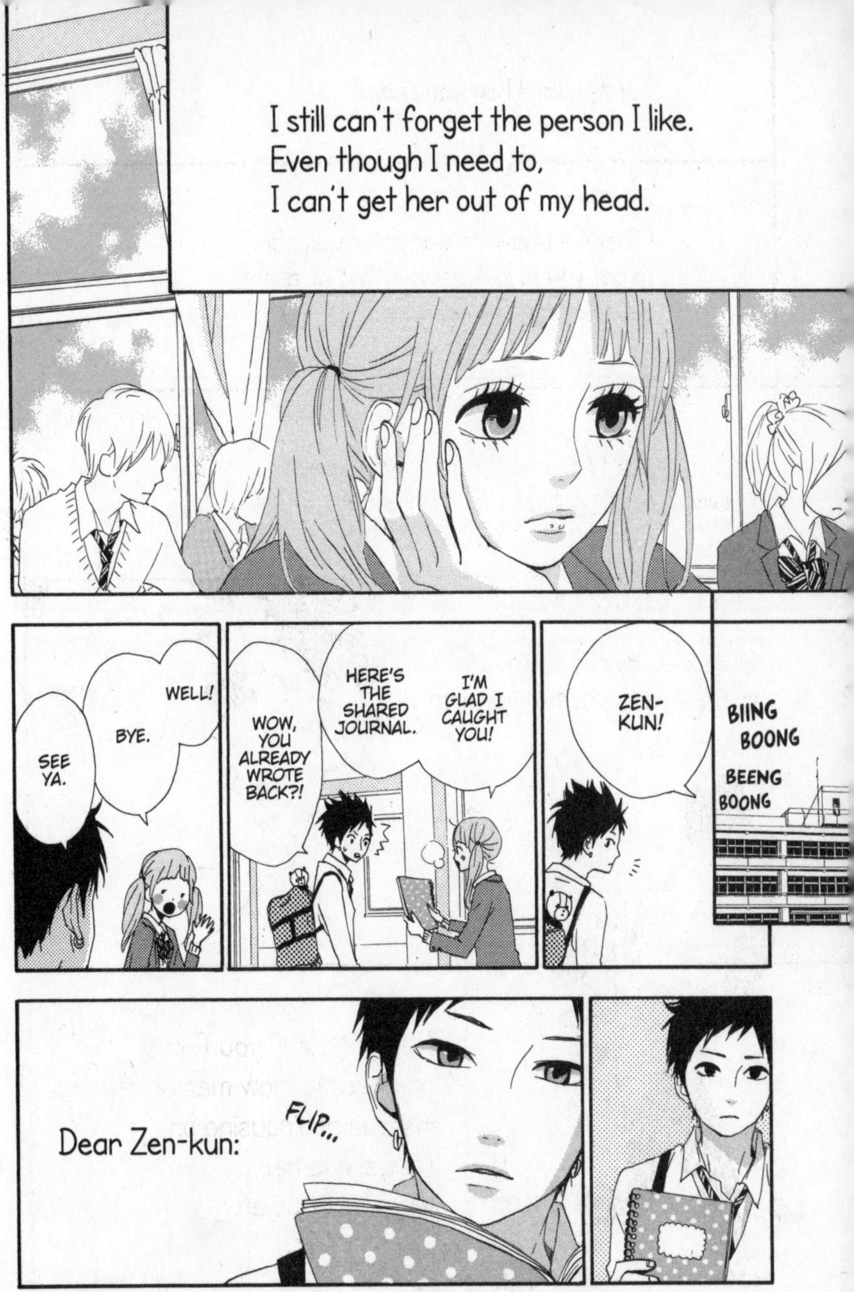
I still can't forget the person I like.
Even though I need to,
I can't get her out of my head.
BIING BOONG
BEENG BOONG
ZEN-KUN!
I'M GLAD I CAUGHT YOU!
HERE'S THE SHARED JOURNAL.
WOW, YOU ALREADY WROTE BACK?!
WELL!
BYE.
SEE YA.
FLIP...
Dear Zen-kun:

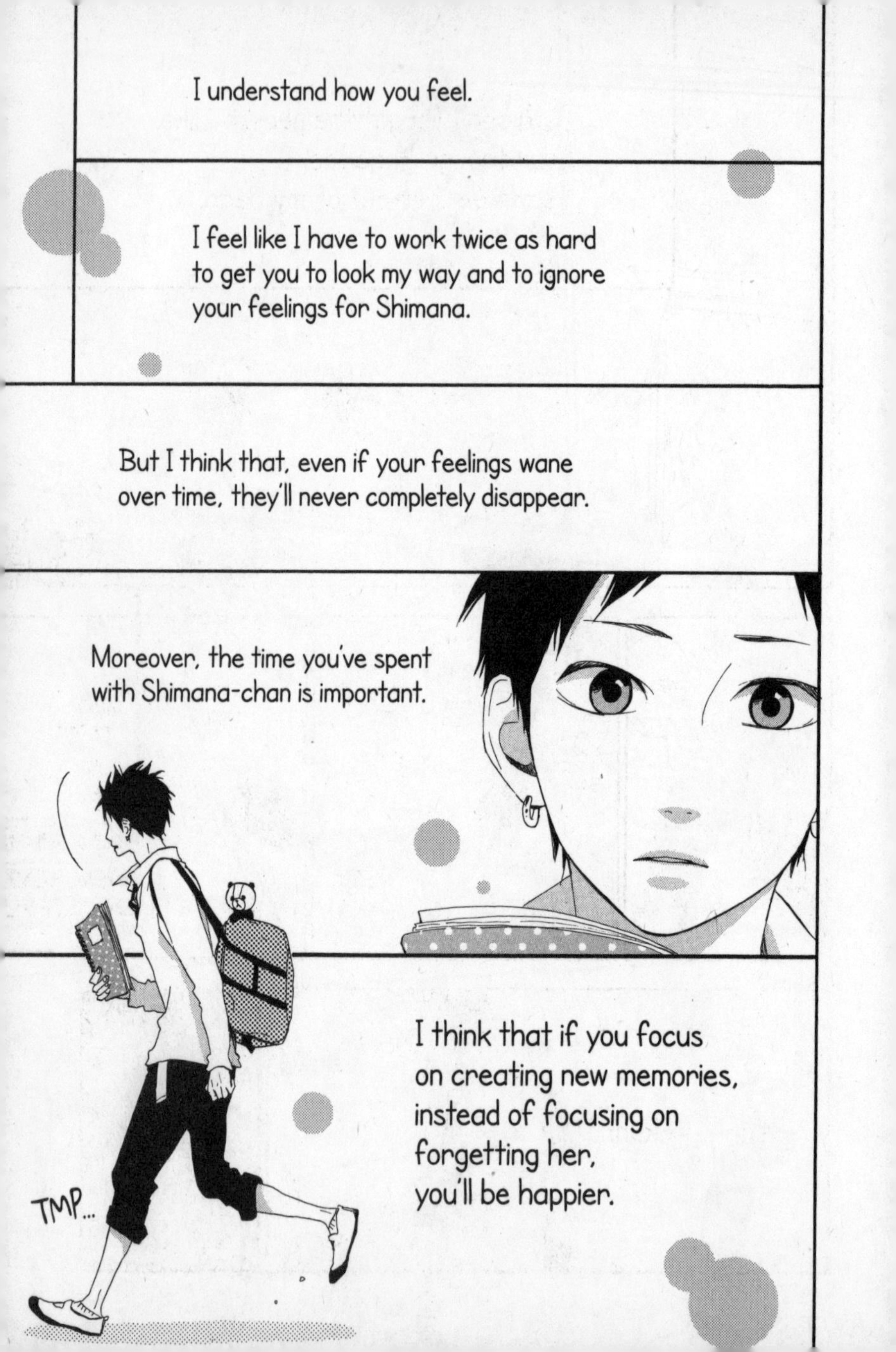
I understand how you feel.
I feel like I have to work twice as hard to get you to look my way and to ignore your feelings for Shimana.
But I think that, even if your feelings wane over time, they'll never completely disappear.
Moreover, the time you've spent with Shimana-chan is important.
I think that if you focus on creating new memories, instead of focusing on forgetting her, you'll be happier.
TMP...

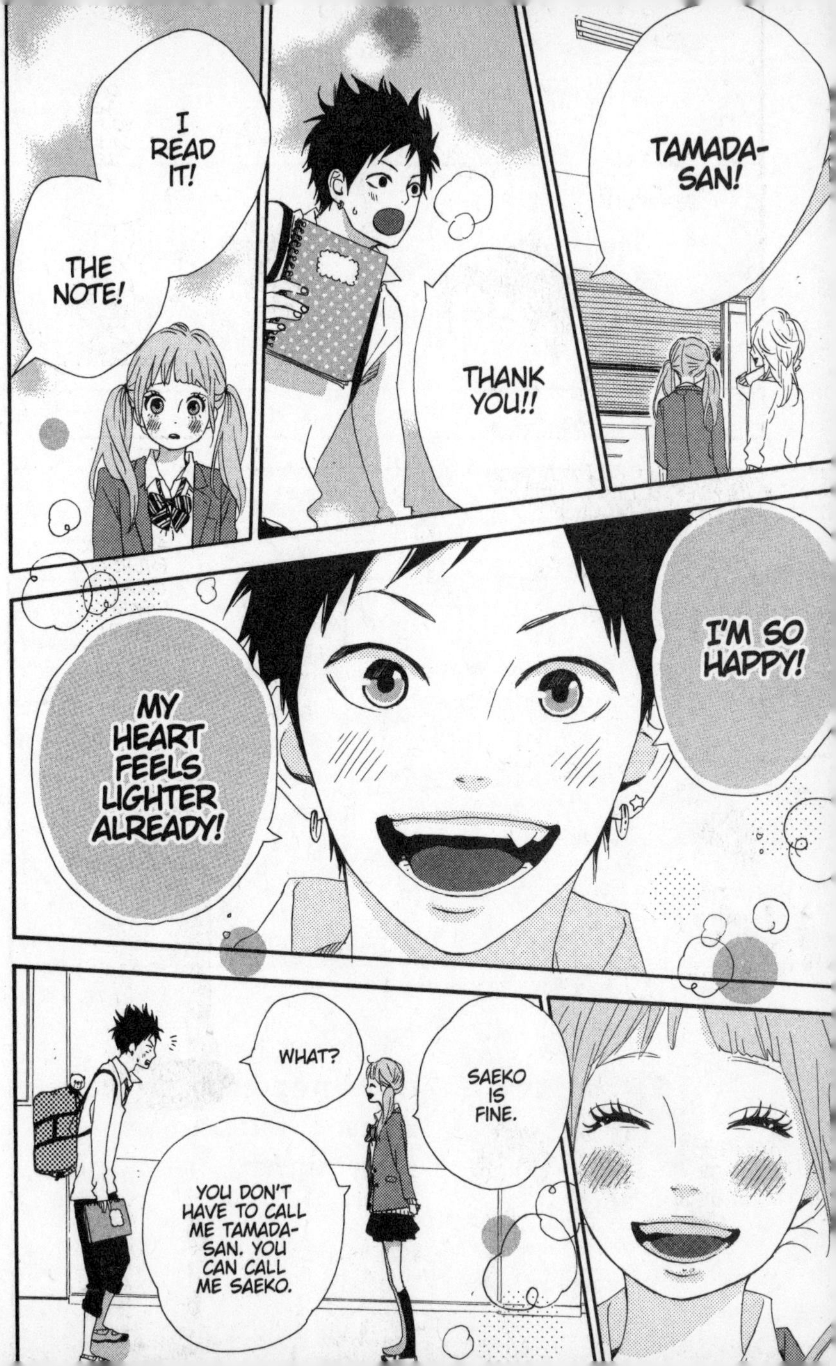
TAMADA-SAN!
THANK YOU!!
I READ IT!
THE NOTE!
I'M SO HAPPY!
MY HEART FEELS LIGHTER ALREADY!
YOU DON'T HAVE TO CALL ME TAMADA-SAN. YOU CAN CALL ME SAEKO.
WHAT?
SAEKO IS FINE.

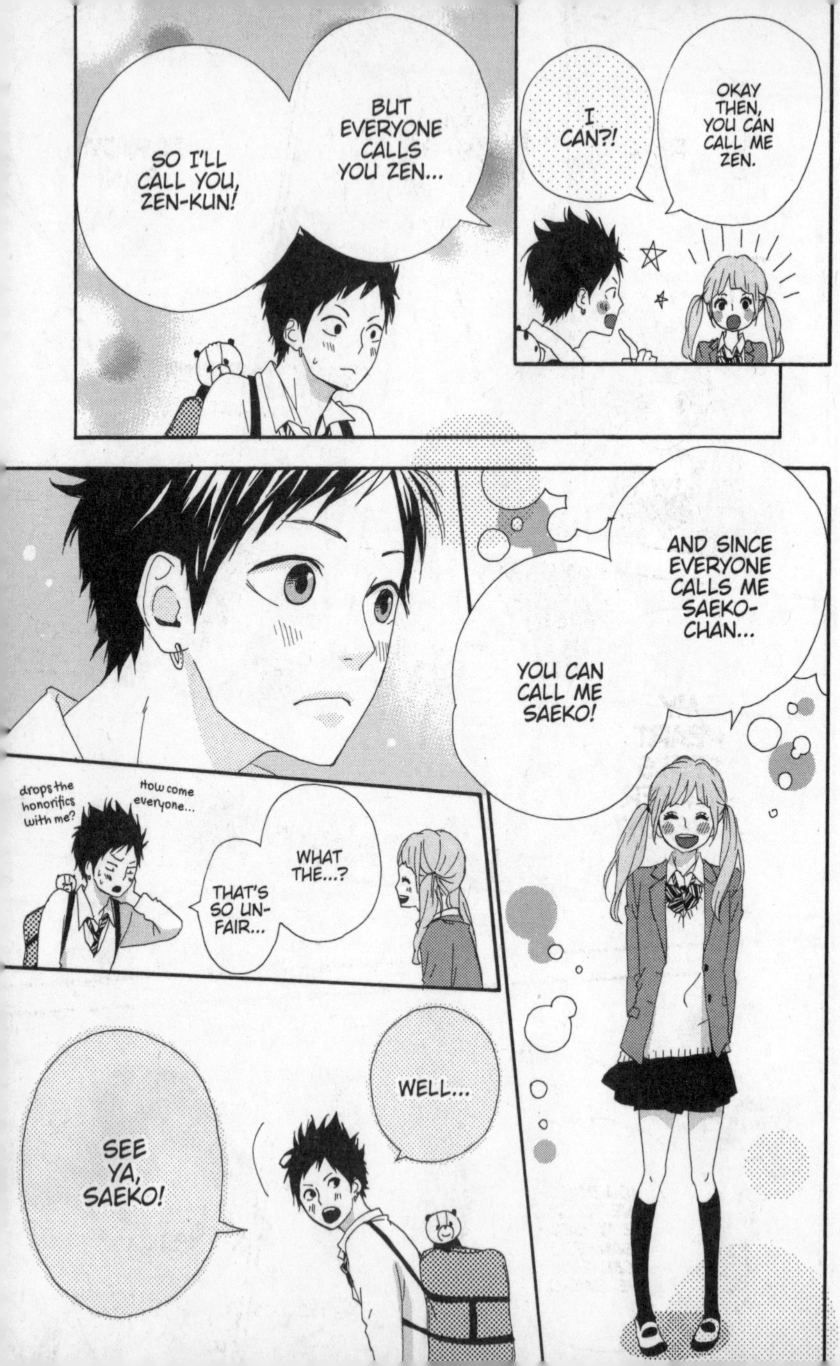
OKAY THEN, YOU CAN CALL ME ZEN.
I CAN?!
BUT EVERYONE CALLS YOU ZEN...
SO I'LL CALL YOU, ZEN-KUN!
AND SINCE EVERYONE CALLS ME SAEKO-CHAN...
YOU CAN CALL ME SAEKO!
WHAT THE...?
THAT'S SO UN-FAIR...
How come everyone...
drops the honorifics with me?
WELL...
SEE YA, SAEKO!

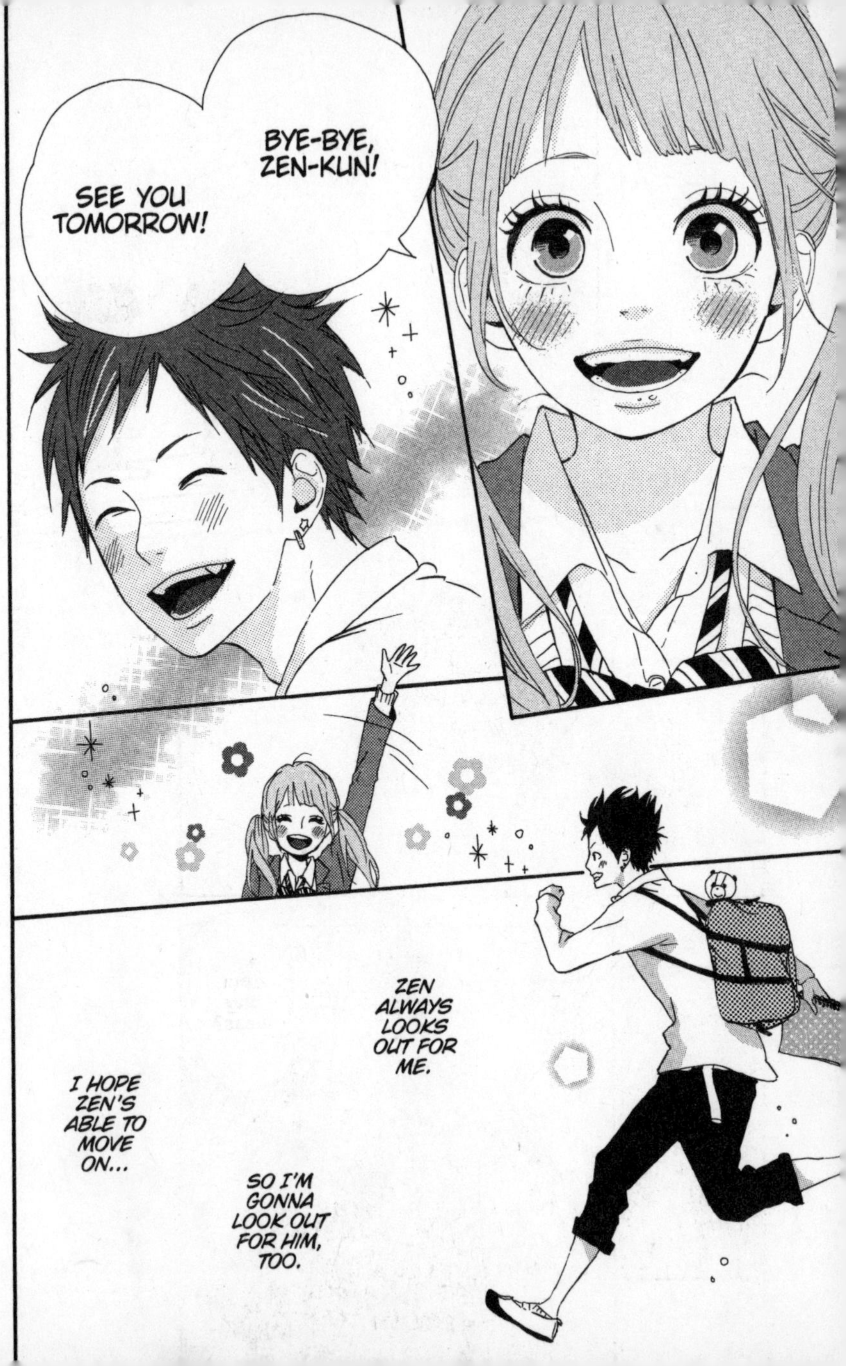
BYE-BYE, ZEN-KUN!
SEE YOU TOMORROW!
ZEN ALWAYS LOOKS OUT FOR ME.
SO I'M GONNA LOOK OUT FOR HIM, TOO.
I HOPE ZEN'S ABLE TO MOVE ON...

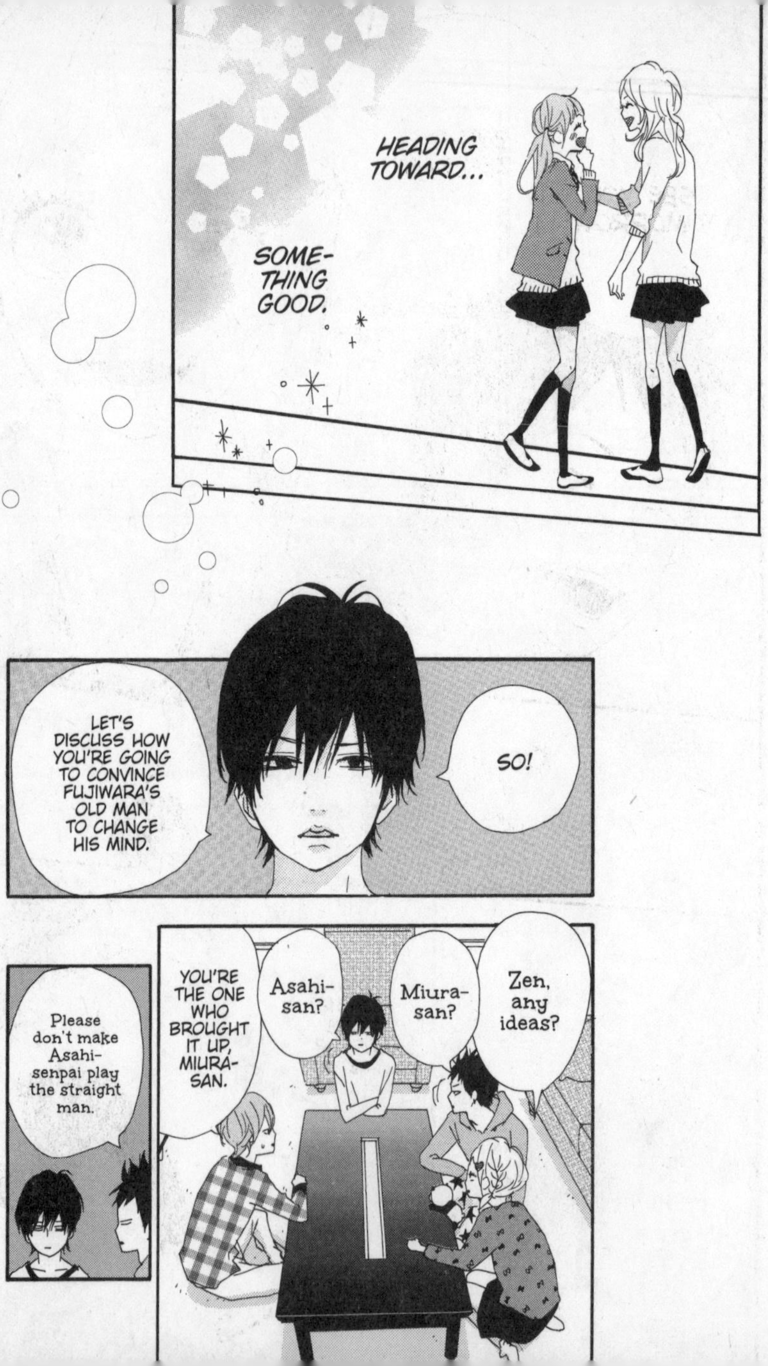
HEADING TOWARD...
SOME-THING GOOD.
SO!
LET'S DISCUSS HOW YOU'RE GOING TO CONVINCE FUJIWARA'S OLD MAN TO CHANGE HIS MIND.
Zen, any ideas?
Miura-san?
Asahi-san?
YOU'RE THE ONE WHO BROUGHT IT UP, MIURA-SAN.
Please don't make Asahi-senpai play the straight man.

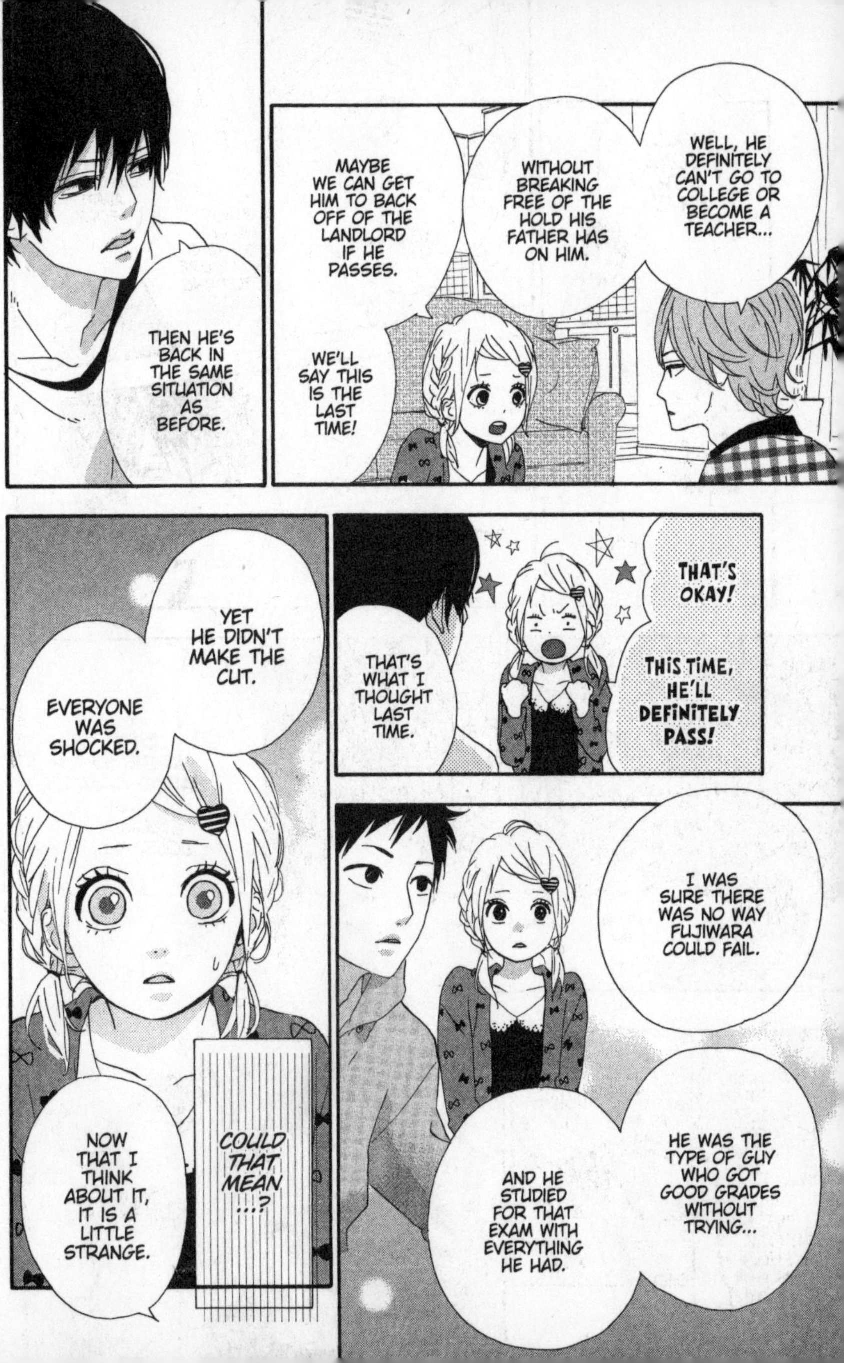
WELL, HE DEFINITELY CAN'T GO TO COLLEGE OR BECOME A TEACHER...
WITHOUT BREAKING FREE OF THE HOLD HIS FATHER HAS ON HIM.
MAYBE WE CAN GET HIM TO BACK OFF OF THE LANDLORD IF HE PASSES.
WE'LL SAY THIS IS THE LAST TIME!
THEN HE'S BACK IN THE SAME SITUATION AS BEFORE.
THAT'S OKAY!
THIS TIME, HE'LL DEFINITELY PASS!
THAT'S WHAT I THOUGHT LAST TIME.
I WAS SURE THERE WAS NO WAY FUJIWARA COULD FAIL.
HE WAS THE TYPE OF GUY WHO GOT GOOD GRADES WITHOUT TRYING...
AND HE STUDIED FOR THAT EXAM WITH EVERYTHING HE HAD.
YET HE DIDN'T MAKE THE CUT.
EVERYONE WAS SHOCKED.
COULD THAT MEAN ...?
NOW THAT I THINK ABOUT IT, IT IS A LITTLE STRANGE.

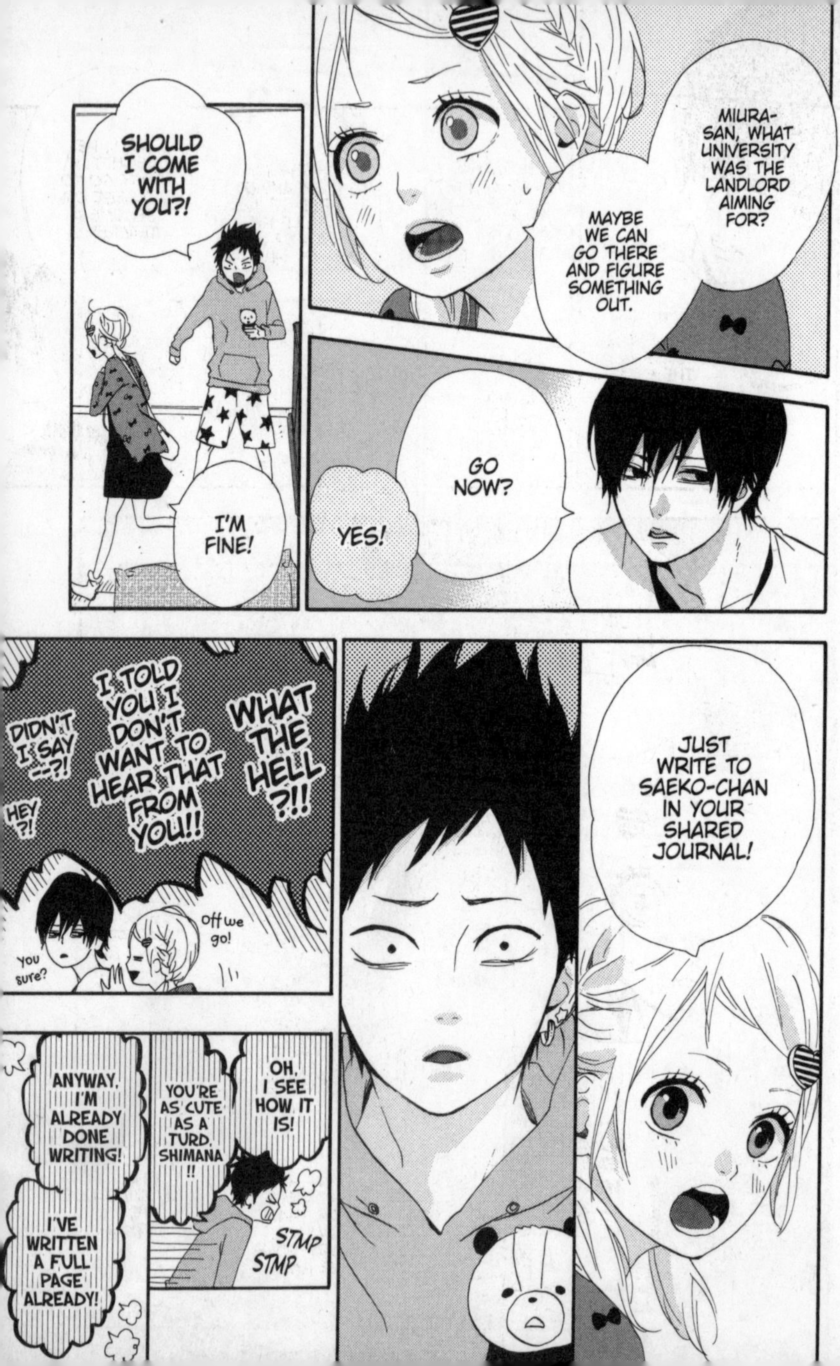
MIURA-SAN, WHAT UNIVERSITY WAS THE LANDLORD AIMING FOR?
MAYBE WE CAN GO THERE AND FIGURE SOMETHING OUT.
GO NOW?
YES!
SHOULD I COME WITH YOU?!
I'M FINE!
JUST WRITE TO SAEKO-CHAN IN YOUR SHARED JOURNAL!
WHAT THE HELL?!!
I TOLD YOU I DON'T WANT TO HEAR THAT FROM YOU!!
DIDN'T I SAY--?!
HEY?!
Off we go!
You sure?
OH, I SEE HOW IT IS!
YOU'RE AS CUTE AS A TURD, SHIMANA!!
STMP
STMP
ANYWAY, I'M ALREADY DONE WRITING!
I'VE WRITTEN A FULL PAGE ALREADY!

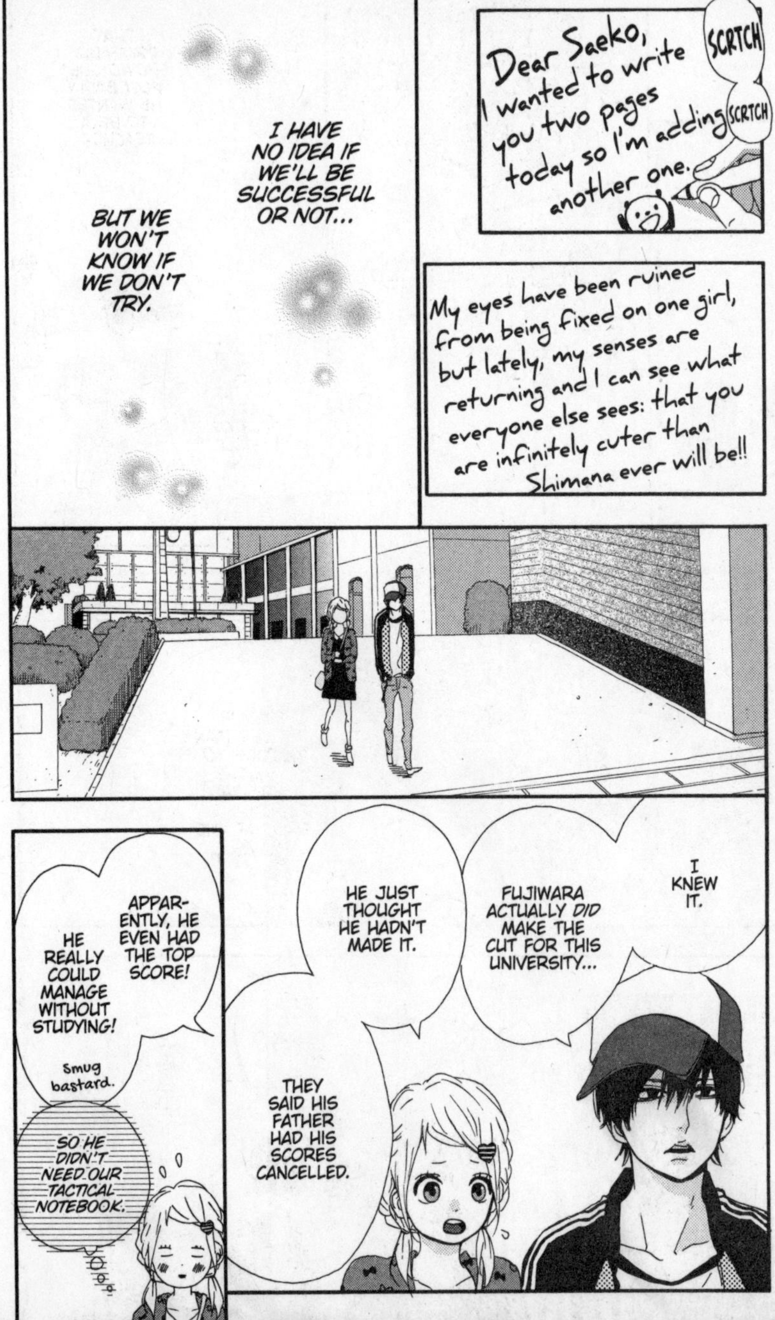
Dear Saeko, I wanted to write you two pages today so I'm adding another one.
SCRTCH
SCRTCH
My eyes have been ruined from being fixed on one girl, but lately, my senses are returning and I can see what everyone else sees: that you are infinitely cuter than Shimana ever will be!!
I HAVE NO IDEA IF WE'LL BE SUCCESSFUL OR NOT...
BUT WE WON'T KNOW IF WE DON'T TRY.
I KNEW IT.
FUJIWARA ACTUALLY *DID* MAKE THE CUT FOR THIS UNIVERSITY...
HE JUST THOUGHT HE HADN'T MADE IT.
THEY SAID HIS FATHER HAD HIS SCORES CANCELLED.
APPARENTLY, HE EVEN HAD THE TOP SCORE!
HE REALLY COULD MANAGE WITHOUT STUDYING!
Smug bastard.
SO HE DIDN'T NEED OUR TACTICAL NOTEBOOK.

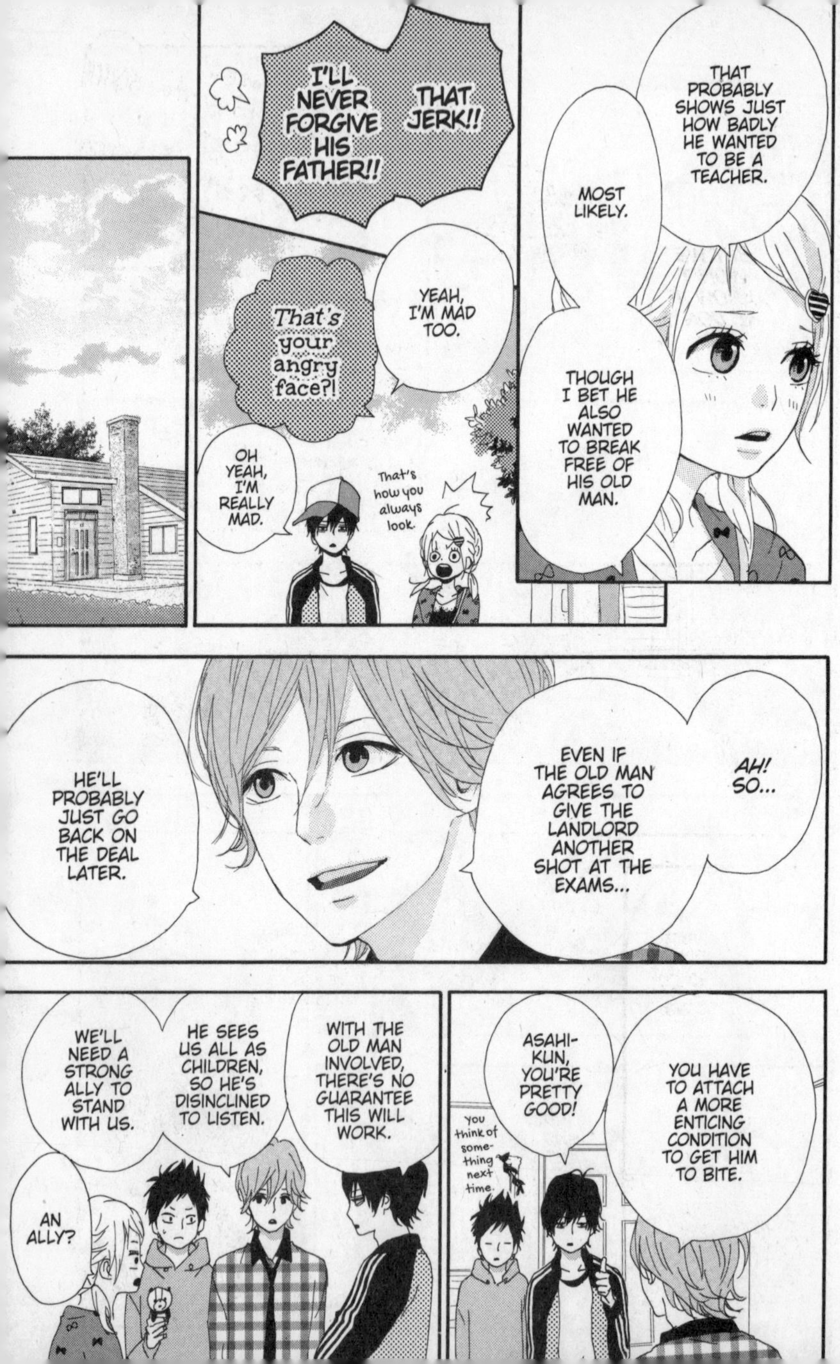
THAT PROBABLY SHOWS JUST HOW BADLY HE WANTED TO BE A TEACHER.
MOST LIKELY.
THOUGH I BET HE ALSO WANTED TO BREAK FREE OF HIS OLD MAN.
I'LL NEVER FORGIVE HIS FATHER!! THAT JERK!!
YEAH, I'M MAD TOO.
That's your angry face?!
OH YEAH, I'M REALLY MAD.
That's how you always look.
AH! SO...
EVEN IF THE OLD MAN AGREES TO GIVE THE LANDLORD ANOTHER SHOT AT THE EXAMS...
HE'LL PROBABLY JUST GO BACK ON THE DEAL LATER.
YOU HAVE TO ATTACH A MORE ENTICING CONDITION TO GET HIM TO BITE.
ASAHI-KUN, YOU'RE PRETTY GOOD!
You think of something next time.
WITH THE OLD MAN INVOLVED, THERE'S NO GUARANTEE THIS WILL WORK.
HE SEES US ALL AS CHILDREN, SO HE'S DISINCLINED TO LISTEN.
WE'LL NEED A STRONG ALLY TO STAND WITH US.
AN ALLY?

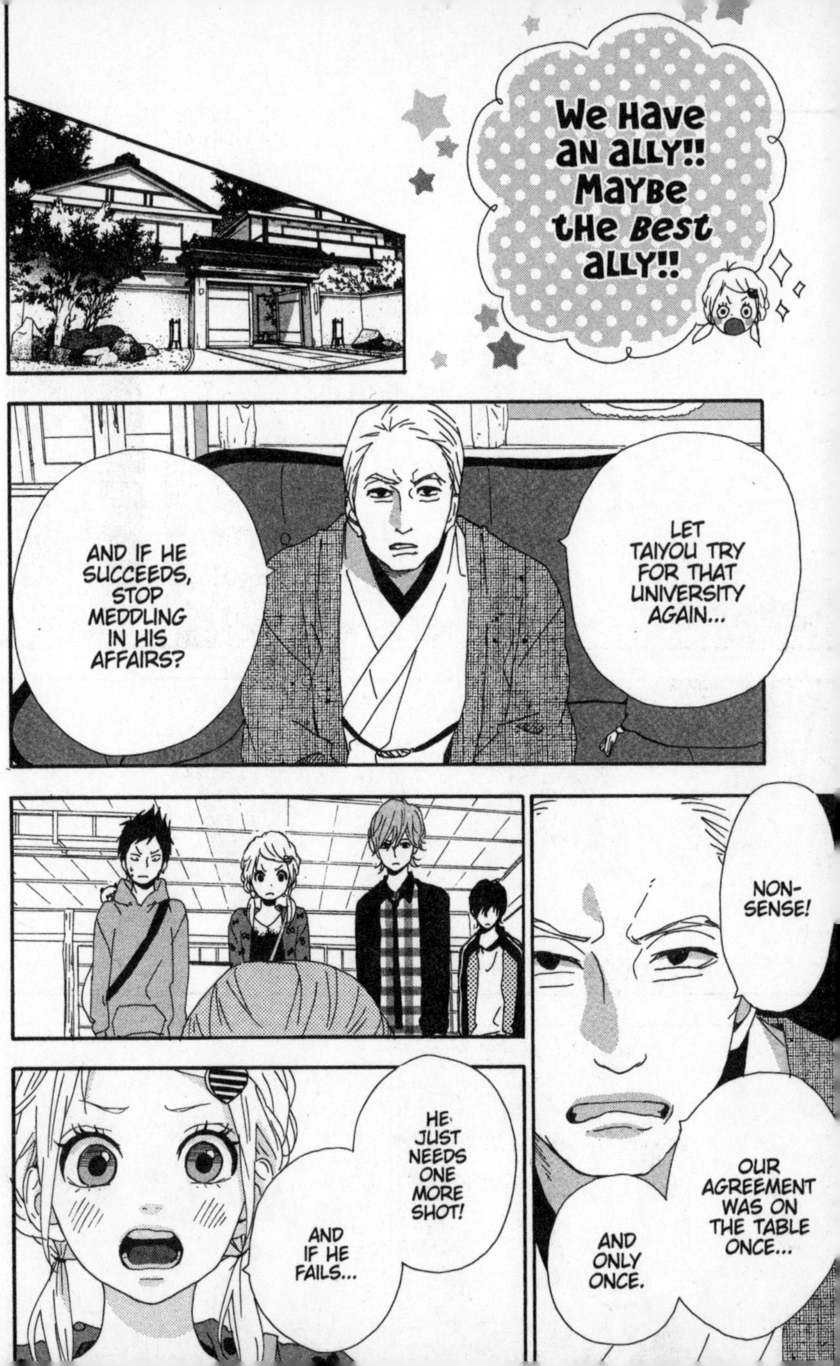
We Have an ALLY!! Maybe the Best ALLY!!
LET TAIYOU TRY FOR THAT UNIVERSITY AGAIN...
AND IF HE SUCCEEDS, STOP MEDDLING IN HIS AFFAIRS?
NON-SENSE!
OUR AGREEMENT WAS ON THE TABLE ONCE...
AND ONLY ONCE.
HE JUST NEEDS ONE MORE SHOT!
AND IF HE FAILS...

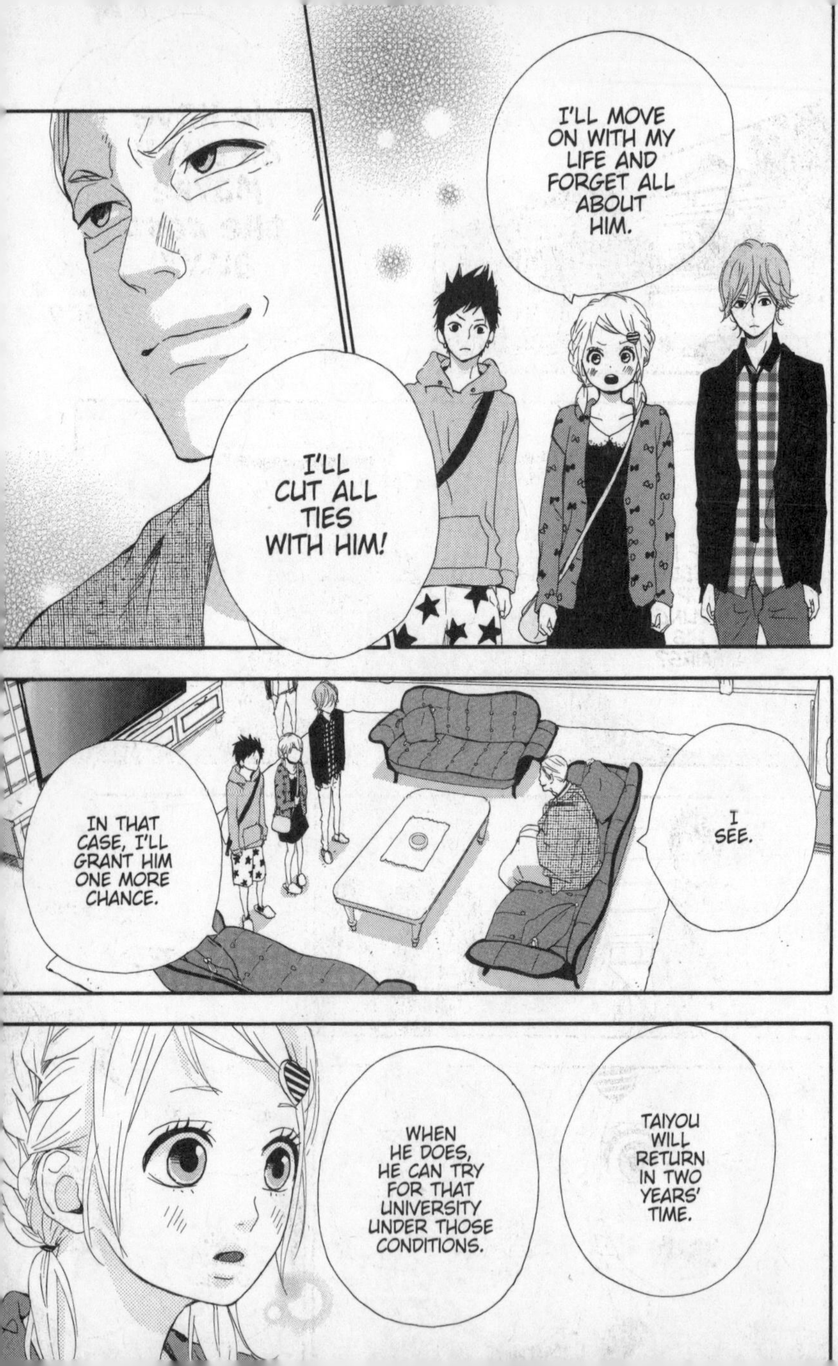
I'LL MOVE ON WITH MY LIFE AND FORGET ALL ABOUT HIM.
I'LL CUT ALL TIES WITH HIM!
I SEE.
IN THAT CASE, I'LL GRANT HIM ONE MORE CHANCE.
TAIYOU WILL RETURN IN TWO YEARS' TIME.
WHEN HE DOES, HE CAN TRY FOR THAT UNIVERSITY UNDER THOSE CONDITIONS.

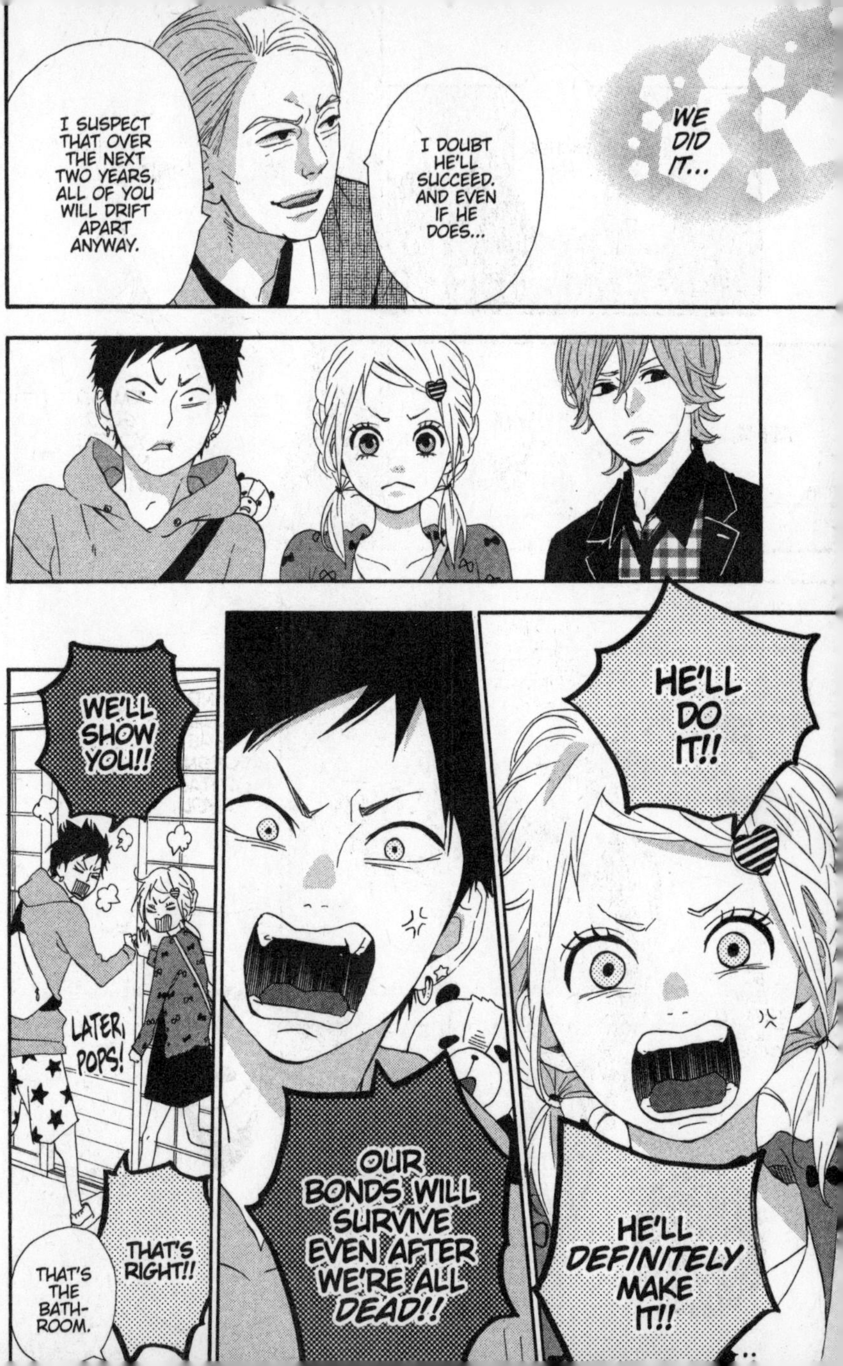
WE DID IT...
I DOUBT HE'LL SUCCEED. AND EVEN IF HE DOES...
I SUSPECT THAT OVER THE NEXT TWO YEARS, ALL OF YOU WILL DRIFT APART ANYWAY.
HE'LL DO IT!!
HE'LL DEFINITELY MAKE IT!!
OUR BONDS WILL SURVIVE EVEN AFTER WE'RE ALL DEAD!!
WE'LL SHOW YOU!!
THAT'S RIGHT!!
LATER, POPS!
THAT'S THE BATH-ROOM.

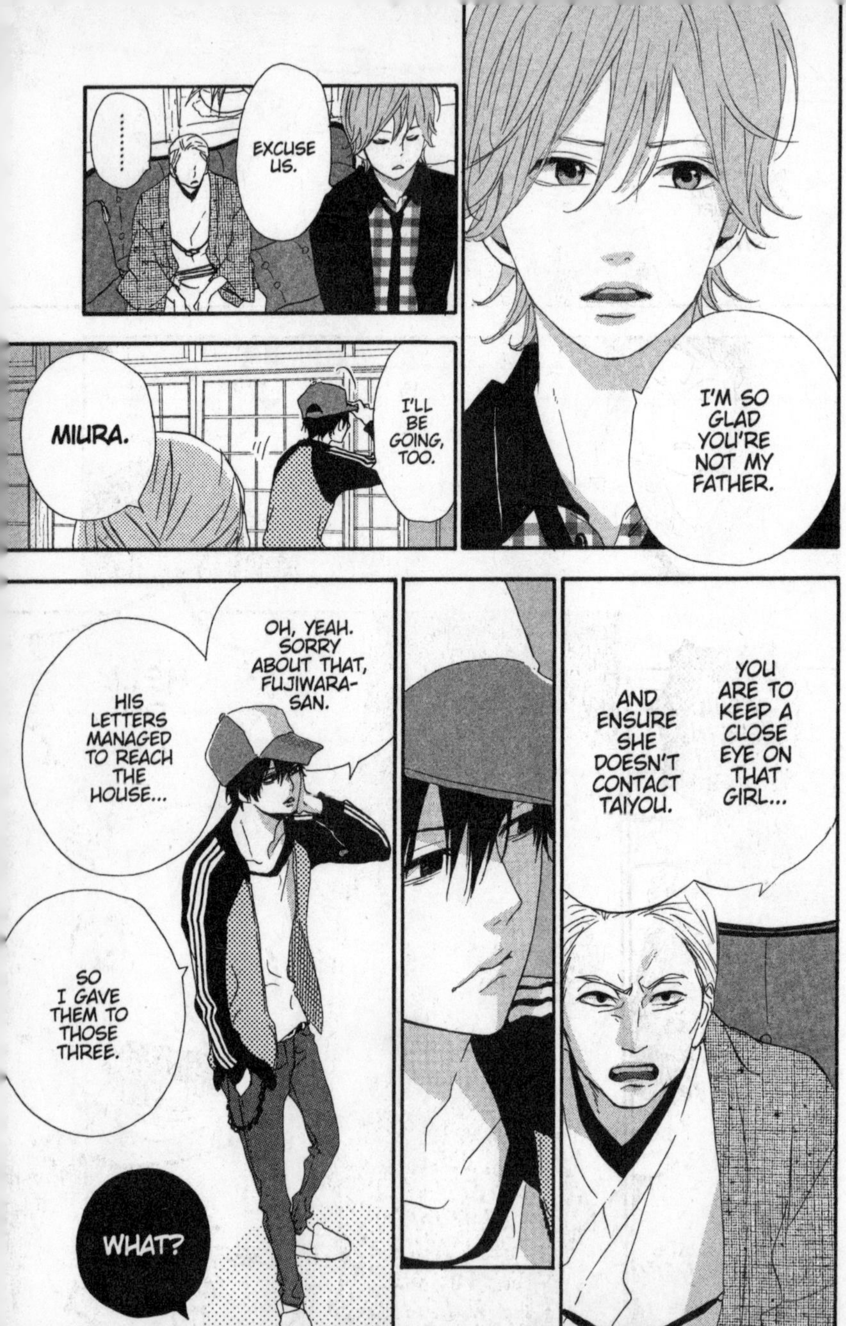
I'M SO GLAD YOU'RE NOT MY FATHER.
EXCUSE US.
......
I'LL BE GOING, TOO.
MIURA.
YOU ARE TO KEEP A CLOSE EYE ON THAT GIRL...
AND ENSURE SHE DOESN'T CONTACT TAIYOU.
OH, YEAH. SORRY ABOUT THAT, FUJIWARA-SAN.
HIS LETTERS MANAGED TO REACH THE HOUSE...
SO I GAVE THEM TO THOSE THREE.
WHAT?

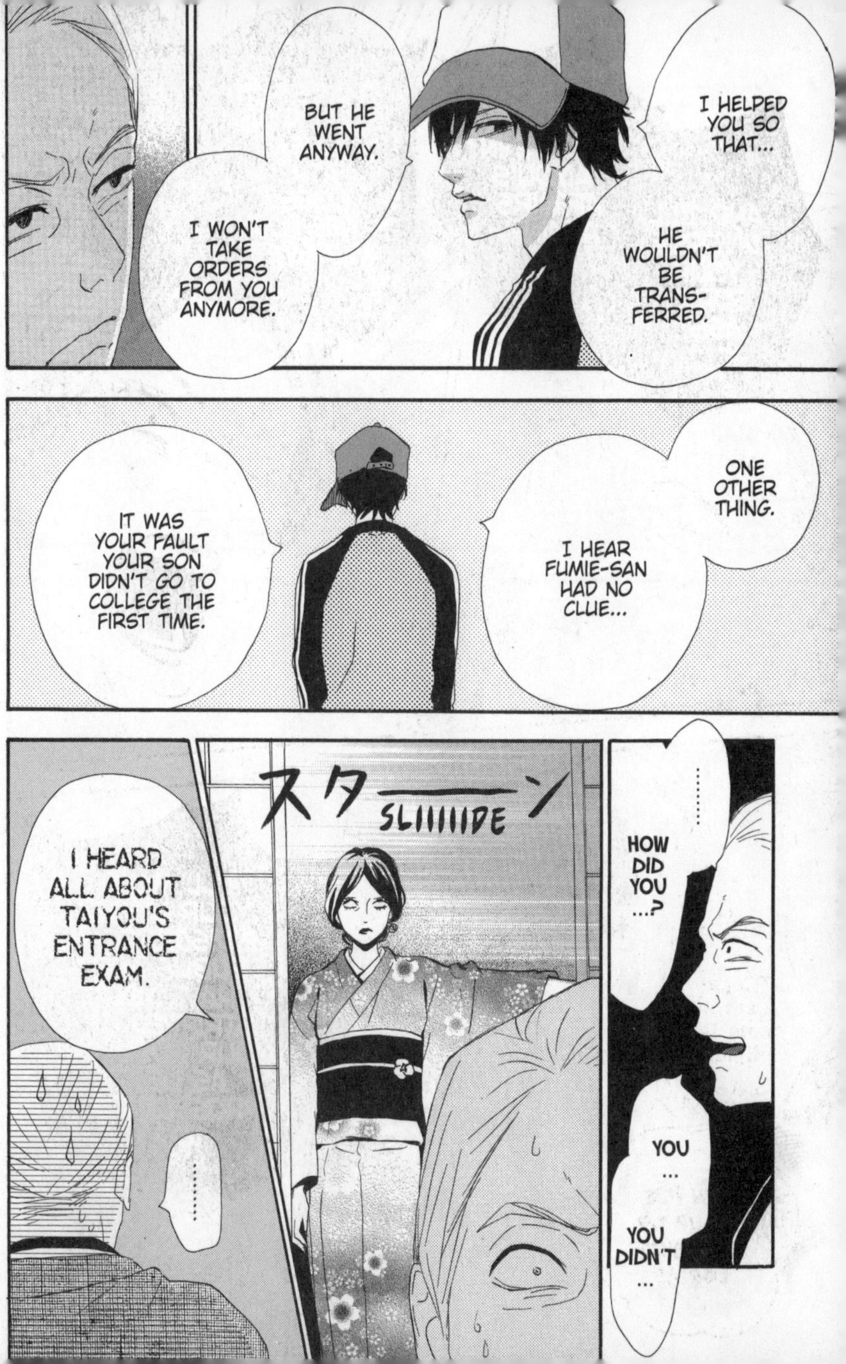
I HELPED YOU SO THAT...
HE WOULDN'T BE TRANS-FERRED.
BUT HE WENT ANYWAY.
I WON'T TAKE ORDERS FROM YOU ANYMORE.
ONE OTHER THING.
I HEAR FUMIE-SAN HAD NO CLUE...
IT WAS YOUR FAULT YOUR SON DIDN'T GO TO COLLEGE THE FIRST TIME.
......
HOW DID YOU ...?
YOU ...
YOU DIDN'T ...
スターーーン
SLIIIIIDE
I HEARD ALL ABOUT TAIYOU'S ENTRANCE EXAM.
......

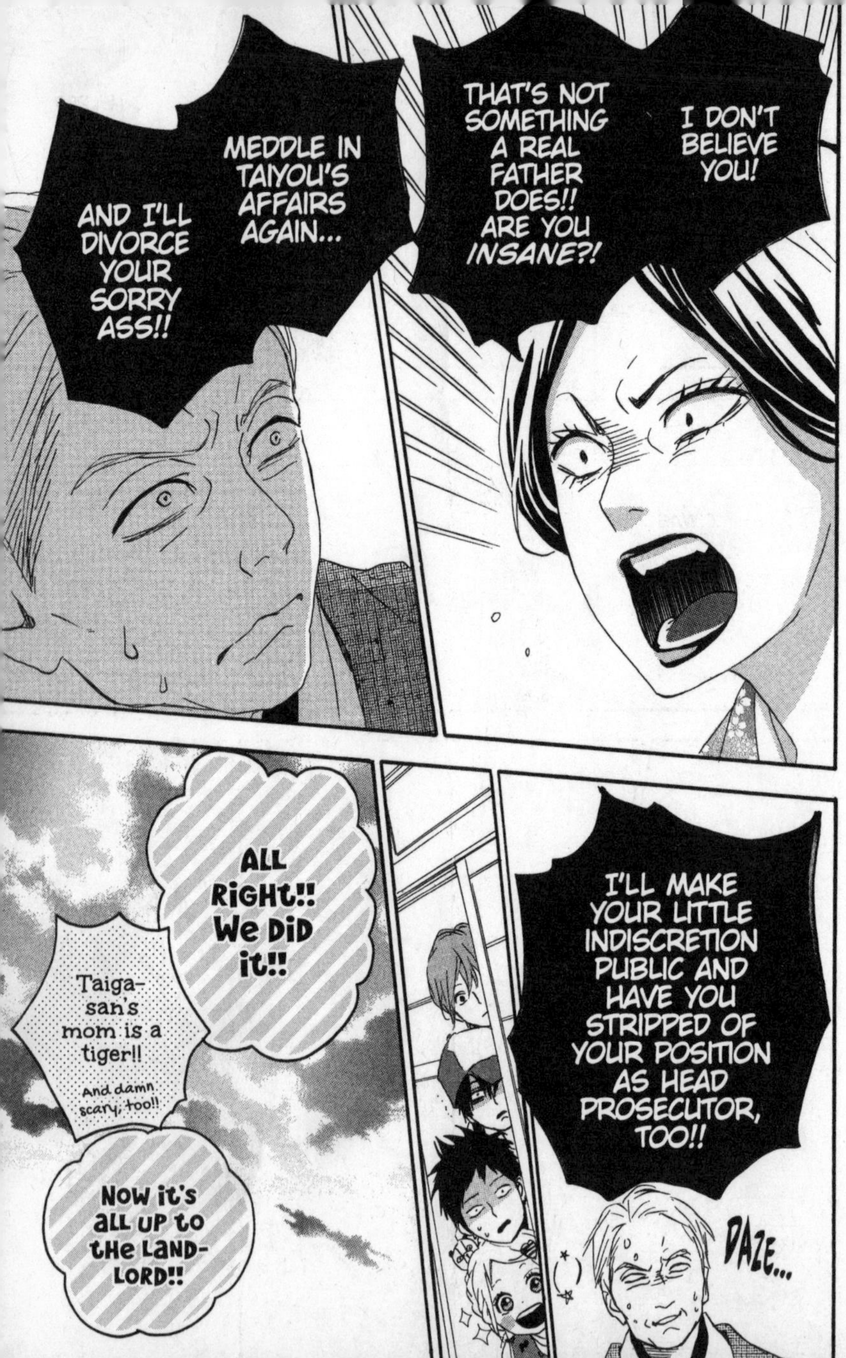
I DON'T BELIEVE YOU!
THAT'S NOT SOMETHING A REAL FATHER DOES!! ARE YOU INSANE?!
MEDDLE IN TAIYOU'S AFFAIRS AGAIN...
AND I'LL DIVORCE YOUR SORRY ASS!!
I'LL MAKE YOUR LITTLE INDISCRETION PUBLIC AND HAVE YOU STRIPPED OF YOUR POSITION AS HEAD PROSECUTOR, TOO!!
DAZE...
ALL RIGHT!! We DID it!!
Taiga-san's mom is a tiger!!
And damn scary, too!!
Now it's all up to the LAND-LORD!!

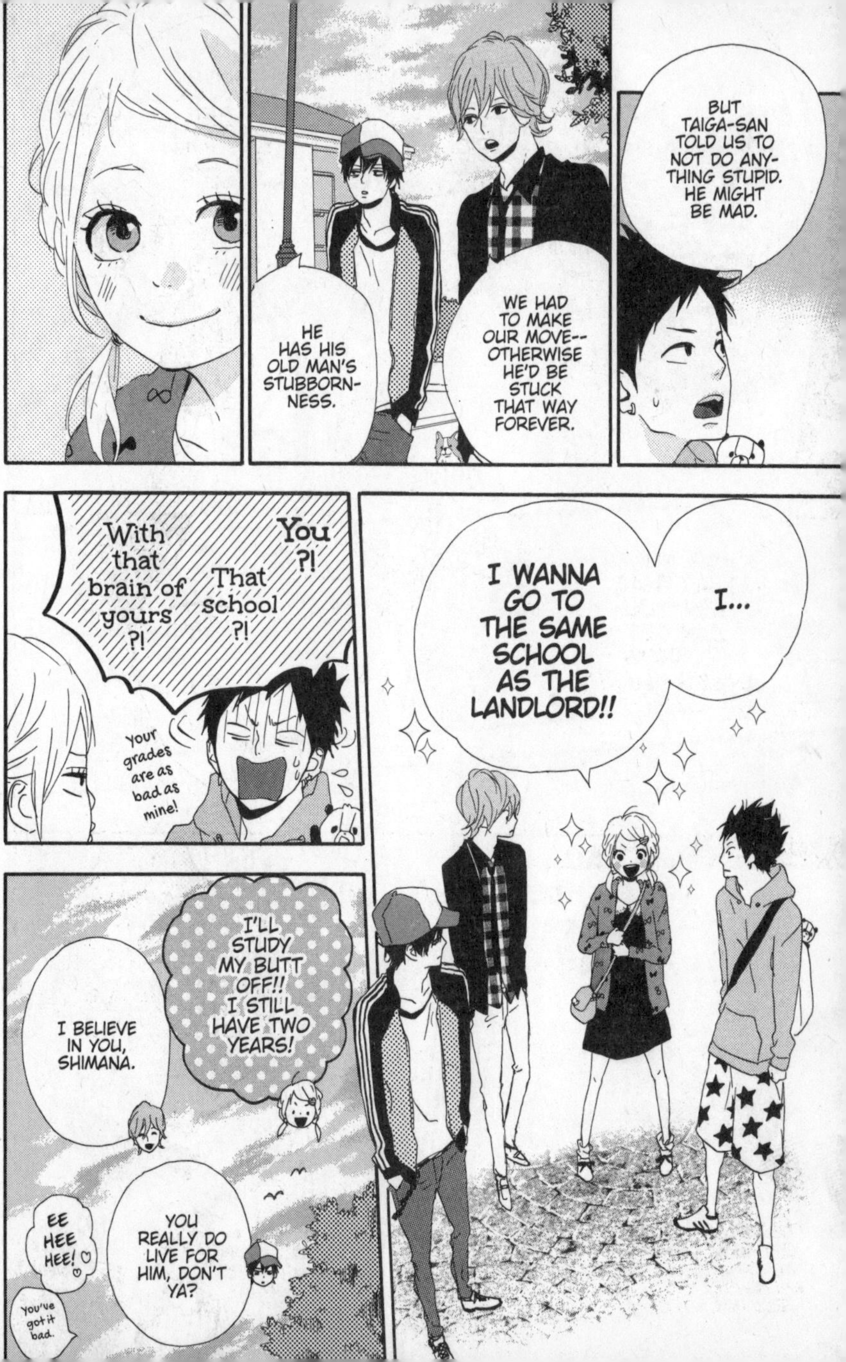
BUT TAIGA-SAN TOLD US TO NOT DO ANYTHING STUPID. HE MIGHT BE MAD.
WE HAD TO MAKE OUR MOVE-- OTHERWISE HE'D BE STUCK THAT WAY FOREVER.
HE HAS HIS OLD MAN'S STUBBORNNESS.
I...
I WANNA GO TO THE SAME SCHOOL AS THE LANDLORD!!
You?!
That school?!
With that brain of yours?!
Your grades are as bad as mine!
I'LL STUDY MY BUTT OFF!! I STILL HAVE TWO YEARS!
I BELIEVE IN YOU, SHIMANA.
YOU REALLY DO LIVE FOR HIM, DON'T YA?
EE HEE HEE! ♡
You've got it bad.

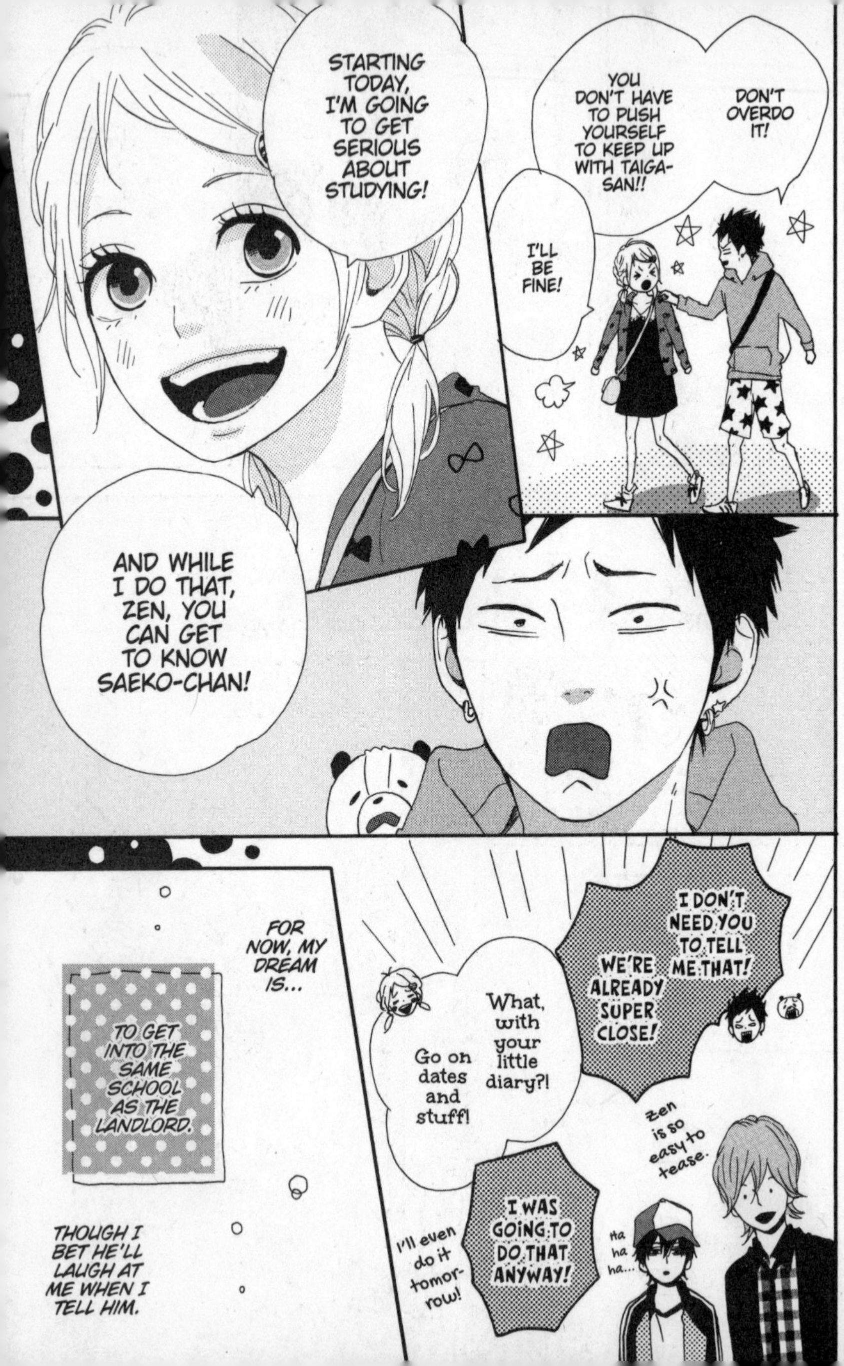
DON'T OVERDO IT!
YOU DON'T HAVE TO PUSH YOURSELF TO KEEP UP WITH TAIGA-SAN!!
I'LL BE FINE!
STARTING TODAY, I'M GOING TO GET SERIOUS ABOUT STUDYING!
AND WHILE I DO THAT, ZEN, YOU CAN GET TO KNOW SAEKO-CHAN!
I DON'T NEED YOU TO TELL ME THAT!
WE'RE ALREADY SUPER CLOSE!
What, with your little diary?!
Go on dates and stuff!
Zen is so easy to tease.
I WAS GOING TO DO THAT ANYWAY!
I'll even do it tomorrow!
Ha ha ha...
FOR NOW, MY DREAM IS...
TO GET INTO THE SAME SCHOOL AS THE LANDLORD.
THOUGH I BET HE'LL LAUGH AT ME WHEN I TELL HIM.

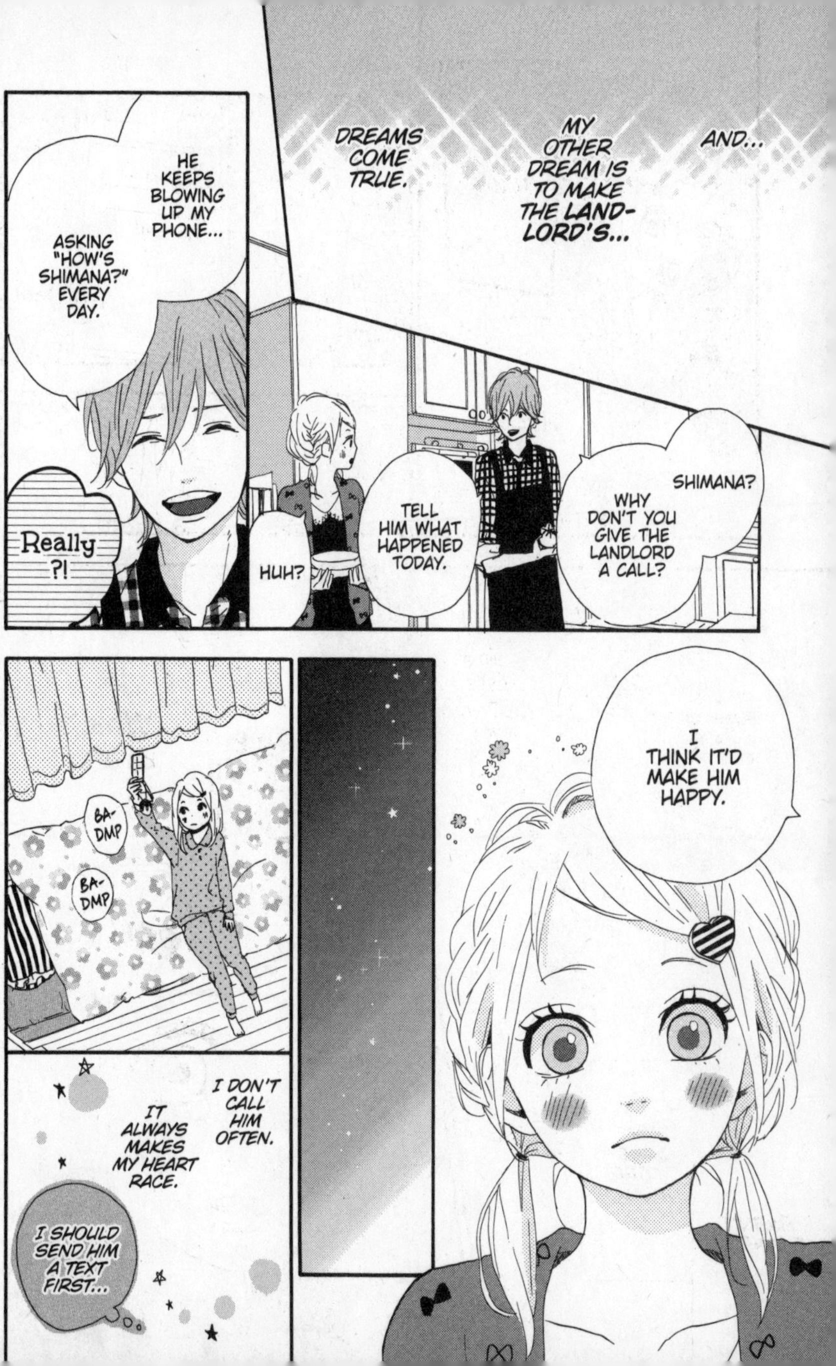
AND...
MY OTHER DREAM IS TO MAKE THE LANDLORD'S...
DREAMS COME TRUE.
SHIMANA?
WHY DON'T YOU GIVE THE LANDLORD A CALL?
TELL HIM WHAT HAPPENED TODAY.
HUH?
HE KEEPS BLOWING UP MY PHONE...
ASKING "HOW'S SHIMANA?" EVERY DAY.
Really?!
I THINK IT'D MAKE HIM HAPPY.
BA-DMP
BA-DMP
I DON'T CALL HIM OFTEN.
IT ALWAYS MAKES MY HEART RACE.
I SHOULD SEND HIM A TEXT FIRST...

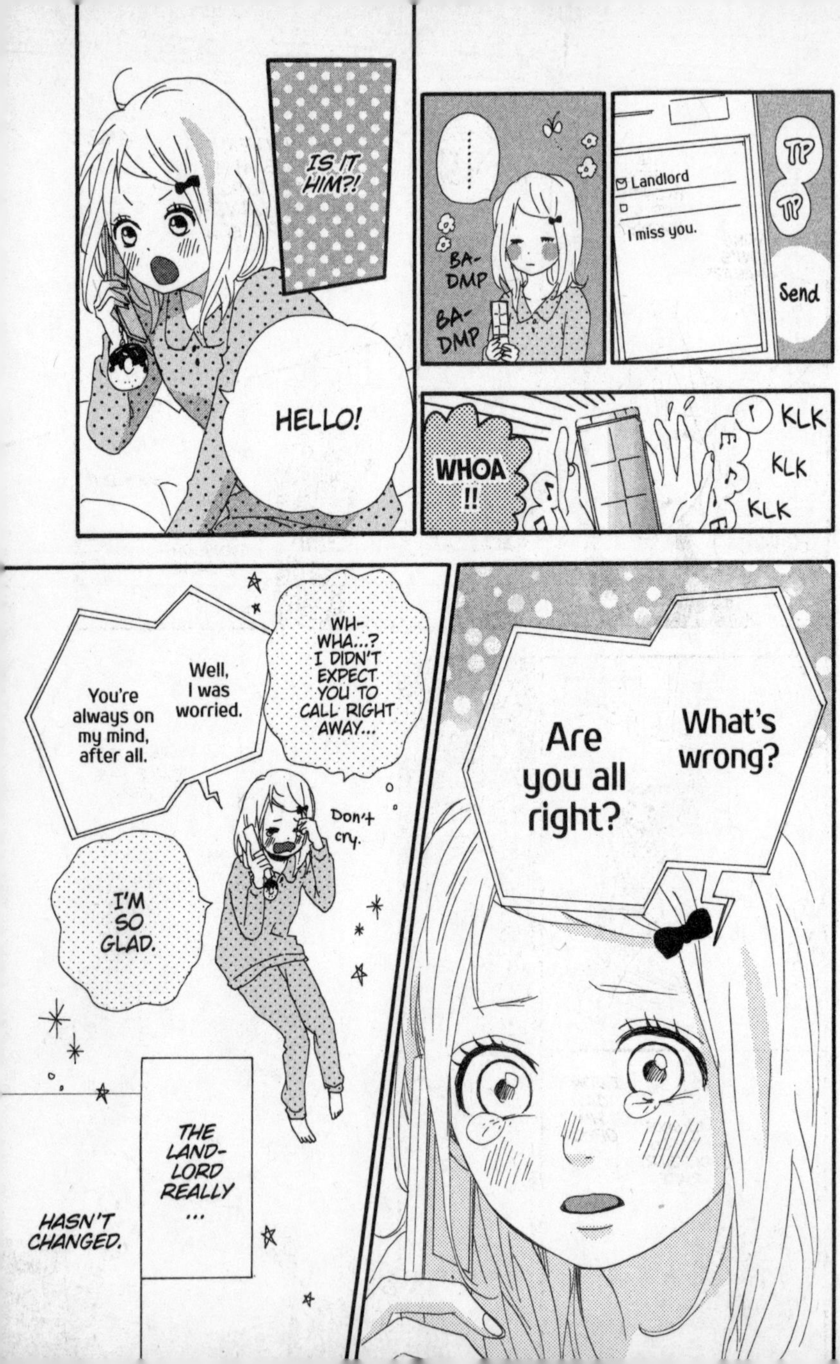
Landlord
I miss you.
TP
TP
Send
......
BA-DMP
BA-DMP
WHOA !!
KLK
KLK
KLK
IS IT HIM?!
HELLO!
What's wrong?
Are you all right?
WH-WHA...? I DIDN'T EXPECT YOU TO CALL RIGHT AWAY...
Well, I was worried.
You're always on my mind, after all.
Don't cry.
I'M SO GLAD.
THE LANDLORD REALLY...
HASN'T CHANGED.

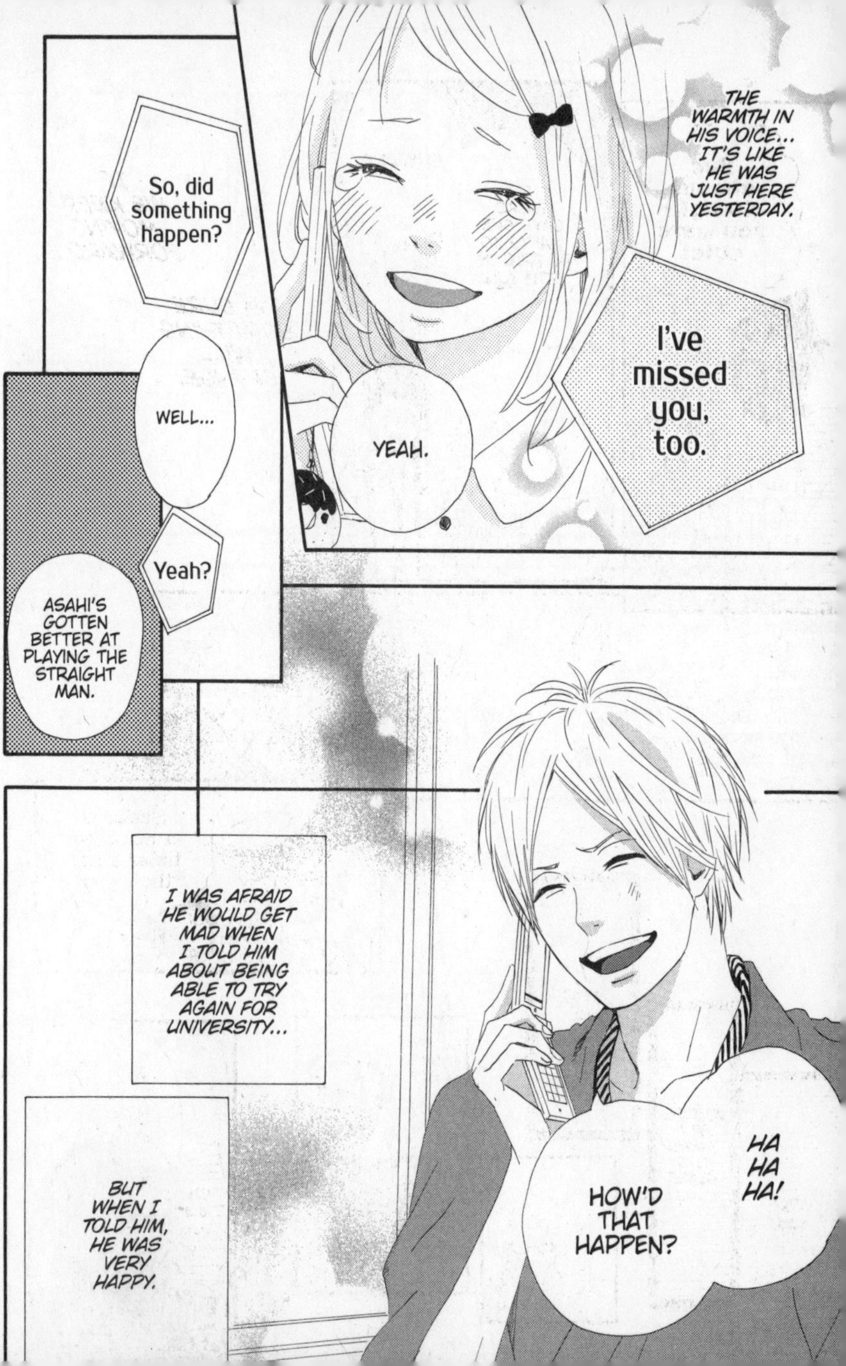
THE WARMTH IN HIS VOICE... IT'S LIKE HE WAS JUST HERE YESTERDAY.
I've missed you, too.
YEAH.
So, did something happen?
WELL...
Yeah?
ASAHI'S GOTTEN BETTER AT PLAYING THE STRAIGHT MAN.
HA HA HA!
HOW'D THAT HAPPEN?
I WAS AFRAID HE WOULD GET MAD WHEN I TOLD HIM ABOUT BEING ABLE TO TRY AGAIN FOR UNIVERSITY...
BUT WHEN I TOLD HIM, HE WAS VERY HAPPY.

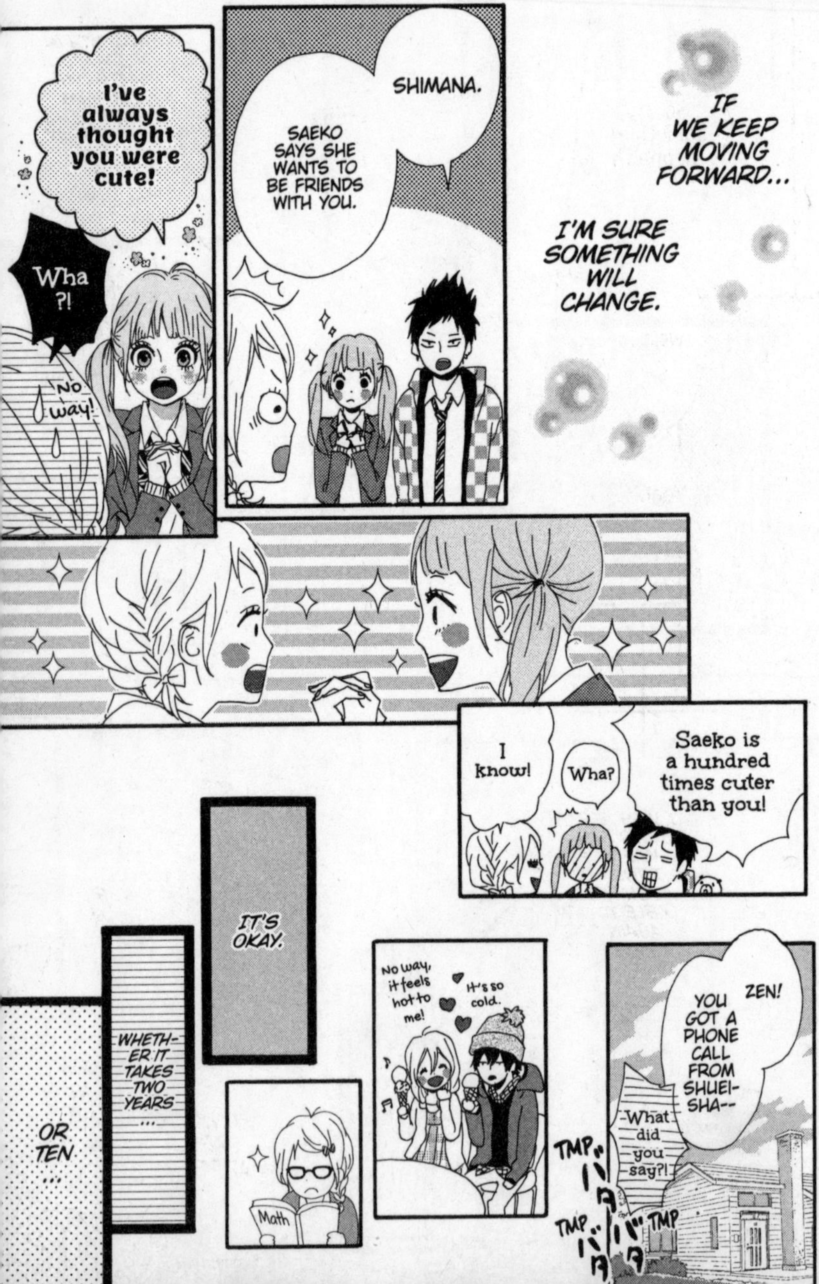
IF WE KEEP MOVING FORWARD...
I'M SURE SOMETHING WILL CHANGE.
SHIMANA.
SAEKO SAYS SHE WANTS TO BE FRIENDS WITH YOU.
I've always thought you were cute!
Wha ?!
No way!
Saeko is a hundred times cuter than you!
Wha?
I know!
ZEN!
YOU GOT A PHONE CALL FROM SHUEI-SHA--
What did you say?!
TMP
TMP
TMP
It's so cold.
No way, it feels hot to me!
IT'S OKAY.
Math
WHETHER IT TAKES TWO YEARS...
OR TEN...

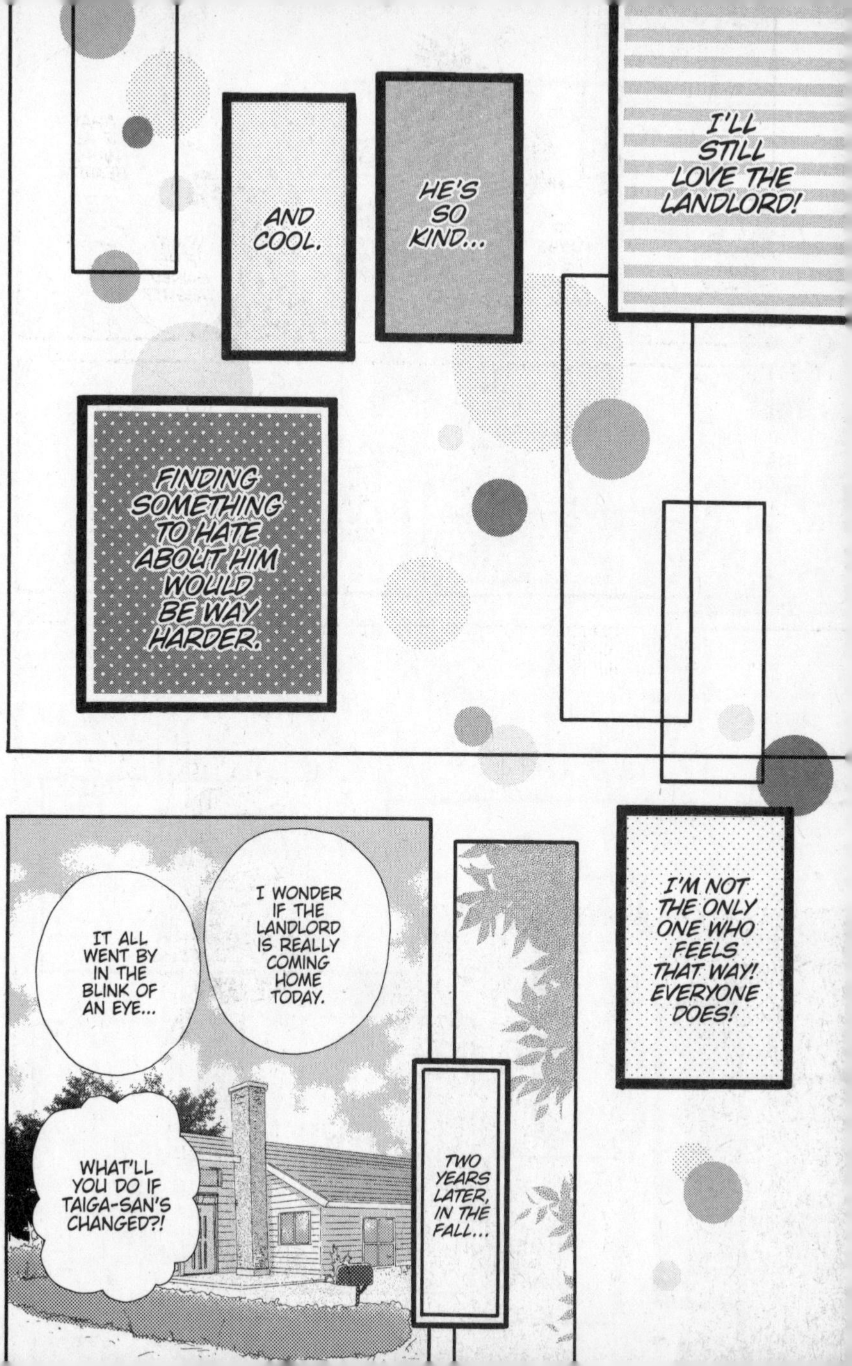
I'LL STILL LOVE THE LANDLORD!
HE'S SO KIND...
AND COOL.
FINDING SOMETHING TO HATE ABOUT HIM WOULD BE WAY HARDER.
I'M NOT THE ONLY ONE WHO FEELS THAT WAY! EVERYONE DOES!
TWO YEARS LATER, IN THE FALL...
I WONDER IF THE LANDLORD IS REALLY COMING HOME TODAY.
IT ALL WENT BY IN THE BLINK OF AN EYE...
WHAT'LL YOU DO IF TAIGA-SAN'S CHANGED?!

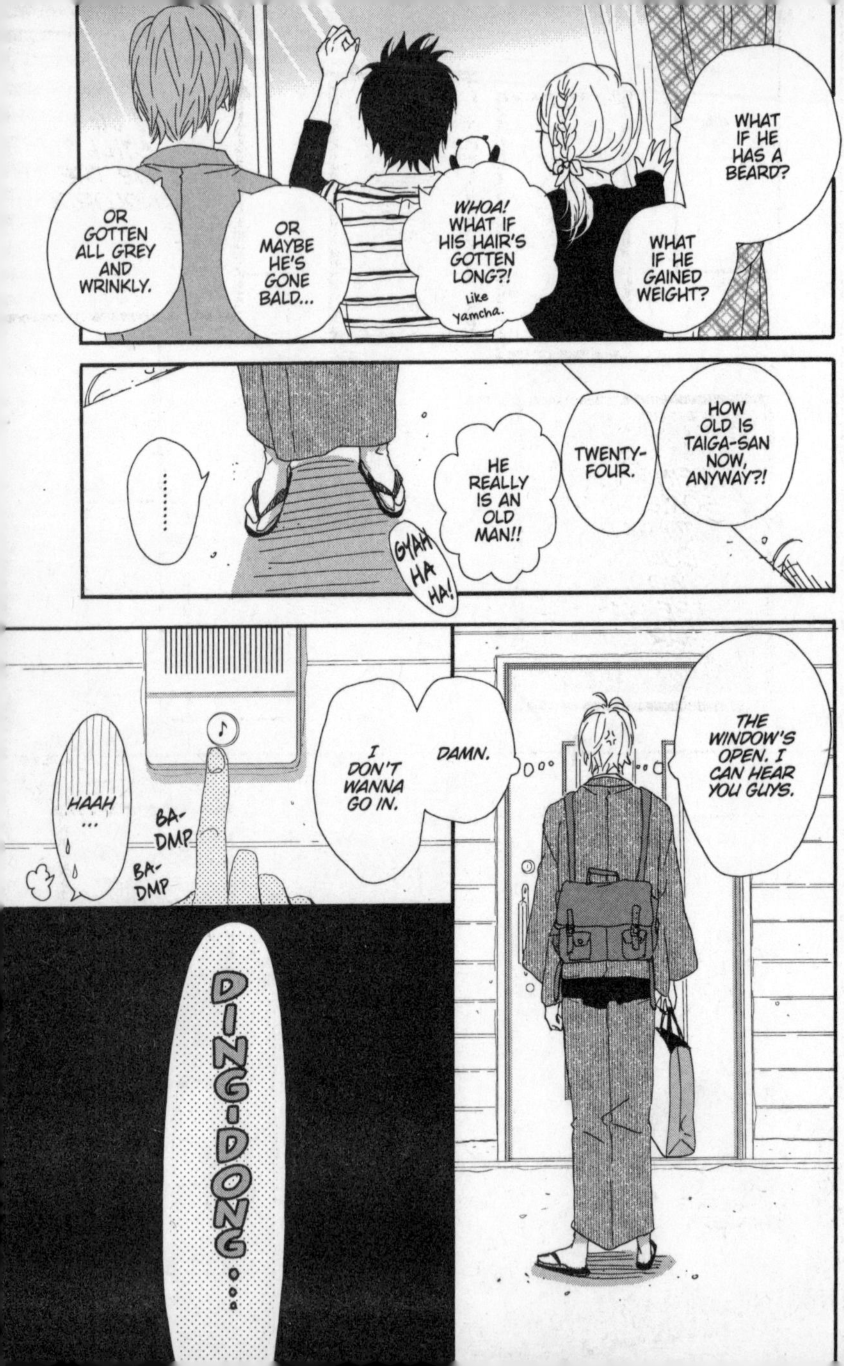
WHAT IF HE HAS A BEARD?
WHAT IF HE GAINED WEIGHT?
WHOA! WHAT IF HIS HAIR'S GOTTEN LONG?!
Like Yamcha.
OR MAYBE HE'S GONE BALD...
OR GOTTEN ALL GREY AND WRINKLY.
HOW OLD IS TAIGA-SAN NOW, ANYWAY?!
TWENTY-FOUR.
HE REALLY IS AN OLD MAN!!
GYAH HA HA!
......
THE WINDOW'S OPEN. I CAN HEAR YOU GUYS.
DAMN.
I DON'T WANNA GO IN.
HAAH ...
BA-DMP
BA-DMP
DING-DONG...

Picture by: Landlord

Subject: Panda

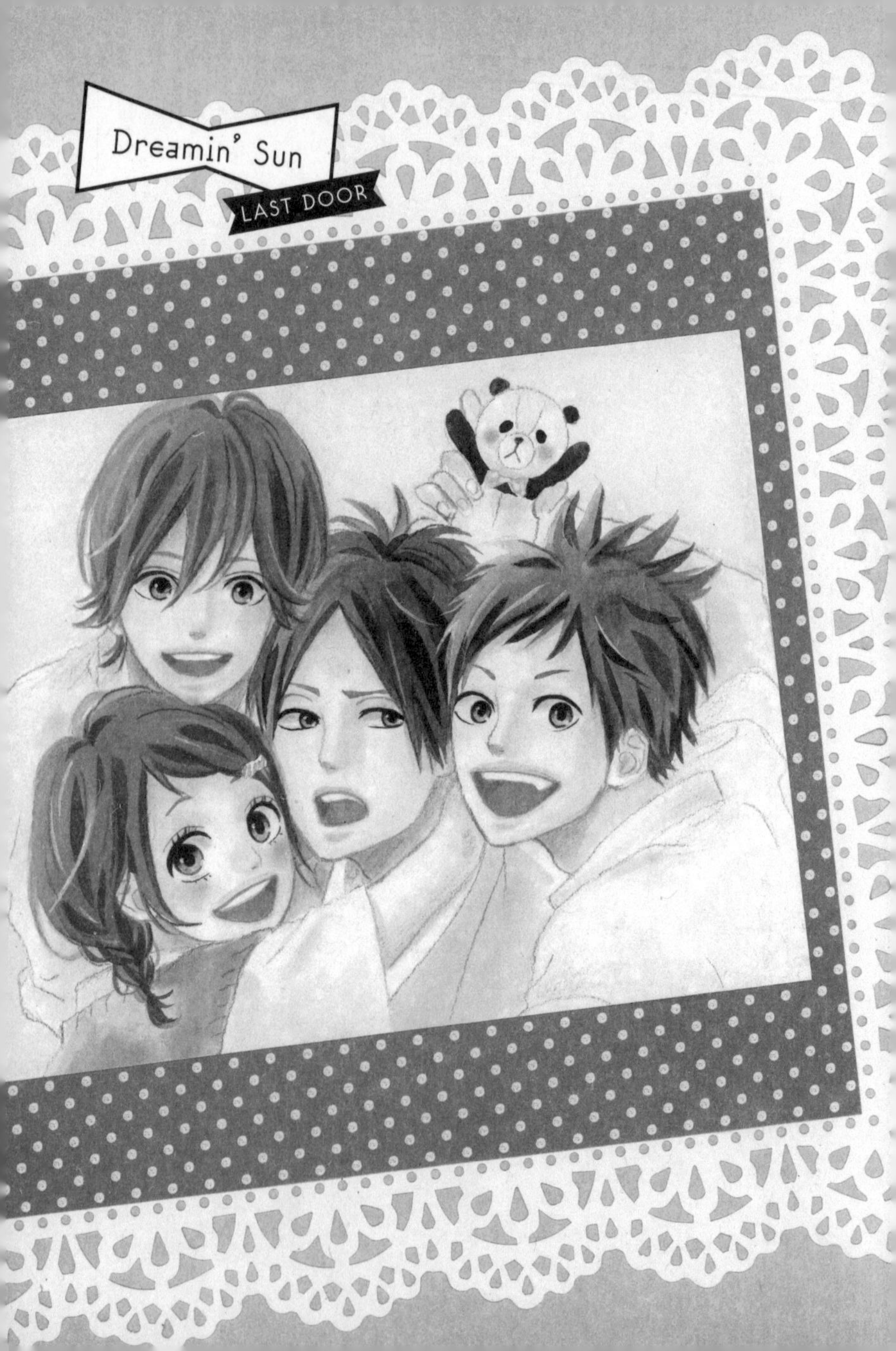
Dreamin' Sun
LAST DOOR

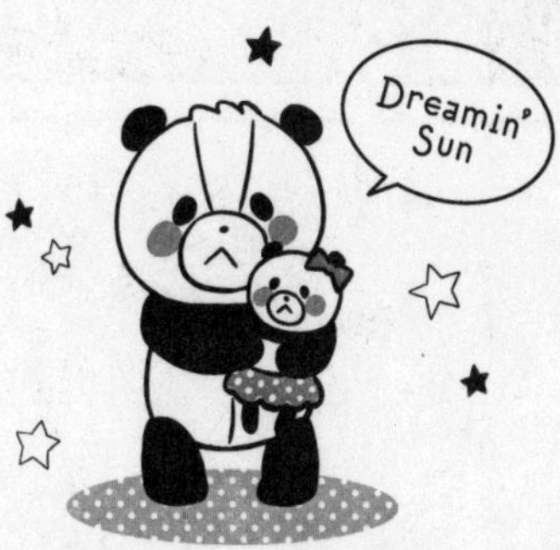
Dreamin' Sun

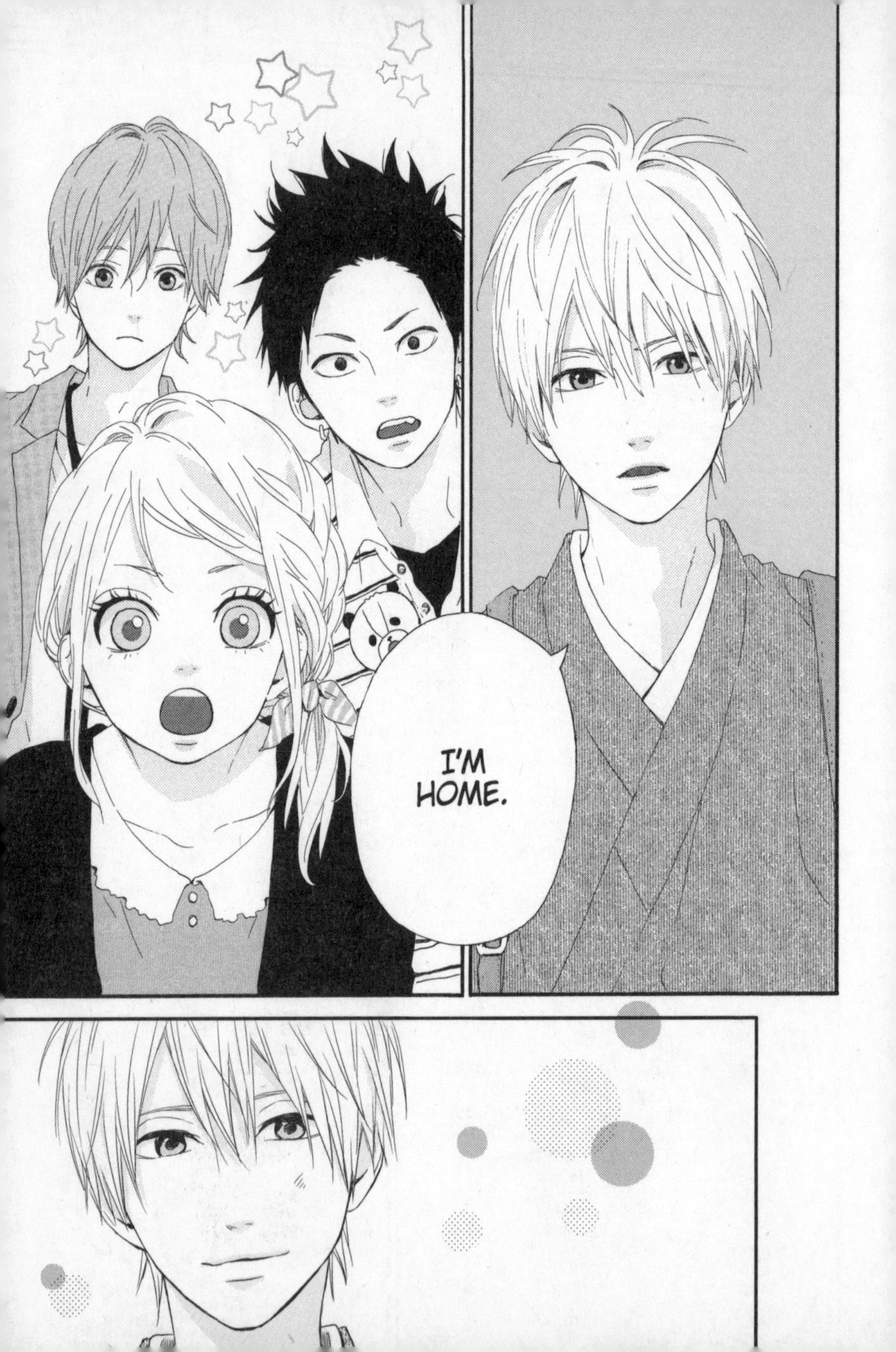
I'M HOME.

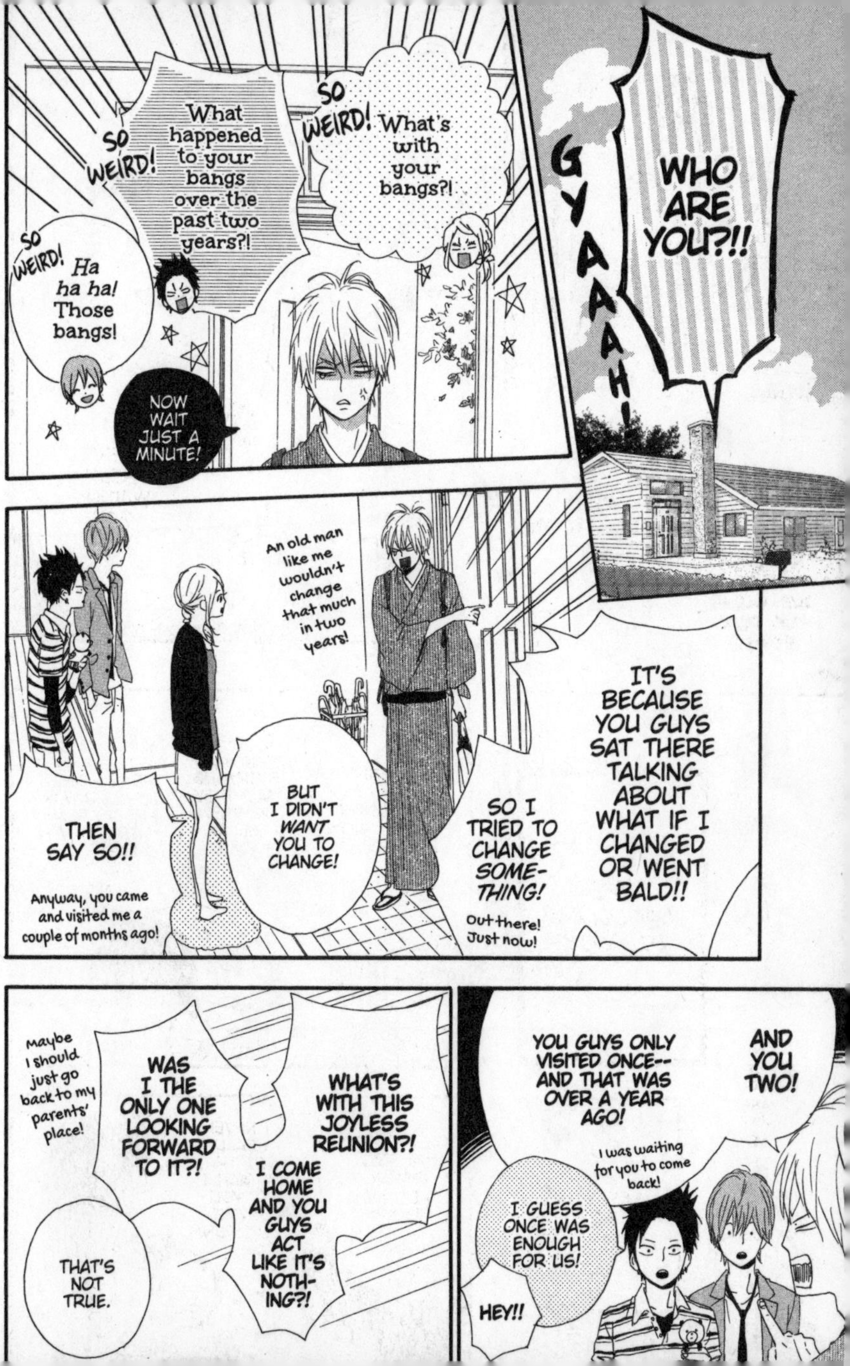
WHO ARE YOU?!!
GYAAAH!
SO WEIRD!
What's with your bangs?!
SO WEIRD!
What happened to your bangs over the past two years?!
SO WEIRD!
Ha ha ha! Those bangs!
NOW WAIT JUST A MINUTE!
IT'S BECAUSE YOU GUYS SAT THERE TALKING ABOUT WHAT IF I CHANGED OR WENT BALD!!
SO I TRIED TO CHANGE SOME-THING!
Out there! Just now!
An old man like me wouldn't change that much in two years!
BUT I DIDN'T WANT YOU TO CHANGE!
THEN SAY SO!!
Anyway, you came and visited me a couple of months ago!
AND YOU TWO!
YOU GUYS ONLY VISITED ONCE-- AND THAT WAS OVER A YEAR AGO!
I was waiting for you to come back!
I GUESS ONCE WAS ENOUGH FOR US!
HEY!!
WHAT'S WITH THIS JOYLESS REUNION?!
WAS I THE ONLY ONE LOOKING FORWARD TO IT?!
Maybe I should just go back to my parents' place!
I COME HOME AND YOU GUYS ACT LIKE IT'S NOTH-ING?!
THAT'S NOT TRUE.

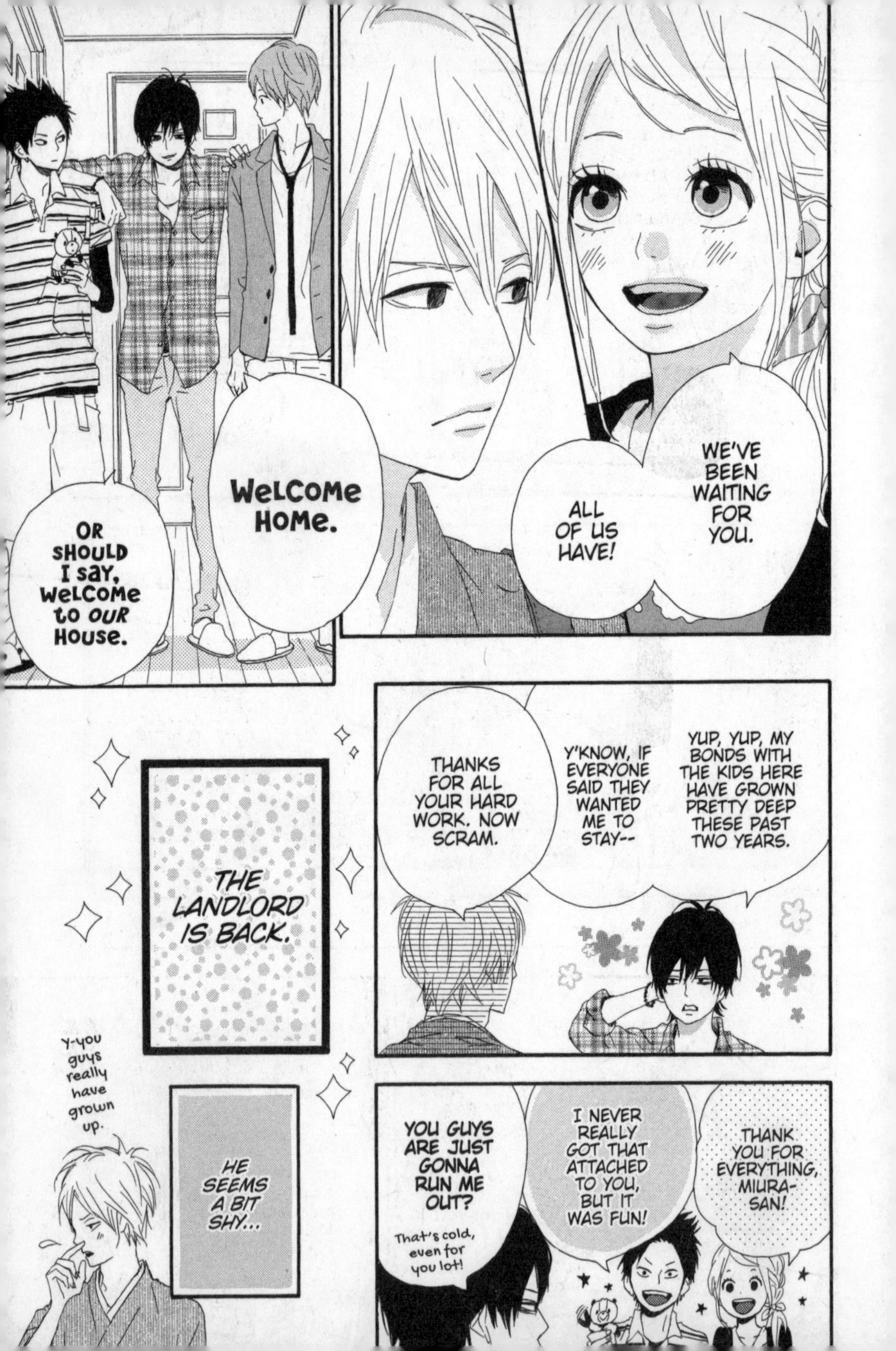
WE'VE BEEN WAITING FOR YOU.
ALL OF US HAVE!
WELCOME HOME.
OR SHOULD I SAY, WELCOME TO OUR HOUSE.
YUP, YUP, MY BONDS WITH THE KIDS HERE HAVE GROWN PRETTY DEEP THESE PAST TWO YEARS.
Y'KNOW, IF EVERYONE SAID THEY WANTED ME TO STAY--
THANKS FOR ALL YOUR HARD WORK. NOW SCRAM.
THE LANDLORD IS BACK.
THANK YOU FOR EVERYTHING, MIURA-SAN!
I NEVER REALLY GOT THAT ATTACHED TO YOU, BUT IT WAS FUN!
YOU GUYS ARE JUST GONNA RUN ME OUT?
That's cold, even for you lot!
HE SEEMS A BIT SHY...
Y-you guys really have grown up.

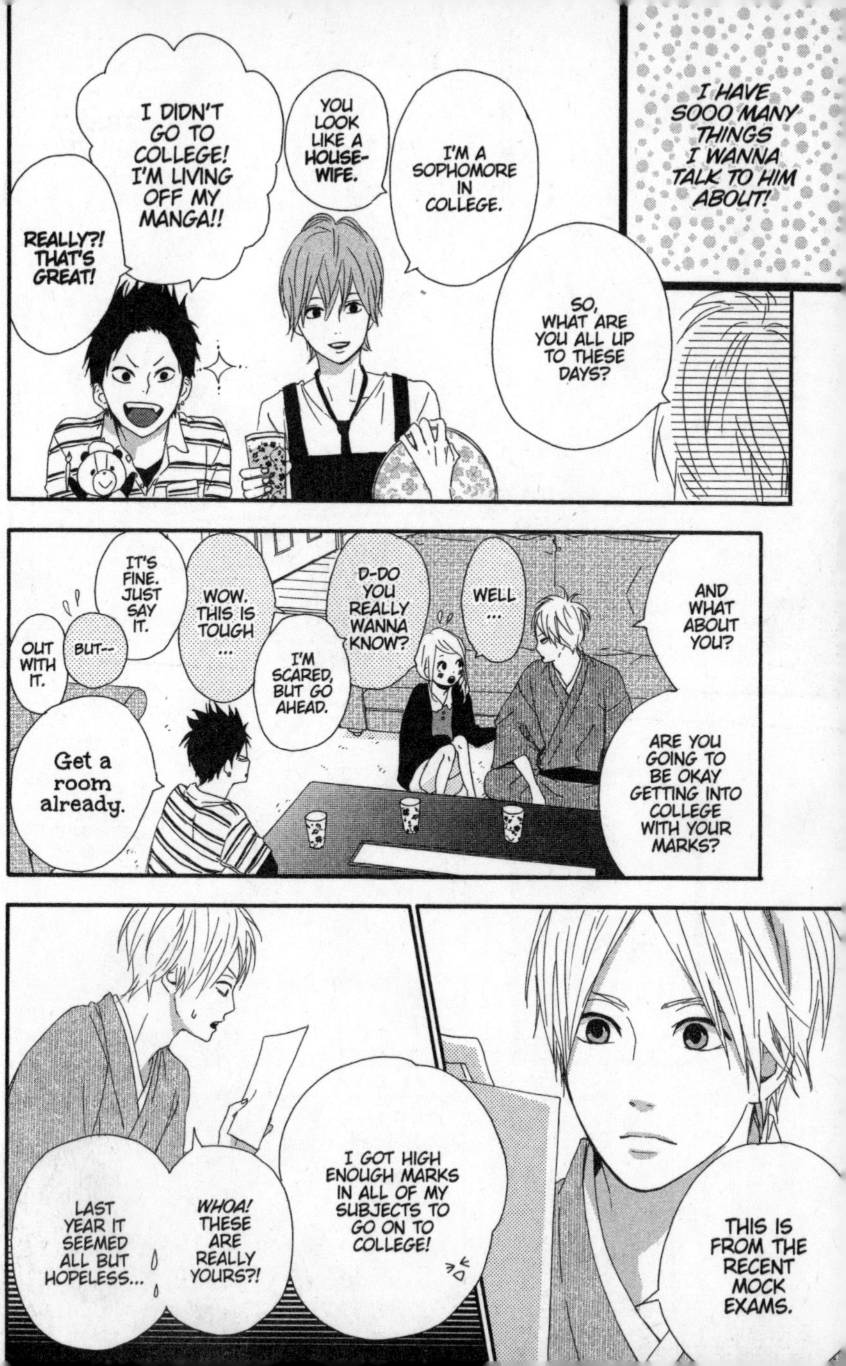
I HAVE SOOO MANY THINGS I WANNA TALK TO HIM ABOUT!
SO, WHAT ARE YOU ALL UP TO THESE DAYS?
I'M A SOPHOMORE IN COLLEGE.
YOU LOOK LIKE A HOUSE-WIFE.
I DIDN'T GO TO COLLEGE! I'M LIVING OFF MY MANGA!!
REALLY?! THAT'S GREAT!
AND WHAT ABOUT YOU?
ARE YOU GOING TO BE OKAY GETTING INTO COLLEGE WITH YOUR MARKS?
WELL ...
D-DO YOU REALLY WANNA KNOW?
I'M SCARED, BUT GO AHEAD.
WOW. THIS IS TOUGH ...
IT'S FINE. JUST SAY IT.
BUT--
OUT WITH IT.
Get a room already.
THIS IS FROM THE RECENT MOCK EXAMS.
I GOT HIGH ENOUGH MARKS IN ALL OF MY SUBJECTS TO GO ON TO COLLEGE!
WHOA! THESE ARE REALLY YOURS?!
LAST YEAR IT SEEMED ALL BUT HOPELESS...

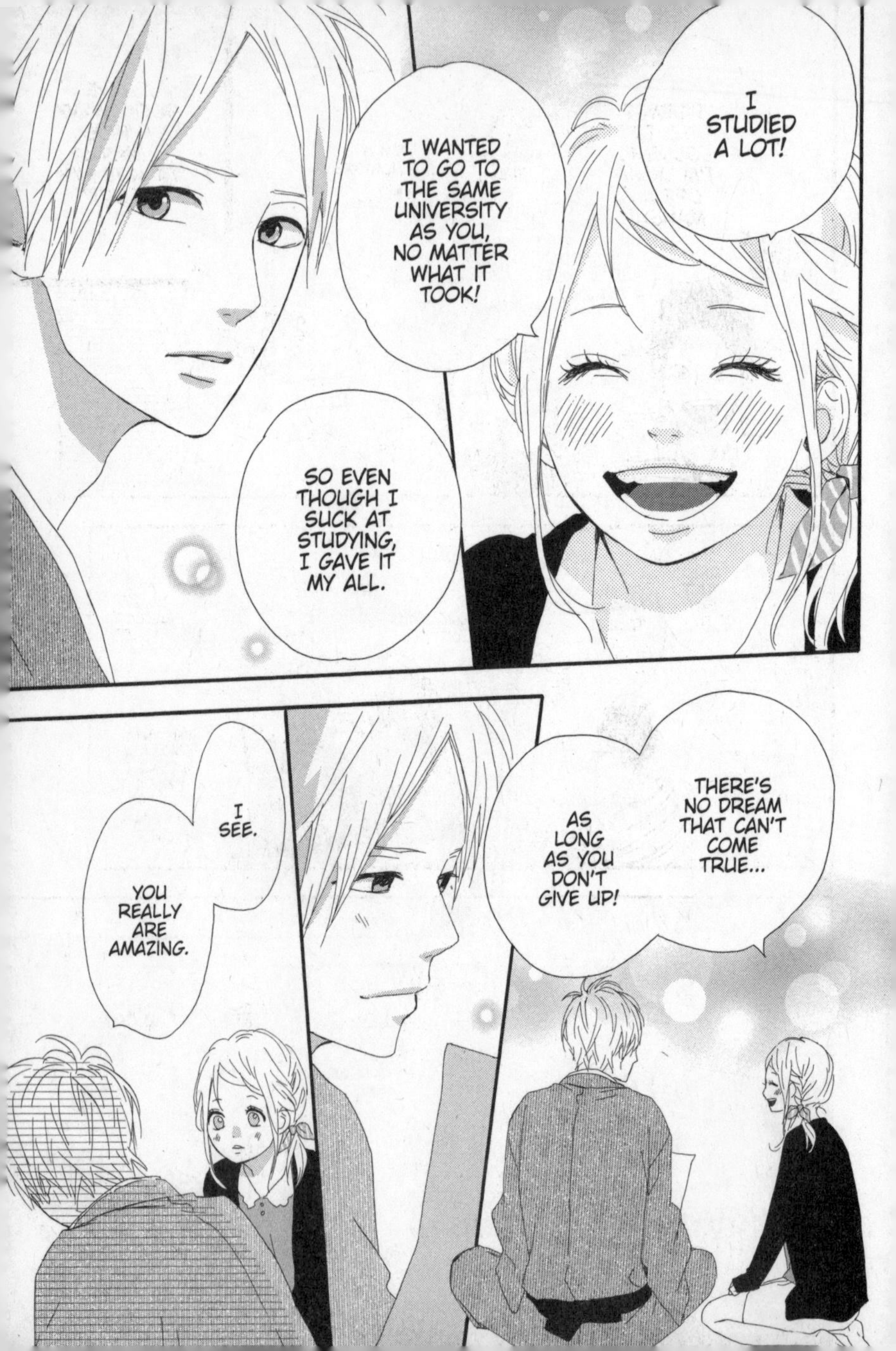
I STUDIED A LOT!
I WANTED TO GO TO THE SAME UNIVERSITY AS YOU, NO MATTER WHAT IT TOOK!
SO EVEN THOUGH I SUCK AT STUDYING, I GAVE IT MY ALL.
THERE'S NO DREAM THAT CAN'T COME TRUE...
AS LONG AS YOU DON'T GIVE UP!
I SEE.
YOU REALLY ARE AMAZING.

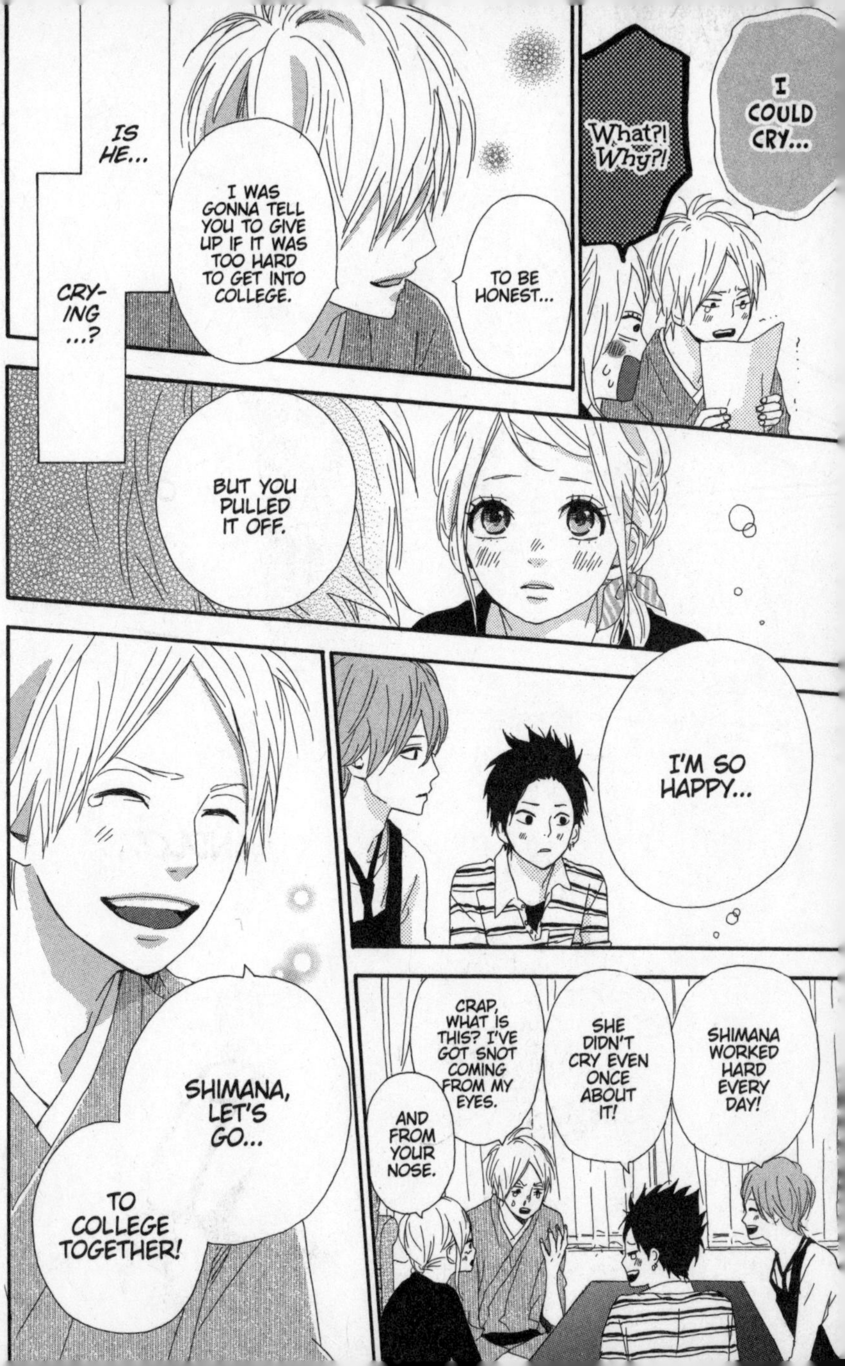
I COULD CRY...
What?! Why?!
TO BE HONEST...
I WAS GONNA TELL YOU TO GIVE UP IF IT WAS TOO HARD TO GET INTO COLLEGE.
IS HE...
CRY-ING ...?
BUT YOU PULLED IT OFF.
I'M SO HAPPY...
SHIMANA WORKED HARD EVERY DAY!
SHE DIDN'T CRY EVEN ONCE ABOUT IT!
CRAP, WHAT IS THIS? I'VE GOT SNOT COMING FROM MY EYES.
AND FROM YOUR NOSE.
SHIMANA, LET'S GO...
TO COLLEGE TOGETHER!

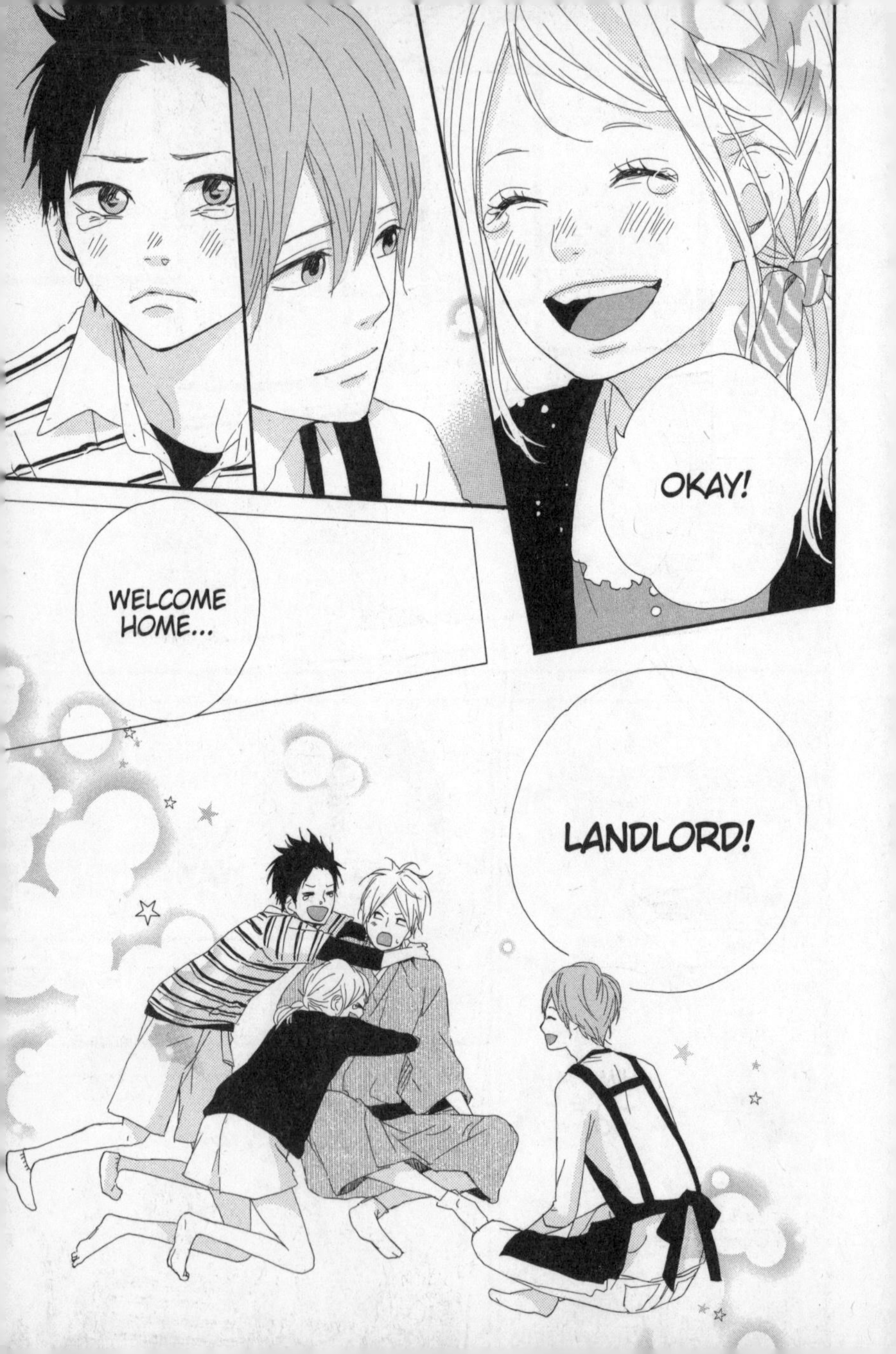
OKAY!
WELCOME HOME...
LANDLORD!

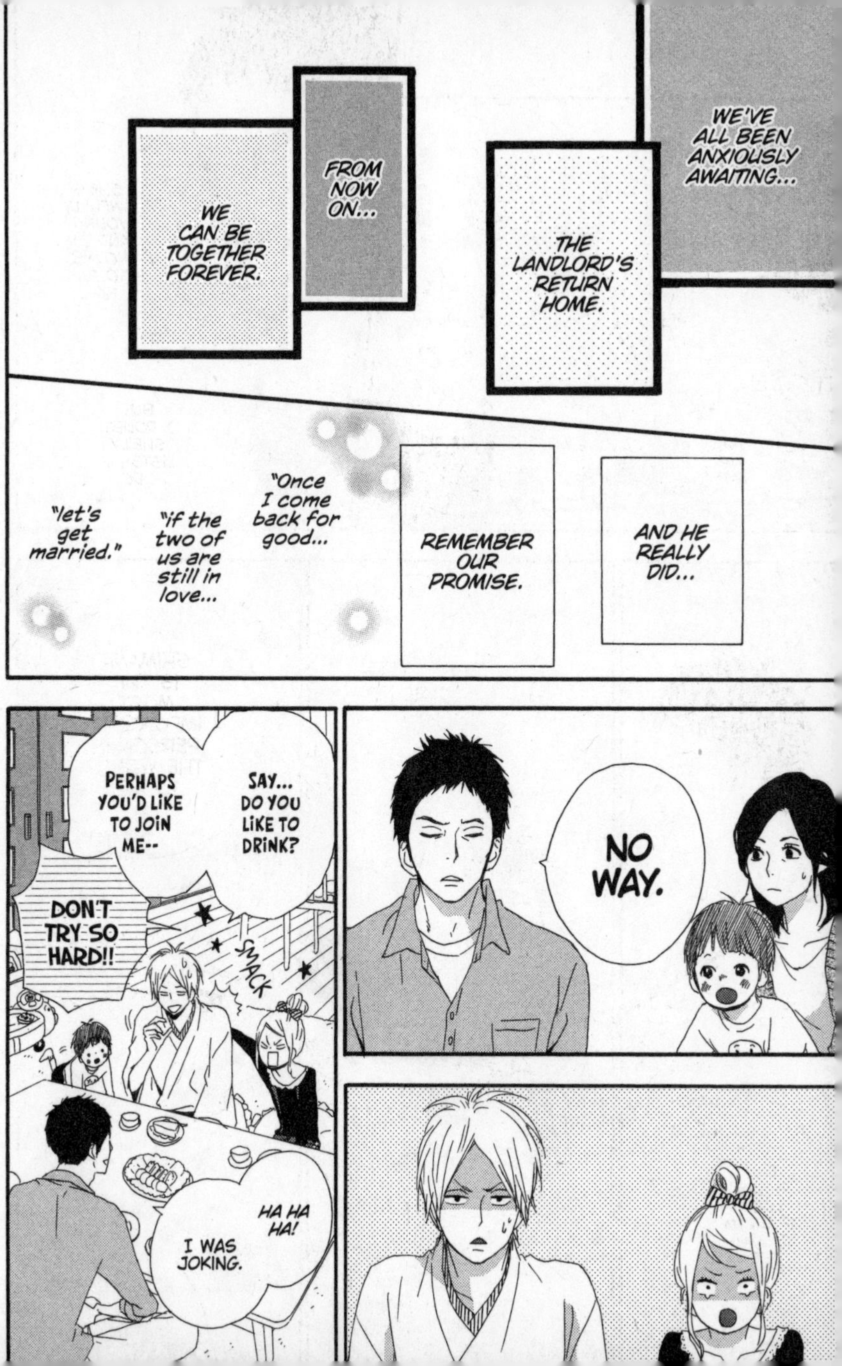
WE'VE ALL BEEN ANXIOUSLY AWAITING...
THE LANDLORD'S RETURN HOME.
FROM NOW ON...
WE CAN BE TOGETHER FOREVER.
AND HE REALLY DID...
REMEMBER OUR PROMISE.
"Once I come back for good...
"if the two of us are still in love...
"let's get married."
NO WAY.
SAY... DO YOU LIKE TO DRINK?
PERHAPS YOU'D LIKE TO JOIN ME--
DON'T TRY SO HARD!!
SMACK
HA HA HA!
I WAS JOKING.

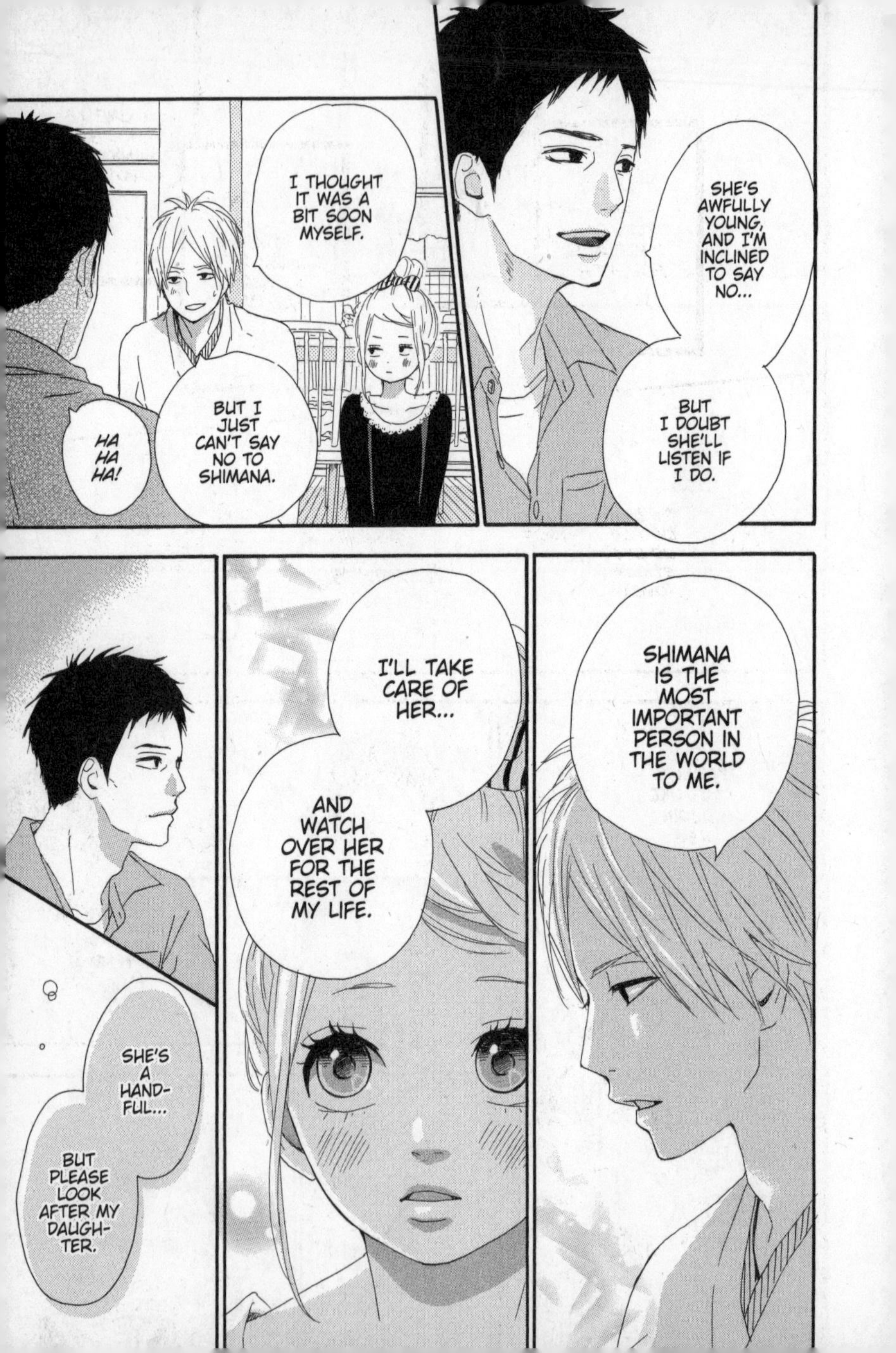
SHE'S AWFULLY YOUNG, AND I'M INCLINED TO SAY NO...
BUT I DOUBT SHE'LL LISTEN IF I DO.
I THOUGHT IT WAS A BIT SOON MYSELF.
BUT I JUST CAN'T SAY NO TO SHIMANA.
HA HA HA!
SHIMANA IS THE MOST IMPORTANT PERSON IN THE WORLD TO ME.
I'LL TAKE CARE OF HER...
AND WATCH OVER HER FOR THE REST OF MY LIFE.
SHE'S A HAND-FUL...
BUT PLEASE LOOK AFTER MY DAUGH-TER.

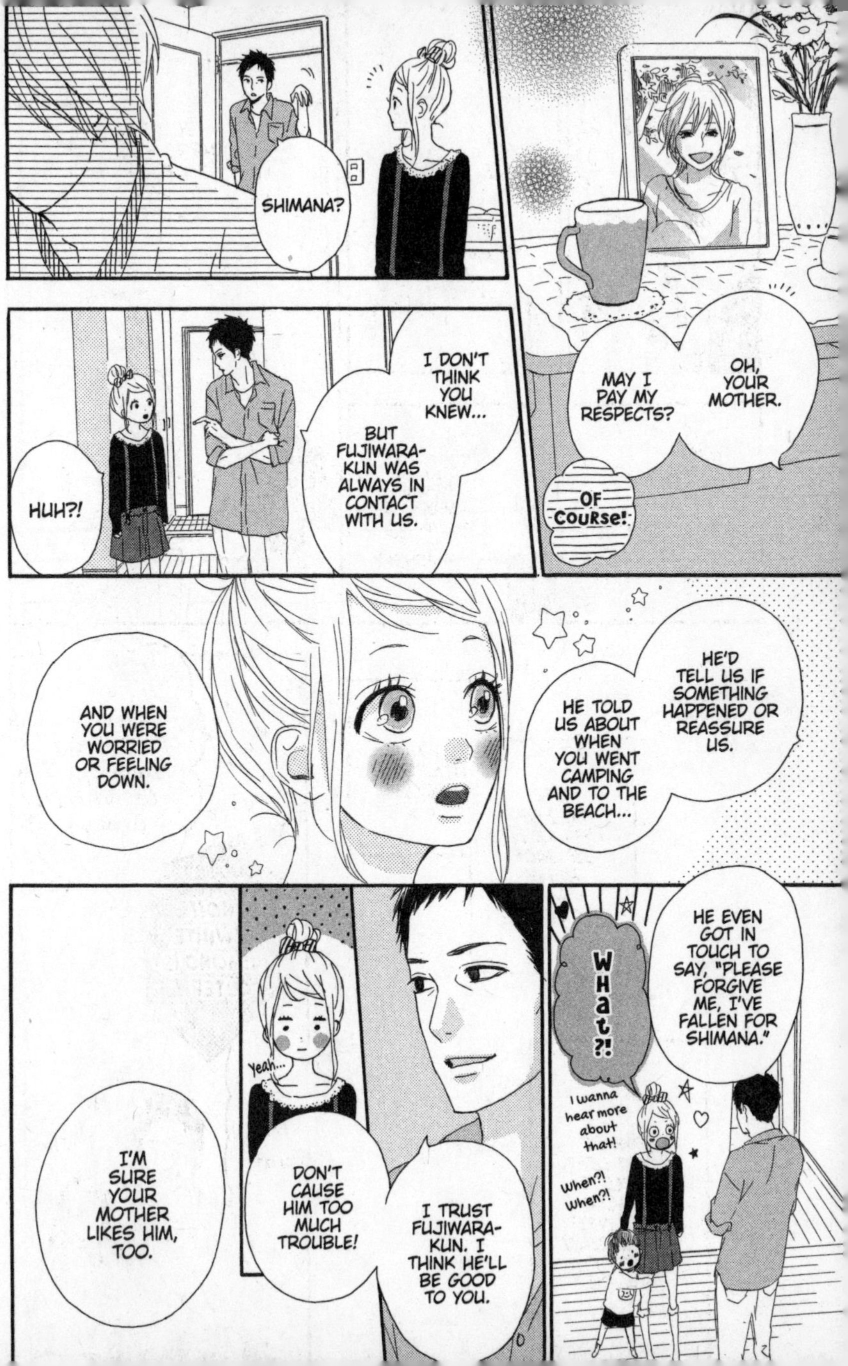
SHIMANA?
OH, YOUR MOTHER.
MAY I PAY MY RESPECTS?
OF COURSE!
I DON'T THINK YOU KNEW... BUT FUJIWARA-KUN WAS ALWAYS IN CONTACT WITH US.
HUH?!
HE'D TELL US IF SOMETHING HAPPENED OR REASSURE US.
HE TOLD US ABOUT WHEN YOU WENT CAMPING AND TO THE BEACH...
AND WHEN YOU WERE WORRIED OR FEELING DOWN.
HE EVEN GOT IN TOUCH TO SAY, "PLEASE FORGIVE ME, I'VE FALLEN FOR SHIMANA."
What?!
I wanna hear more about that!
When?! When?!
I TRUST FUJIWARA-KUN. I THINK HE'LL BE GOOD TO YOU.
DON'T CAUSE HIM TOO MUCH TROUBLE!
Yeah...
I'M SURE YOUR MOTHER LIKES HIM, TOO.

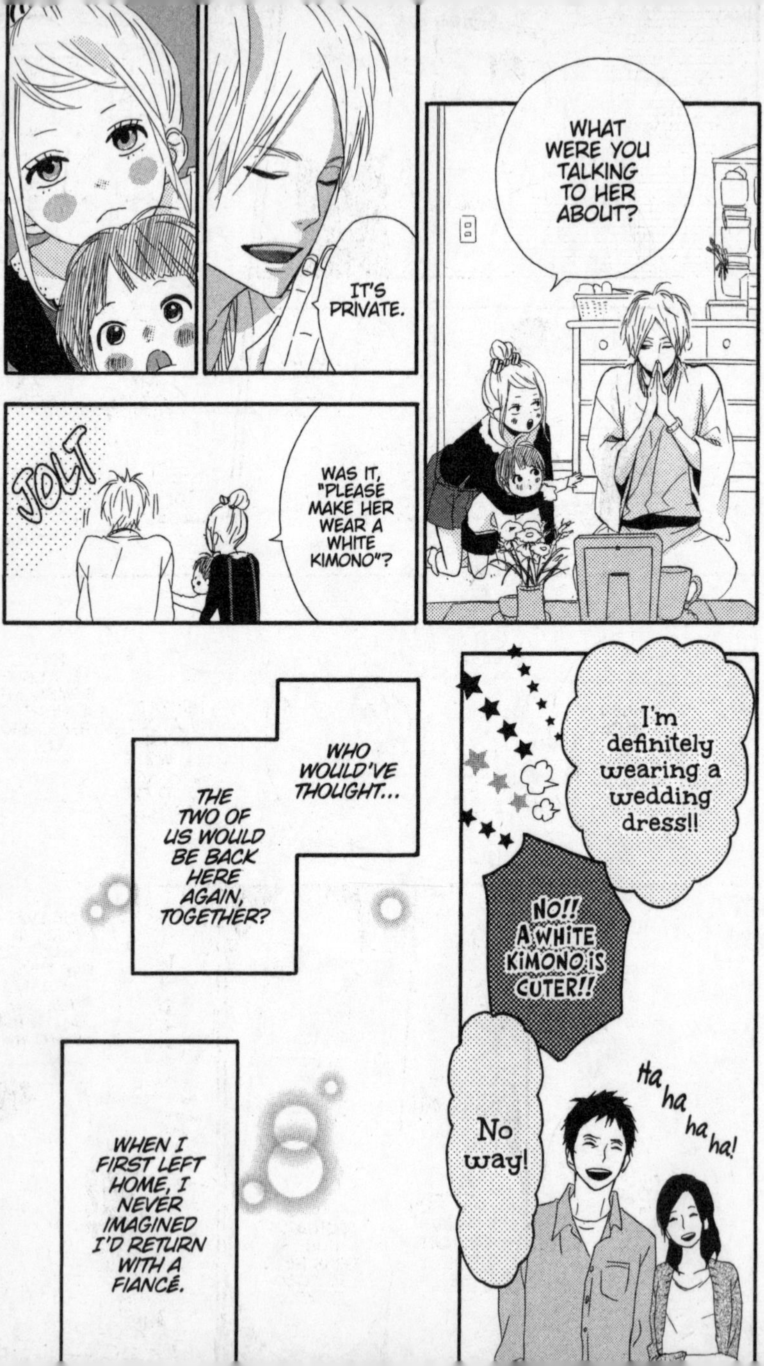
WHAT WERE YOU TALKING TO HER ABOUT?
IT'S PRIVATE.
WAS IT, "PLEASE MAKE HER WEAR A WHITE KIMONO"?
JOLT
I'm definitely wearing a wedding dress!!
NO!! A WHITE KIMONO IS CUTER!!
No way!
Ha ha ha ha!
WHO WOULD'VE THOUGHT...
THE TWO OF US WOULD BE BACK HERE AGAIN, TOGETHER?
WHEN I FIRST LEFT HOME, I NEVER IMAGINED I'D RETURN WITH A FIANCÉ.

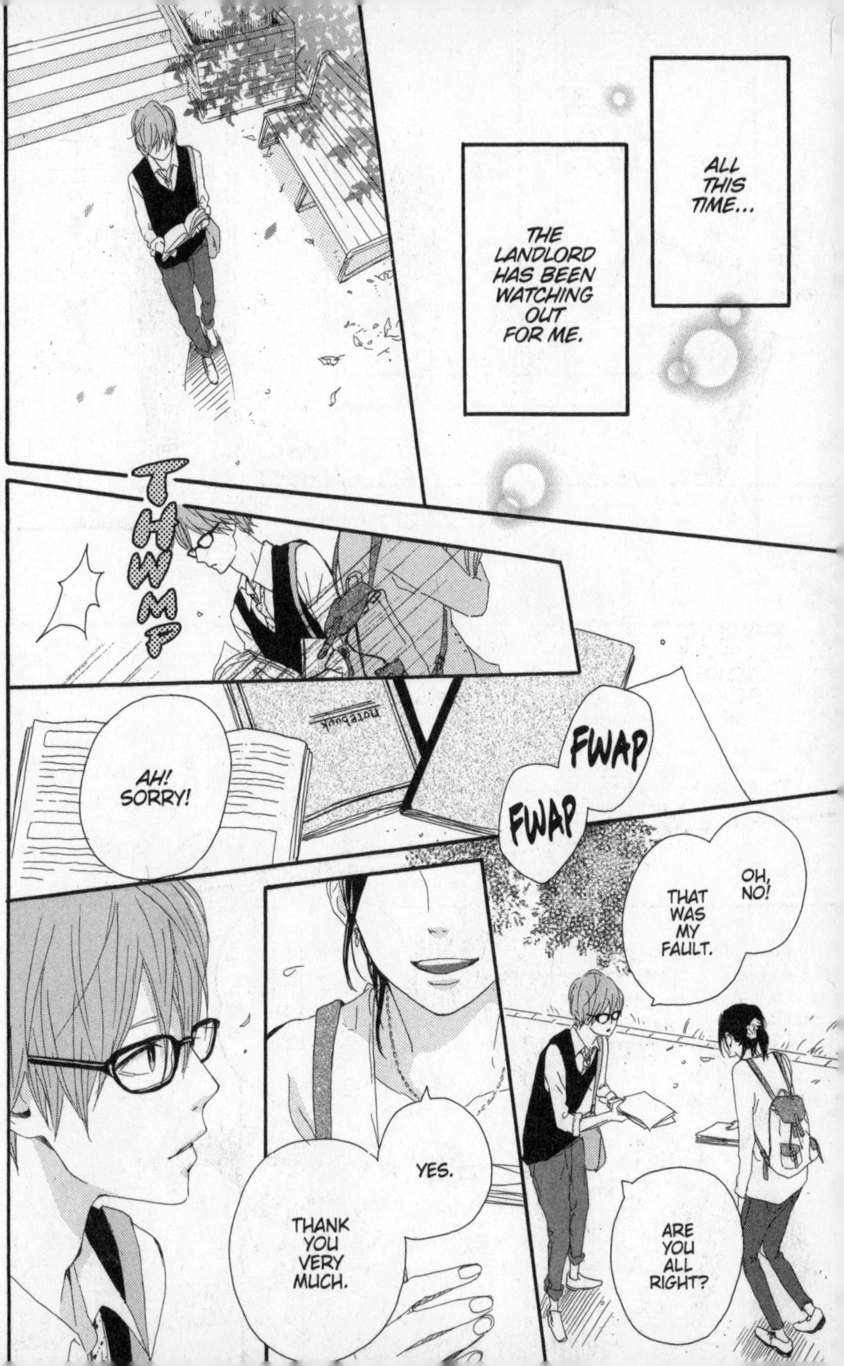
ALL THIS TIME...
THE LANDLORD HAS BEEN WATCHING OUT FOR ME.
THWMP
FWAP
FWAP
AH! SORRY!
OH, NO!
THAT WAS MY FAULT.
ARE YOU ALL RIGHT?
YES.
THANK YOU VERY MUCH.

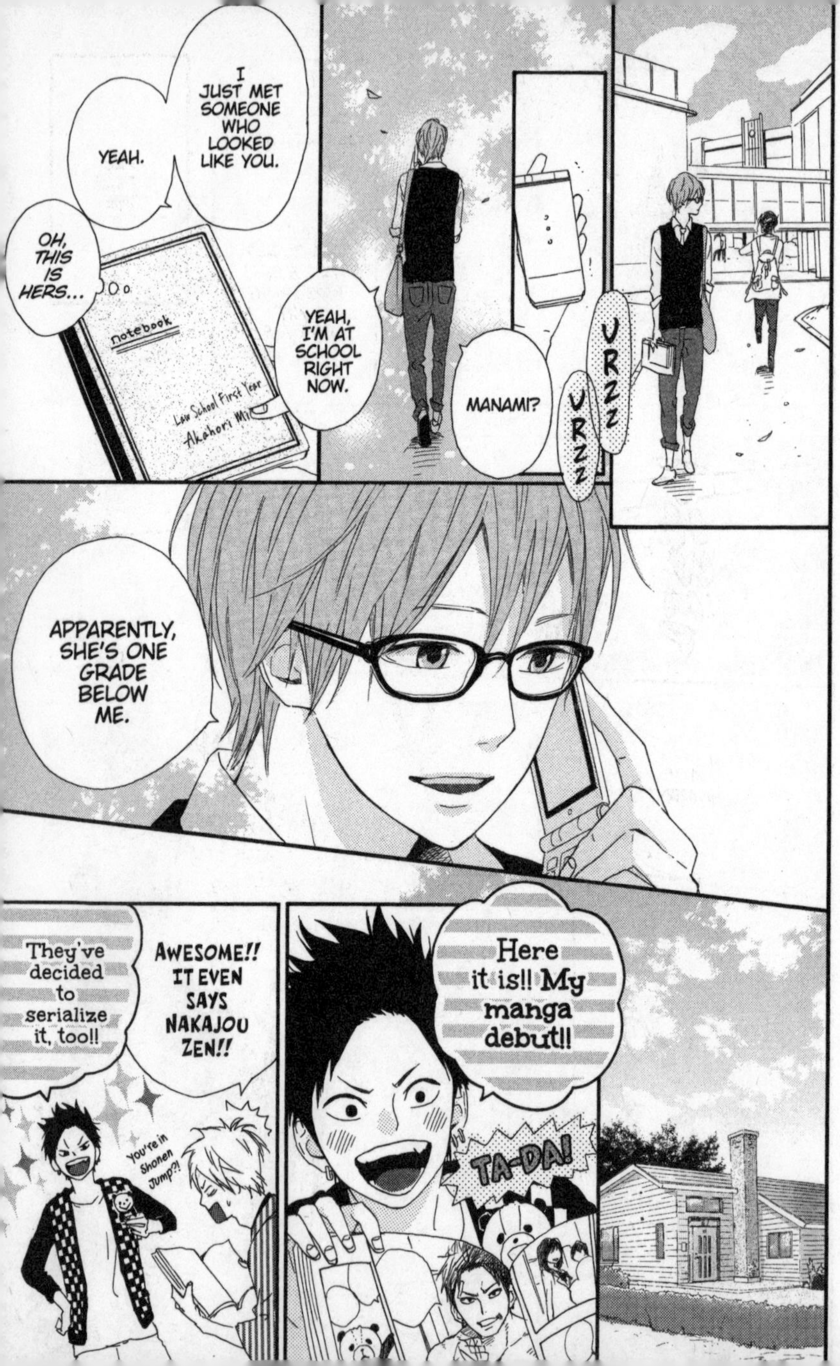
URZZ
URZZ
MANAMI?
YEAH, I'M AT SCHOOL RIGHT NOW.
I JUST MET SOMEONE WHO LOOKED LIKE YOU.
YEAH.
OH, THIS IS HERS...
notebook
Law School First Year
Akahori Mi
APPARENTLY, SHE'S ONE GRADE BELOW ME.
Here it is!! My manga debut!!
TA-DA!
AWESOME!! IT EVEN SAYS NAKAJOU ZEN!!
They've decided to serialize it, too!!
You're in Shonen Jump?!

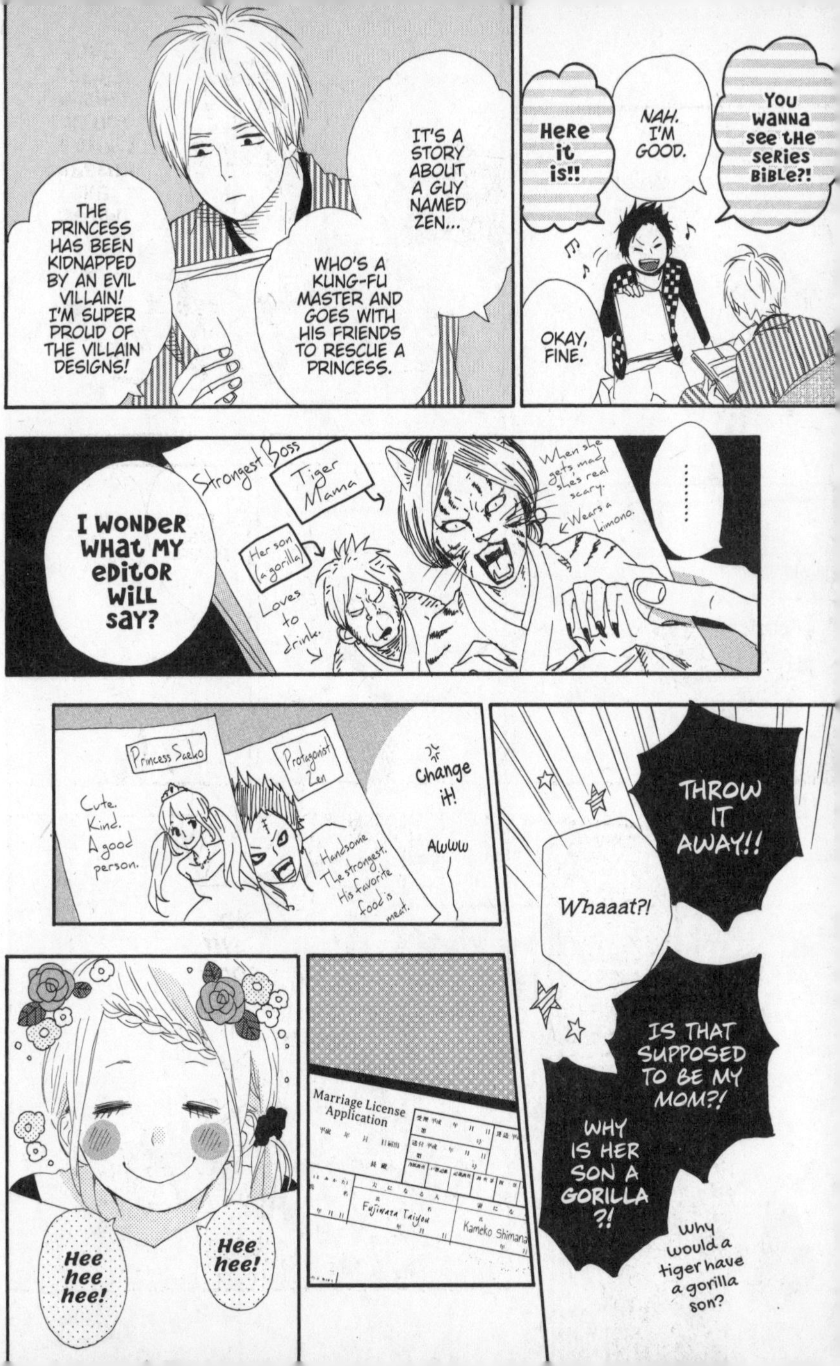
You wanna see the series Bible?!
Nah. I'm good.
Here it is!!
Okay, fine.
It's a story about a guy named Zen...
Who's a kung-fu master and goes with his friends to rescue a princess.
The princess has been kidnapped by an evil villain! I'm super proud of the villain designs!
......
Strongest Boss
Tiger Mama
When she gets mad she's real scary.
Wears a kimono.
Her son (a gorilla)
Loves to drink.
I wonder what my editor will say?
Throw it away!!
Whaaat?!
Princess Saeko
Cute. Kind. A good person.
Protagonist Zen
Handsome The strongest. His favorite food is meat.
Change it!
Awww
Is that supposed to be my mom?!
Why is her son a gorilla?!
Why would a tiger have a gorilla son?
Marriage License Application
Fujiwara Taiyou
Kameko Shimana
Hee hee!
Hee hee hee!

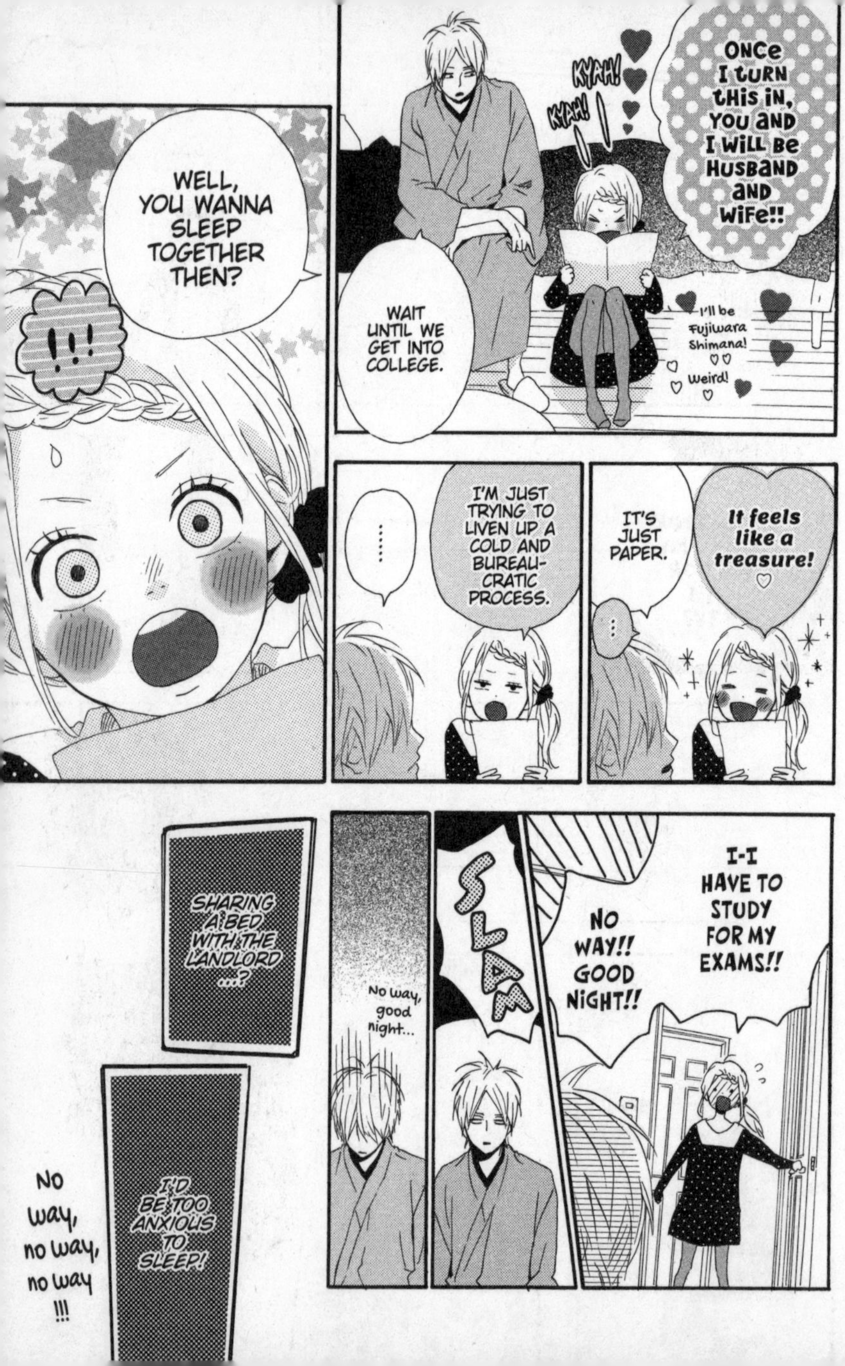
ONCE I TURN THIS IN, YOU AND I WILL BE HUSBAND AND WIFE!!
KYAH! KYAH!
I'll be Fujiwara Shimana! ♡♡
Weird! ♡
WAIT UNTIL WE GET INTO COLLEGE.
It feels like a treasure! ♡
IT'S JUST PAPER.
...
I'M JUST TRYING TO LIVEN UP A COLD AND BUREAUCRATIC PROCESS.
......
WELL, YOU WANNA SLEEP TOGETHER THEN?
!!!
I-I HAVE TO STUDY FOR MY EXAMS!!
NO WAY!! GOOD NIGHT!!
SLAM
No way, good night...
SHARING A BED WITH THE LANDLORD ...?
I'D BE TOO ANXIOUS TO SLEEP!
No way, no way, no way !!!

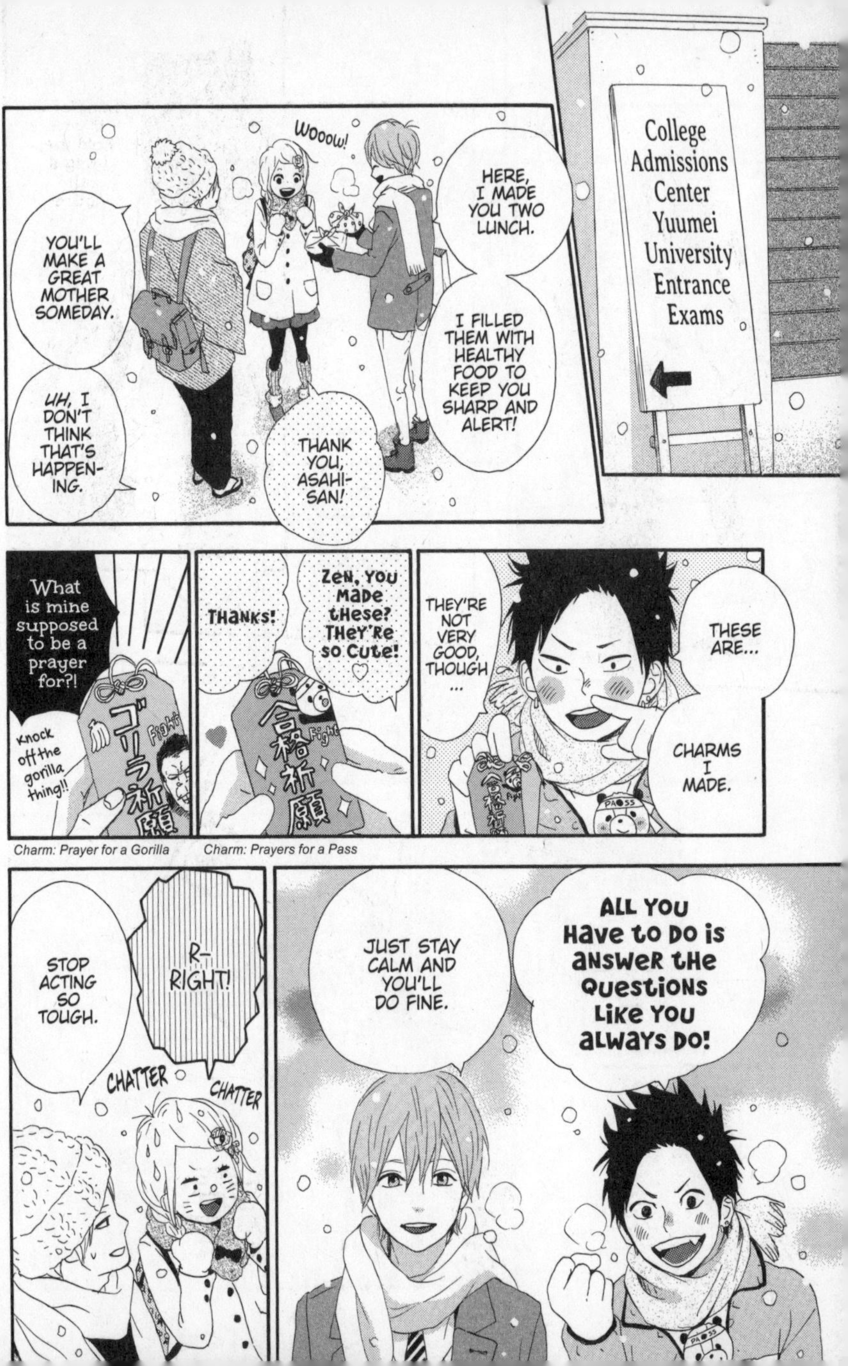
College Admissions Center Yuumei University Entrance Exams
HERE, I MADE YOU TWO LUNCH.
I FILLED THEM WITH HEALTHY FOOD TO KEEP YOU SHARP AND ALERT!
WOOOW!
THANK YOU, ASAHI-SAN!
YOU'LL MAKE A GREAT MOTHER SOMEDAY.
UH, I DON'T THINK THAT'S HAPPENING.
THESE ARE...
CHARMS I MADE.
THEY'RE NOT VERY GOOD, THOUGH...
ZEN, YOU MADE THESE? THEY'RE SO CUTE!
THANKS!
合格祈願
What is mine supposed to be a prayer for?!
ゴリラ祈願
Knock off the gorilla thing!!
ALL YOU HAVE TO DO IS ANSWER THE QUESTIONS LIKE YOU ALWAYS DO!
JUST STAY CALM AND YOU'LL DO FINE.
R-RIGHT!
STOP ACTING SO TOUGH.
CHATTER
CHATTER

Charm: Prayer for a Gorilla

Charm: Prayers for a Pass

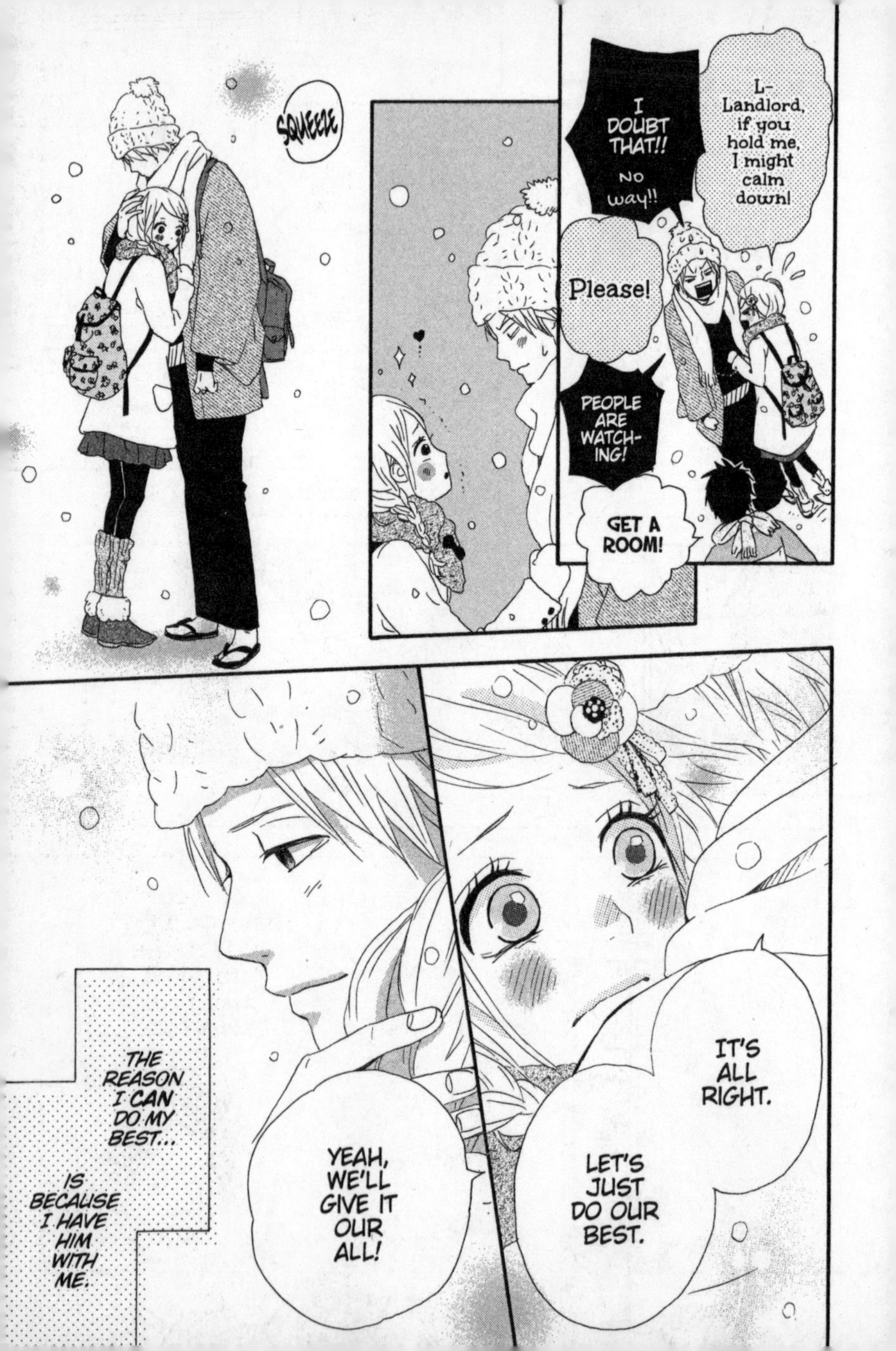
L-Landlord, if you hold me, I might calm down!
I DOUBT THAT!!
No way!!
Please!
PEOPLE ARE WATCHING!
GET A ROOM!
SQUEEZE
IT'S ALL RIGHT.
LET'S JUST DO OUR BEST.
YEAH, WE'LL GIVE IT OUR ALL!
THE REASON I CAN DO MY BEST...
IS BECAUSE I HAVE HIM WITH ME.

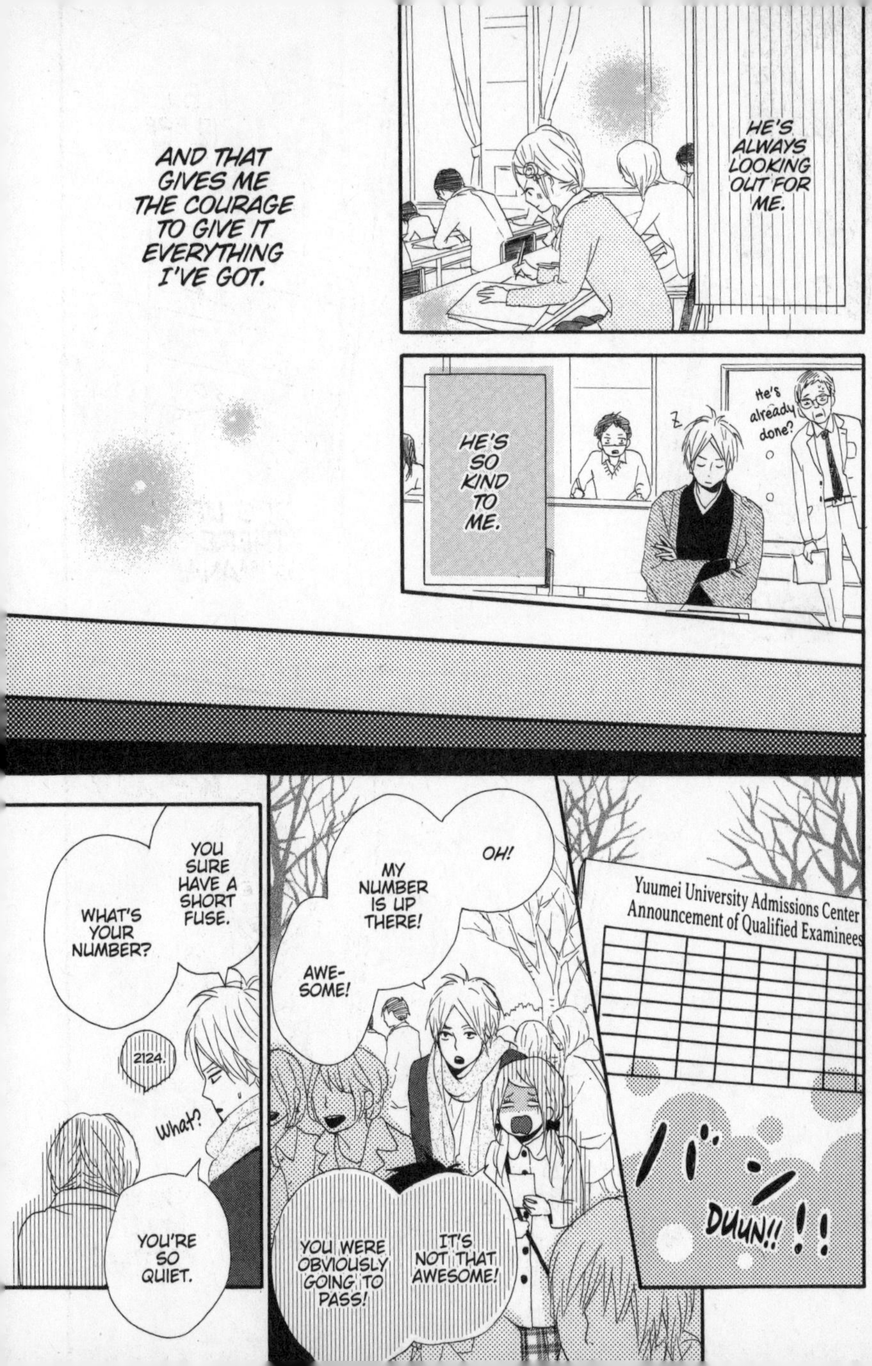
HE'S ALWAYS LOOKING OUT FOR ME.
He's already done?
HE'S SO KIND TO ME.
AND THAT GIVES ME THE COURAGE TO GIVE IT EVERYTHING I'VE GOT.
Yuumei University Admissions Center
Announcement of Qualified Examinees
DUUN!! ! !
OH!
MY NUMBER IS UP THERE!
AWESOME!
IT'S NOT THAT AWESOME!
YOU WERE OBVIOUSLY GOING TO PASS!
YOU SURE HAVE A SHORT FUSE.
WHAT'S YOUR NUMBER?
2124.
What?
YOU'RE SO QUIET.

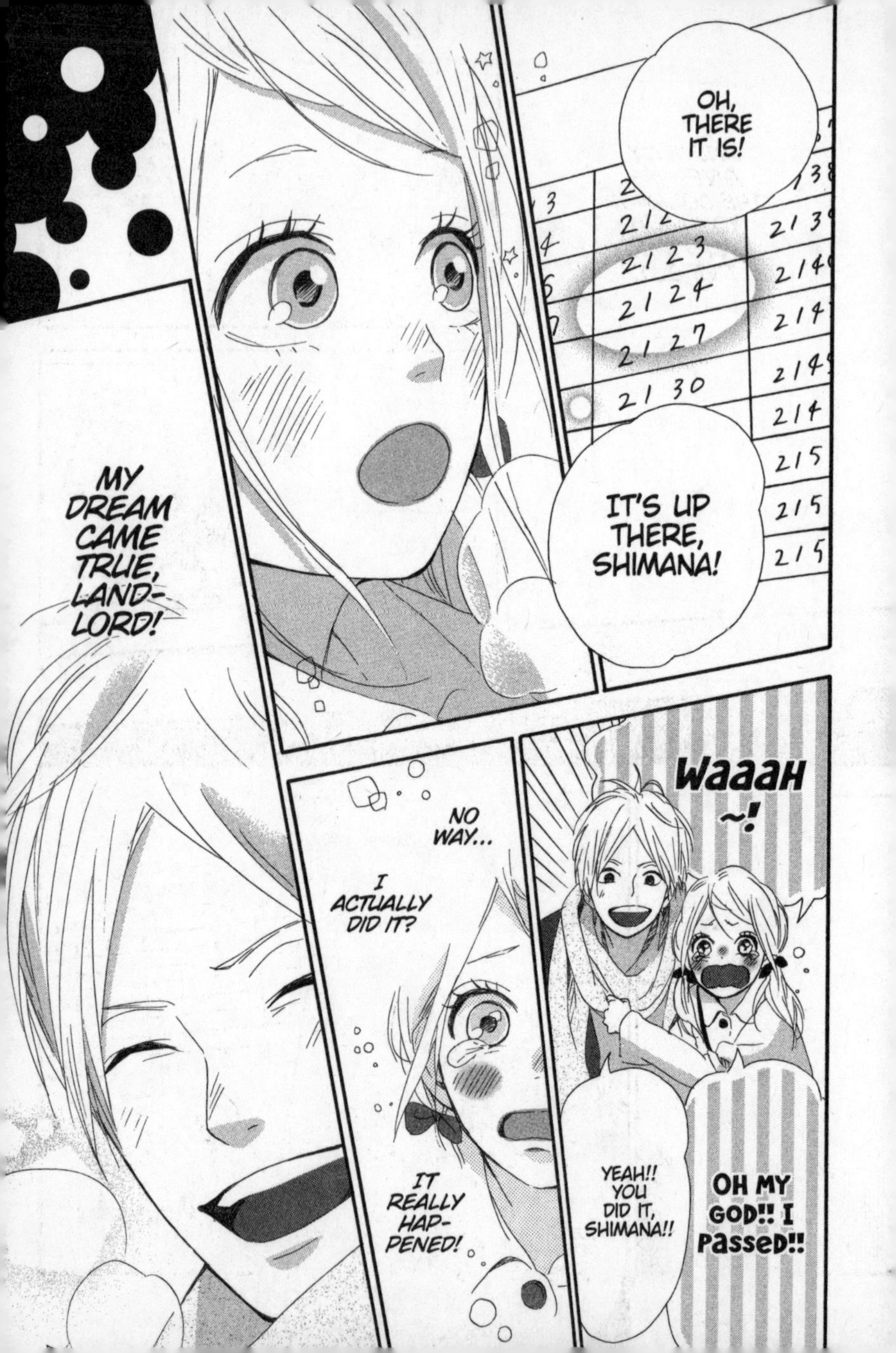
OH, THERE IT IS!
IT'S UP THERE, SHIMANA!
WaaaH ~!
YEAH!! YOU DID IT, SHIMANA!!
OH MY GOD!! I Passed!!
NO WAY...
I ACTUALLY DID IT?
IT REALLY HAP-PENED!
MY DREAM CAME TRUE, LAND-LORD!

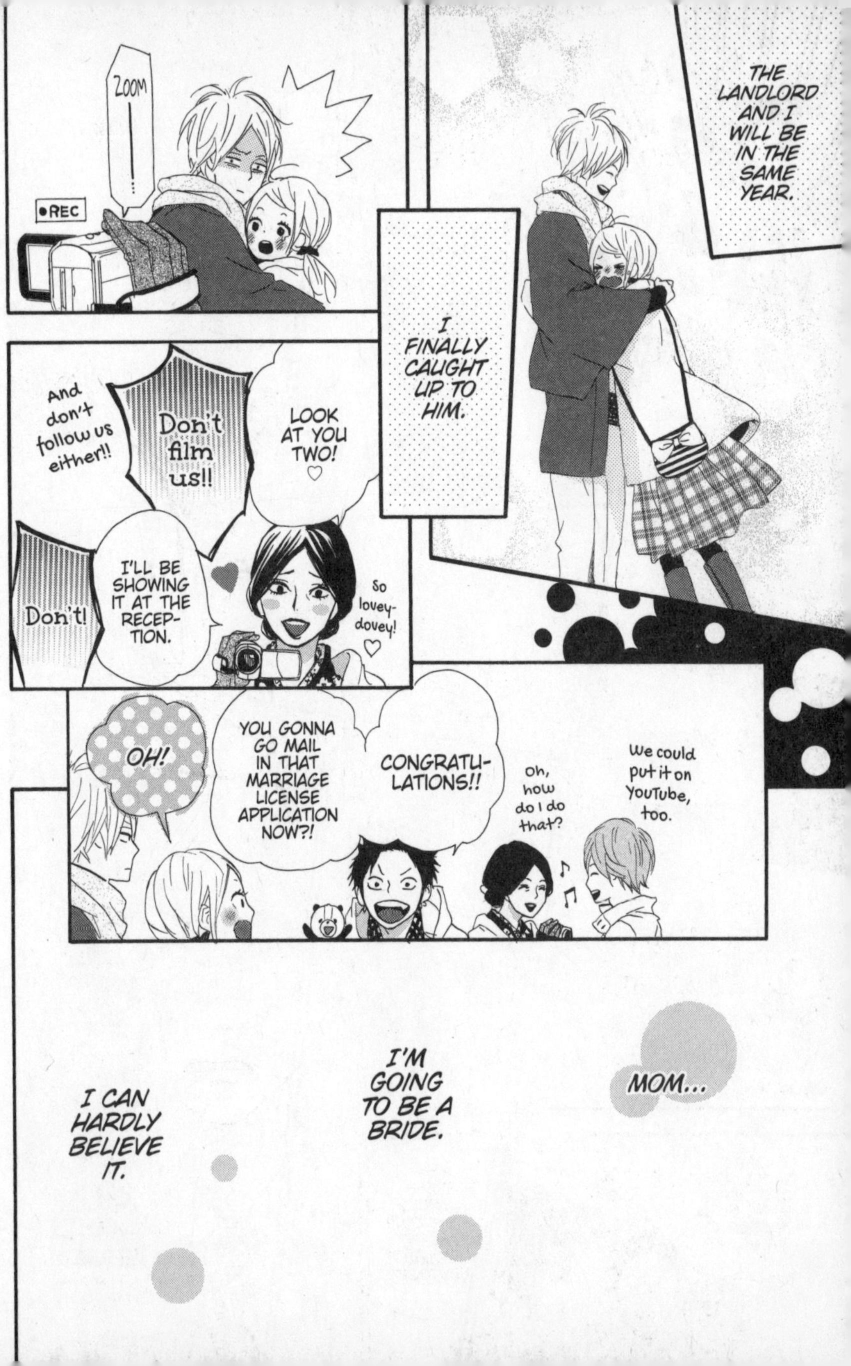
THE LANDLORD AND I WILL BE IN THE SAME YEAR.
I FINALLY CAUGHT UP TO HIM.
ZOOM
●REC
LOOK AT YOU TWO! ♡
Don't film us!!
And don't follow us either!!
So lovey-dovey! ♡
I'LL BE SHOWING IT AT THE RECEPTION.
Don't!
We could put it on YouTube, too.
Oh, how do I do that?
CONGRATULATIONS!!
YOU GONNA GO MAIL IN THAT MARRIAGE LICENSE APPLICATION NOW?!
OH!
MOM...
I'M GOING TO BE A BRIDE.
I CAN HARDLY BELIEVE IT.

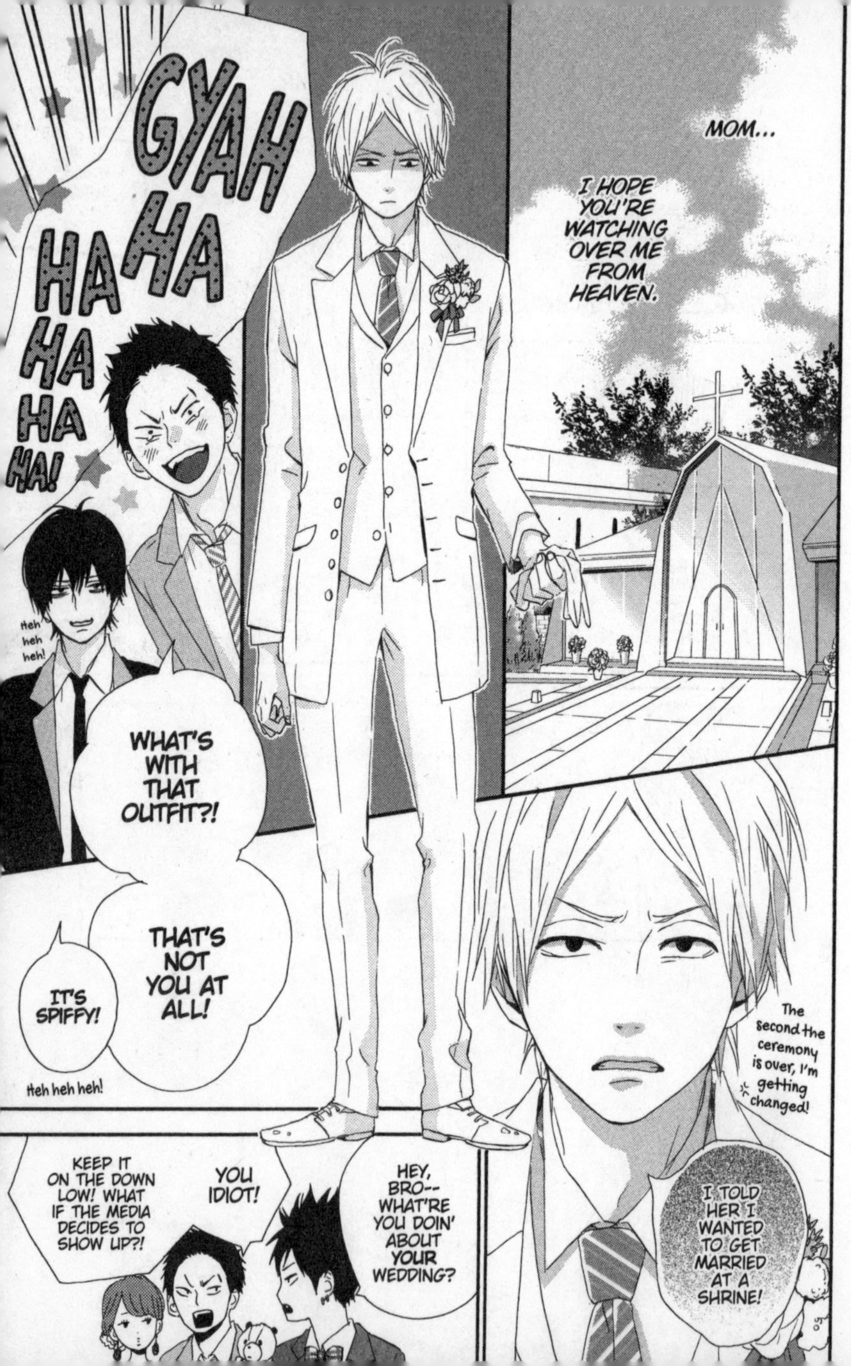
MOM...
I HOPE YOU'RE WATCHING OVER ME FROM HEAVEN.
GYAH HAHA HAHA HA HA HA!
heh heh heh!
WHAT'S WITH THAT OUTFIT?!
THAT'S NOT YOU AT ALL!
IT'S SPIFFY!
heh heh heh!
The second the ceremony is over, I'm getting changed!
I TOLD HER I WANTED TO GET MARRIED AT A SHRINE!
HEY, BRO-- WHAT'RE YOU DOIN' ABOUT YOUR WEDDING?
YOU IDIOT!
KEEP IT ON THE DOWN LOW! WHAT IF THE MEDIA DECIDES TO SHOW UP?!

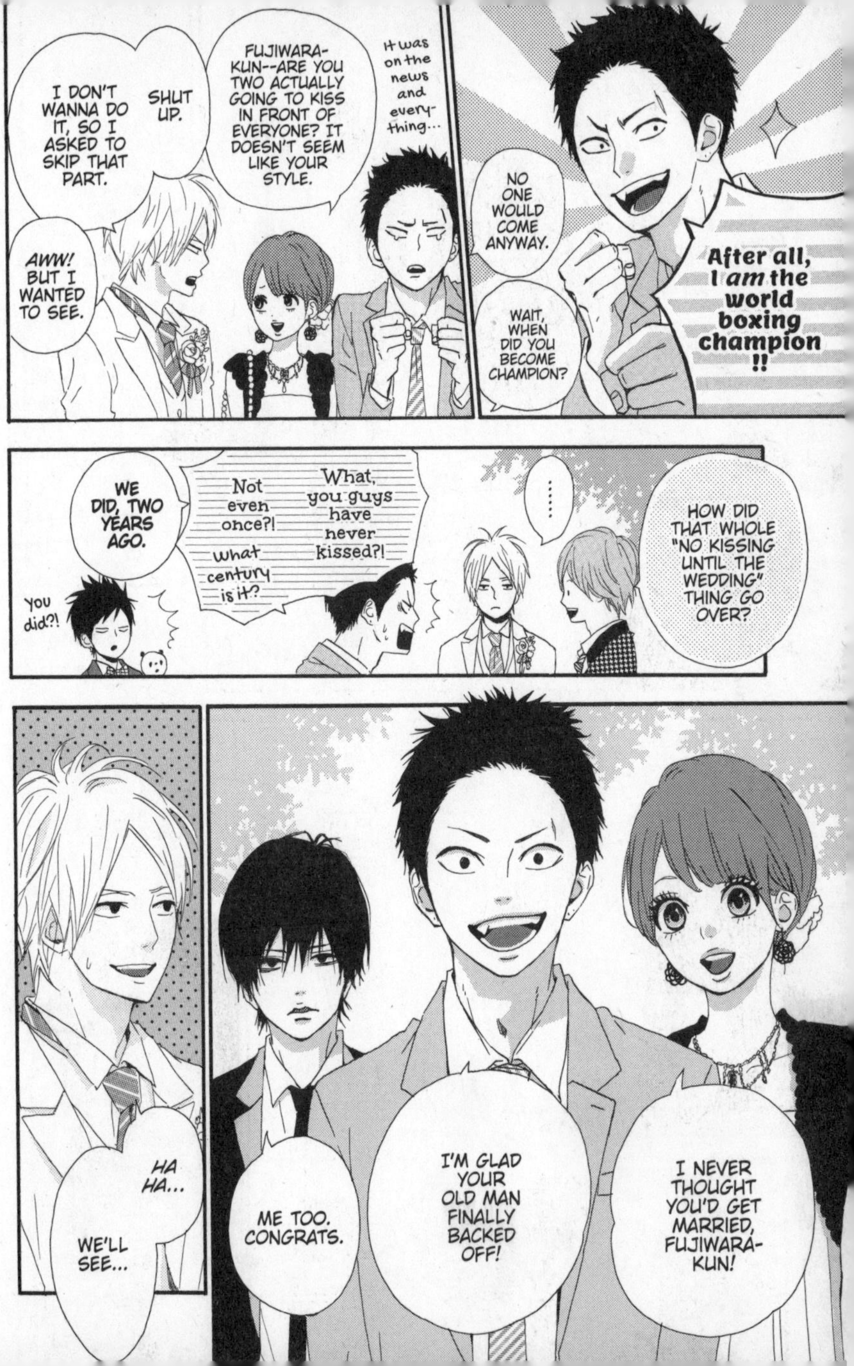
NO ONE WOULD COME ANYWAY.
After all, I *am* the world boxing champion!!
WAIT, WHEN DID YOU BECOME CHAMPION?
It was on the news and every-thing...
FUJIWARA-KUN--ARE YOU TWO ACTUALLY GOING TO KISS IN FRONT OF EVERYONE? IT DOESN'T SEEM LIKE YOUR STYLE.
SHUT UP.
I DON'T WANNA DO IT, SO I ASKED TO SKIP THAT PART.
AWW! BUT I WANTED TO SEE.
HOW DID THAT WHOLE "NO KISSING UNTIL THE WEDDING" THING GO OVER?
......
What, you guys have never kissed?!
Not even once?!
what century is it?
WE DID, TWO YEARS AGO.
You did?!
I NEVER THOUGHT YOU'D GET MARRIED, FUJIWARA-KUN!
I'M GLAD YOUR OLD MAN FINALLY BACKED OFF!
ME TOO. CONGRATS.
HA HA...
WE'LL SEE...

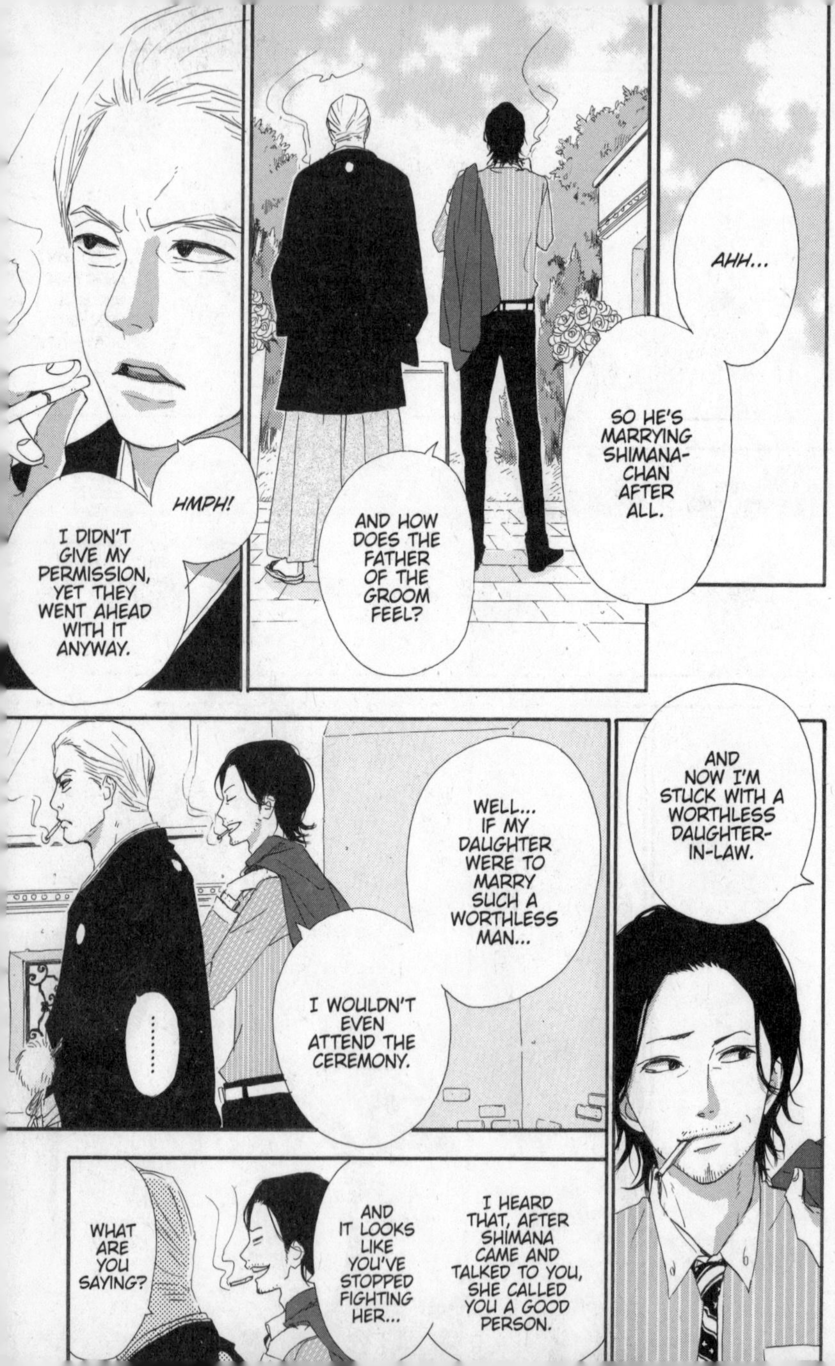
AHH...
SO HE'S MARRYING SHIMANA-CHAN AFTER ALL.
AND HOW DOES THE FATHER OF THE GROOM FEEL?
HMPH!
I DIDN'T GIVE MY PERMISSION, YET THEY WENT AHEAD WITH IT ANYWAY.
AND NOW I'M STUCK WITH A WORTHLESS DAUGHTER-IN-LAW.
WELL... IF MY DAUGHTER WERE TO MARRY SUCH A WORTHLESS MAN...
I WOULDN'T EVEN ATTEND THE CEREMONY.
......
I HEARD THAT, AFTER SHIMANA CAME AND TALKED TO YOU, SHE CALLED YOU A GOOD PERSON.
AND IT LOOKS LIKE YOU'VE STOPPED FIGHTING HER...
WHAT ARE YOU SAYING?

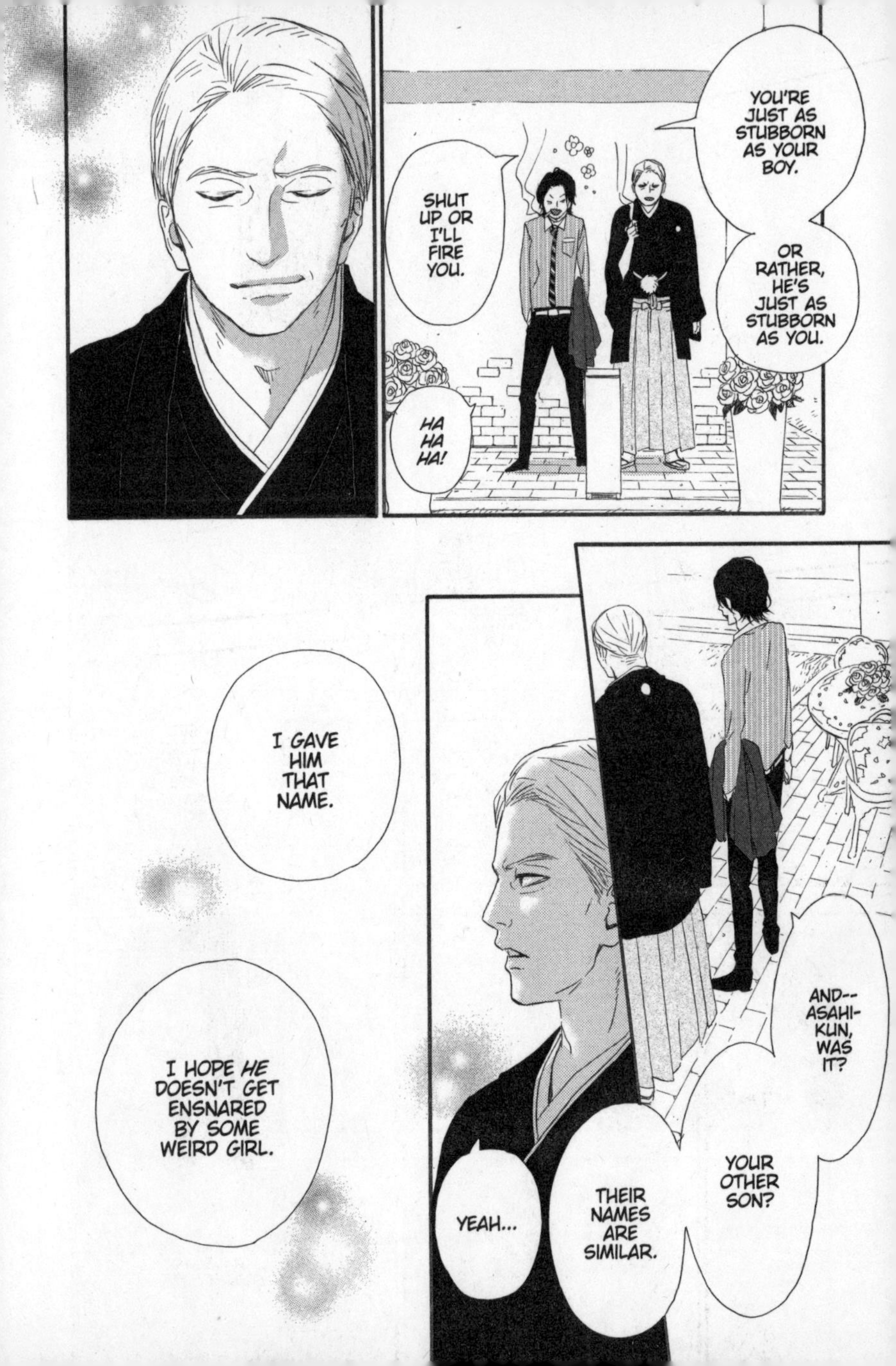
YOU'RE JUST AS STUBBORN AS YOUR BOY.
OR RATHER, HE'S JUST AS STUBBORN AS YOU.
SHUT UP OR I'LL FIRE YOU.
HA HA HA!
AND-- ASAHI-KUN, WAS IT?
YOUR OTHER SON?
THEIR NAMES ARE SIMILAR.
YEAH...
I GAVE HIM THAT NAME.
I HOPE *HE* DOESN'T GET ENSNARED BY SOME WEIRD GIRL.

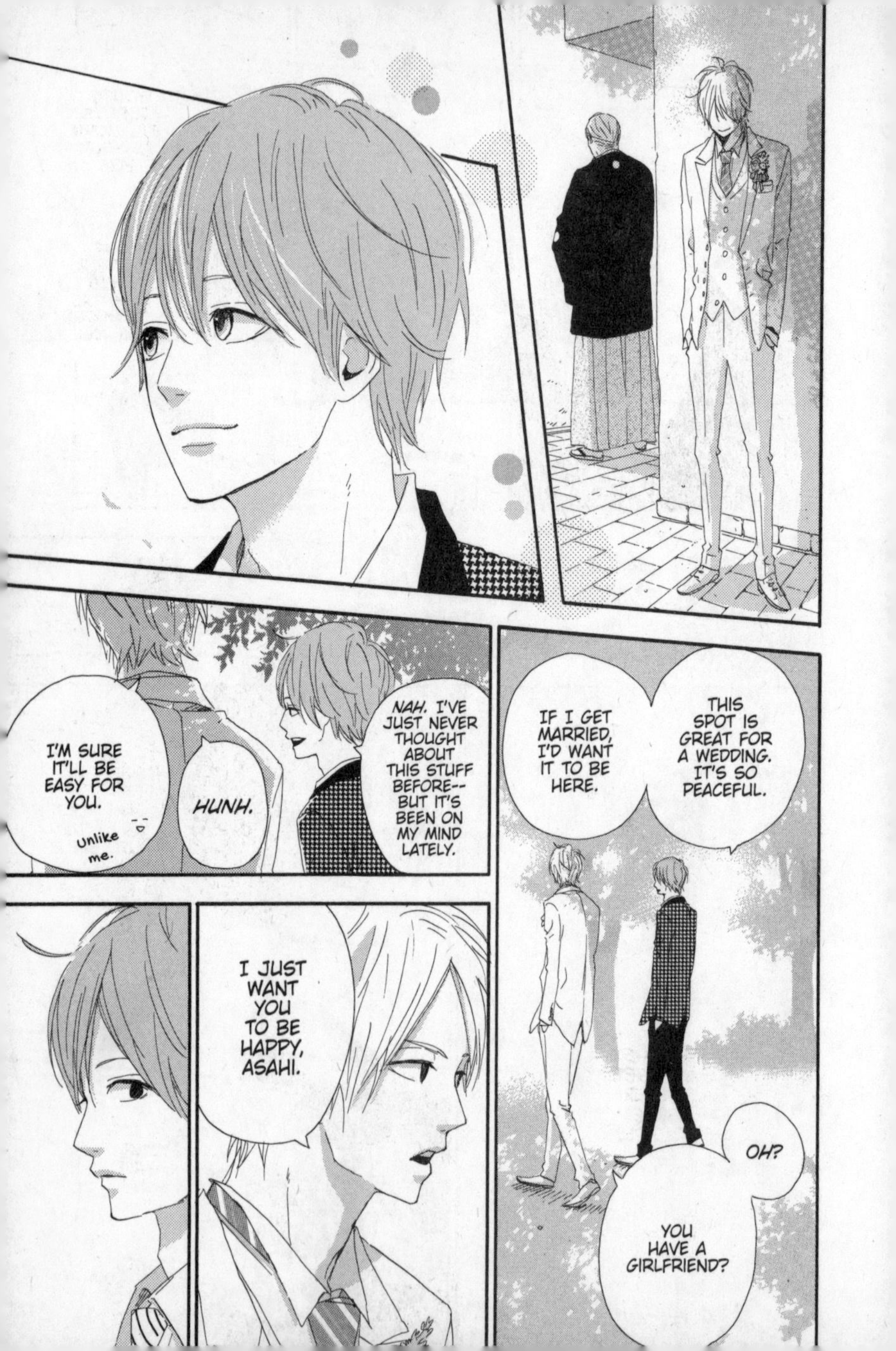
THIS SPOT IS GREAT FOR A WEDDING. IT'S SO PEACEFUL.
IF I GET MARRIED, I'D WANT IT TO BE HERE.
OH?
YOU HAVE A GIRLFRIEND?
NAH. I'VE JUST NEVER THOUGHT ABOUT THIS STUFF BEFORE-- BUT IT'S BEEN ON MY MIND LATELY.
HUNH.
I'M SURE IT'LL BE EASY FOR YOU.
Unlike me.
I JUST WANT YOU TO BE HAPPY, ASAHI.

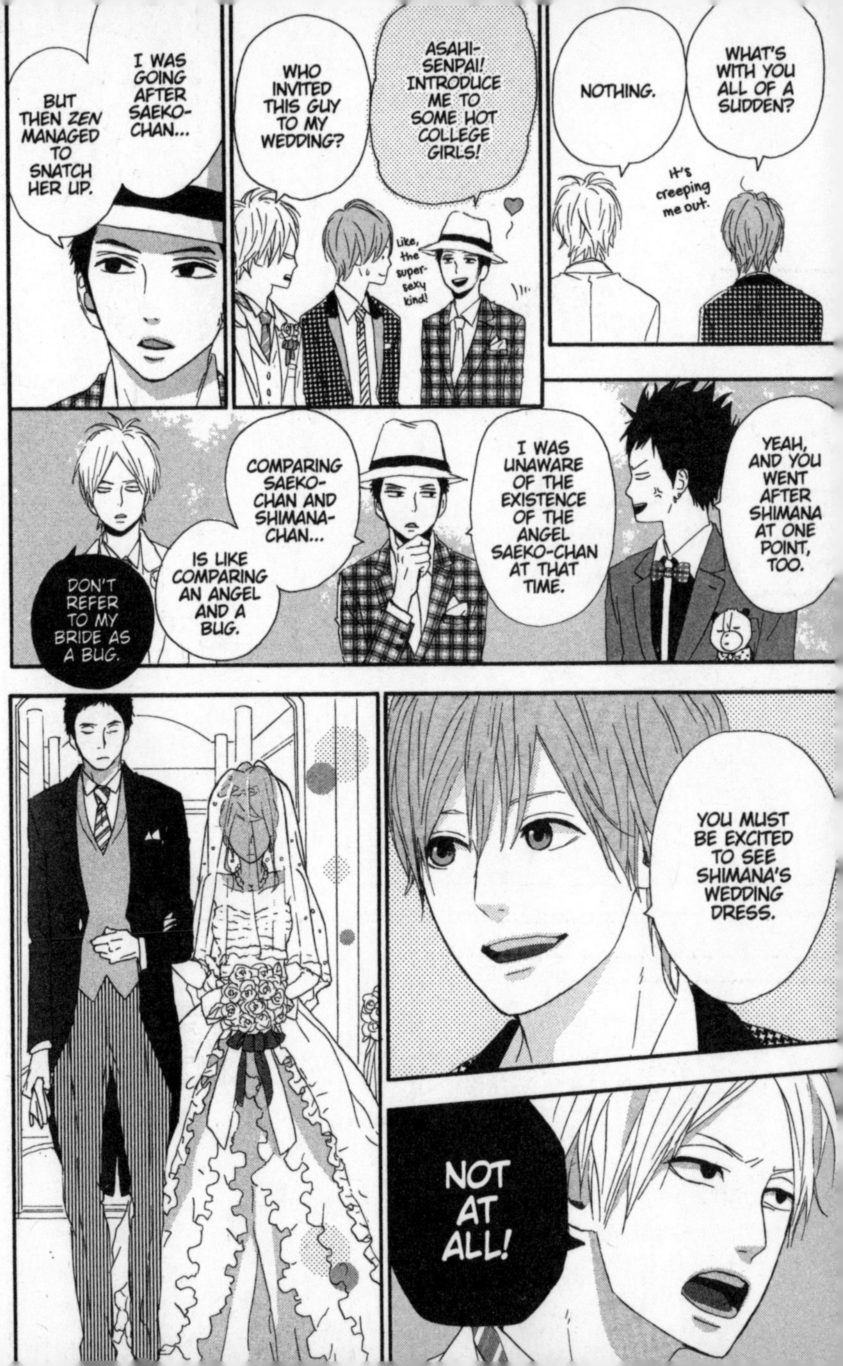
WHAT'S WITH YOU ALL OF A SUDDEN?
NOTHING.
It's creeping me out.
ASAHI-SENPAI! INTRODUCE ME TO SOME HOT COLLEGE GIRLS!
Like, the super-sexy kind!
WHO INVITED THIS GUY TO MY WEDDING?
I WAS GOING AFTER SAEKO-CHAN...
BUT THEN ZEN MANAGED TO SNATCH HER UP.
YEAH, AND YOU WENT AFTER SHIMANA AT ONE POINT, TOO.
I WAS UNAWARE OF THE EXISTENCE OF THE ANGEL SAEKO-CHAN AT THAT TIME.
COMPARING SAEKO-CHAN AND SHIMANA-CHAN...
IS LIKE COMPARING AN ANGEL AND A BUG.
DON'T REFER TO MY BRIDE AS A BUG.
YOU MUST BE EXCITED TO SEE SHIMANA'S WEDDING DRESS.
NOT AT ALL!

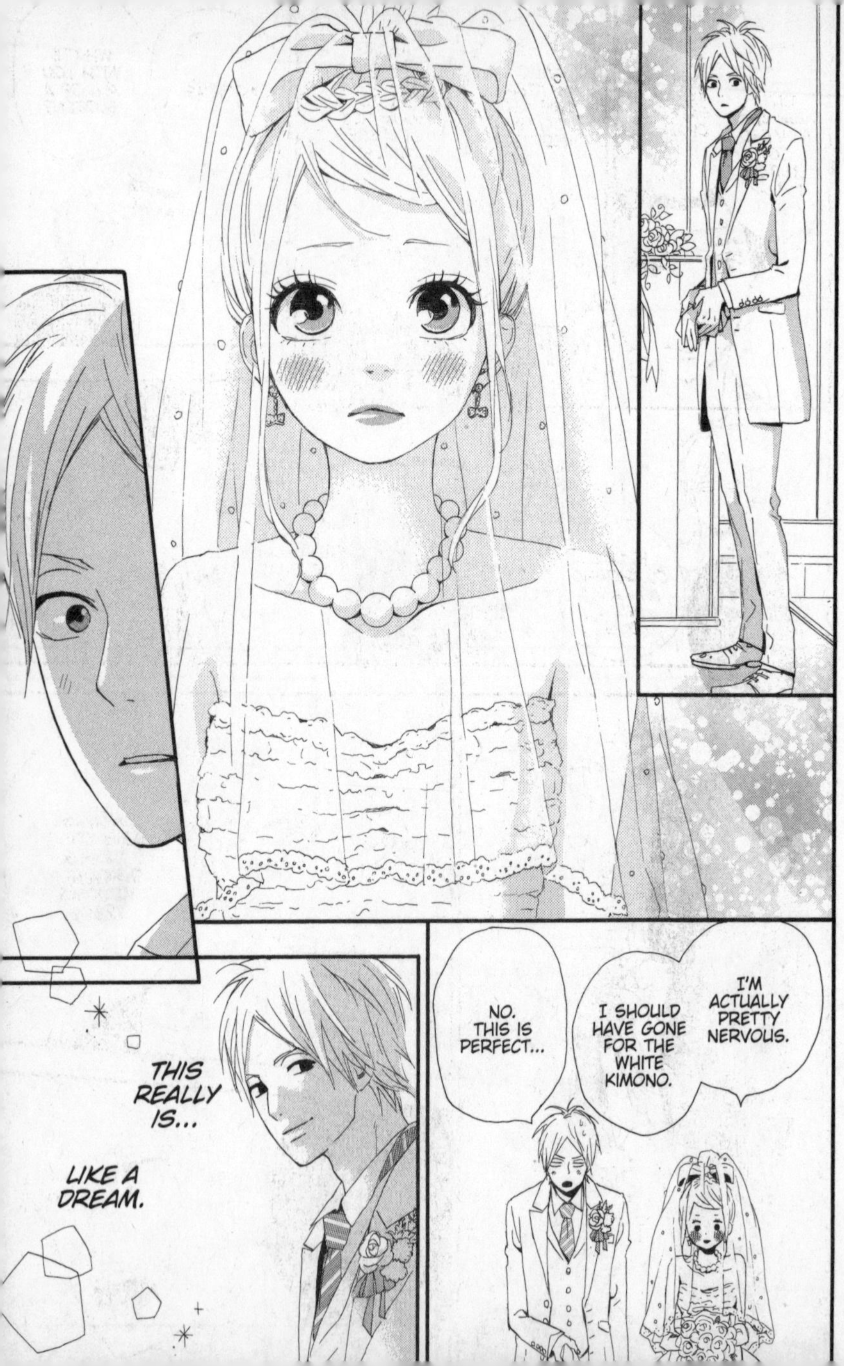
I'M ACTUALLY PRETTY NERVOUS.
I SHOULD HAVE GONE FOR THE WHITE KIMONO.
NO. THIS IS PERFECT...
THIS REALLY IS...
LIKE A DREAM.

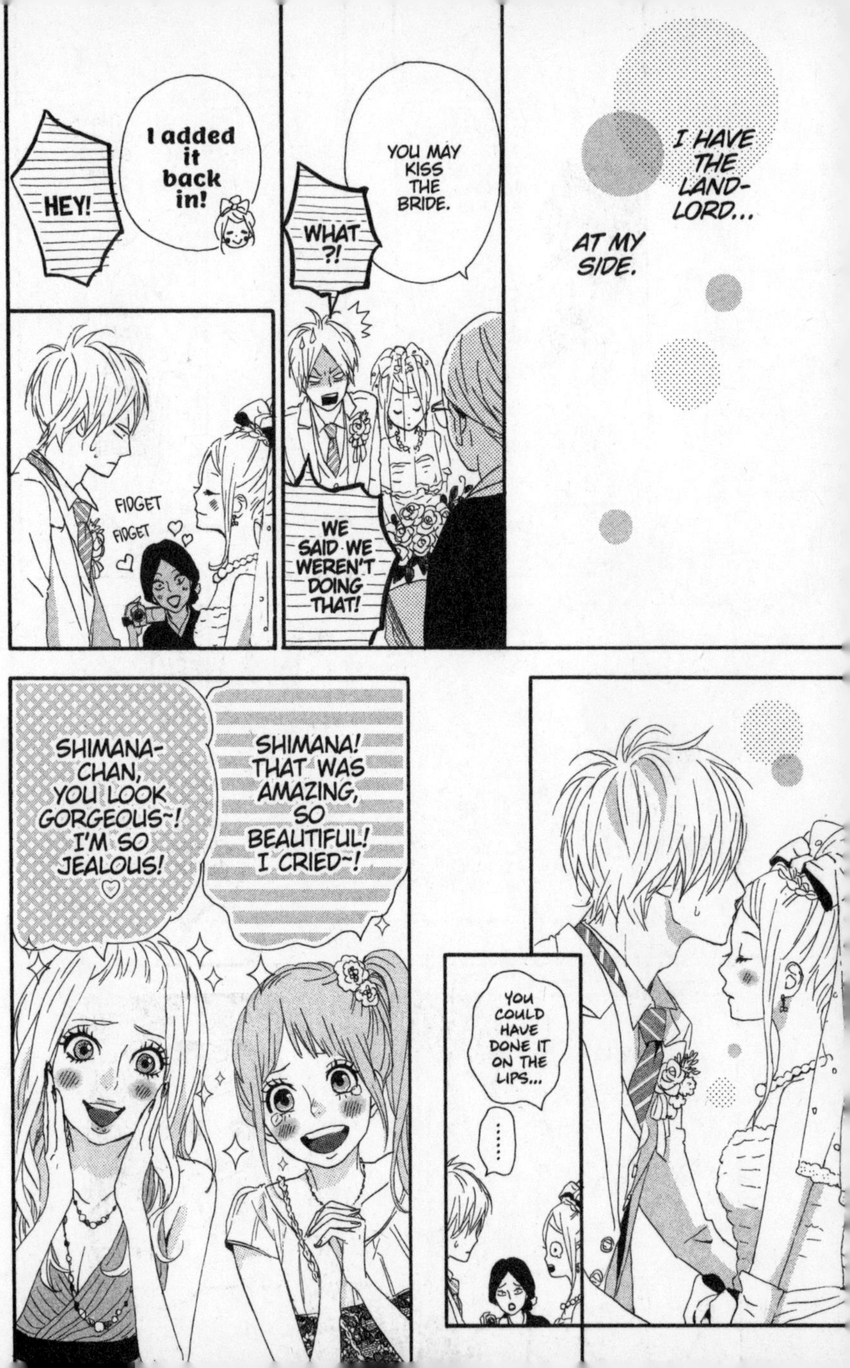
I HAVE THE LAND-LORD...
AT MY SIDE.
YOU MAY KISS THE BRIDE.
WHAT?!
WE SAID WE WEREN'T DOING THAT!
HEY!
I added it back in!
FIDGET
FIDGET
YOU COULD HAVE DONE IT ON THE LIPS...
......
SHIMANA! THAT WAS AMAZING, SO BEAUTIFUL! I CRIED~!
SHIMANA-CHAN, YOU LOOK GORGEOUS~! I'M SO JEALOUS!

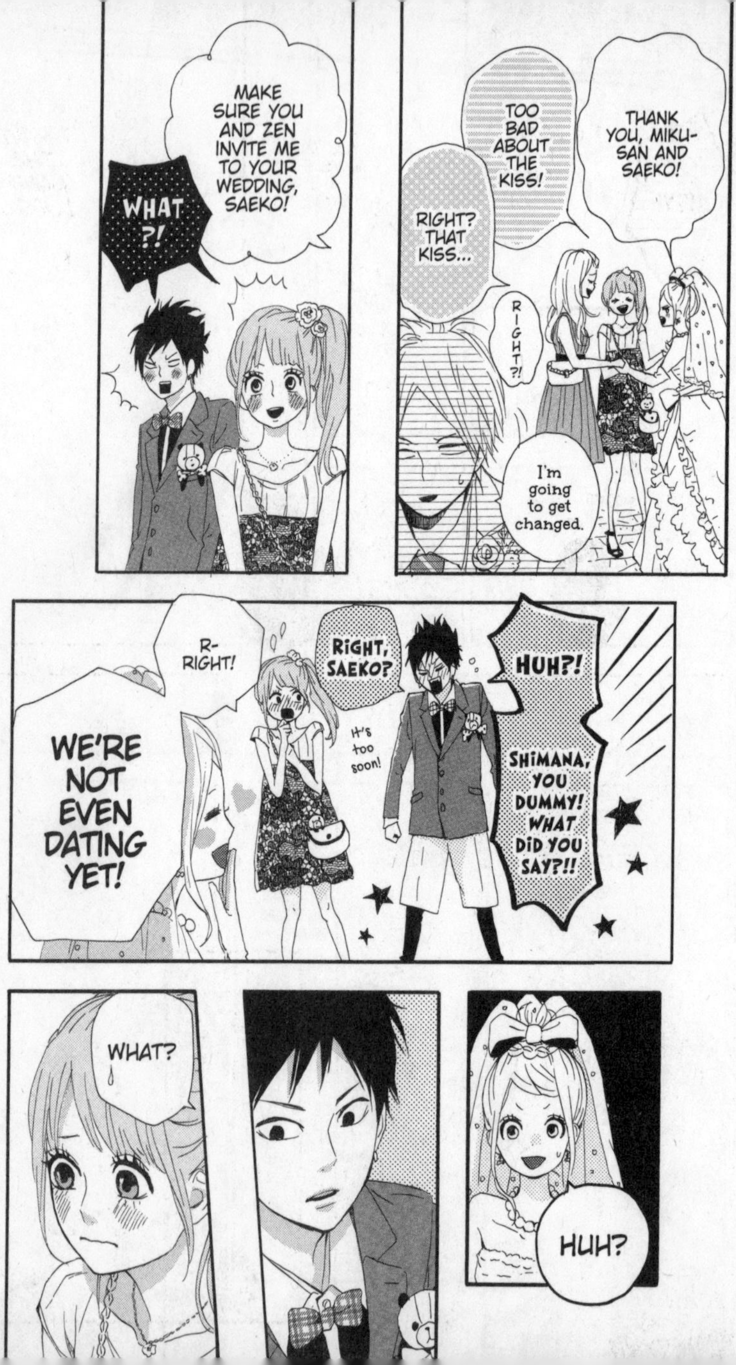
THANK YOU, MIKU-SAN AND SAEKO!
TOO BAD ABOUT THE KISS!
RIGHT? THAT KISS...
RIGHT?!
I'm going to get changed.
MAKE SURE YOU AND ZEN INVITE ME TO YOUR WEDDING, SAEKO!
WHAT?!
HUH?!
SHIMANA, YOU DUMMY! WHAT DID YOU SAY?!!
RIGHT, SAEKO?
R-RIGHT!
It's too soon!
WE'RE NOT EVEN DATING YET!
HUH?
WHAT?

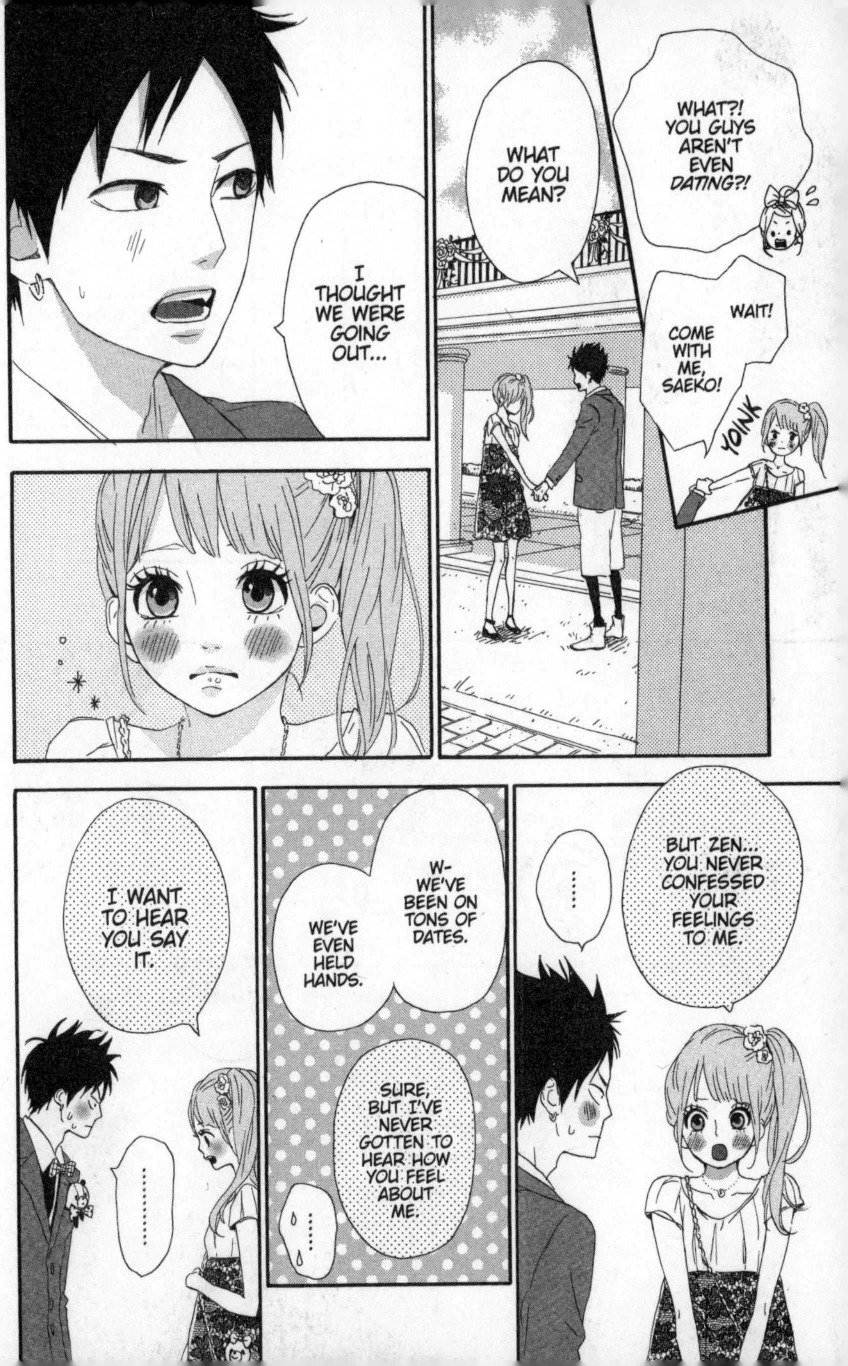
WHAT?! YOU GUYS AREN'T EVEN DATING?!
WAIT!
COME WITH ME, SAEKO!
YOINK
WHAT DO YOU MEAN?
I THOUGHT WE WERE GOING OUT...
BUT ZEN... YOU NEVER CONFESSED YOUR FEELINGS TO ME.
......
W- WE'VE BEEN ON TONS OF DATES.
WE'VE EVEN HELD HANDS.
SURE, BUT I'VE NEVER GOTTEN TO HEAR HOW YOU FEEL ABOUT ME.
......
I WANT TO HEAR YOU SAY IT.
....

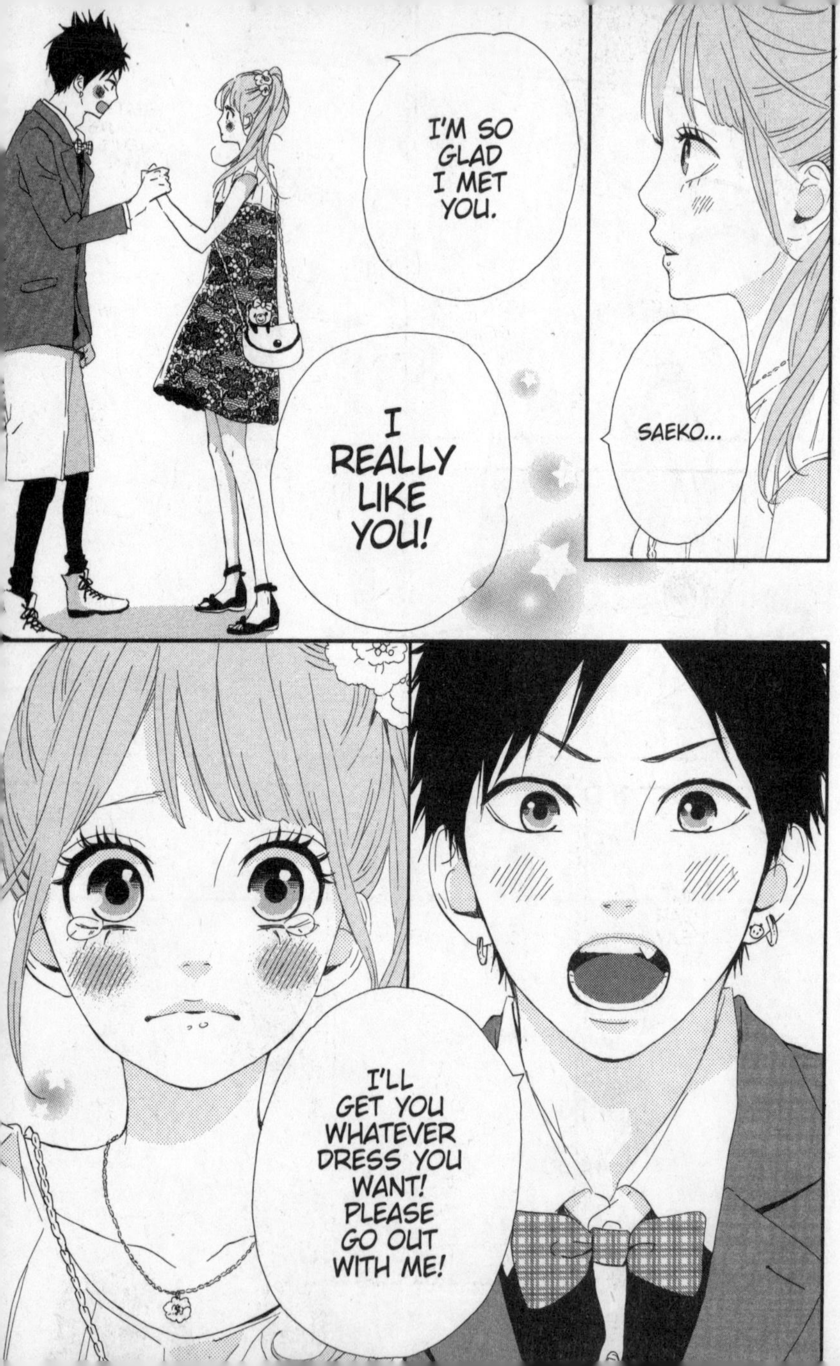
SAEKO...
I'M SO GLAD I MET YOU.
I REALLY LIKE YOU!
I'LL GET YOU WHATEVER DRESS YOU WANT! PLEASE GO OUT WITH ME!

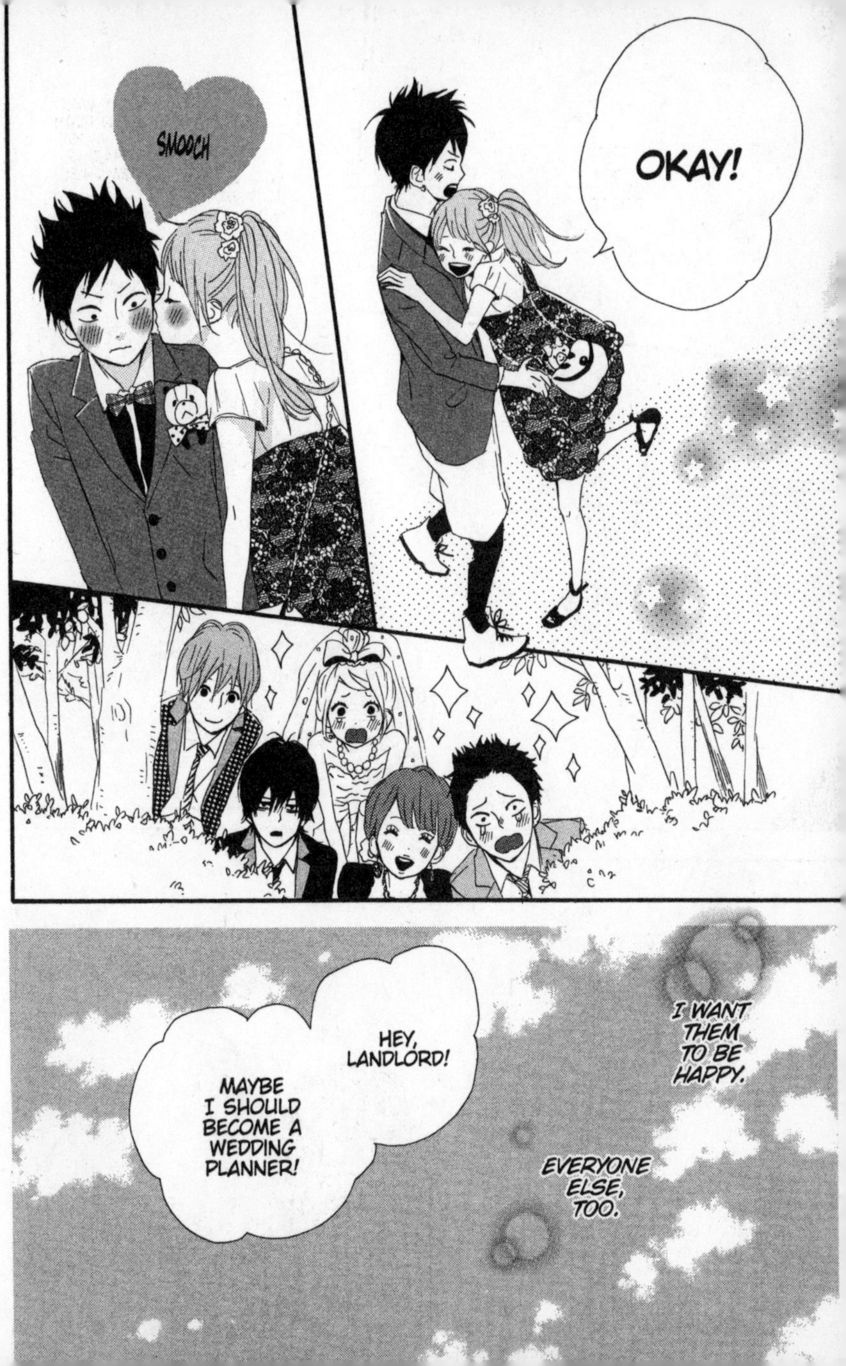
OKAY!
SMOOCH
I WANT THEM TO BE HAPPY.
EVERYONE ELSE, TOO.
HEY, LANDLORD!
MAYBE I SHOULD BECOME A WEDDING PLANNER!

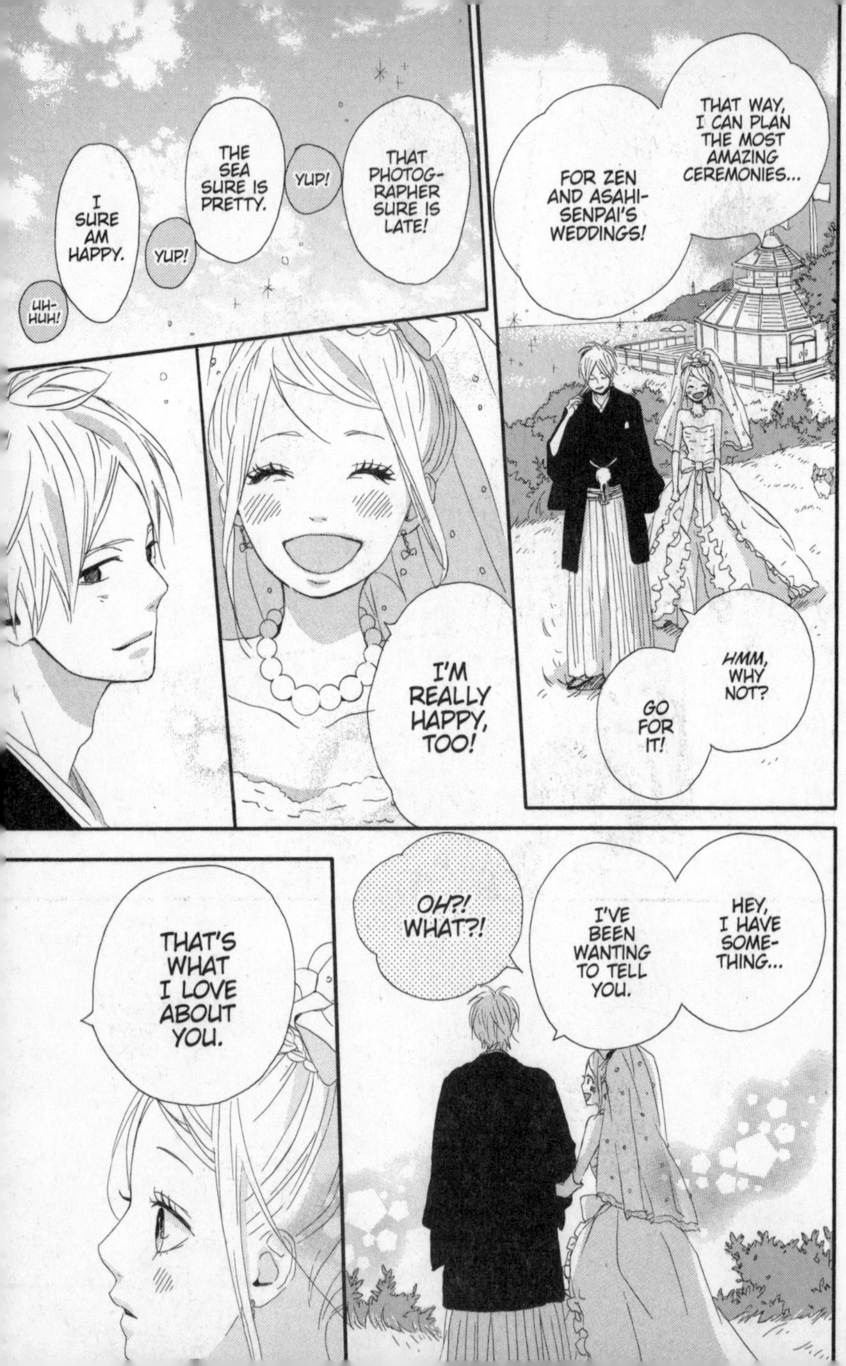
THAT WAY, I CAN PLAN THE MOST AMAZING CEREMONIES...
FOR ZEN AND ASAHI-SENPAI'S WEDDINGS!
HMM, WHY NOT?
GO FOR IT!
THAT PHOTOG-RAPHER SURE IS LATE!
YUP!
THE SEA SURE IS PRETTY.
YUP!
I SURE AM HAPPY.
UH-HUH!
I'M REALLY HAPPY, TOO!
HEY, I HAVE SOME-THING...
I'VE BEEN WANTING TO TELL YOU.
OH?! WHAT?!
THAT'S WHAT I LOVE ABOUT YOU.

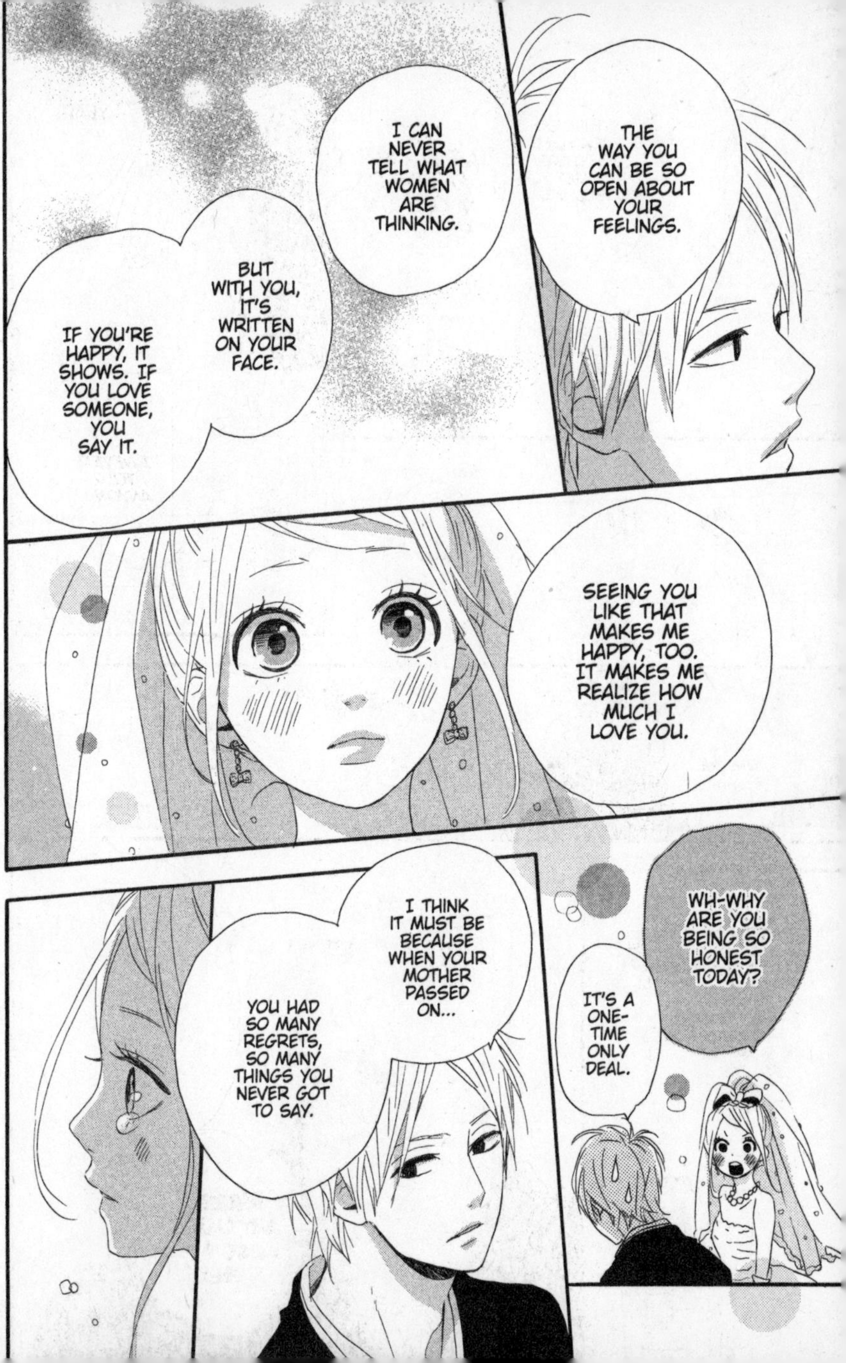
THE WAY YOU CAN BE SO OPEN ABOUT YOUR FEELINGS.
I CAN NEVER TELL WHAT WOMEN ARE THINKING.
BUT WITH YOU, IT'S WRITTEN ON YOUR FACE.
IF YOU'RE HAPPY, IT SHOWS. IF YOU LOVE SOMEONE, YOU SAY IT.
SEEING YOU LIKE THAT MAKES ME HAPPY, TOO. IT MAKES ME REALIZE HOW MUCH I LOVE YOU.
WH-WHY ARE YOU BEING SO HONEST TODAY?
IT'S A ONE-TIME ONLY DEAL.
I THINK IT MUST BE BECAUSE WHEN YOUR MOTHER PASSED ON...
YOU HAD SO MANY REGRETS, SO MANY THINGS YOU NEVER GOT TO SAY.

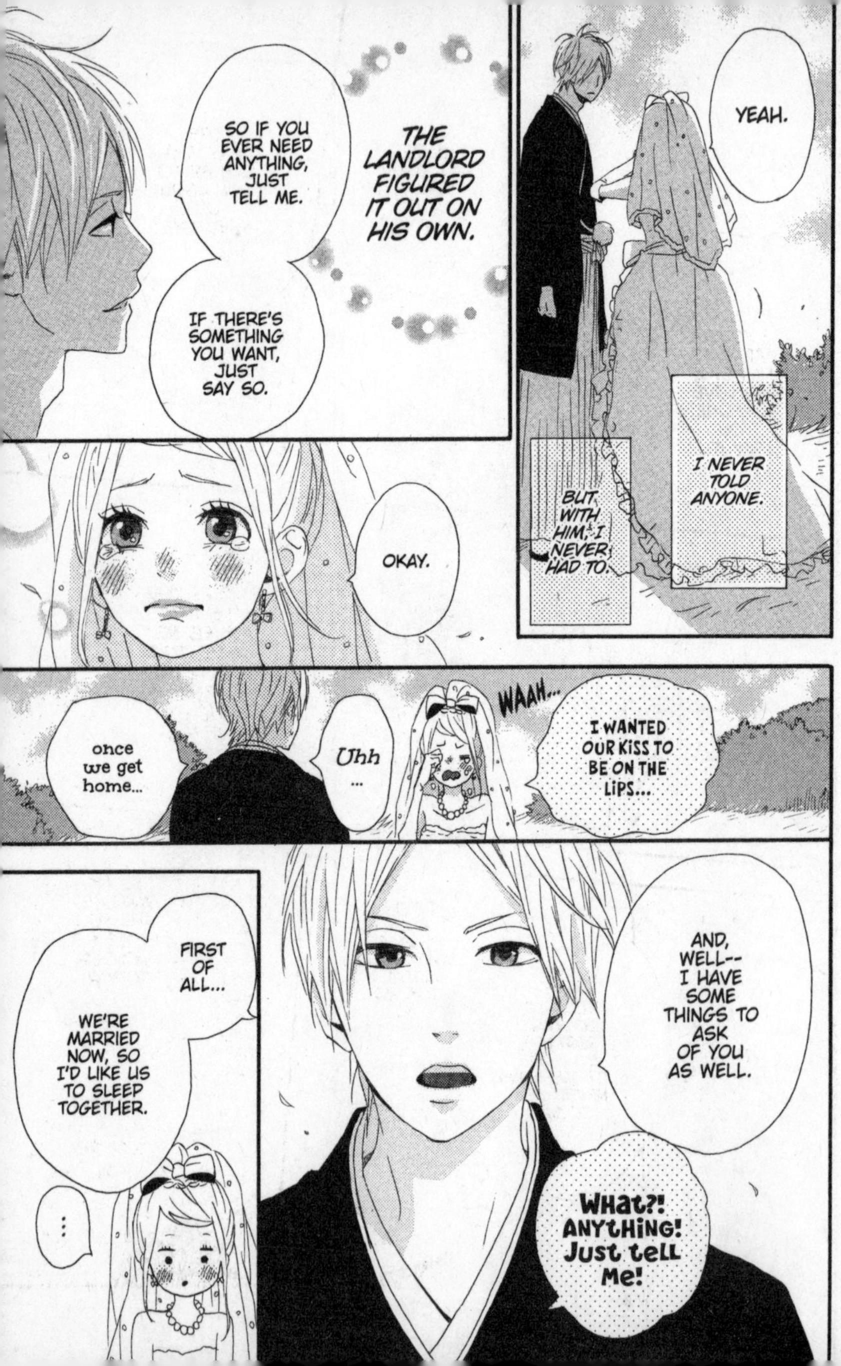
YEAH.
I NEVER TOLD ANYONE.
BUT, WITH HIM, I NEVER HAD TO.
THE LANDLORD FIGURED IT OUT ON HIS OWN.
SO IF YOU EVER NEED ANYTHING, JUST TELL ME.
IF THERE'S SOMETHING YOU WANT, JUST SAY SO.
OKAY.
WAAH...
I WANTED OUR KISS TO BE ON THE LIPS...
Uhh ...
once we get home...
AND, WELL-- I HAVE SOME THINGS TO ASK OF YOU AS WELL.
What?! ANYTHING! Just tell Me!
FIRST OF ALL...
WE'RE MARRIED NOW, SO I'D LIKE US TO SLEEP TOGETHER.
...

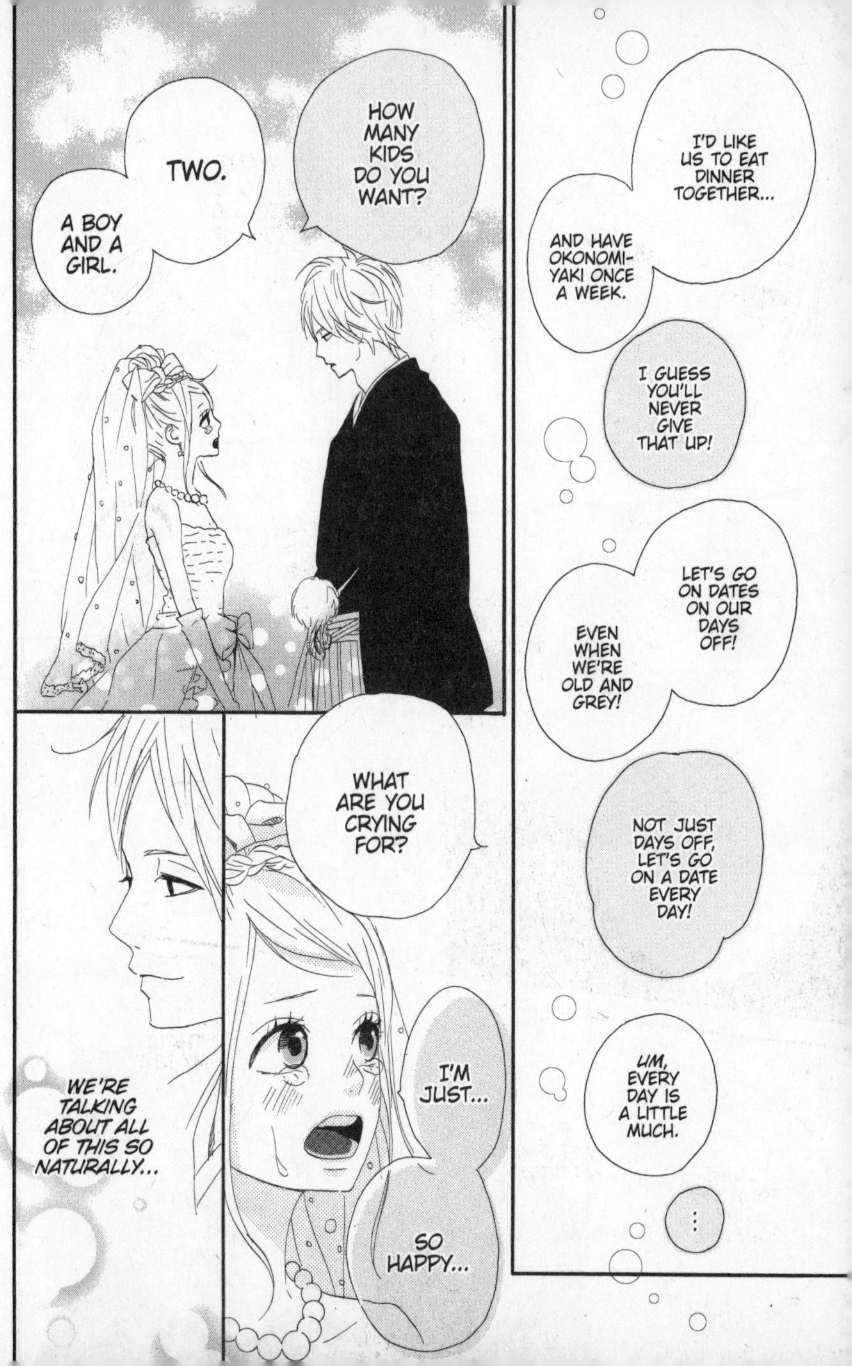

I'D LIKE US TO EAT DINNER TOGETHER...
AND HAVE OKONOMI-YAKI ONCE A WEEK.
I GUESS YOU'LL NEVER GIVE THAT UP!
LET'S GO ON DATES ON OUR DAYS OFF!
EVEN WHEN WE'RE OLD AND GREY!
NOT JUST DAYS OFF, LET'S GO ON A DATE EVERY DAY!
UM, EVERY DAY IS A LITTLE MUCH.
...
HOW MANY KIDS DO YOU WANT?
TWO.
A BOY AND A GIRL.
WHAT ARE YOU CRYING FOR?
I'M JUST...
SO HAPPY...
WE'RE TALKING ABOUT ALL OF THIS SO NATURALLY...

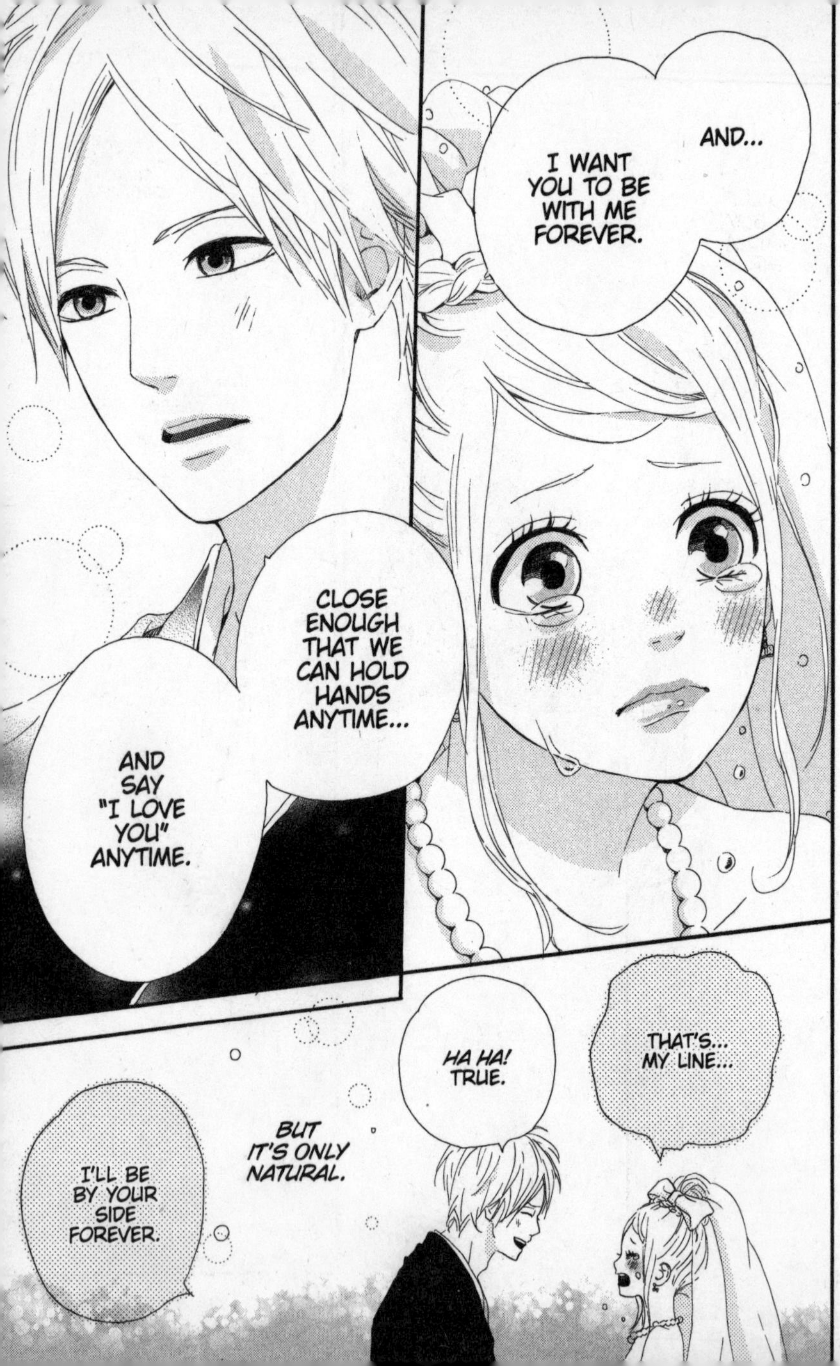
AND...
I WANT YOU TO BE WITH ME FOREVER.
CLOSE ENOUGH THAT WE CAN HOLD HANDS ANYTIME...
AND SAY "I LOVE YOU" ANYTIME.
THAT'S... MY LINE...
HA HA! TRUE.
BUT IT'S ONLY NATURAL.
I'LL BE BY YOUR SIDE FOREVER.

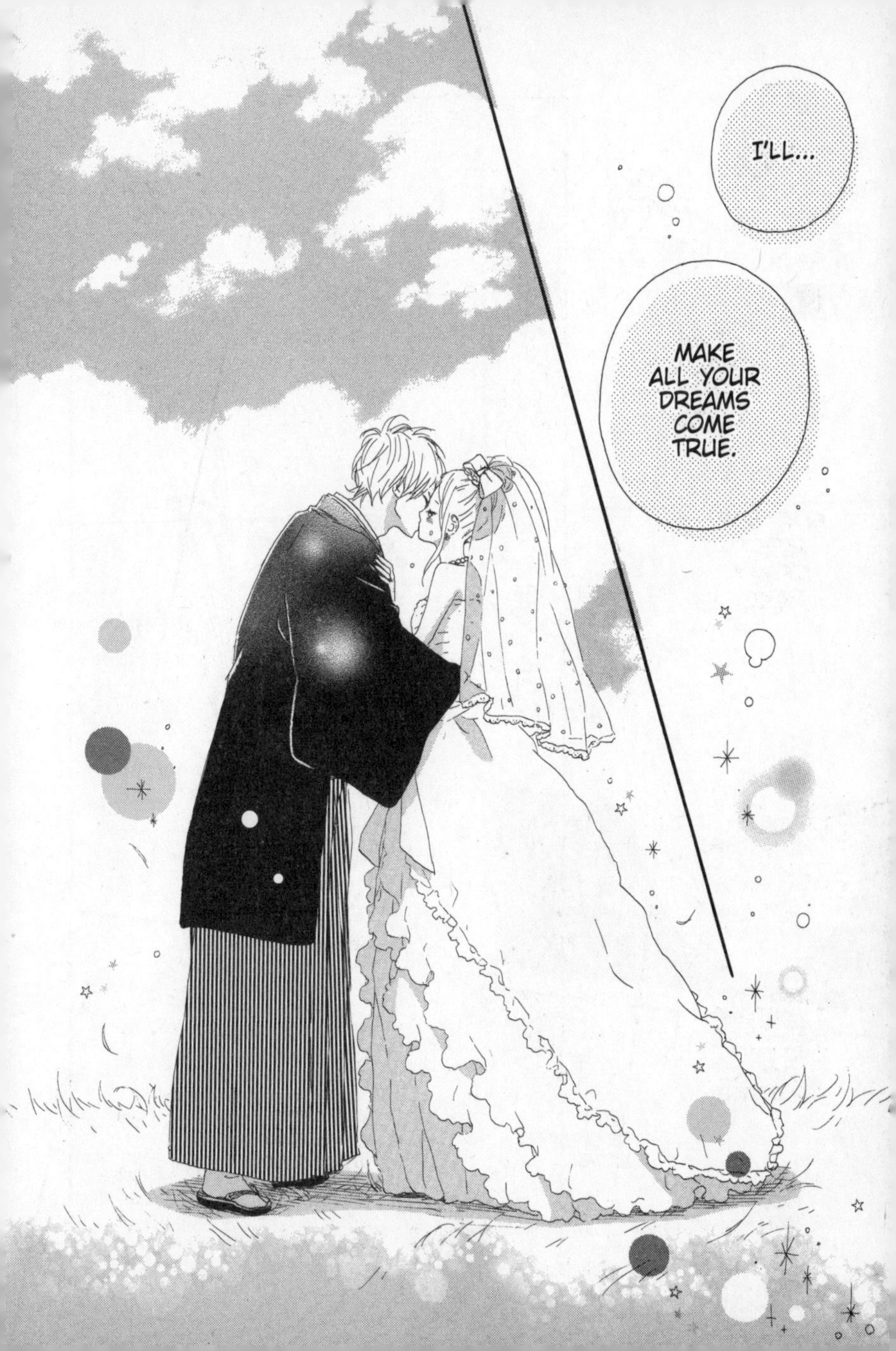
I'LL...
MAKE ALL YOUR DREAMS COME TRUE.

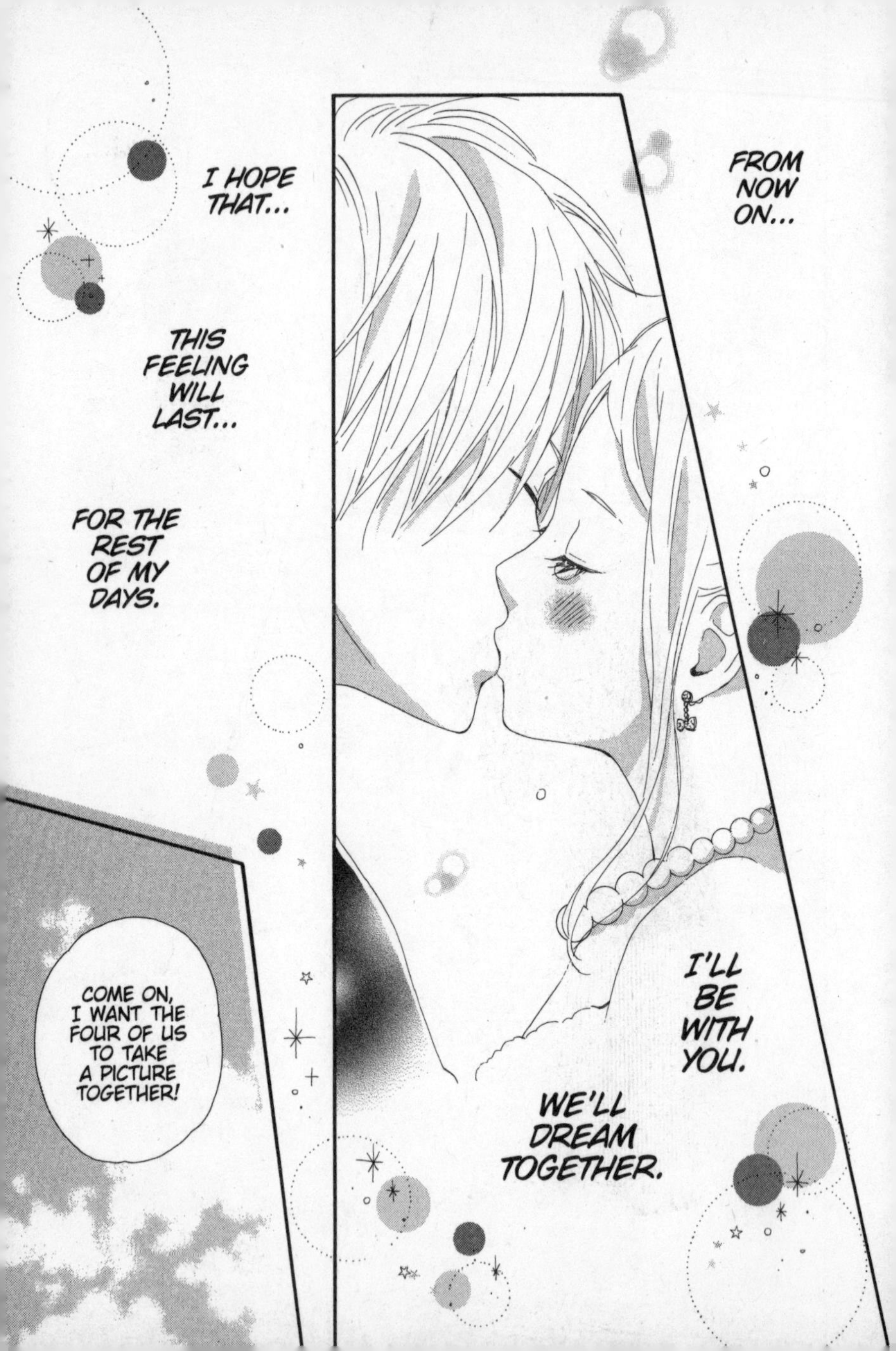
FROM NOW ON...
I'LL BE WITH YOU.
WE'LL DREAM TOGETHER.
I HOPE THAT...
THIS FEELING WILL LAST...
FOR THE REST OF MY DAYS.
COME ON, I WANT THE FOUR OF US TO TAKE A PICTURE TOGETHER!

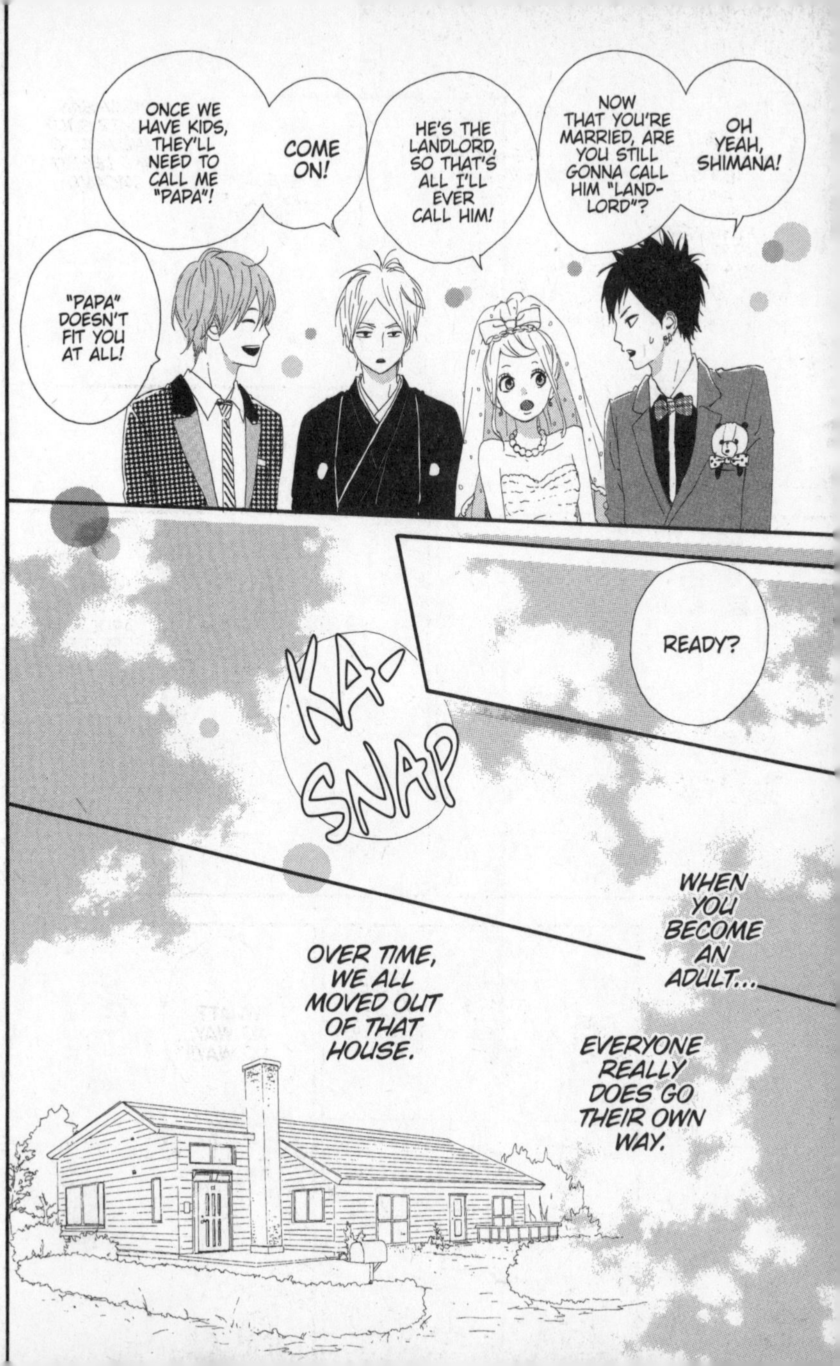
OH YEAH, SHIMANA!
NOW THAT YOU'RE MARRIED, ARE YOU STILL GONNA CALL HIM "LANDLORD"?
HE'S THE LANDLORD, SO THAT'S ALL I'LL EVER CALL HIM!
COME ON!
ONCE WE HAVE KIDS, THEY'LL NEED TO CALL ME "PAPA"!
"PAPA" DOESN'T FIT YOU AT ALL!
READY?
KA-SNAP
WHEN YOU BECOME AN ADULT...
EVERYONE REALLY DOES GO THEIR OWN WAY.
OVER TIME, WE ALL MOVED OUT OF THAT HOUSE.

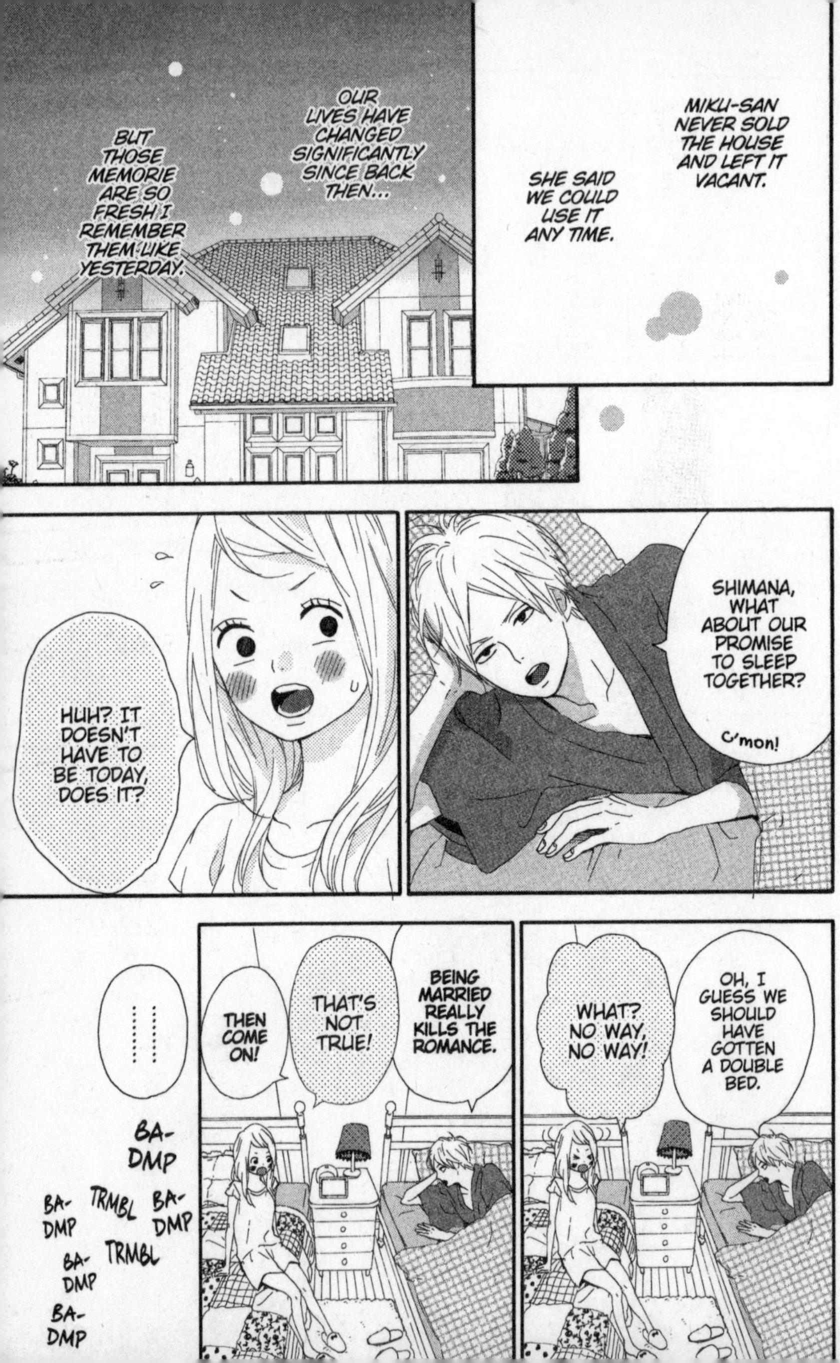
MIKU-SAN NEVER SOLD THE HOUSE AND LEFT IT VACANT.
SHE SAID WE COULD USE IT ANY TIME.
OUR LIVES HAVE CHANGED SIGNIFICANTLY SINCE BACK THEN...
BUT THOSE MEMORIE ARE SO FRESH I REMEMBER THEM LIKE YESTERDAY.
SHIMANA, WHAT ABOUT OUR PROMISE TO SLEEP TOGETHER?
C'mon!
HUH? IT DOESN'T HAVE TO BE TODAY, DOES IT?
OH, I GUESS WE SHOULD HAVE GOTTEN A DOUBLE BED.
WHAT? NO WAY, NO WAY!
BEING MARRIED REALLY KILLS THE ROMANCE.
THAT'S NOT TRUE!
THEN COME ON!
......
BA-DMP
BA-DMP
TRMBL
BA-DMP
BA-DMP
TRMBL
BA-DMP

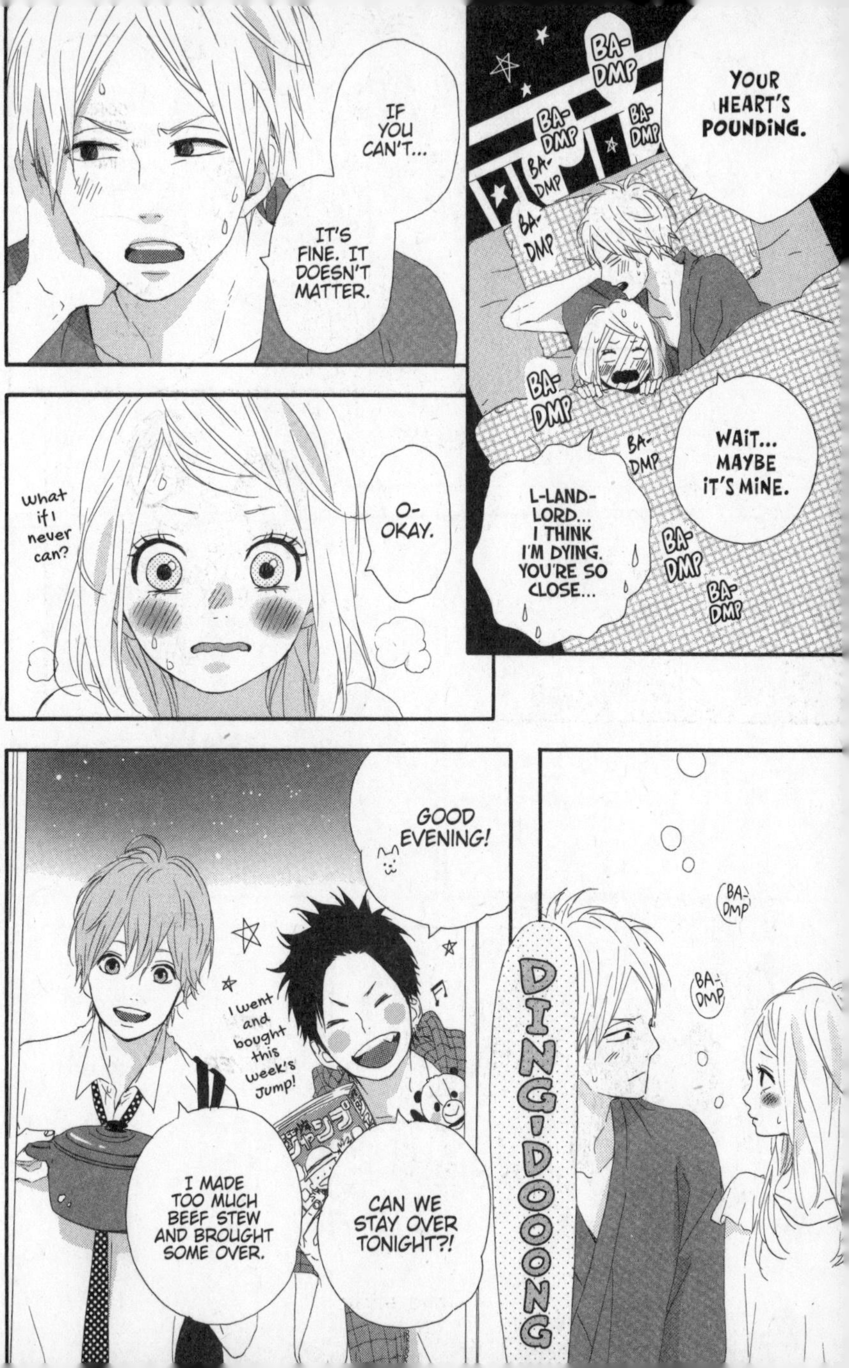
BA-DMP
YOUR HEART'S POUNDING.
BA-DMP
BA-DMP
BA-DMP
BA-DMP
BA-DMP
WAIT... MAYBE IT'S MINE.
BA-DMP
L-LANDLORD... I THINK I'M DYING. YOU'RE SO CLOSE...
BA-DMP
BA-DMP
IF YOU CAN'T...
IT'S FINE. IT DOESN'T MATTER.
O-OKAY.
What if I never can?
BA-DMP
BA-DMP
DING-DOOONG
GOOD EVENING!
I went and bought this week's Jump!
CAN WE STAY OVER TONIGHT?!
I MADE TOO MUCH BEEF STEW AND BROUGHT SOME OVER.

Magazine: Weekly Shonen Jump.

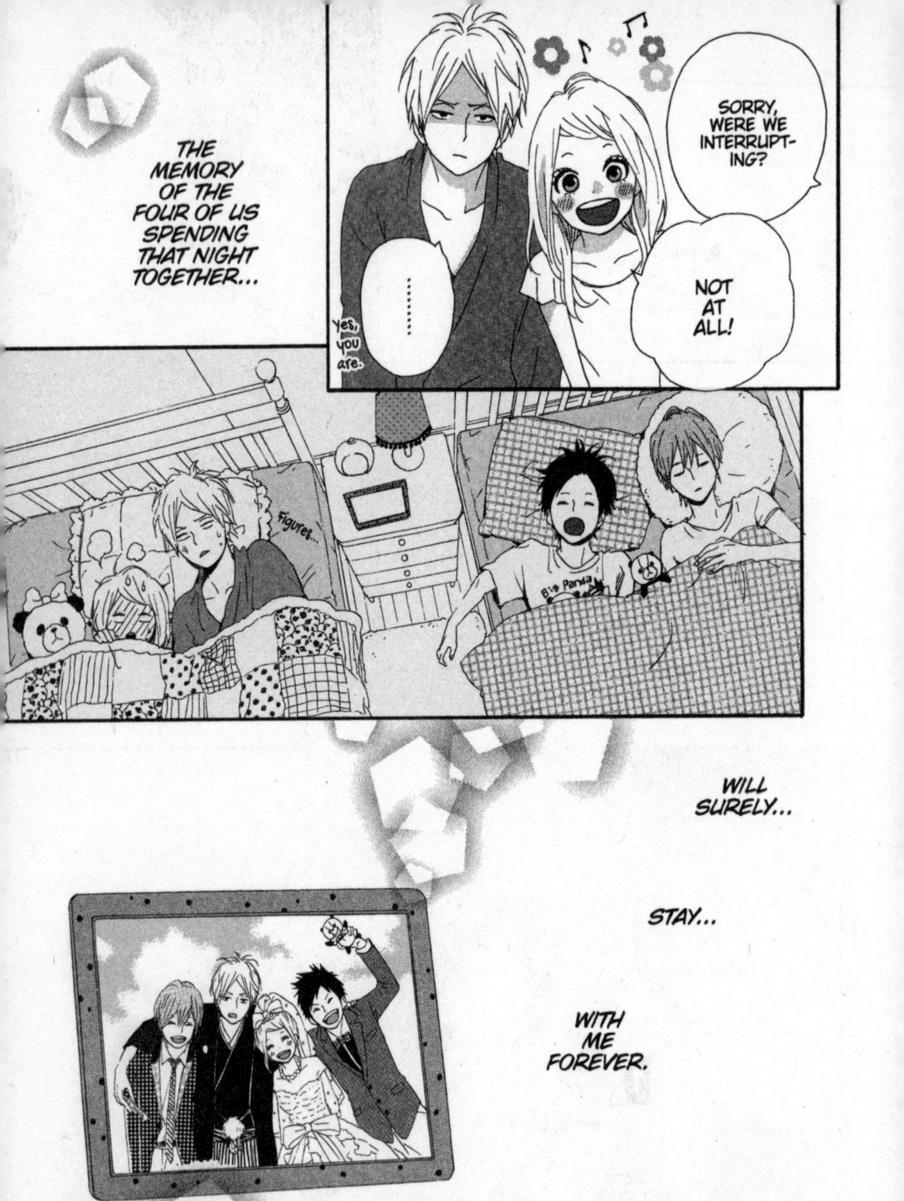
SORRY, WERE WE INTERRUPTING?
NOT AT ALL!
......
Yes, you are.
THE MEMORY OF THE FOUR OF US SPENDING THAT NIGHT TOGETHER...
Figures...
WILL SURELY...
STAY...
WITH ME FOREVER.

‹‹the end››

Thank you

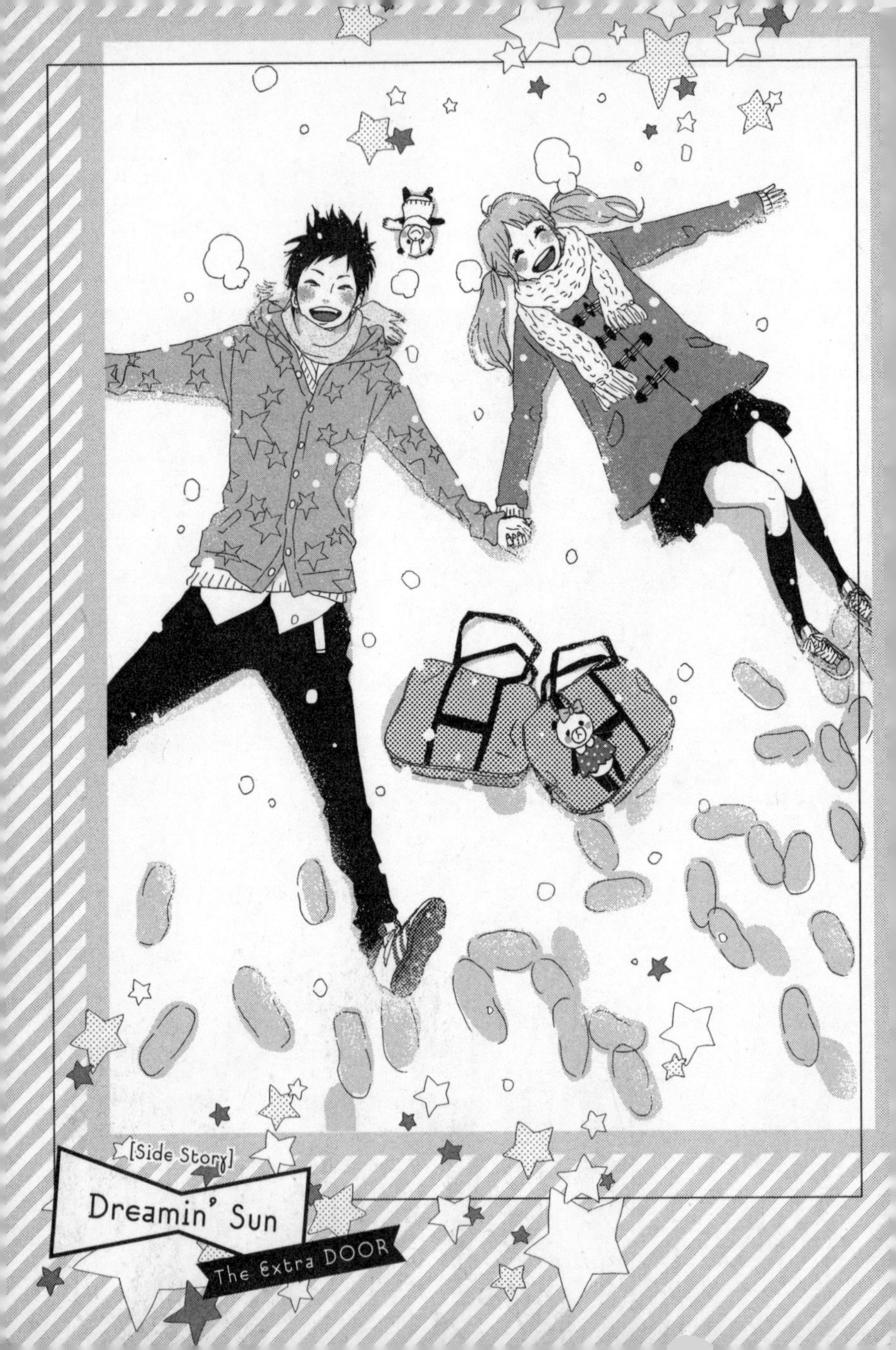
[Side Story]
Dreamin' Sun
The Extra DOOR

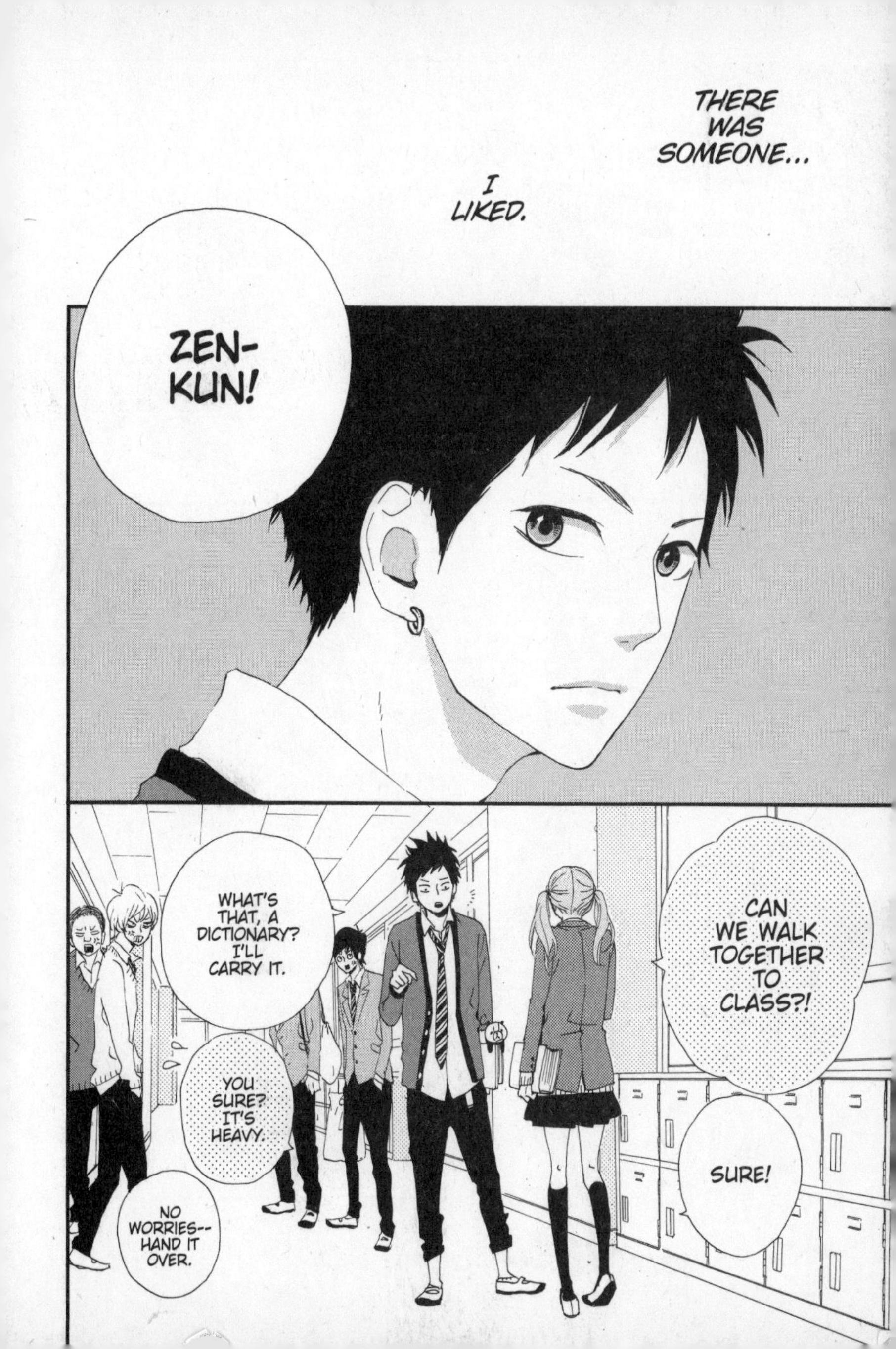
THERE WAS SOMEONE...
I LIKED.
ZEN-KUN!
CAN WE WALK TOGETHER TO CLASS?!
SURE!
WHAT'S THAT, A DICTIONARY? I'LL CARRY IT.
YOU SURE? IT'S HEAVY.
NO WORRIES-- HAND IT OVER.

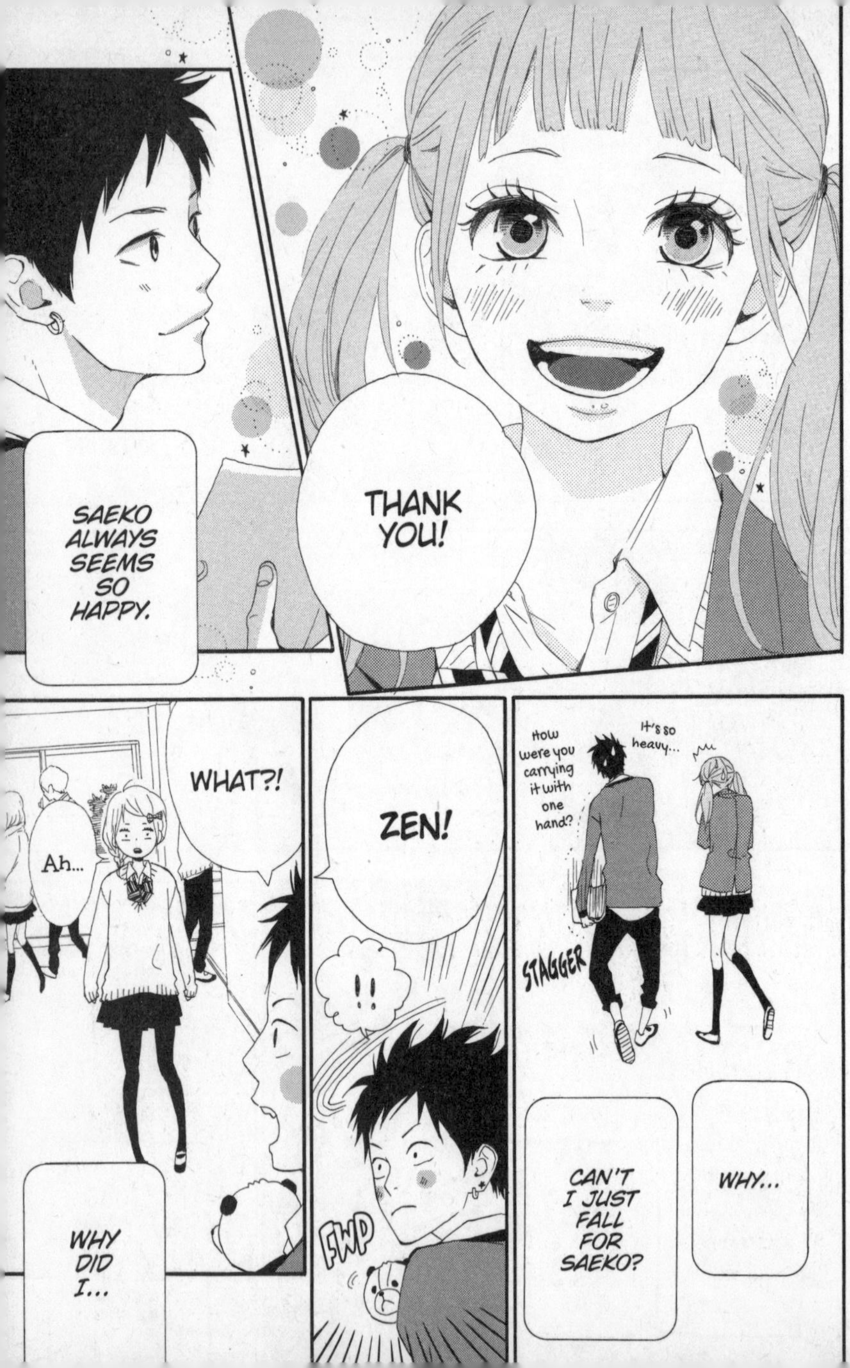
THANK YOU!
SAEKO ALWAYS SEEMS SO HAPPY.
It's so heavy...
How were you carrying it with one hand?
STAGGER
WHY...
CAN'T I JUST FALL FOR SAEKO?
ZEN!
!!
FWP
WHAT?!
Ah...
WHY DID I...

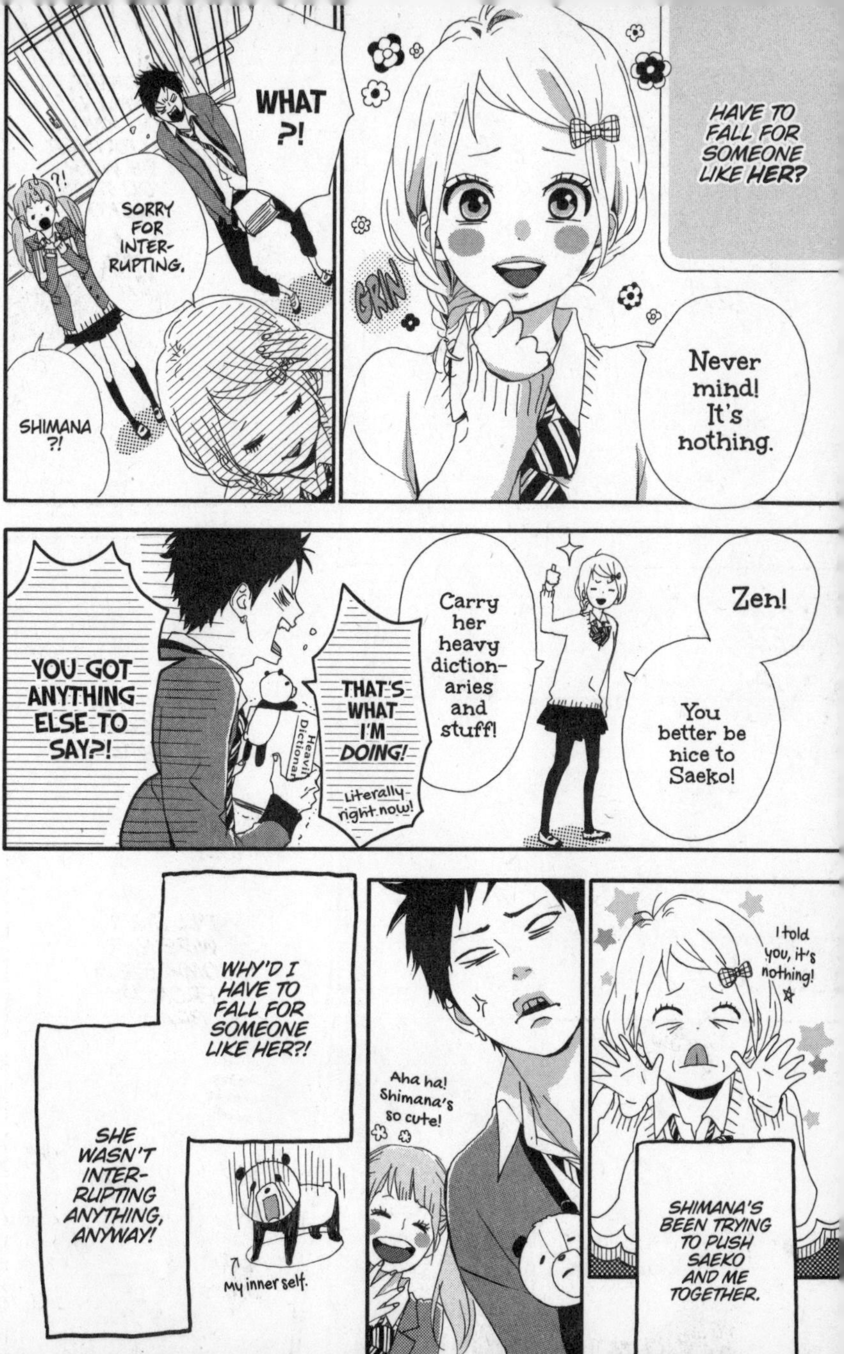
HAVE TO FALL FOR SOMEONE LIKE HER?
GRIN
Never mind! It's nothing.
WHAT?!
SORRY FOR INTER-RUPTING.
?!
SHIMANA?!
Zen!
You better be nice to Saeko!
Carry her heavy diction-aries and stuff!
THAT'S WHAT I'M DOING!
Literally right now!
YOU GOT ANYTHING ELSE TO SAY?!
I told you, it's nothing!
SHIMANA'S BEEN TRYING TO PUSH SAEKO AND ME TOGETHER.
Aha ha! Shimana's so cute!
WHY'D I HAVE TO FALL FOR SOMEONE LIKE HER?!
My inner self.
SHE WASN'T INTER-RUPTING ANYTHING, ANYWAY!

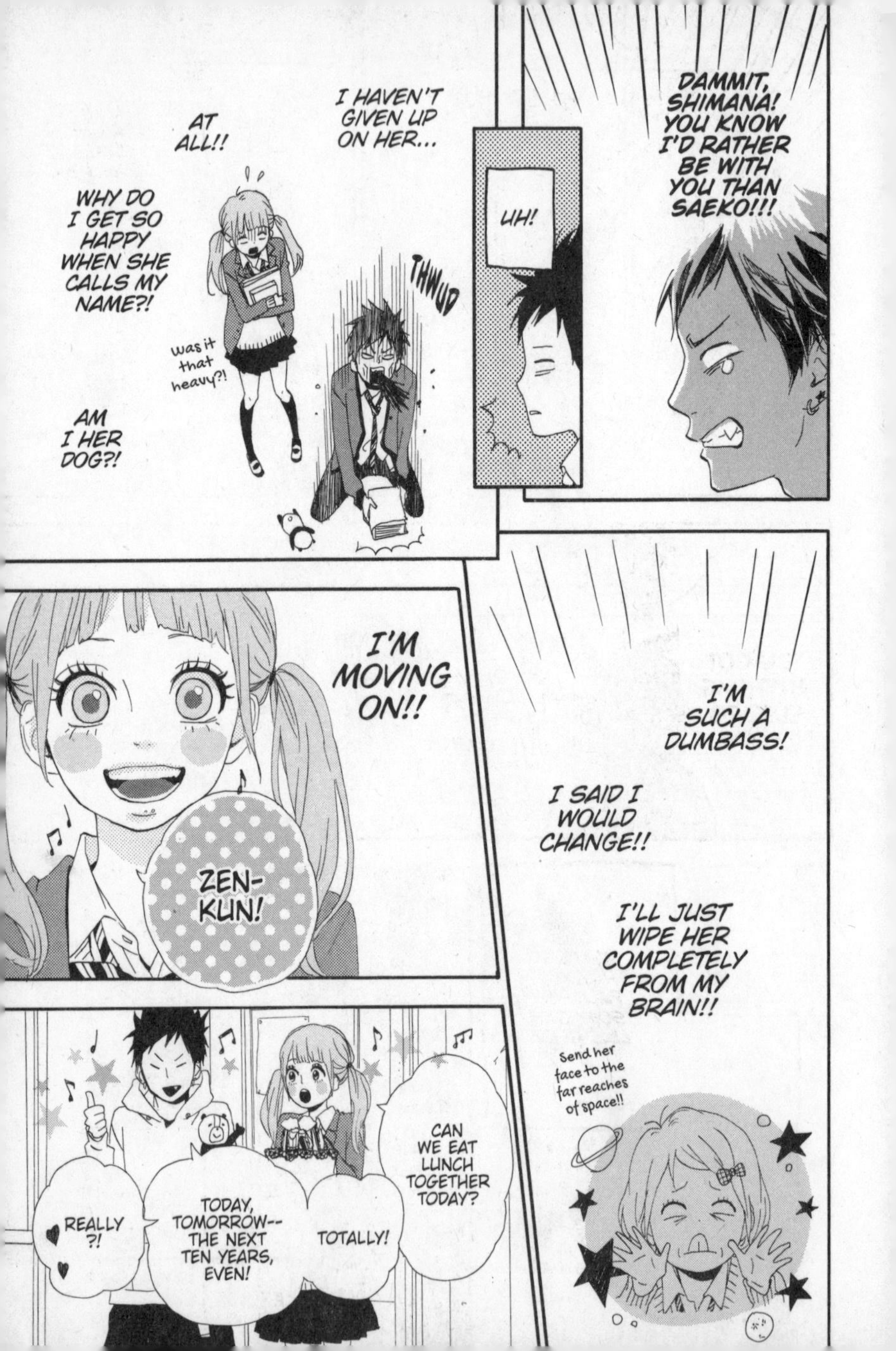
DAMMIT, SHIMANA! YOU KNOW I'D RATHER BE WITH YOU THAN SAEKO!!!
UH!
THWUD
I HAVEN'T GIVEN UP ON HER...
AT ALL!!
WHY DO I GET SO HAPPY WHEN SHE CALLS MY NAME?!
was it that heavy?!
AM I HER DOG?!
I'M SUCH A DUMBASS!
I SAID I WOULD CHANGE!!
I'LL JUST WIPE HER COMPLETELY FROM MY BRAIN!!
Send her face to the far reaches of space!!
I'M MOVING ON!!
ZEN-KUN!
CAN WE EAT LUNCH TOGETHER TODAY?
TOTALLY!
TODAY, TOMORROW-- THE NEXT TEN YEARS, EVEN!
REALLY?!

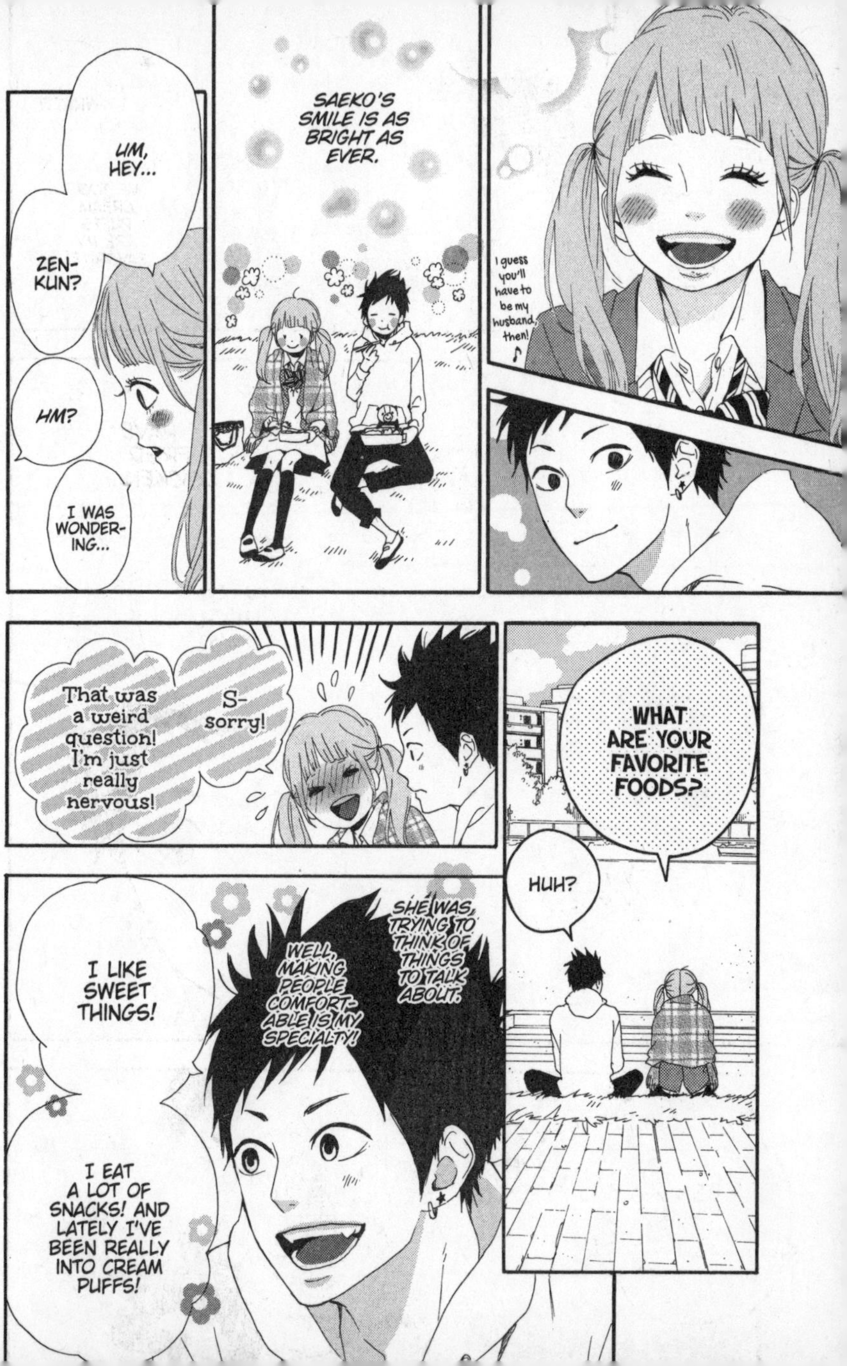
I guess you'll have to be my husband, then! ♪
SAEKO'S SMILE IS AS BRIGHT AS EVER.
UM, HEY...
ZEN-KUN?
HM?
I WAS WONDERING...
WHAT ARE YOUR FAVORITE FOODS?
HUH?
S-sorry!
That was a weird question! I'm just really nervous!
SHE WAS TRYING TO THINK OF THINGS TO TALK ABOUT.
WELL, MAKING PEOPLE COMFORTABLE IS MY SPECIALTY!
I LIKE SWEET THINGS!
I EAT A LOT OF SNACKS! AND LATELY I'VE BEEN REALLY INTO CREAM PUFFS!

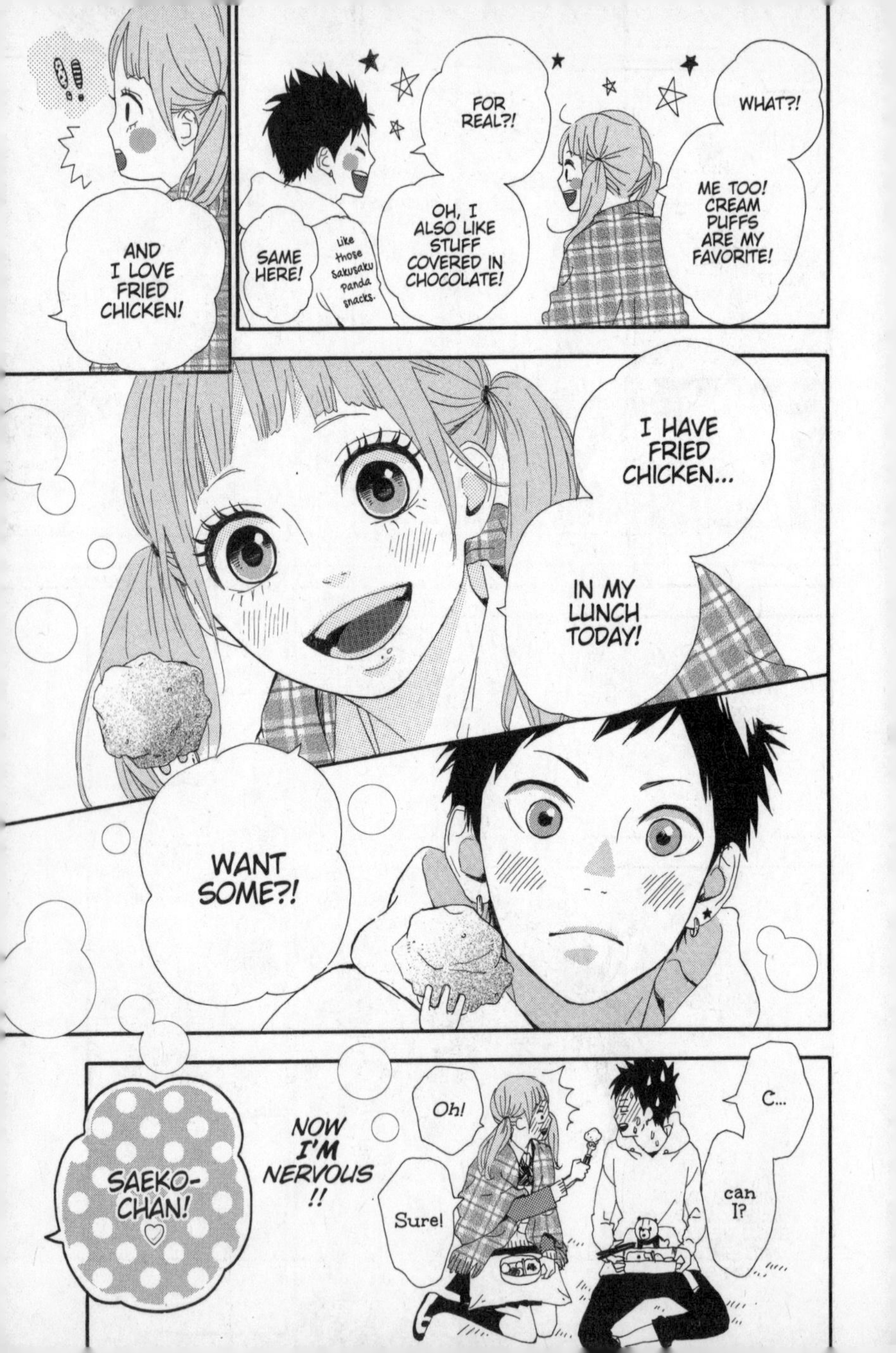
WHAT?!
ME TOO! CREAM PUFFS ARE MY FAVORITE!
FOR REAL?!
OH, I ALSO LIKE STUFF COVERED IN CHOCOLATE!
Like those Sakusaku Panda snacks.
SAME HERE!
AND I LOVE FRIED CHICKEN!
I HAVE FRIED CHICKEN...
IN MY LUNCH TODAY!
WANT SOME?!
C...
can I?
Oh!
Sure!
NOW I'M NERVOUS !!
SAEKO-CHAN! ♡

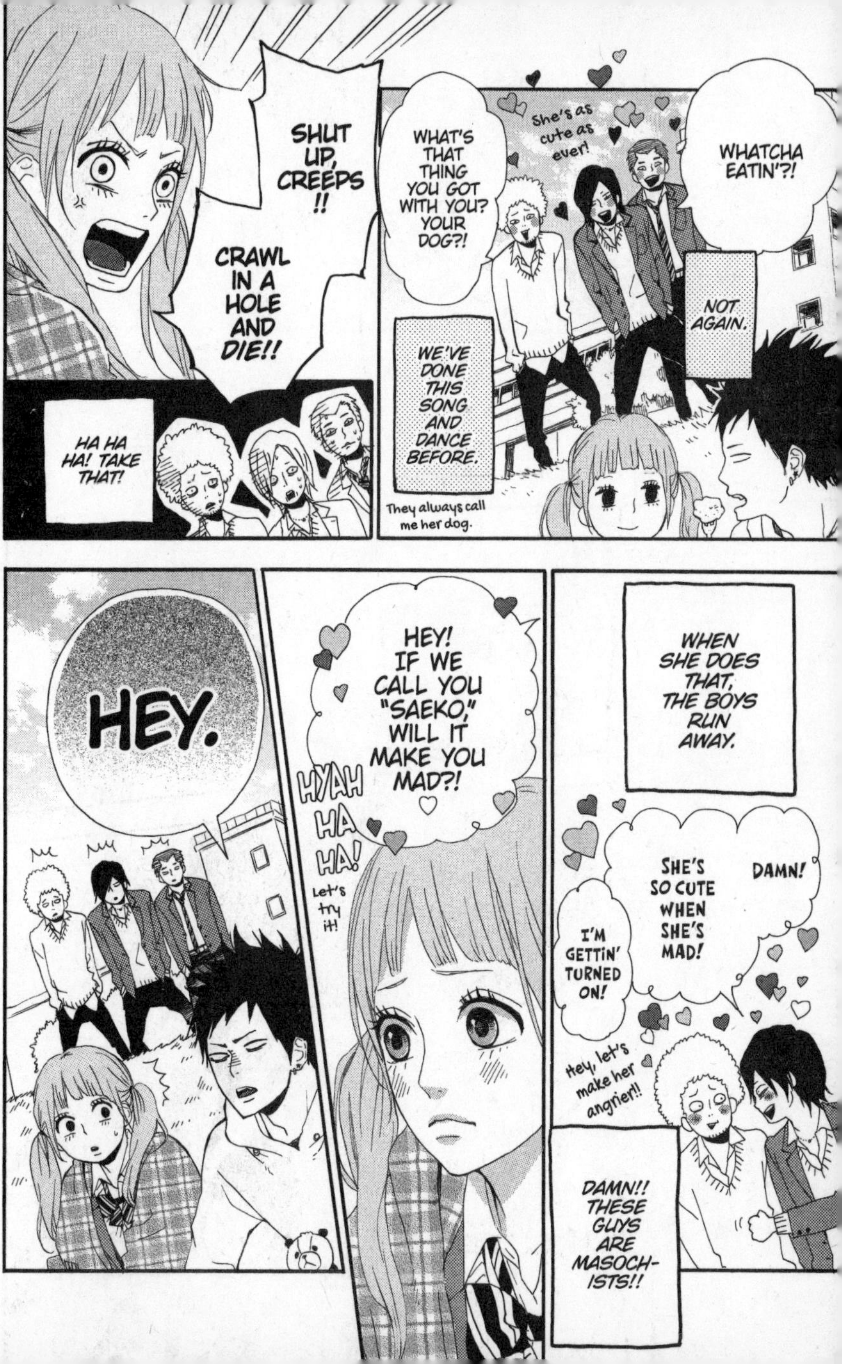
WHATCHA EATIN'?!
She's as cute as ever!
WHAT'S THAT THING YOU GOT WITH YOU? YOUR DOG?!
NOT AGAIN.
WE'VE DONE THIS SONG AND DANCE BEFORE.
They always call me her dog.
SHUT UP, CREEPS!!
CRAWL IN A HOLE AND DIE!!
HA HA HA! TAKE THAT!
WHEN SHE DOES THAT, THE BOYS RUN AWAY.
DAMN!
SHE'S SO CUTE WHEN SHE'S MAD!
I'M GETTIN' TURNED ON!
Hey, let's make her angrier!!
DAMN!! THESE GUYS ARE MASOCHISTS!!
HEY! IF WE CALL YOU "SAEKO," WILL IT MAKE YOU MAD?!
HYAH HA HA!
Let's try it!
HEY.

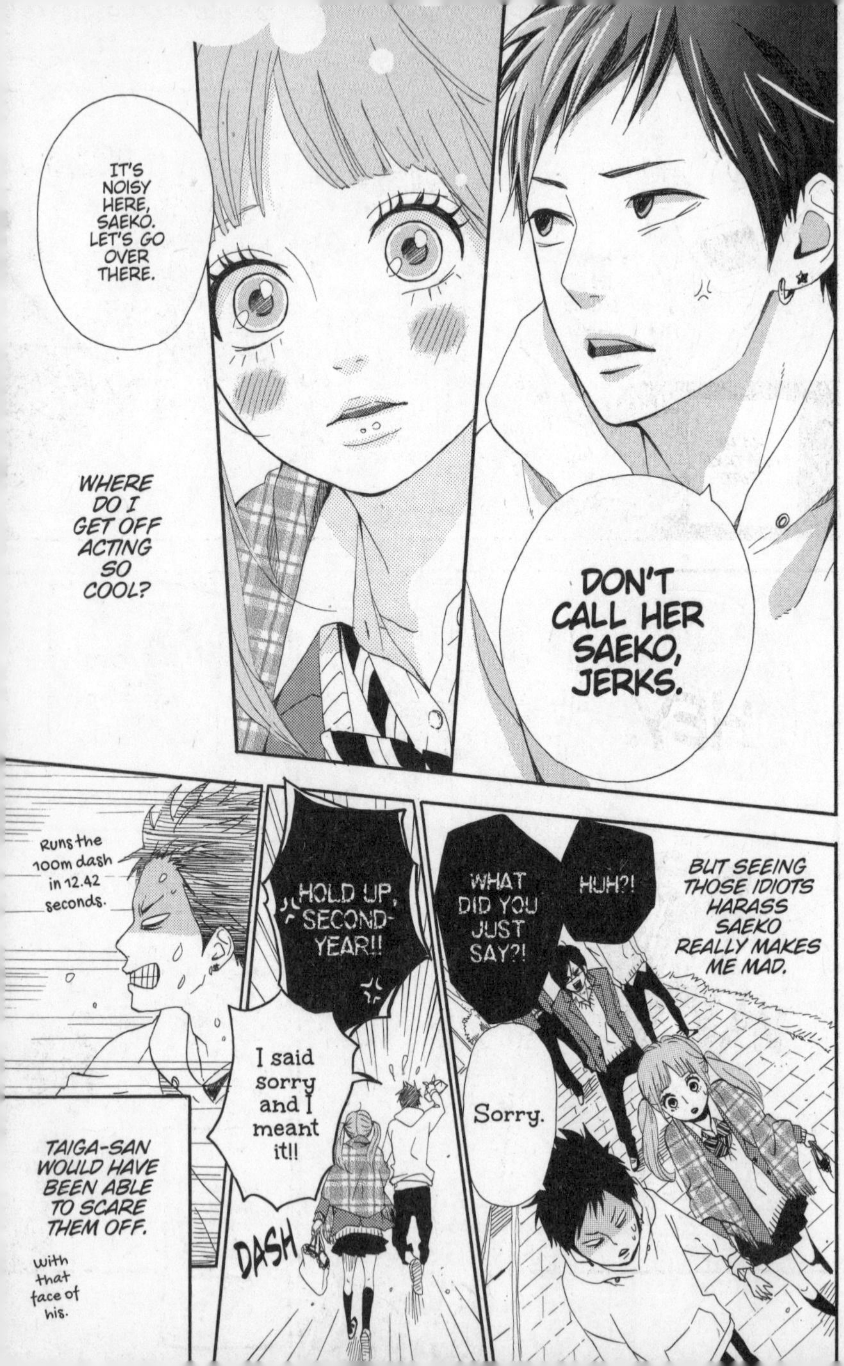
IT'S NOISY HERE, SAEKO. LET'S GO OVER THERE.
DON'T CALL HER SAEKO, JERKS.
WHERE DO I GET OFF ACTING SO COOL?
BUT SEEING THOSE IDIOTS HARASS SAEKO REALLY MAKES ME MAD.
HUH?!
WHAT DID YOU JUST SAY?!
Sorry.
HOLD UP, SECOND-YEAR!!
I said sorry and I meant it!!
DASH
Runs the 100m dash in 12.42 seconds.
TAIGA-SAN WOULD HAVE BEEN ABLE TO SCARE THEM OFF.
With that face of his.

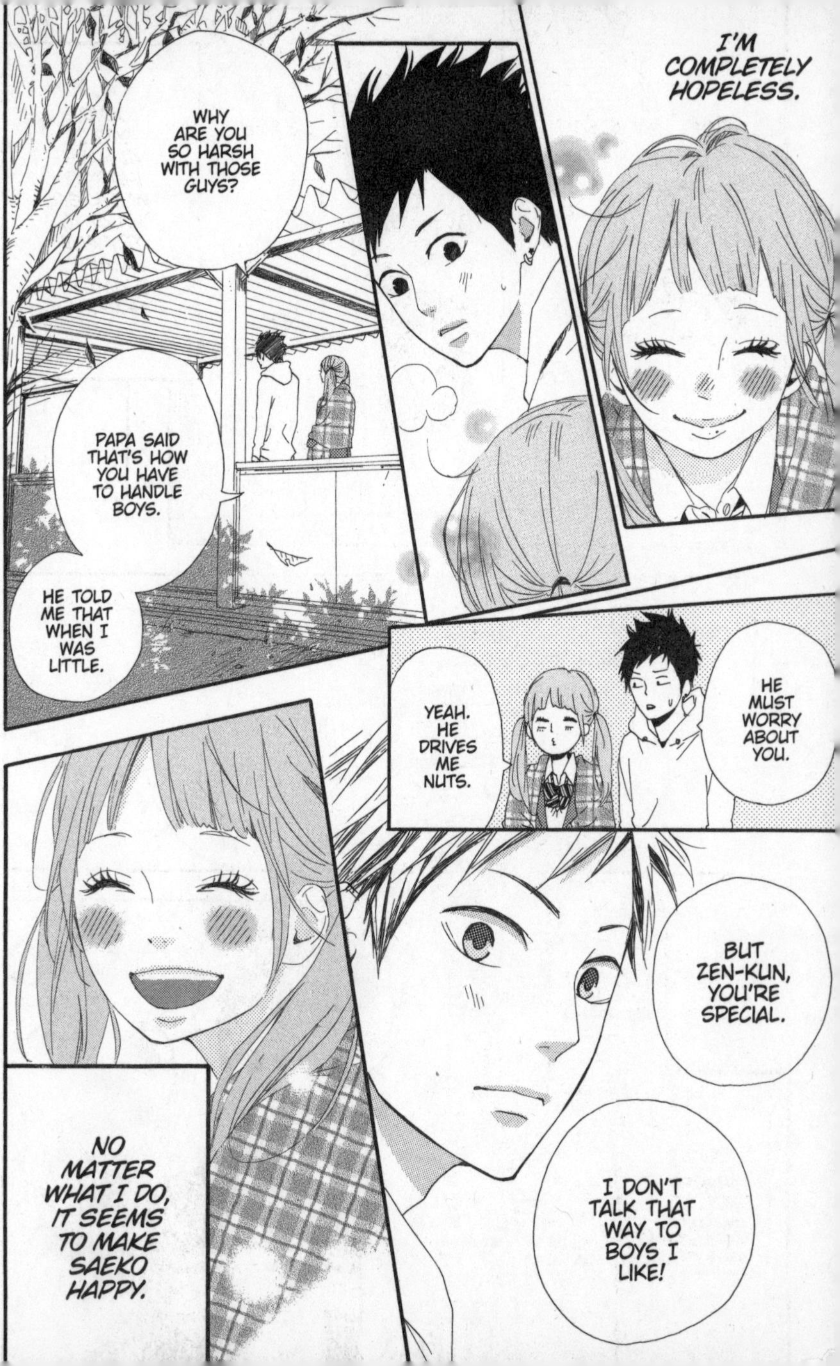
I'M COMPLETELY HOPELESS.
WHY ARE YOU SO HARSH WITH THOSE GUYS?
PAPA SAID THAT'S HOW YOU HAVE TO HANDLE BOYS.
HE TOLD ME THAT WHEN I WAS LITTLE.
HE MUST WORRY ABOUT YOU.
YEAH. HE DRIVES ME NUTS.
BUT ZEN-KUN, YOU'RE SPECIAL.
I DON'T TALK THAT WAY TO BOYS I LIKE!
NO MATTER WHAT I DO, IT SEEMS TO MAKE SAEKO HAPPY.

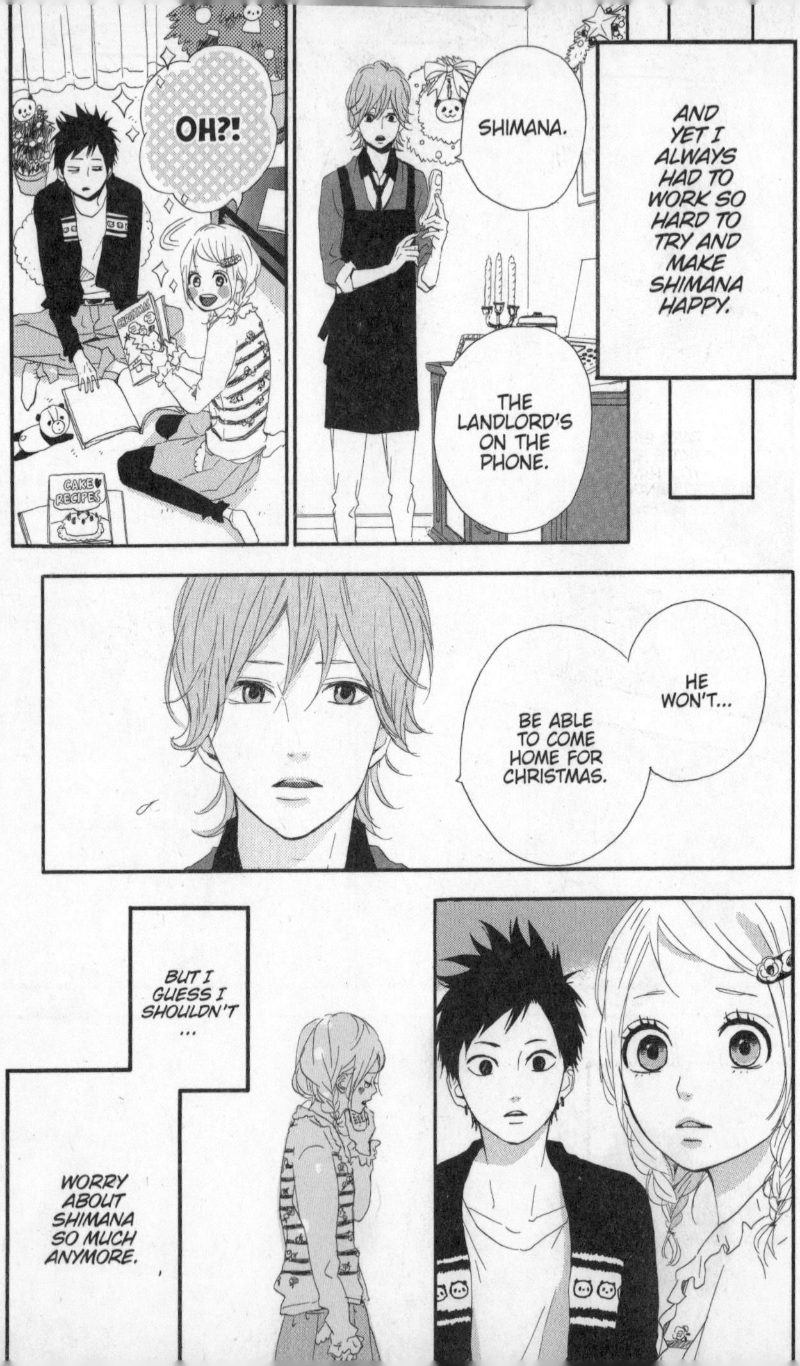
AND YET I ALWAYS HAD TO WORK SO HARD TO TRY AND MAKE SHIMANA HAPPY.
SHIMANA.
THE LANDLORD'S ON THE PHONE.
OH?!
CHRISTMAS
CAKE RECIPES
HE WON'T...
BE ABLE TO COME HOME FOR CHRISTMAS.
BUT I GUESS I SHOULDN'T ...
WORRY ABOUT SHIMANA SO MUCH ANYMORE.

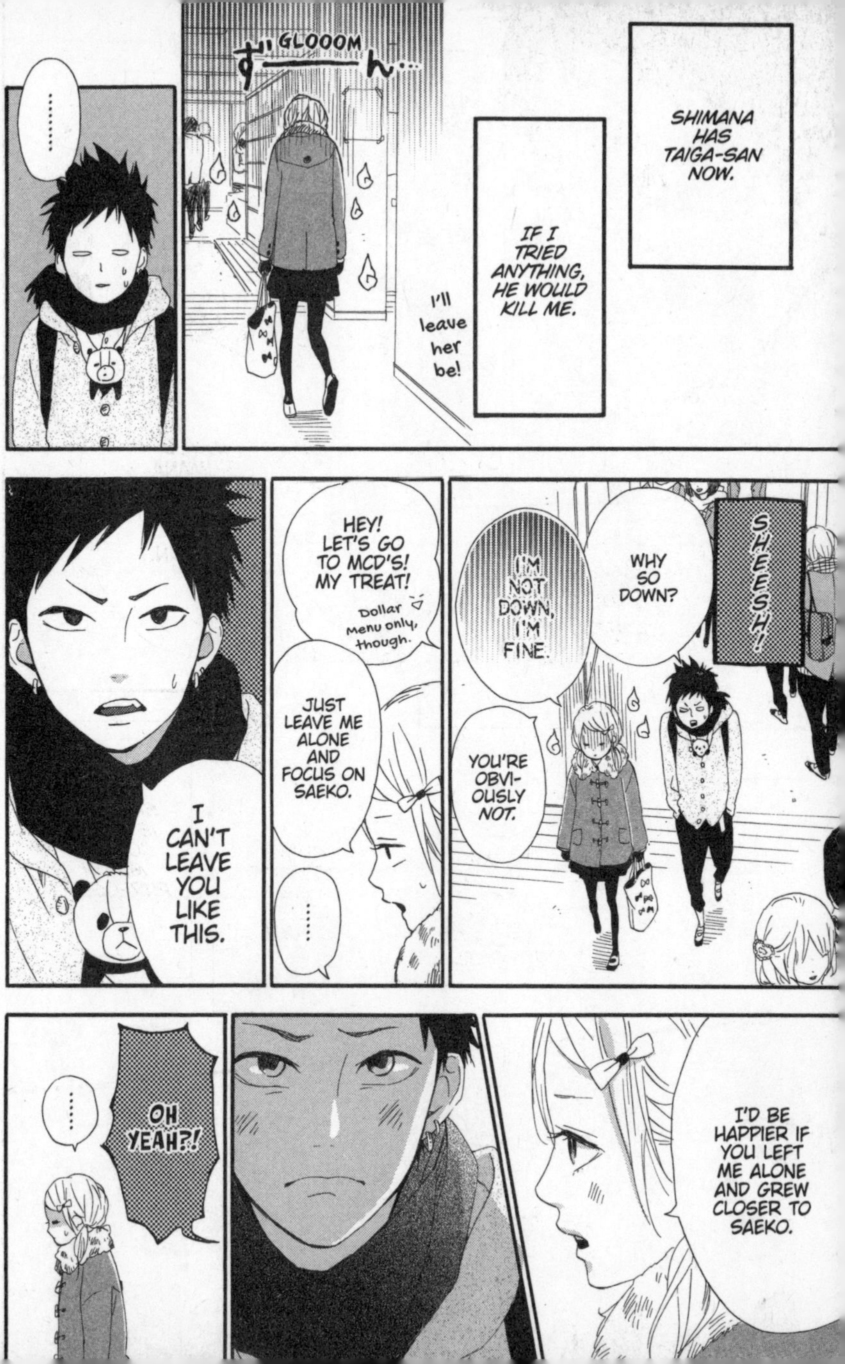
SHIMANA HAS TAIGA-SAN NOW.
IF I TRIED ANYTHING, HE WOULD KILL ME.
I'll leave her be!
ずーん…
GLOOOM
……
SHEESH!
WHY SO DOWN?
I'M NOT DOWN, I'M FINE.
YOU'RE OBVIOUSLY NOT.
HEY! LET'S GO TO MCD'S! MY TREAT!
Dollar Menu only, though.
JUST LEAVE ME ALONE AND FOCUS ON SAEKO.
……
I CAN'T LEAVE YOU LIKE THIS.
I'D BE HAPPIER IF YOU LEFT ME ALONE AND GREW CLOSER TO SAEKO.
OH YEAH?!
……

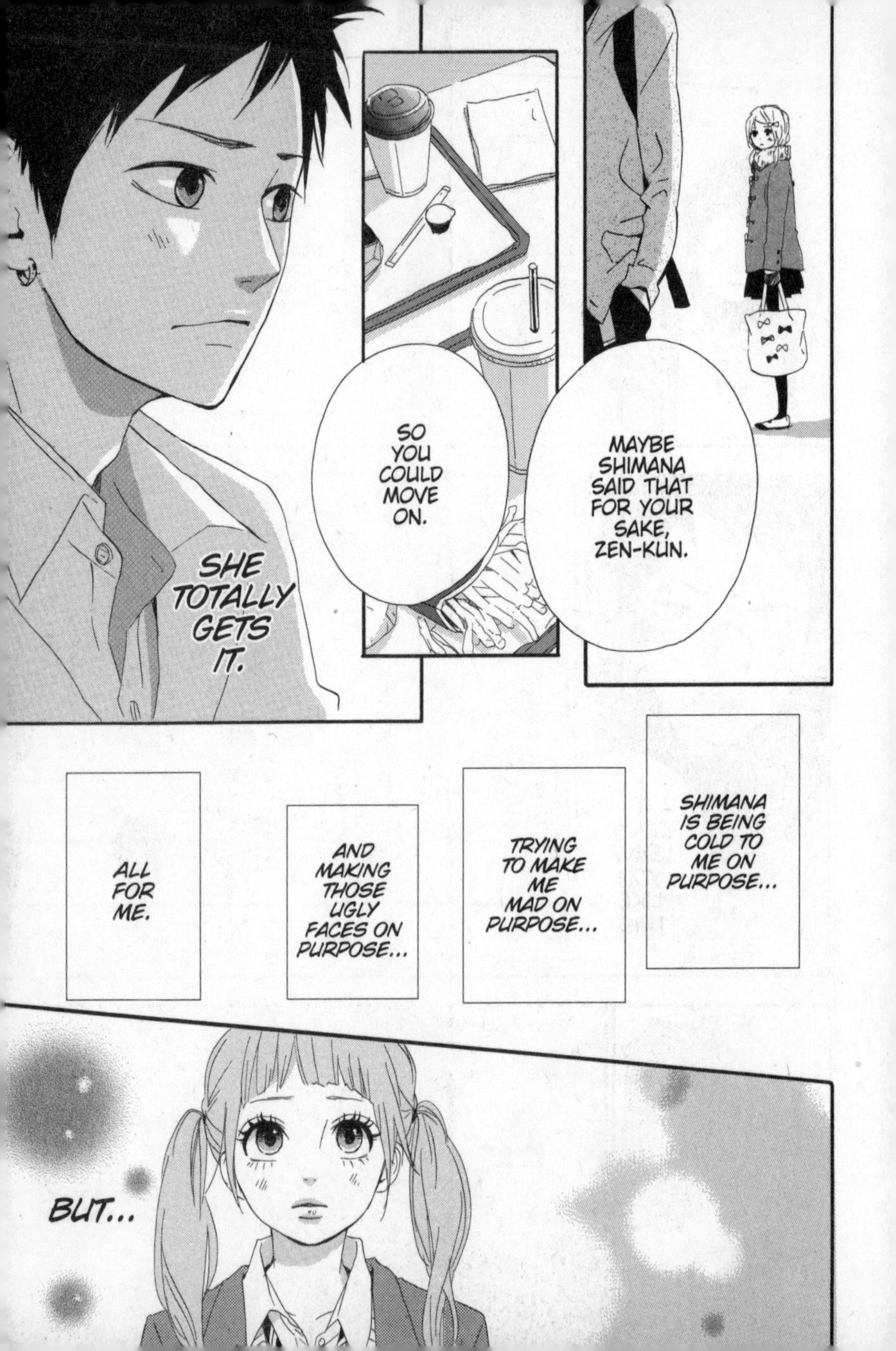
MAYBE SHIMANA SAID THAT FOR YOUR SAKE, ZEN-KUN.
SO YOU COULD MOVE ON.
SHE TOTALLY GETS IT.
SHIMANA IS BEING COLD TO ME ON PURPOSE...
TRYING TO MAKE ME MAD ON PURPOSE...
AND MAKING THOSE UGLY FACES ON PURPOSE...
ALL FOR ME.
BUT...

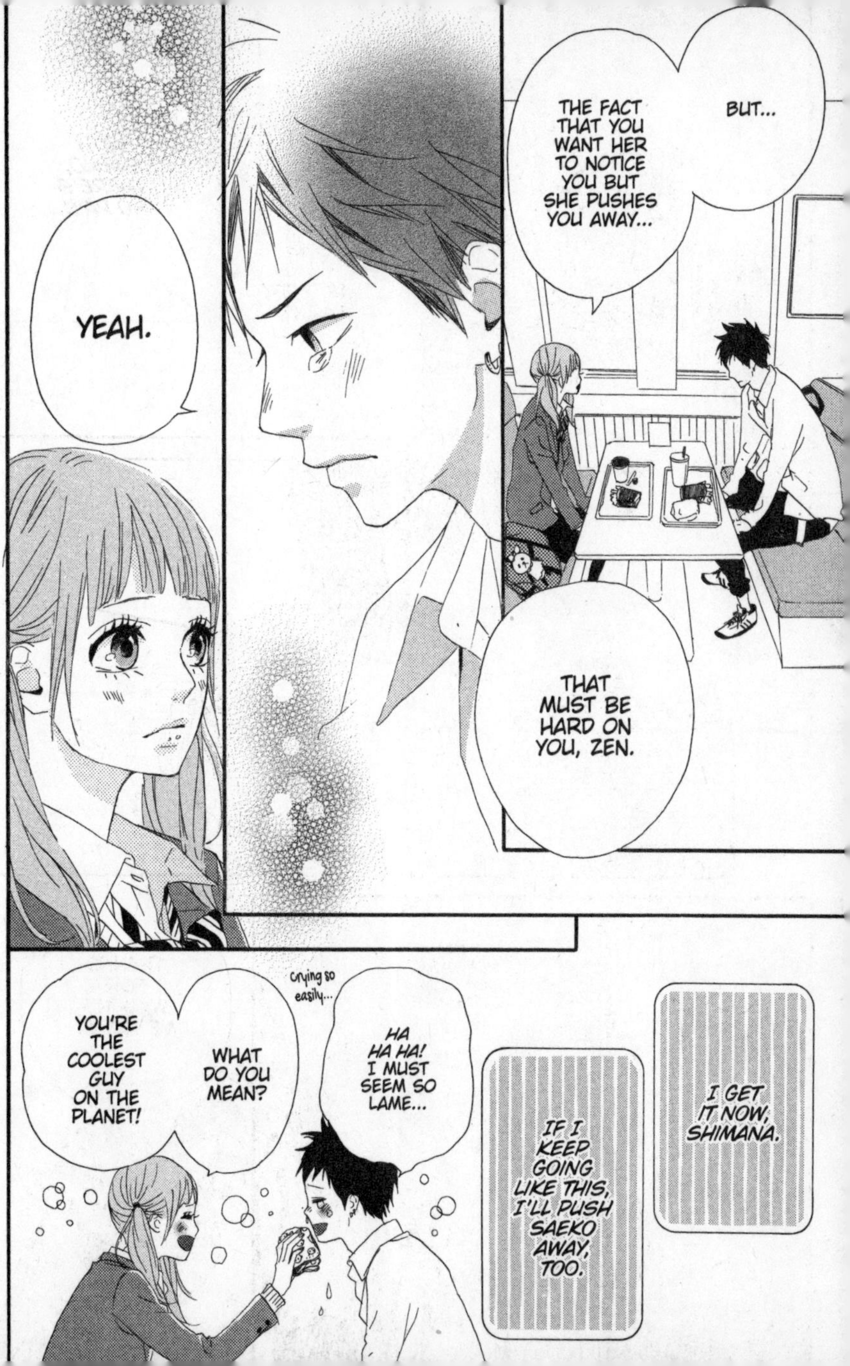
BUT...
THE FACT THAT YOU WANT HER TO NOTICE YOU BUT SHE PUSHES YOU AWAY...
THAT MUST BE HARD ON YOU, ZEN.
YEAH.
I GET IT NOW, SHIMANA.
IF I KEEP GOING LIKE THIS, I'LL PUSH SAEKO AWAY, TOO.
HA HA HA! I MUST SEEM SO LAME...
Crying so easily...
WHAT DO YOU MEAN?
YOU'RE THE COOLEST GUY ON THE PLANET!

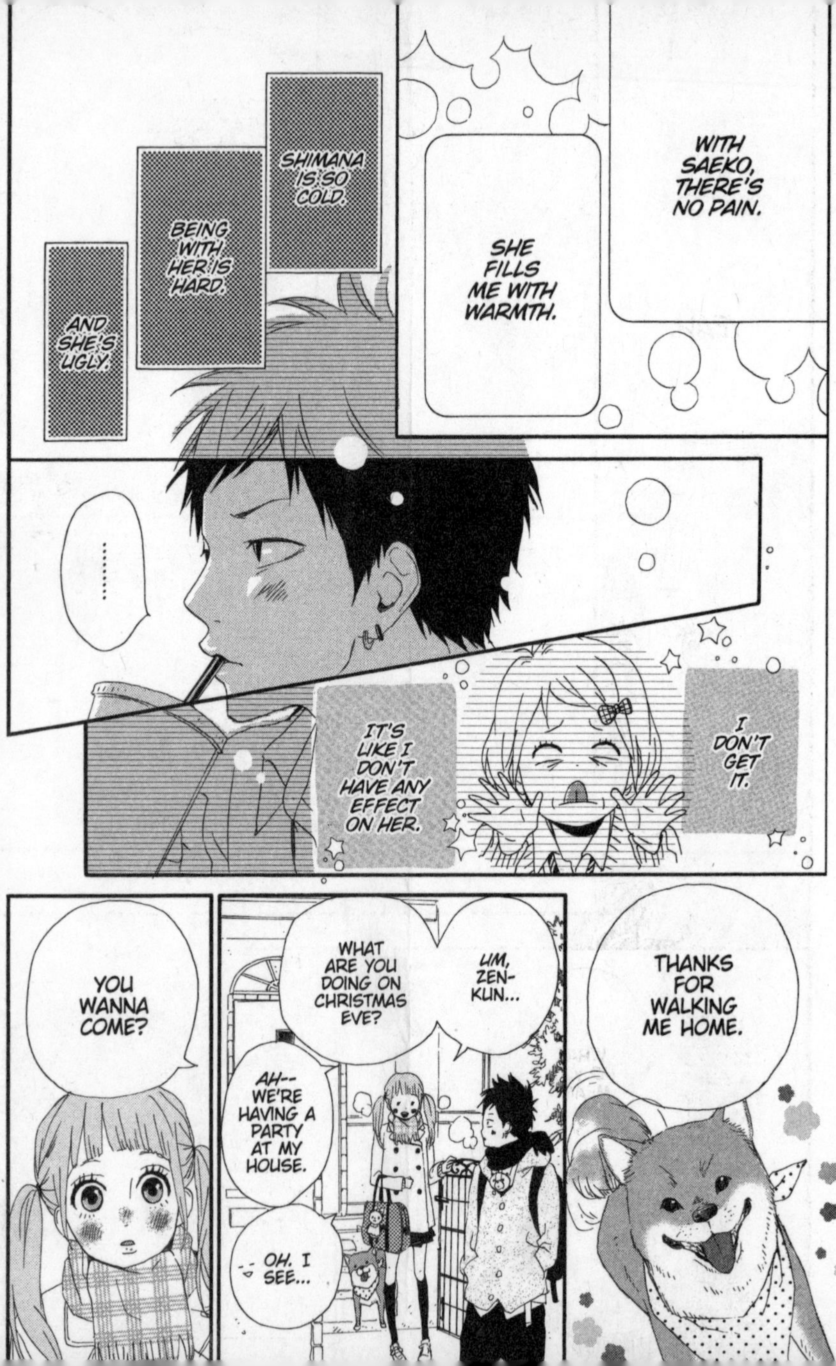
WITH SAEKO, THERE'S NO PAIN.
SHE FILLS ME WITH WARMTH.
SHIMANA IS SO COLD.
BEING WITH HER IS HARD.
AND SHE'S UGLY.
......
I DON'T GET IT.
IT'S LIKE I DON'T HAVE ANY EFFECT ON HER.
THANKS FOR WALKING ME HOME.
UM, ZEN-KUN...
WHAT ARE YOU DOING ON CHRISTMAS EVE?
AH-- WE'RE HAVING A PARTY AT MY HOUSE.
OH. I SEE...
YOU WANNA COME?

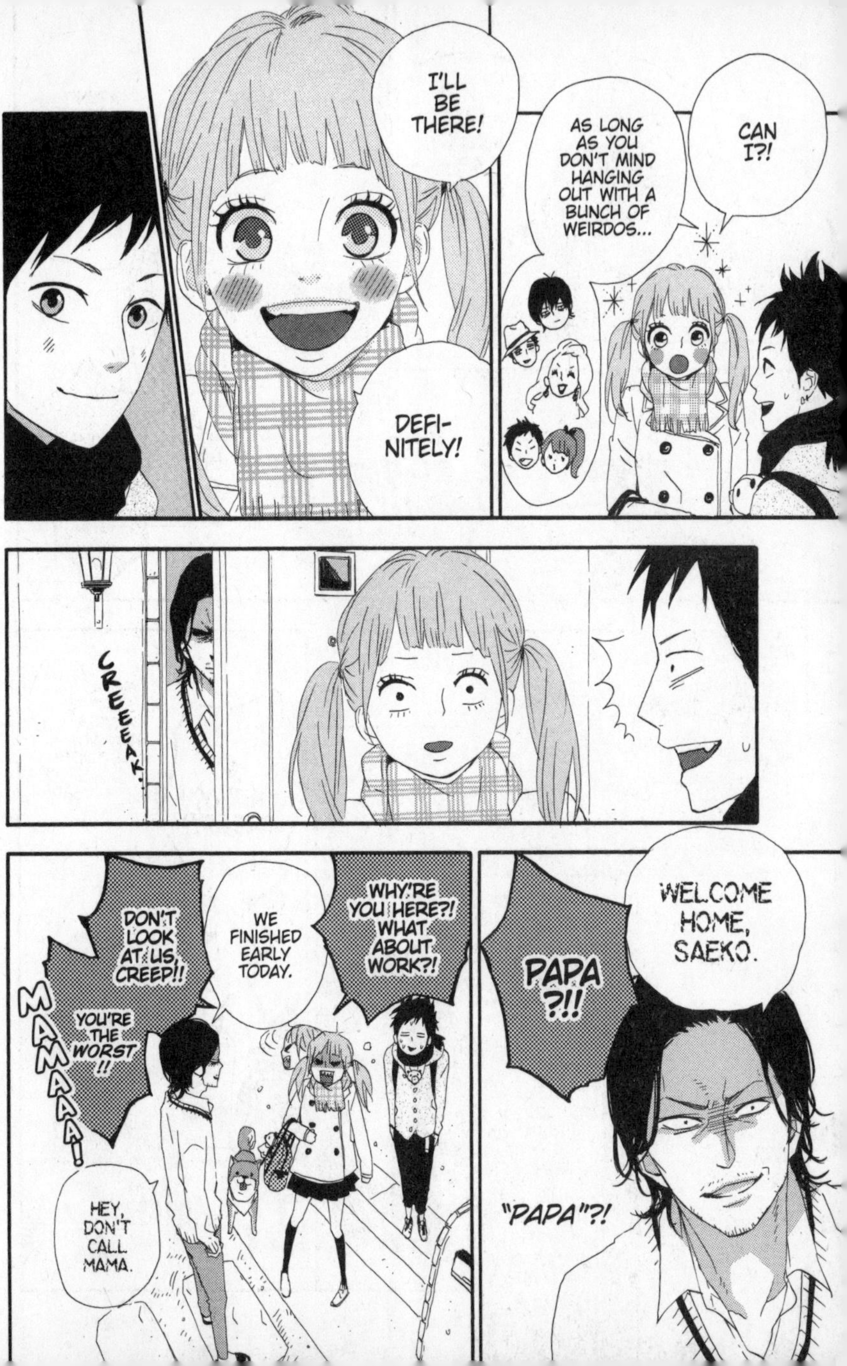
CAN I?!
AS LONG AS YOU DON'T MIND HANGING OUT WITH A BUNCH OF WEIRDOS...
I'LL BE THERE!
DEFI-NITELY!
CREEEAK...
WELCOME HOME, SAEKO.
PAPA ?!!
"PAPA"?!
WHY'RE YOU HERE?! WHAT ABOUT WORK?!
WE FINISHED EARLY TODAY.
DON'T LOOK AT US, CREEP!!
YOU'RE THE WORST!!
MAMAAAA!
HEY, DON'T CALL MAMA.

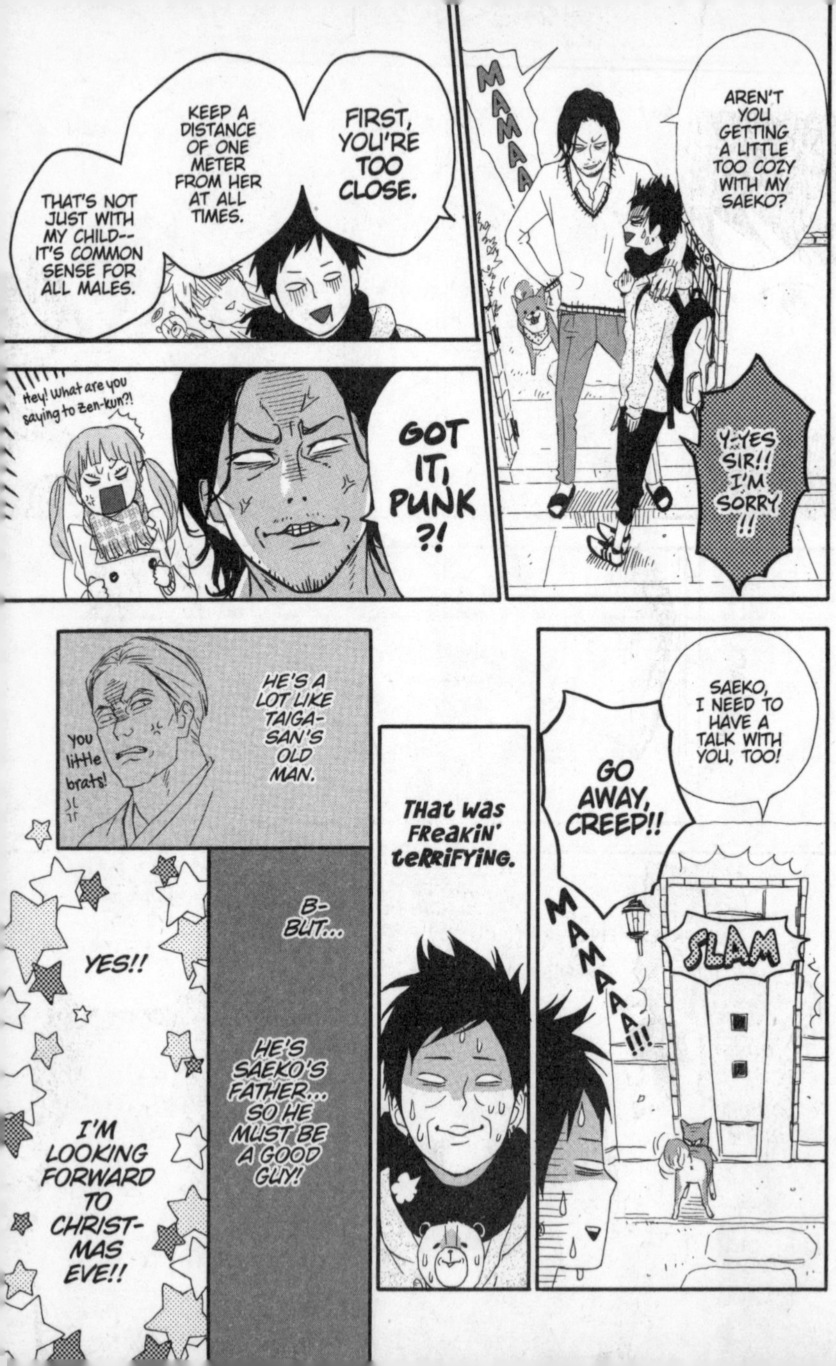
MAMAAA
AREN'T YOU GETTING A LITTLE TOO COZY WITH MY SAEKO?
Y-YES SIR!! I'M SORRY!!
FIRST, YOU'RE TOO CLOSE.
KEEP A DISTANCE OF ONE METER FROM HER AT ALL TIMES.
THAT'S NOT JUST WITH MY CHILD-- IT'S COMMON SENSE FOR ALL MALES.
GOT IT, PUNK?!
Hey! What are you saying to Zen-kun?!
SAEKO, I NEED TO HAVE A TALK WITH YOU, TOO!
GO AWAY, CREEP!!
SLAM
MAMAAAA!!
That was freakin' terrifying.
HE'S A LOT LIKE TAIGA-SAN'S OLD MAN.
You little brats!
B-BUT...
HE'S SAEKO'S FATHER... SO HE MUST BE A GOOD GUY!
YES!!
I'M LOOKING FORWARD TO CHRISTMAS-MAS EVE!!

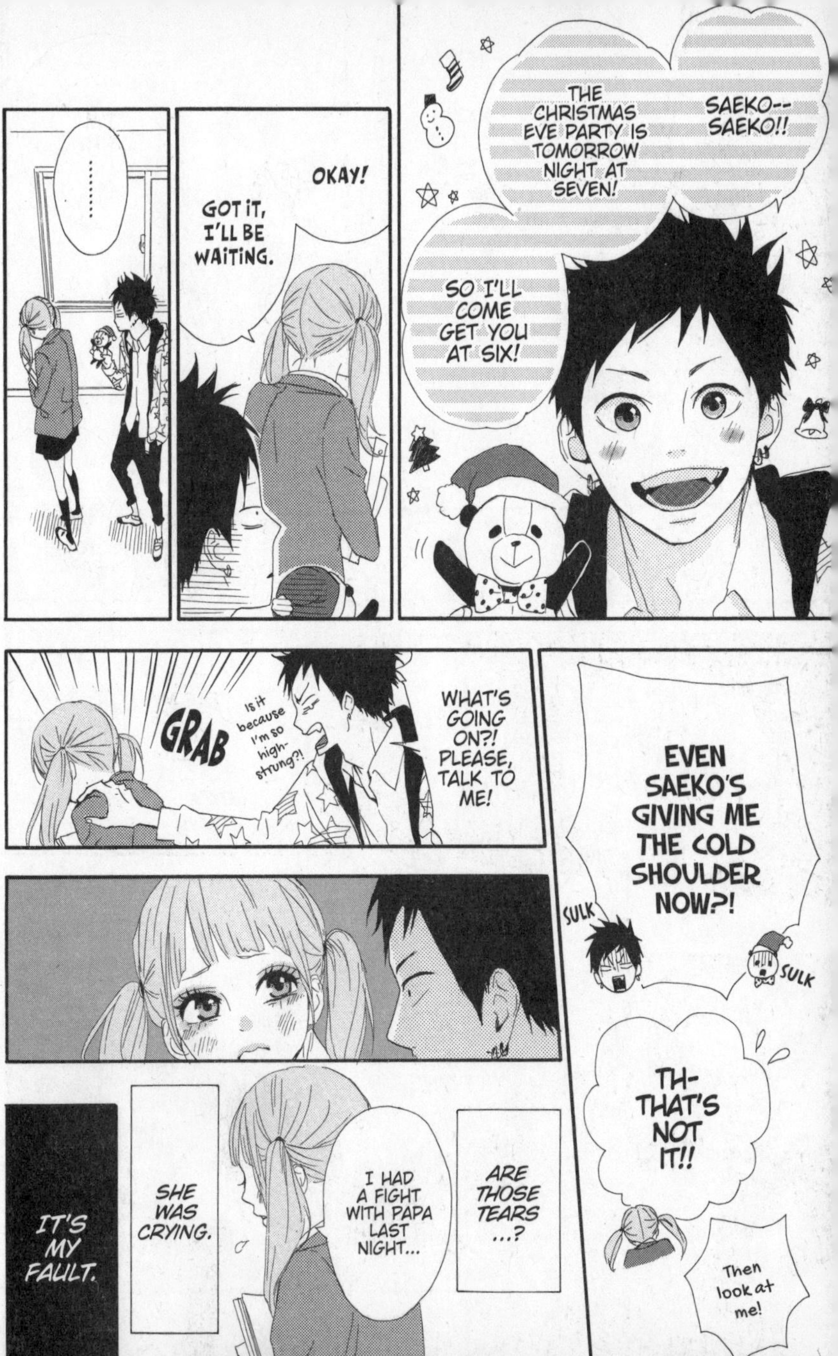
SAEKO-- SAEKO!!
THE CHRISTMAS EVE PARTY IS TOMORROW NIGHT AT SEVEN!
SO I'LL COME GET YOU AT SIX!
OKAY!
GOT IT, I'LL BE WAITING.
......
EVEN SAEKO'S GIVING ME THE COLD SHOULDER NOW?!
SULK
SULK
TH- THAT'S NOT IT!!
Then look at me!
WHAT'S GOING ON?! PLEASE, TALK TO ME!
Is it because I'm so high-strung?!
GRAB
ARE THOSE TEARS ...?
I HAD A FIGHT WITH PAPA LAST NIGHT...
SHE WAS CRYING.
IT'S MY FAULT.

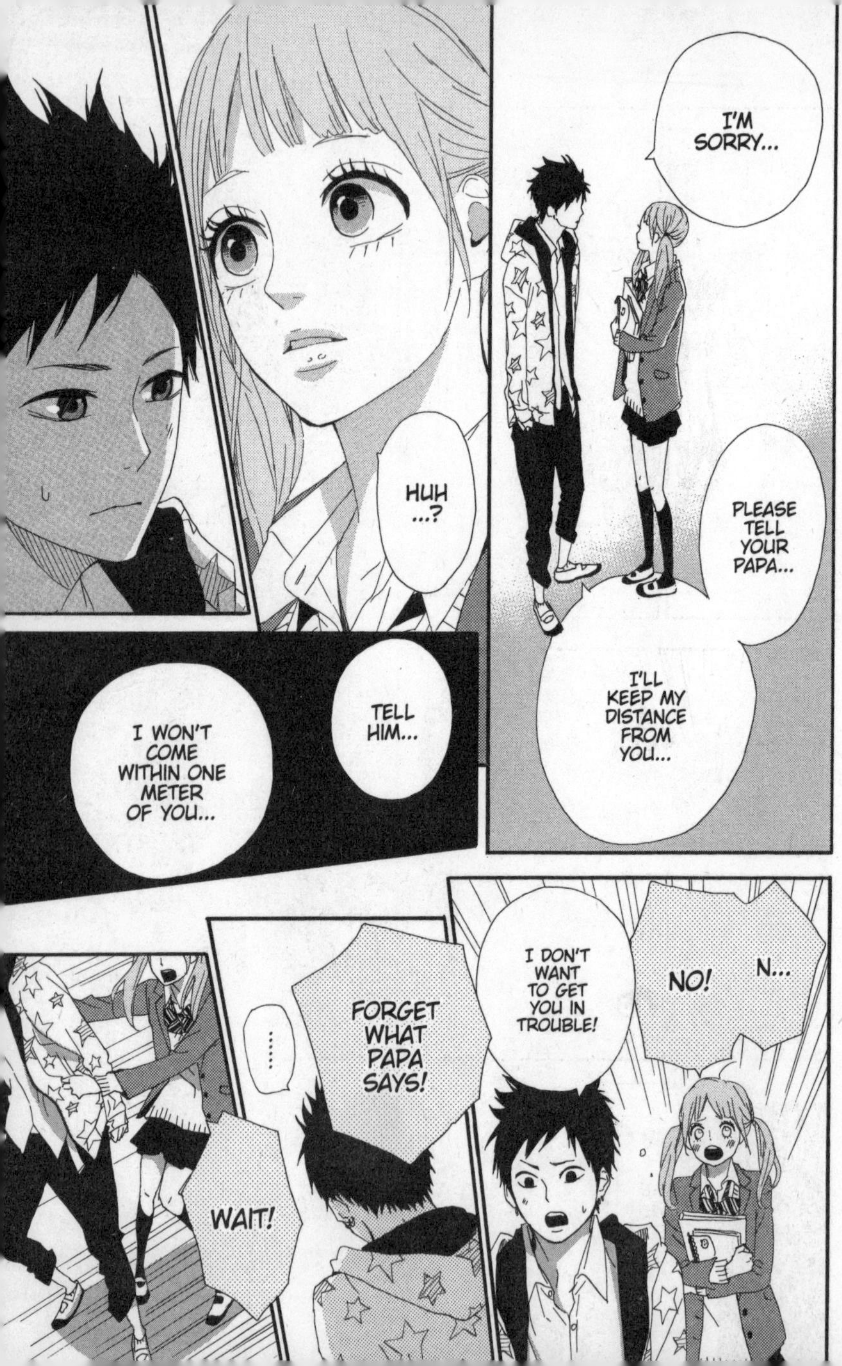

I'M SORRY...
PLEASE TELL YOUR PAPA...
I'LL KEEP MY DISTANCE FROM YOU...
HUH ...?
TELL HIM...
I WON'T COME WITHIN ONE METER OF YOU...
N...
NO!
I DON'T WANT TO GET YOU IN TROUBLE!
FORGET WHAT PAPA SAYS!
......
WAIT!

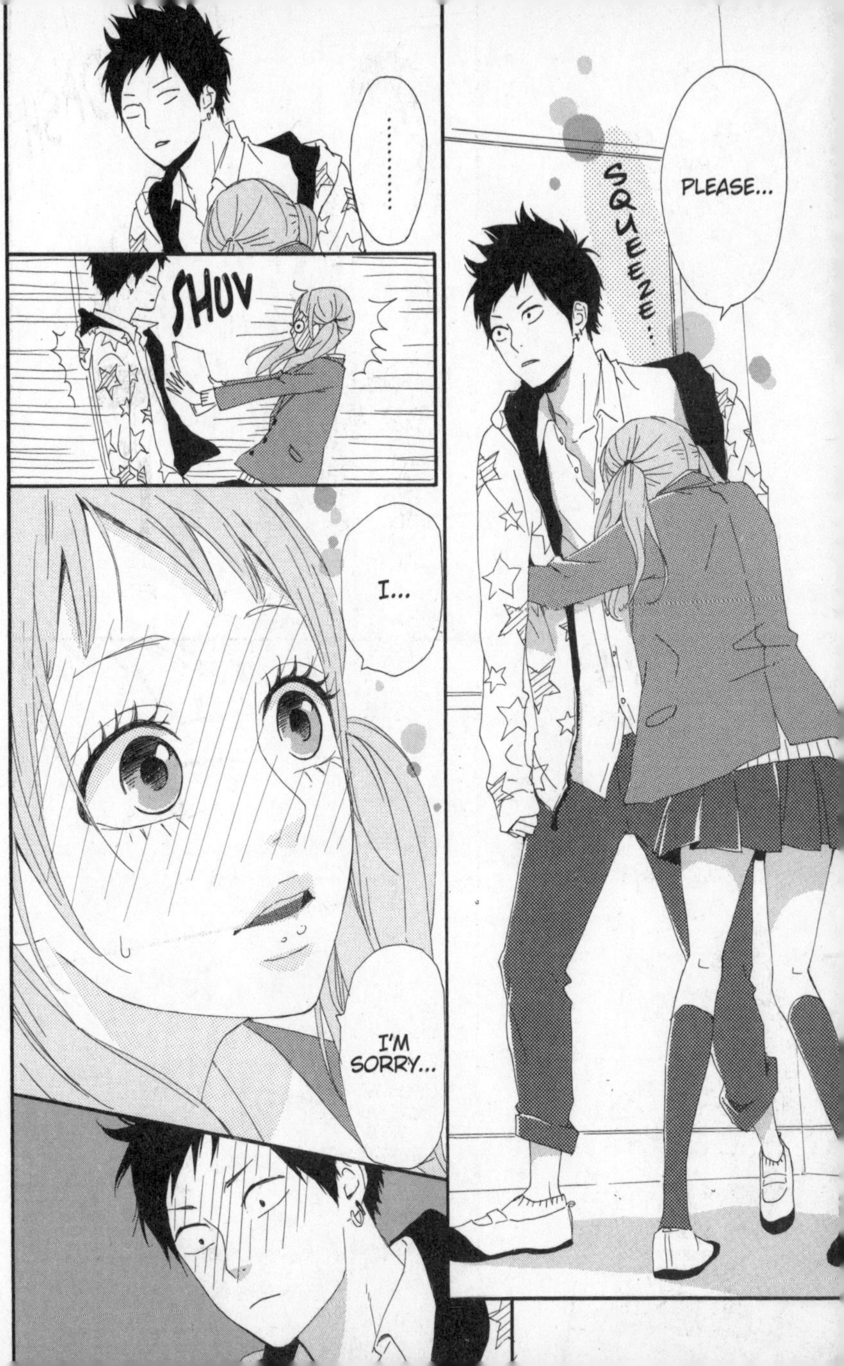

PLEASE...
SQUEEZE...
......
SHUV
I...
I'M SORRY...

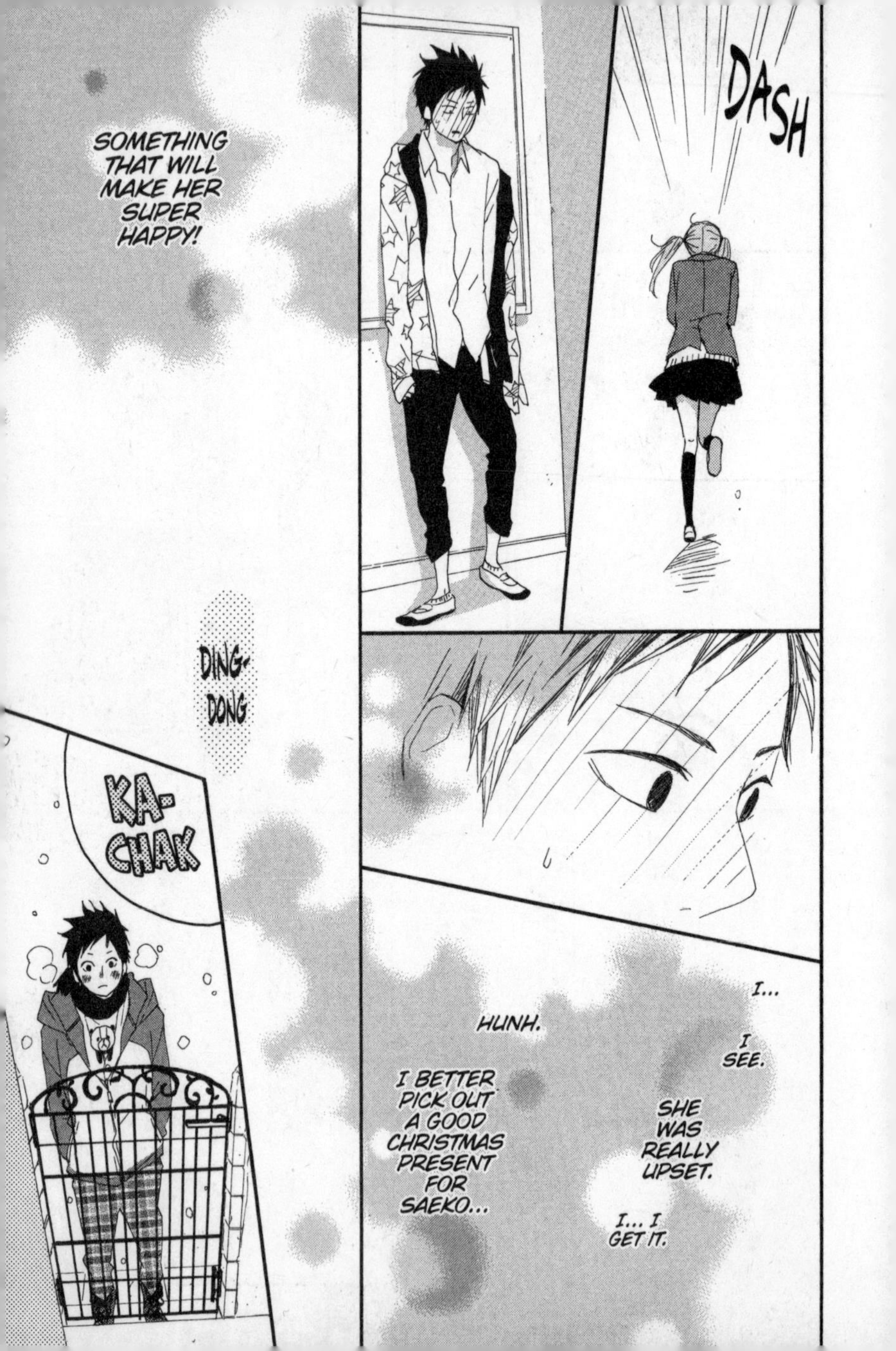
DASH
I...
I SEE.
SHE WAS REALLY UPSET.
I... I GET IT.
HUNH.
I BETTER PICK OUT A GOOD CHRISTMAS PRESENT FOR SAEKO...
SOMETHING THAT WILL MAKE HER SUPER HAPPY!
DING-DONG
KA-CHAK

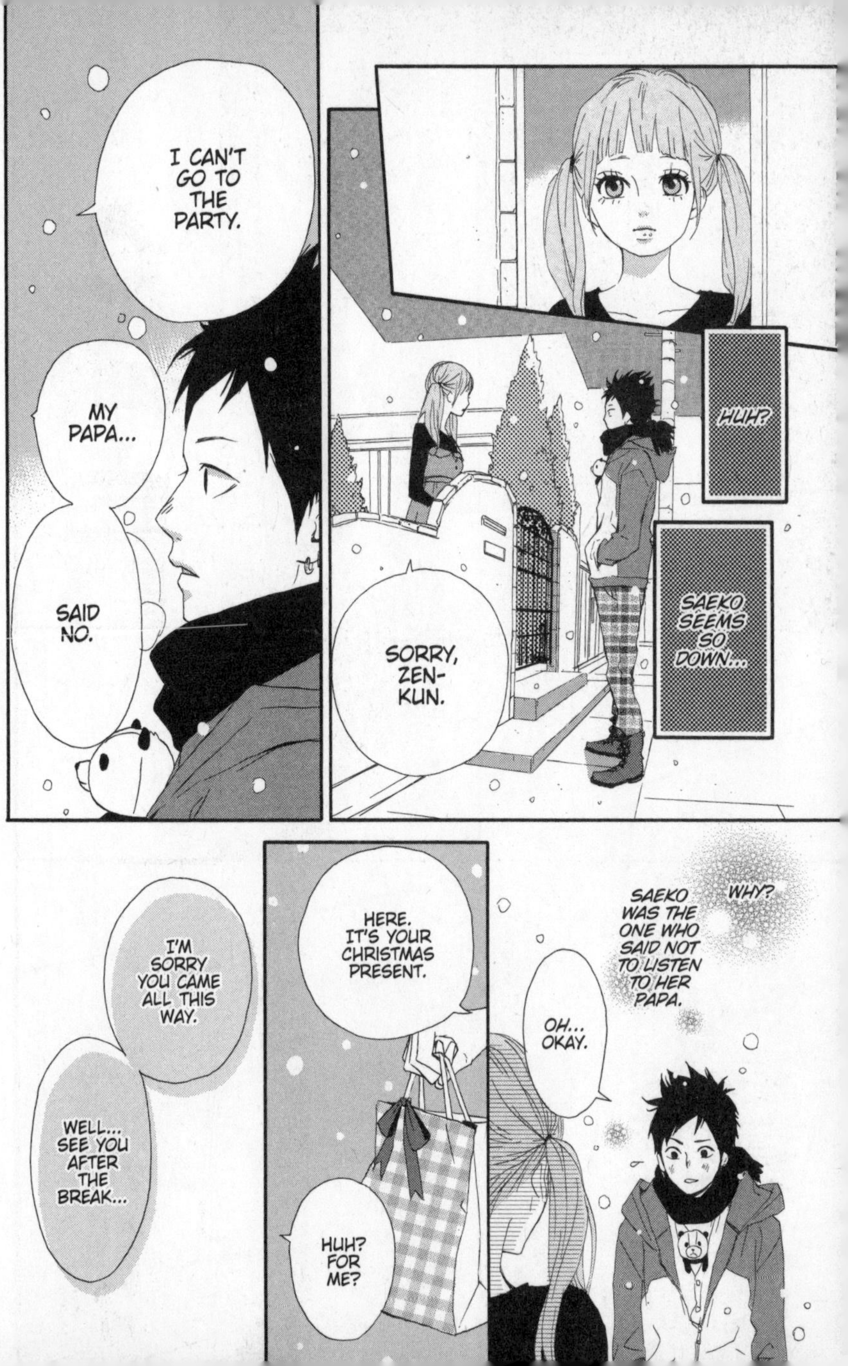
HUH?
SAEKO SEEMS SO DOWN...
SORRY, ZEN-KUN.
I CAN'T GO TO THE PARTY.
MY PAPA...
SAID NO.
WHY?
SAEKO WAS THE ONE WHO SAID NOT TO LISTEN TO HER PAPA.
OH... OKAY.
HERE. IT'S YOUR CHRISTMAS PRESENT.
HUH? FOR ME?
I'M SORRY YOU CAME ALL THIS WAY.
WELL... SEE YOU AFTER THE BREAK...

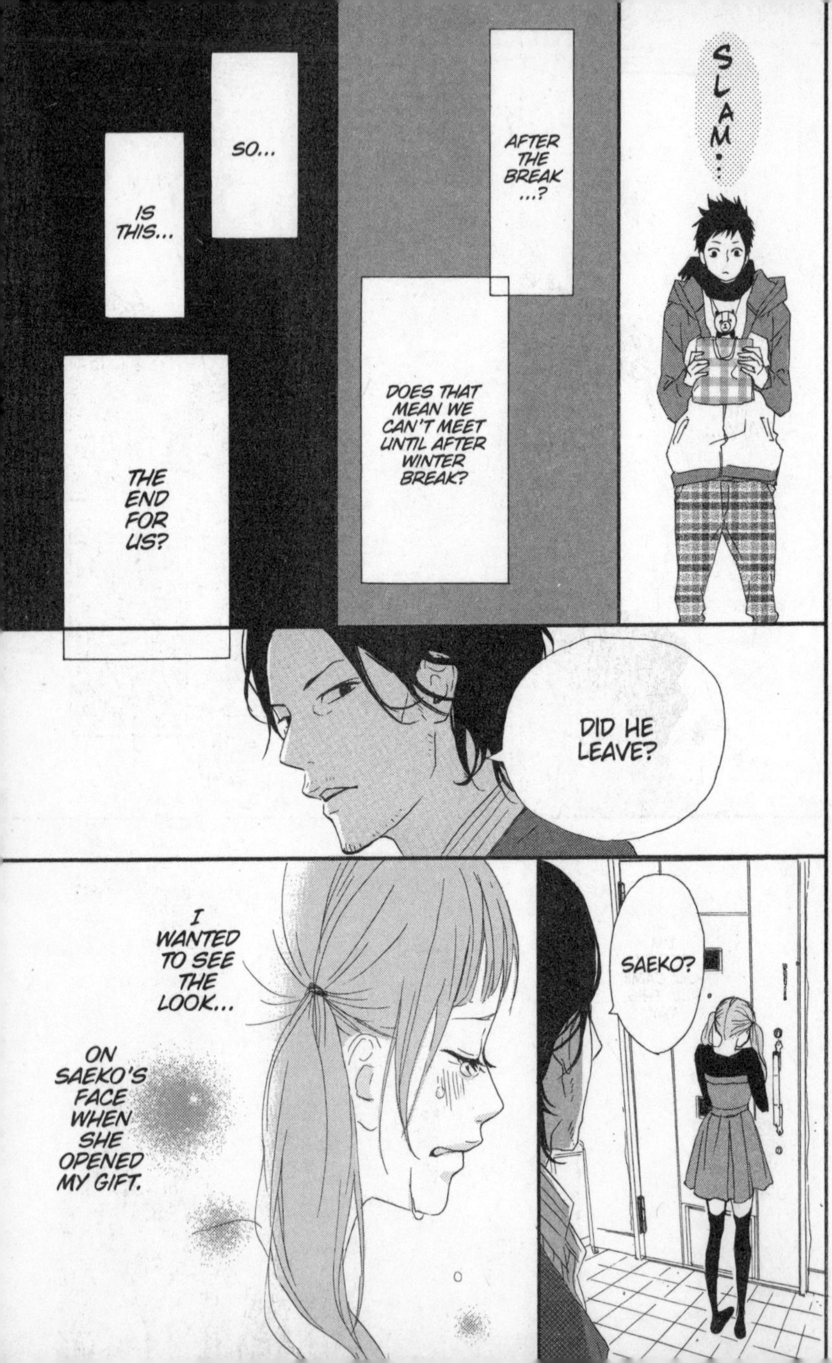
SLAM...
AFTER THE BREAK...?
DOES THAT MEAN WE CAN'T MEET UNTIL AFTER WINTER BREAK?
SO...
IS THIS...
THE END FOR US?
DID HE LEAVE?
SAEKO?
I WANTED TO SEE THE LOOK...
ON SAEKO'S FACE WHEN SHE OPENED MY GIFT.

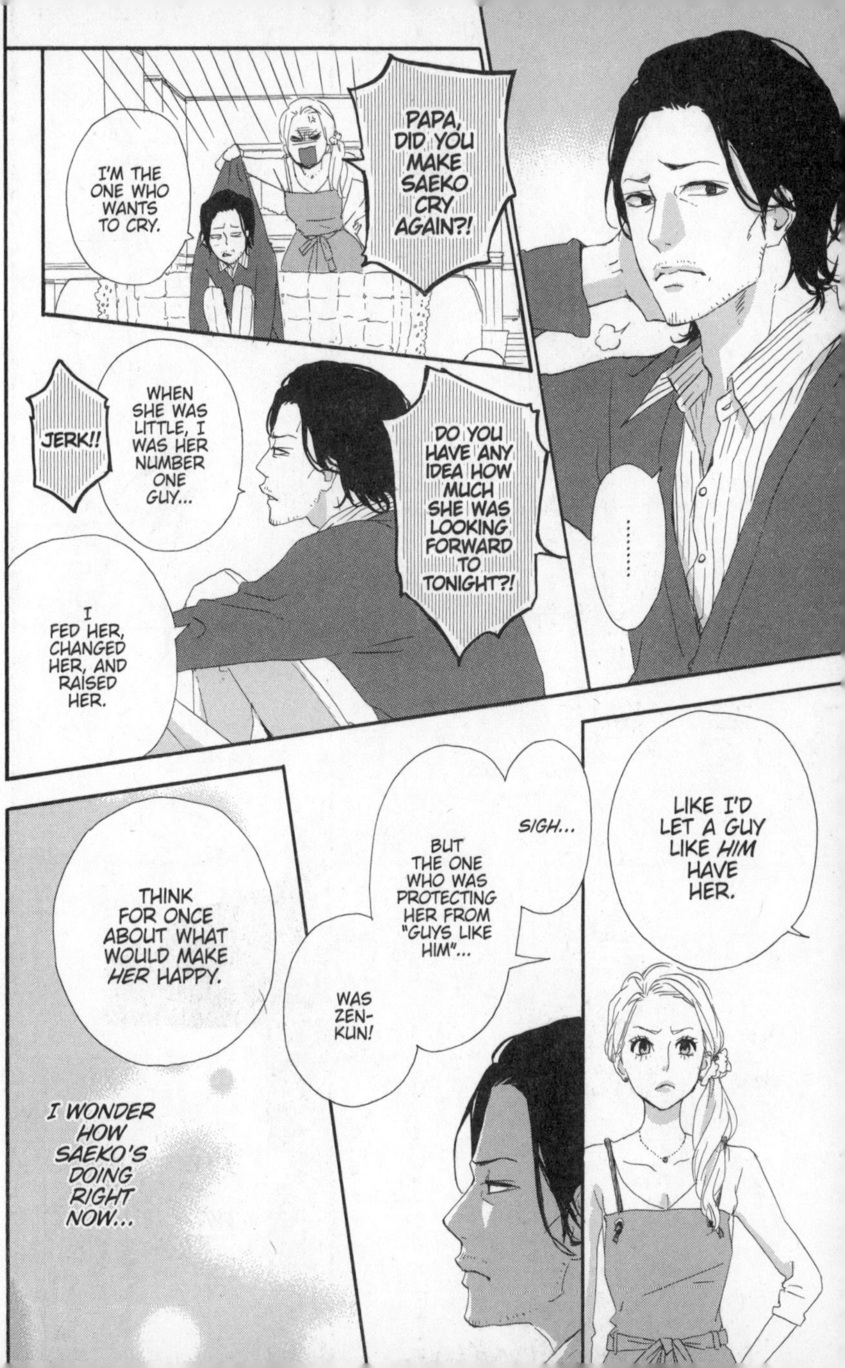
......
PAPA, DID YOU MAKE SAEKO CRY AGAIN?!
I'M THE ONE WHO WANTS TO CRY.
DO YOU HAVE ANY IDEA HOW MUCH SHE WAS LOOKING FORWARD TO TONIGHT?!
WHEN SHE WAS LITTLE, I WAS HER NUMBER ONE GUY...
JERK!!
I FED HER, CHANGED HER, AND RAISED HER.
LIKE I'D LET A GUY LIKE *HIM* HAVE HER.
SIGH...
BUT THE ONE WHO WAS PROTECTING HER FROM "GUYS LIKE HIM"...
WAS ZEN-KUN!
THINK FOR ONCE ABOUT WHAT WOULD MAKE *HER* HAPPY.
I WONDER HOW SAEKO'S DOING RIGHT NOW...

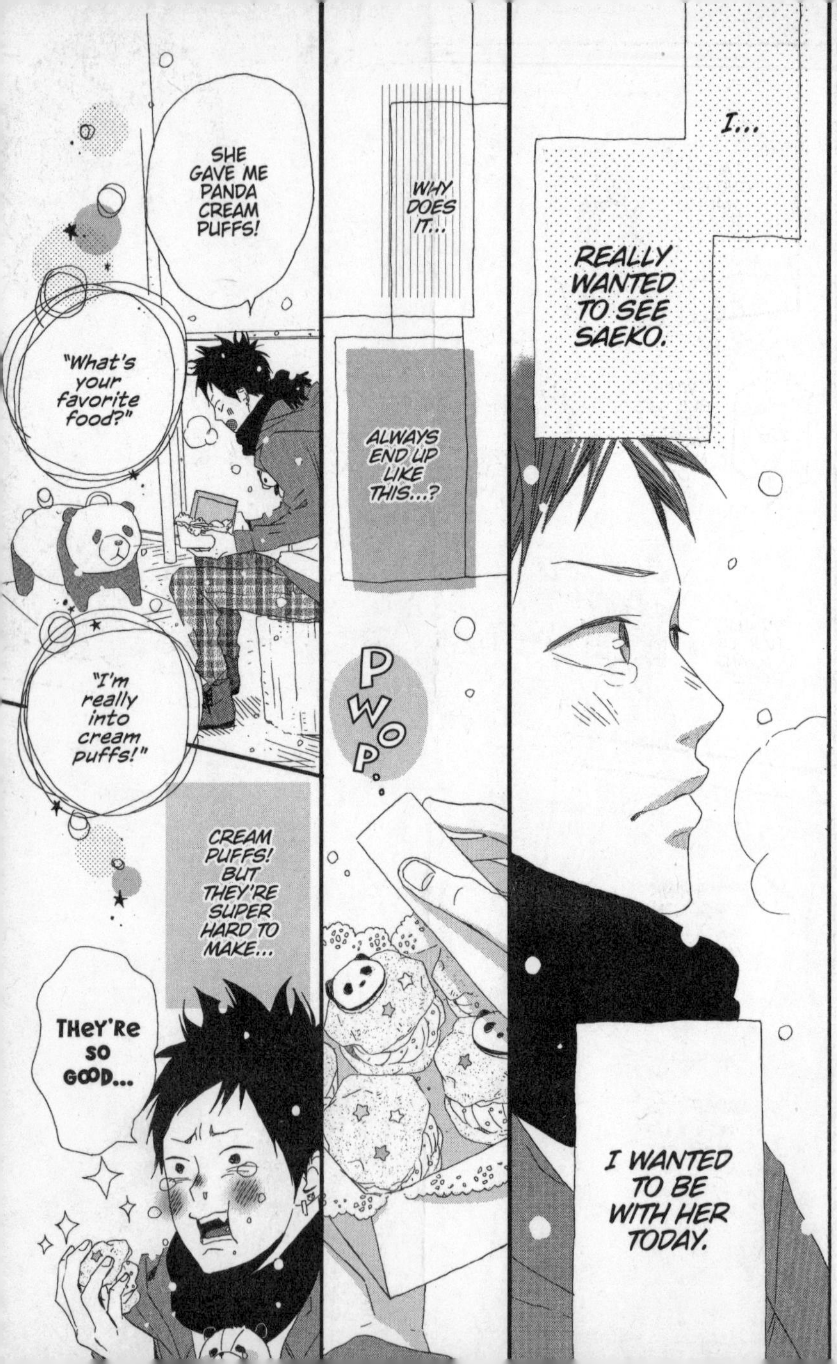
I...
REALLY WANTED TO SEE SAEKO.
I WANTED TO BE WITH HER TODAY.
WHY DOES IT...
ALWAYS END UP LIKE THIS...?
PWOP.
SHE GAVE ME PANDA CREAM PUFFS!
"What's your favorite food?"
"I'm really into cream puffs!"
CREAM PUFFS! BUT THEY'RE SUPER HARD TO MAKE...
THEY'RE SO GOOD...

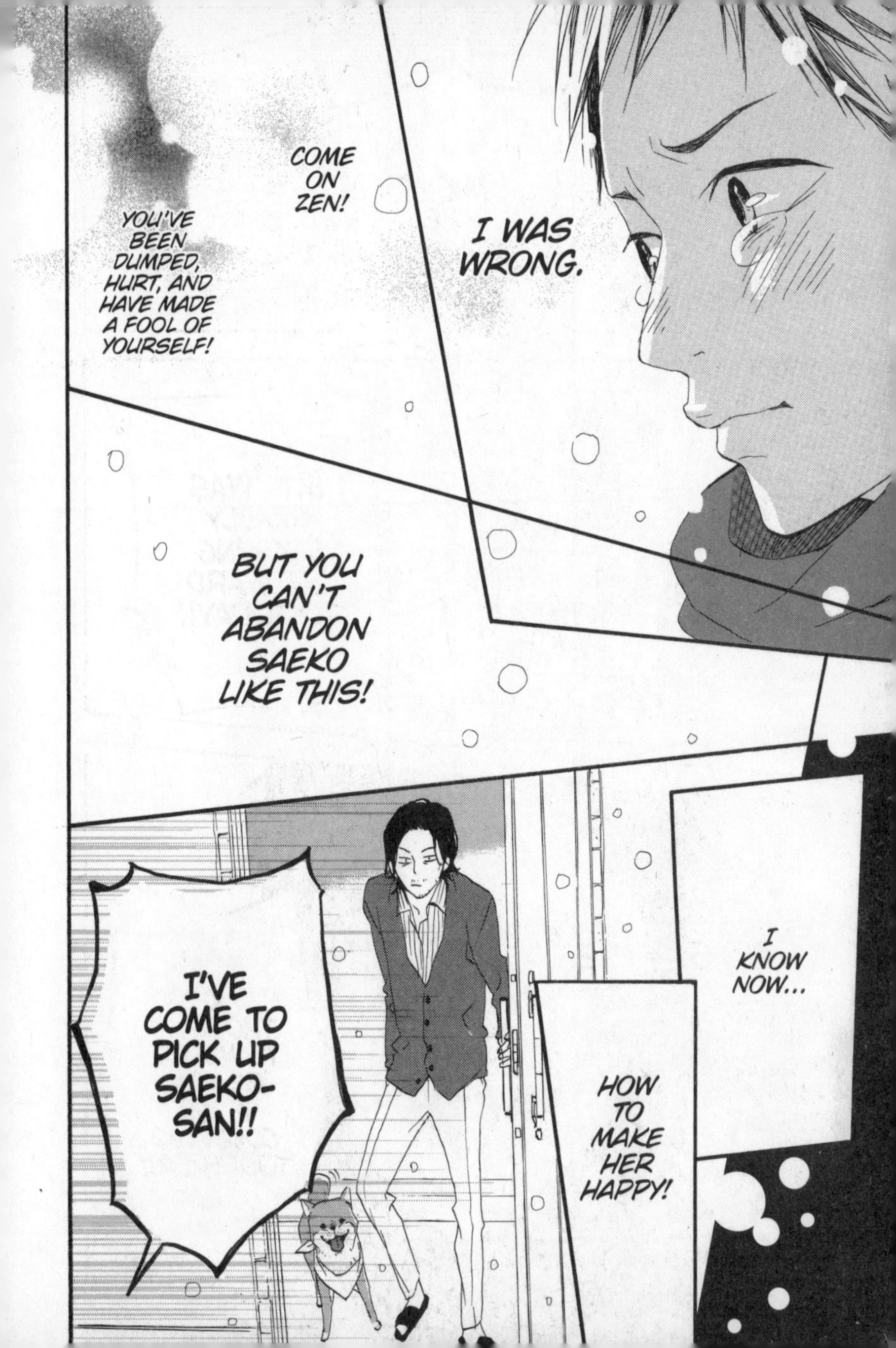
I WAS WRONG.
COME ON ZEN!
YOU'VE BEEN DUMPED, HURT, AND HAVE MADE A FOOL OF YOURSELF!
BUT YOU CAN'T ABANDON SAEKO LIKE THIS!
I KNOW NOW...
HOW TO MAKE HER HAPPY!
I'VE COME TO PICK UP SAEKO-SAN!!

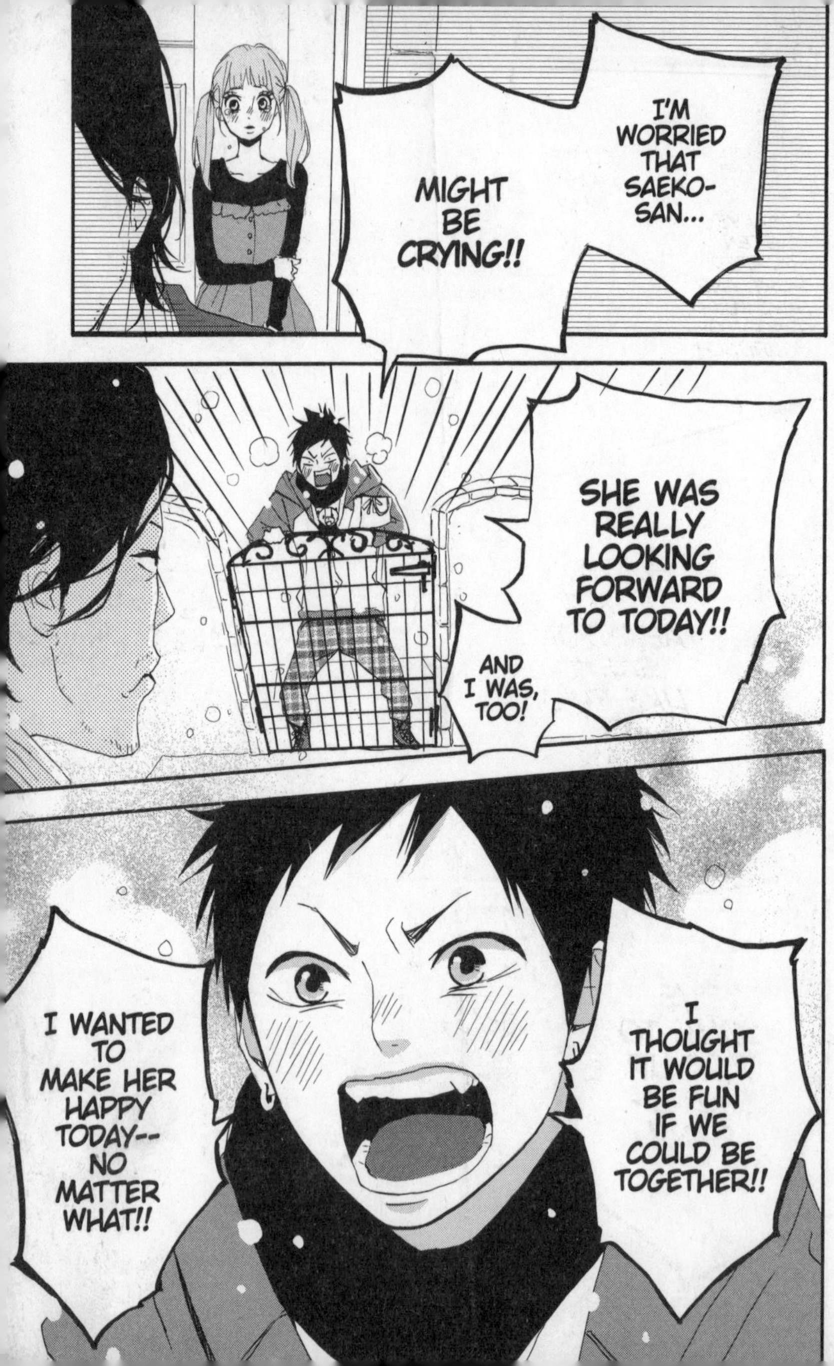
I'M WORRIED THAT SAEKO-SAN...
MIGHT BE CRYING!!
SHE WAS REALLY LOOKING FORWARD TO TODAY!!
AND I WAS, TOO!
I THOUGHT IT WOULD BE FUN IF WE COULD BE TOGETHER!!
I WANTED TO MAKE HER HAPPY TODAY-- NO MATTER WHAT!!

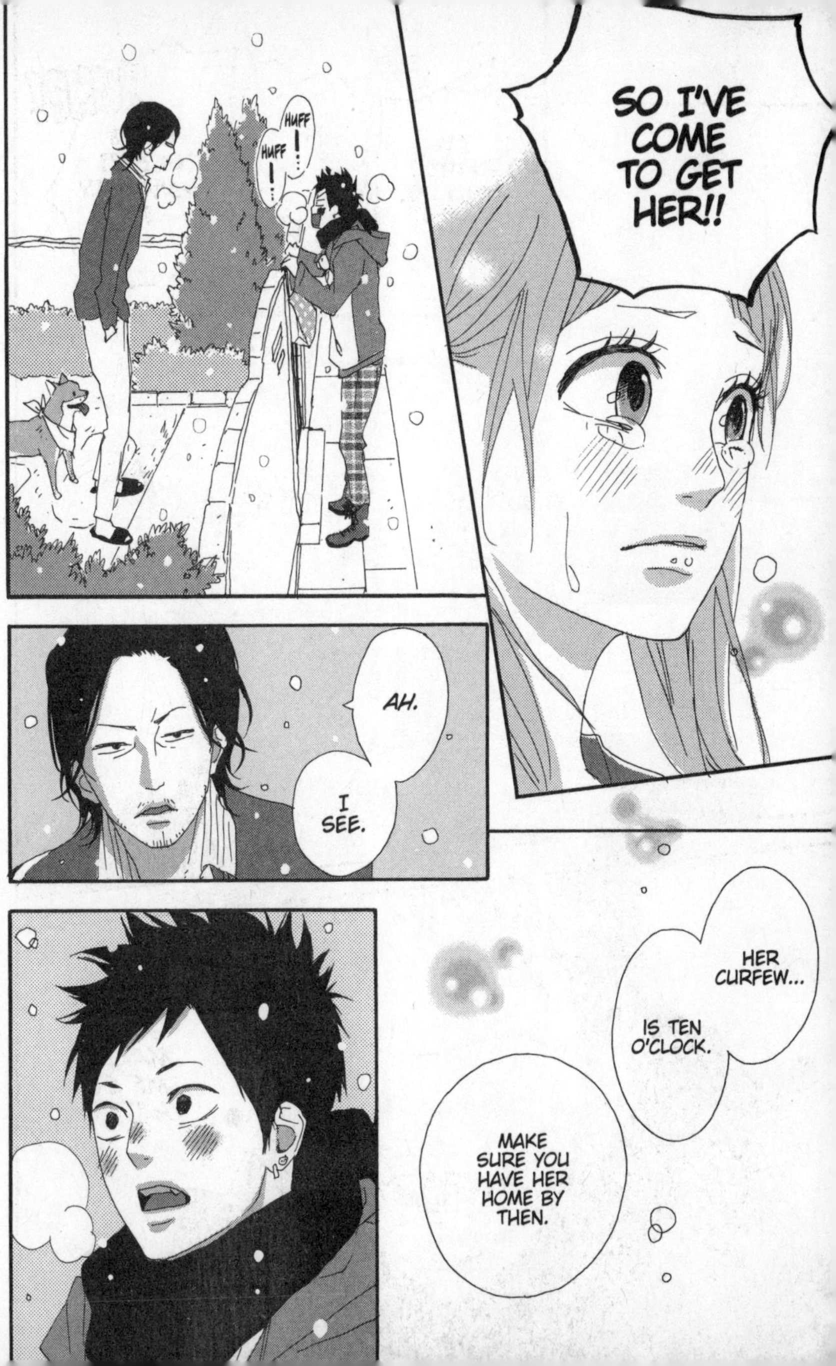
SO I'VE COME TO GET HER!!
HUFF
HUFF
AH.
I SEE.
HER CURFEW...
IS TEN O'CLOCK.
MAKE SURE YOU HAVE HER HOME BY THEN.

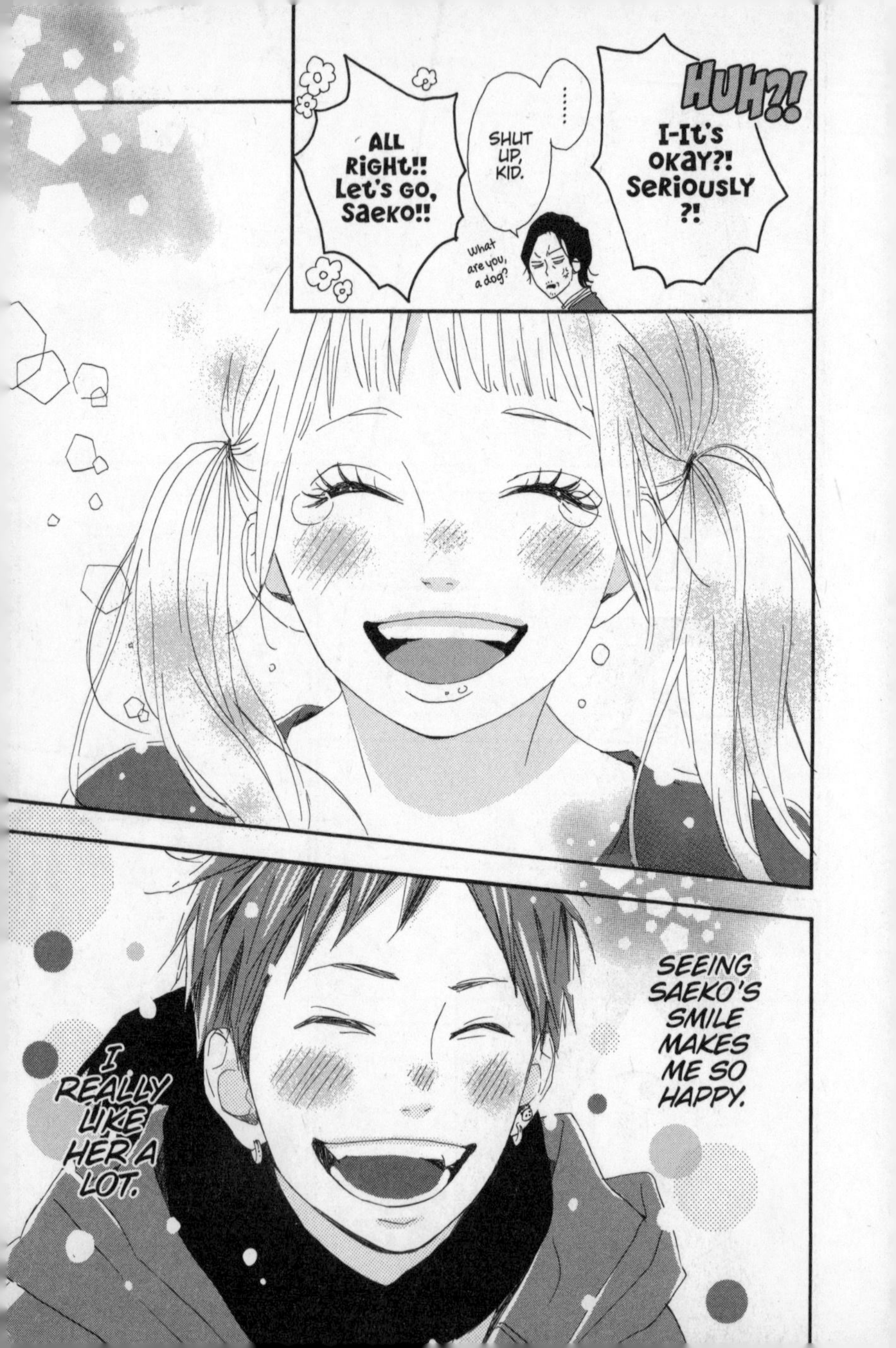
HUH?!
I-It's okay?! Seriously?!
......
Shut up, kid.
What are you, a dog?
All right!! Let's go, Saeko!!
Seeing Saeko's smile makes me so happy.
I really like her a lot.

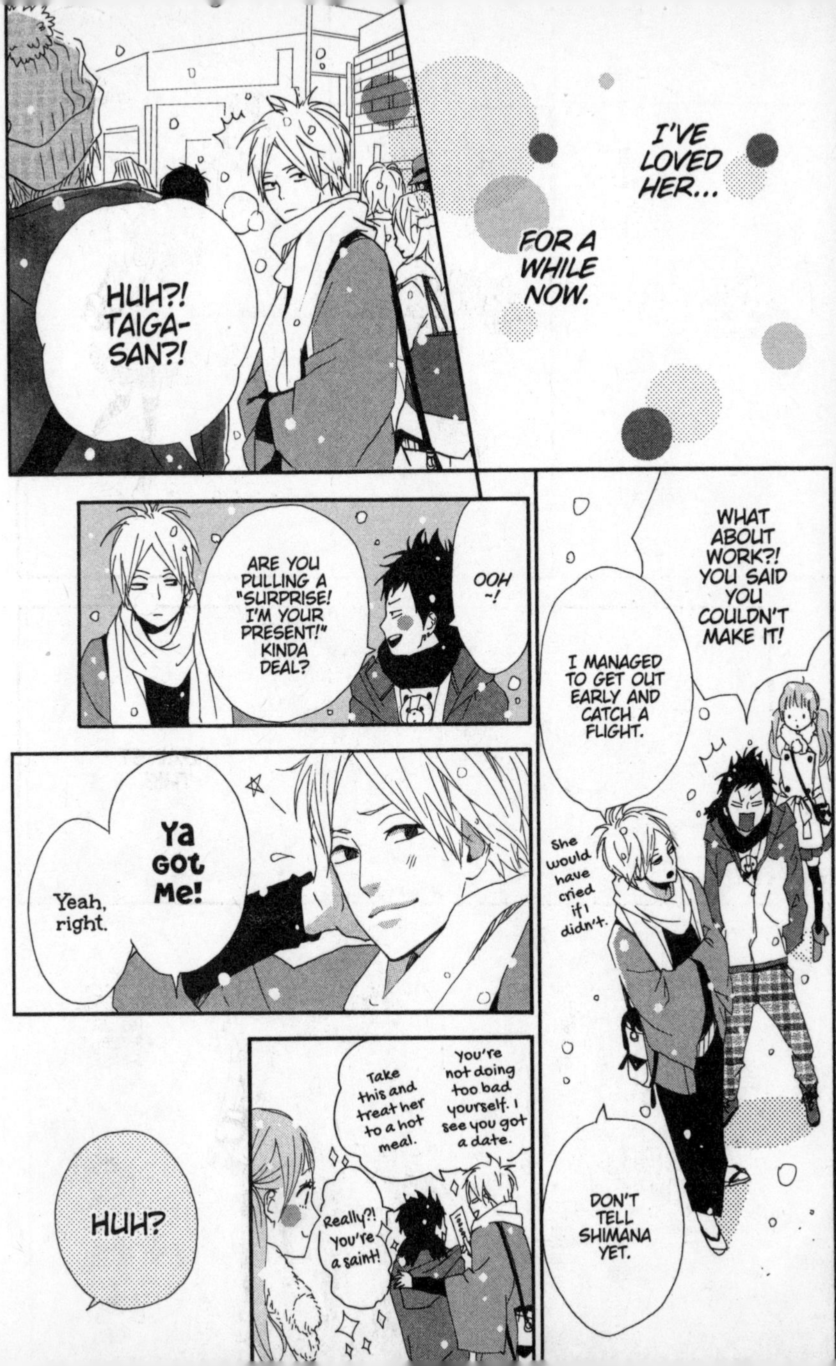
I'VE LOVED HER...
FOR A WHILE NOW.
HUH?! TAIGA-SAN?!
WHAT ABOUT WORK?! YOU SAID YOU COULDN'T MAKE IT!
I MANAGED TO GET OUT EARLY AND CATCH A FLIGHT.
She would have cried if I didn't.
DON'T TELL SHIMANA YET.
OOH~!
ARE YOU PULLING A "SURPRISE! I'M YOUR PRESENT!" KINDA DEAL?
Ya Got Me!
Yeah, right.
You're not doing too bad yourself. I see you got a date.
Take this and treat her to a hot meal.
Really?! You're a saint!
HUH?

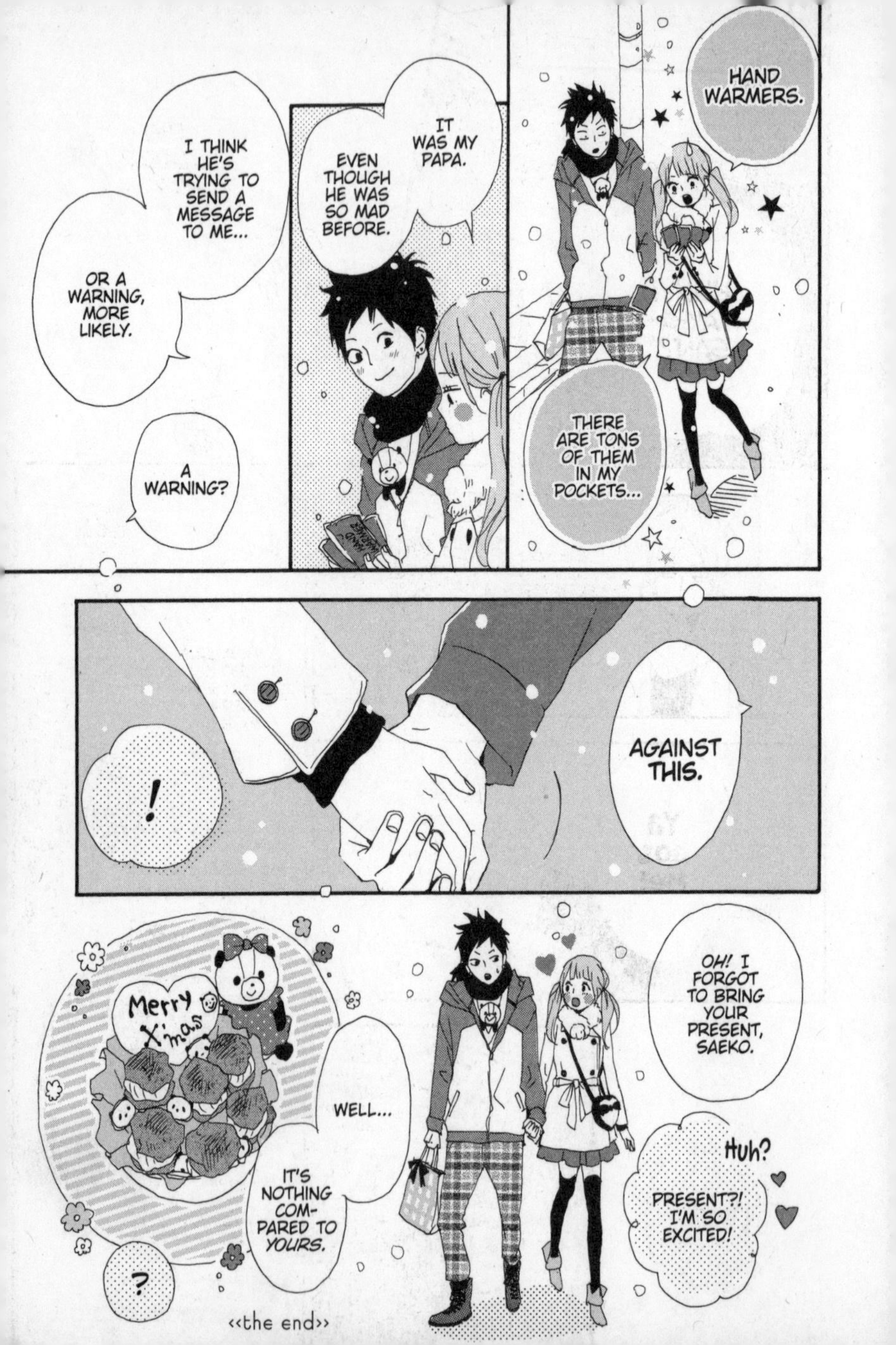
HAND WARMERS.
THERE ARE TONS OF THEM IN MY POCKETS...
IT WAS MY PAPA.
EVEN THOUGH HE WAS SO MAD BEFORE.
I THINK HE'S TRYING TO SEND A MESSAGE TO ME...
OR A WARNING, MORE LIKELY.
A WARNING?
AGAINST THIS.
!
OH! I FORGOT TO BRING YOUR PRESENT, SAEKO.
Huh?
PRESENT?! I'M SO EXCITED!
WELL...
IT'S NOTHING COM-PARED TO YOURS.
Merry X'mas
?

‹‹the end››

THE FIND POKO GAME

Poko is hidden throughout the manga! Find him!

This time, there are 5 Pokos.

Hint: There are no Pokos in the side stories.

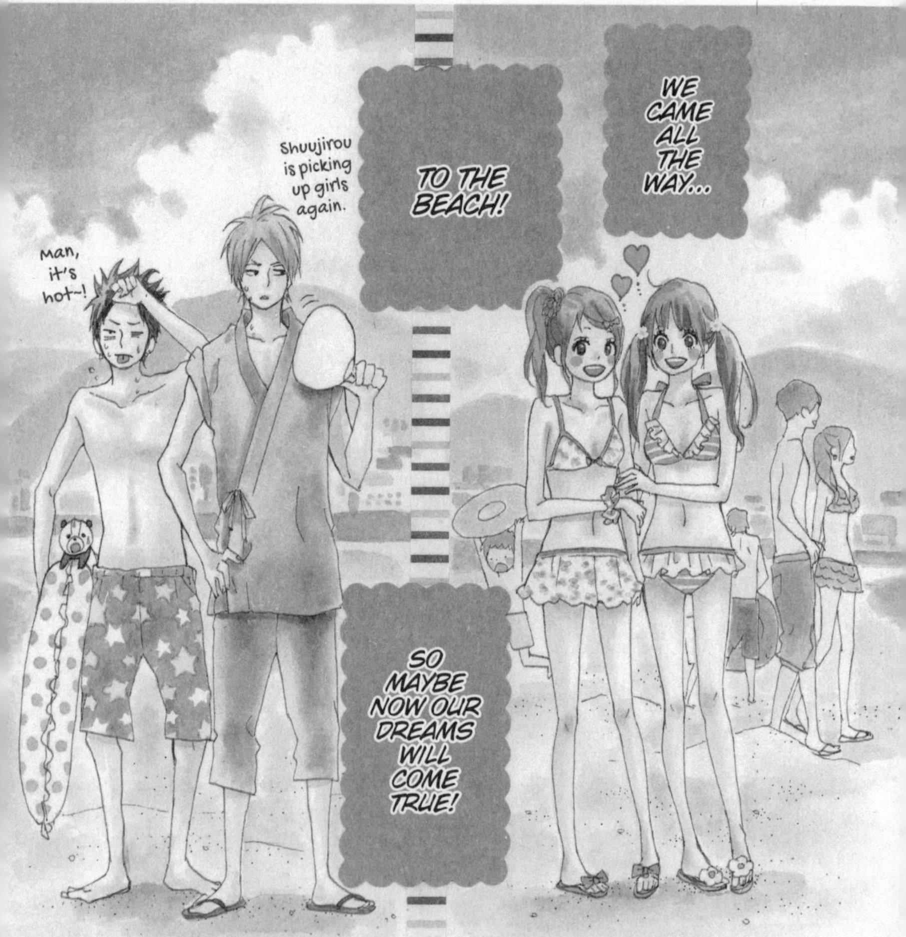
WE CAME ALL THE WAY...
TO THE BEACH!
SO MAYBE NOW OUR DREAMS WILL COME TRUE!
Shuujirou is picking up girls again.
Man, it's hot~!

[Side Story]

Dreamin' Sun

The Extra DOOR

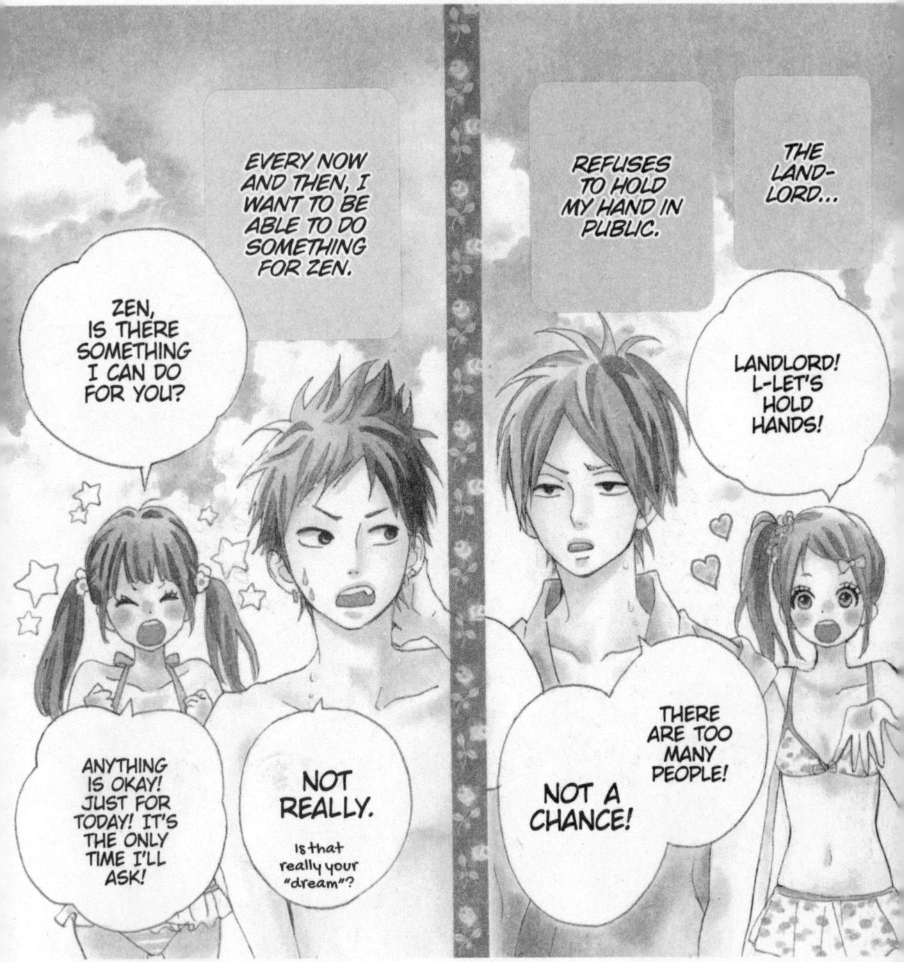
THE LANDLORD...
REFUSES TO HOLD MY HAND IN PUBLIC.
LANDLORD! L-LET'S HOLD HANDS!
THERE ARE TOO MANY PEOPLE!
NOT A CHANCE!
EVERY NOW AND THEN, I WANT TO BE ABLE TO DO SOMETHING FOR ZEN.
ZEN, IS THERE SOMETHING I CAN DO FOR YOU?
NOT REALLY.
Is that really your "dream"?
ANYTHING IS OKAY! JUST FOR TODAY! IT'S THE ONLY TIME I'LL ASK!

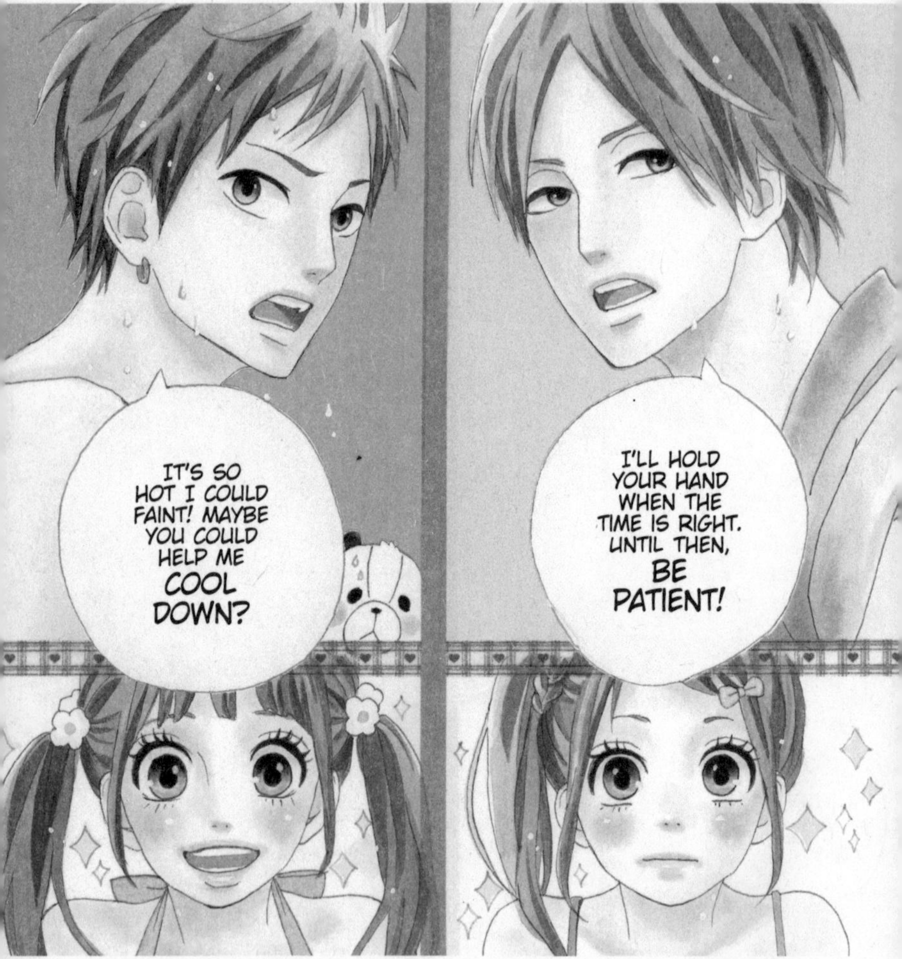
I'LL HOLD YOUR HAND WHEN THE TIME IS RIGHT. UNTIL THEN, BE PATIENT!
IT'S SO HOT I COULD FAINT! MAYBE YOU COULD HELP ME COOL DOWN?

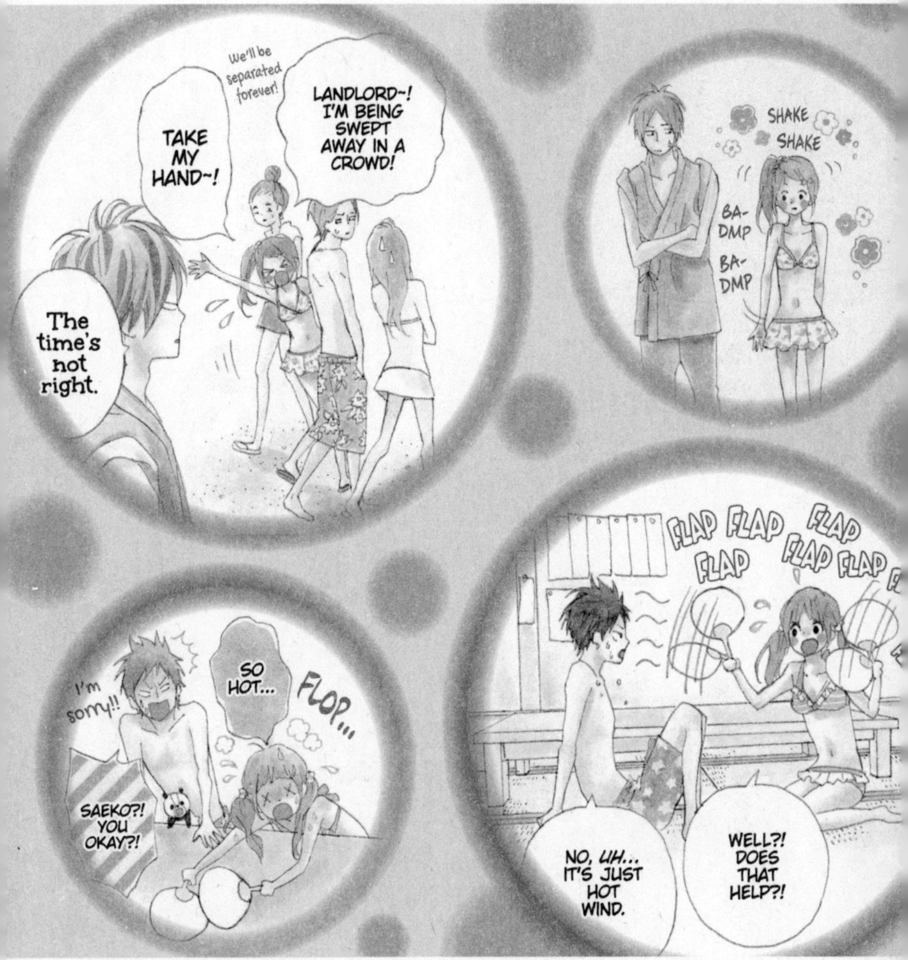
SHAKE
SHAKE
BA-DMP
BA-DMP
LANDLORD~! I'M BEING SWEPT AWAY IN A CROWD!
We'll be separated forever!
TAKE MY HAND~!
The time's not right.
FLAP FLAP FLAP
FLAP
FLAP FLAP FLAP
WELL?! DOES THAT HELP?!
NO, UH... IT'S JUST HOT WIND.
FLOP...
SO HOT...
I'm sorry!!
SAEKO?! YOU OKAY?!

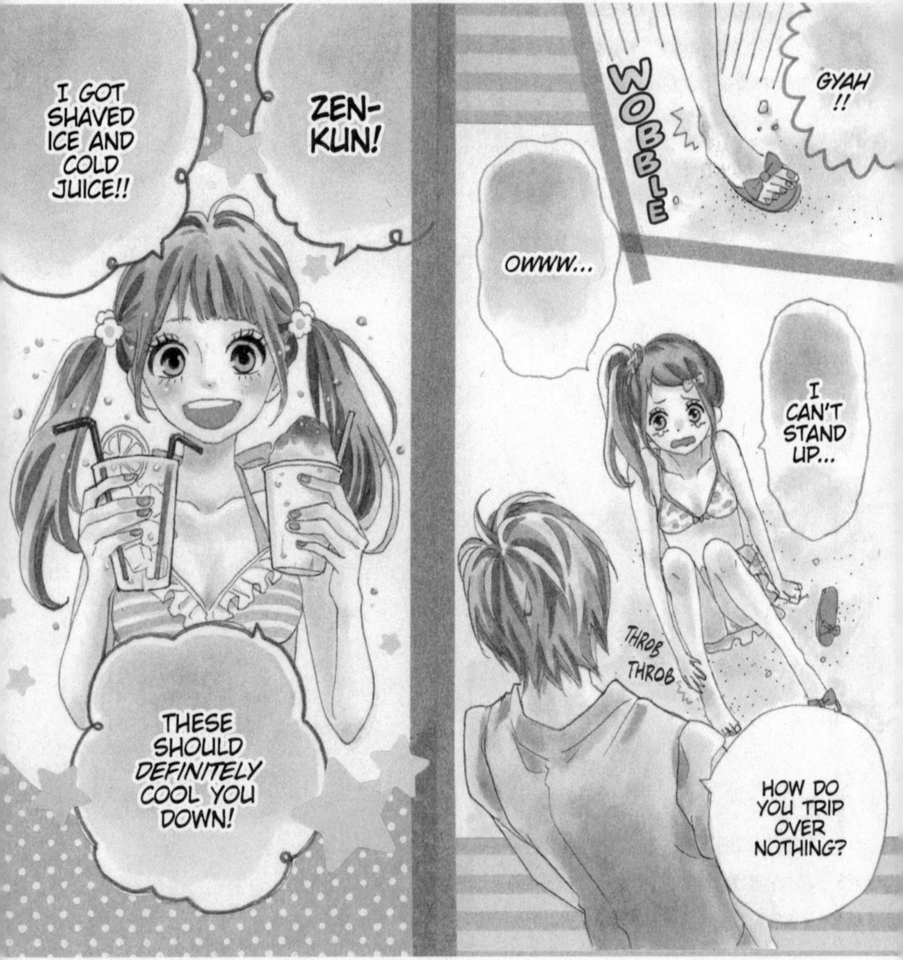
GYAH!!
WOBBLE
OWWW...
I CAN'T STAND UP...
THROB THROB
HOW DO YOU TRIP OVER NOTHING?
ZEN-KUN!
I GOT SHAVED ICE AND COLD JUICE!!
THESE SHOULD DEFINITELY COOL YOU DOWN!

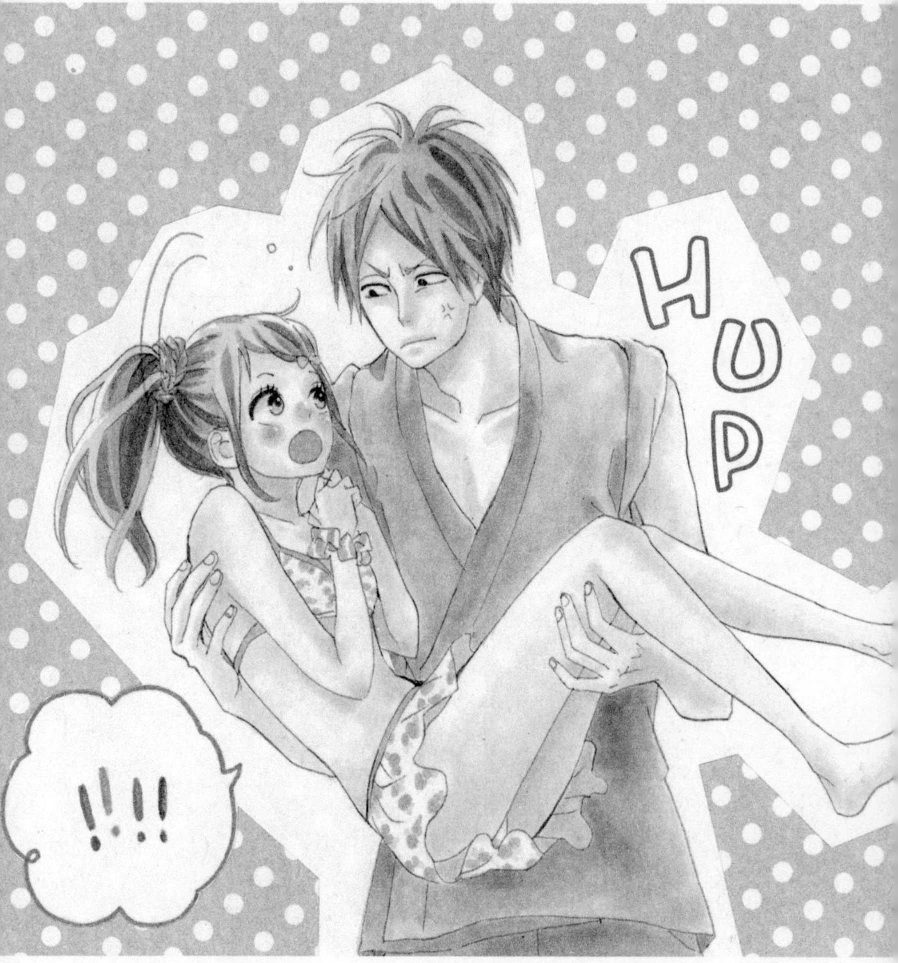
HUP
!!!!

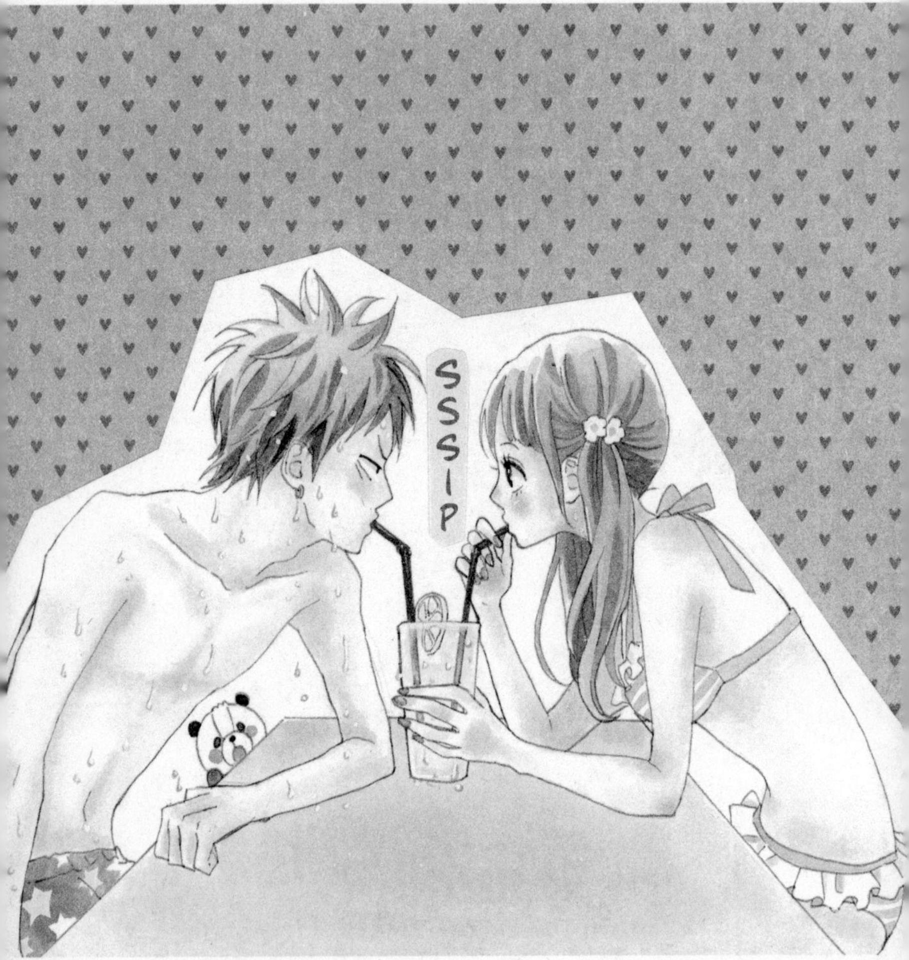
SSSIP

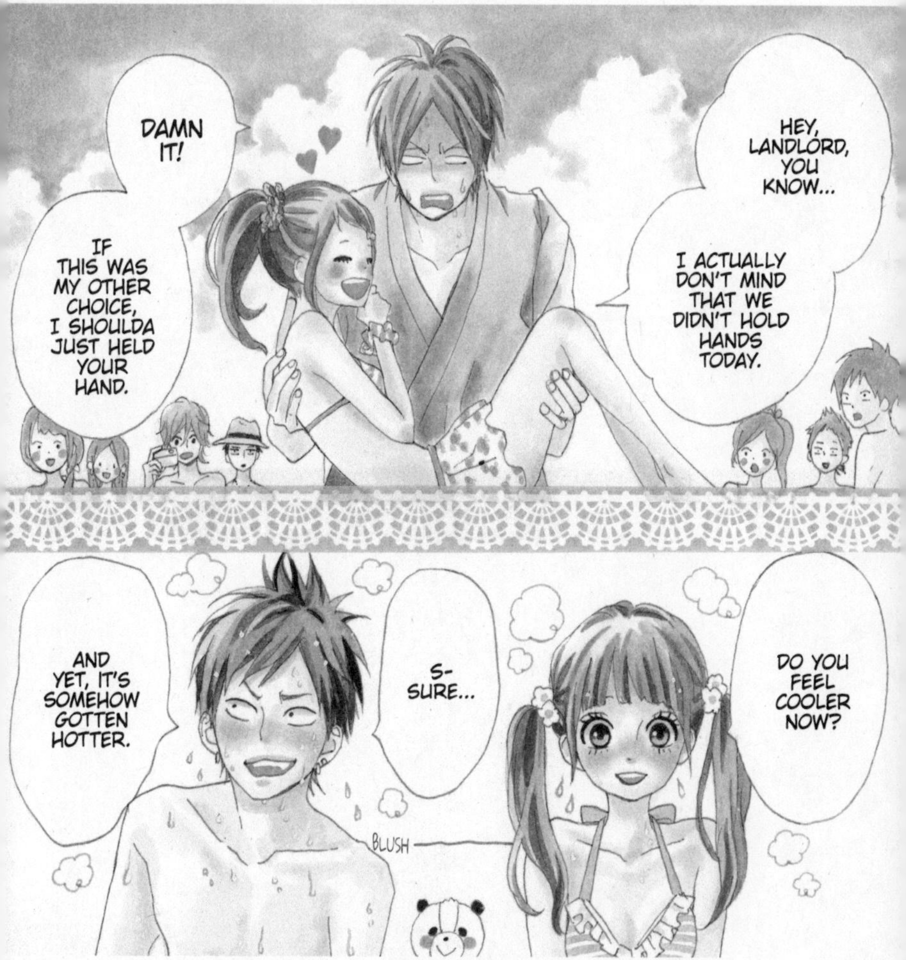
HEY, LANDLORD, YOU KNOW...
I ACTUALLY DON'T MIND THAT WE DIDN'T HOLD HANDS TODAY.
DAMN IT!
IF THIS WAS MY OTHER CHOICE, I SHOULDA JUST HELD YOUR HAND.
DO YOU FEEL COOLER NOW?
S- SURE...
BLUSH
AND YET, IT'S SOMEHOW GOTTEN HOTTER.

THE END

Dreamin' Sun ★

Dreamin' Sun

BONUS MANGA (When He Becomes a Dad...)

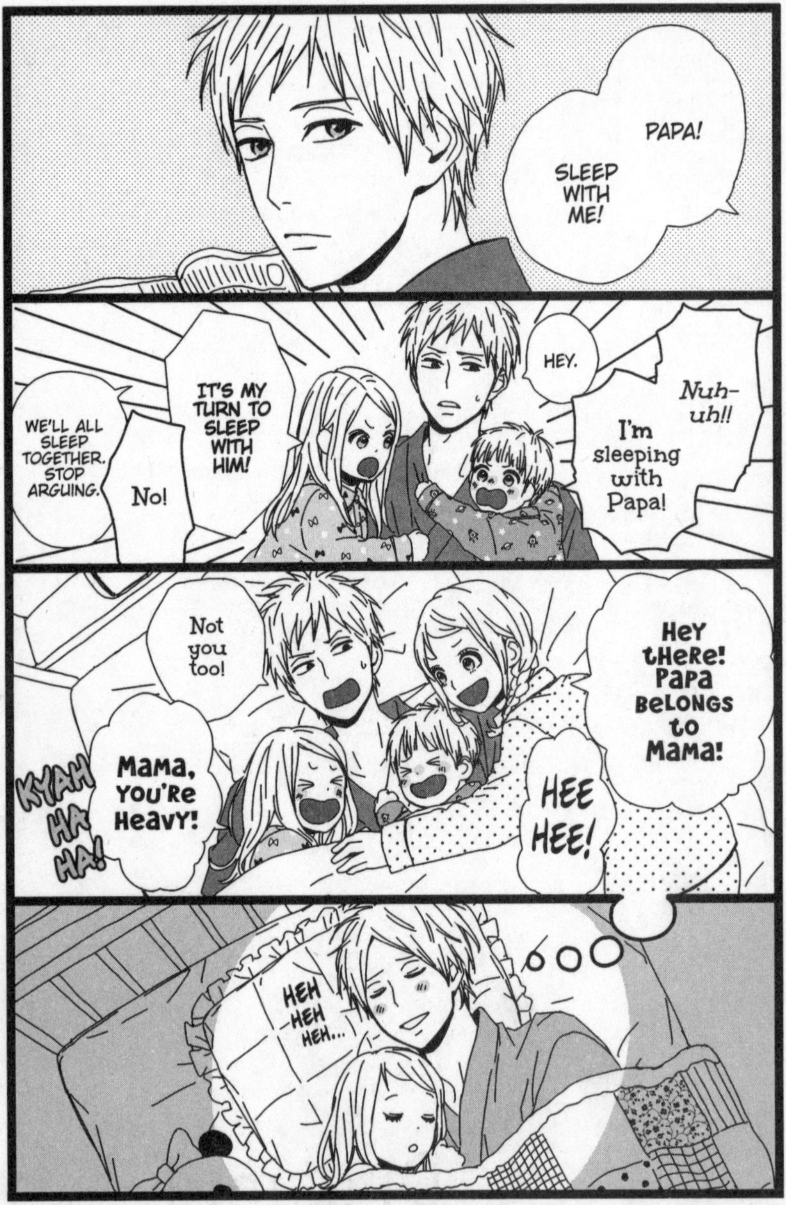
PAPA!
SLEEP WITH ME!
Nuh-uh!!
I'm sleeping with Papa!
HEY.
IT'S MY TURN TO SLEEP WITH HIM!
No!
WE'LL ALL SLEEP TOGETHER. STOP ARGUING.
HEY THERE! PAPA BELONGS TO MAMA!
Not you too!
HEE HEE!
MAMA, YOU'RE HEAVY!
KYAH HA HA!
HEH HEH HEH...

THE END

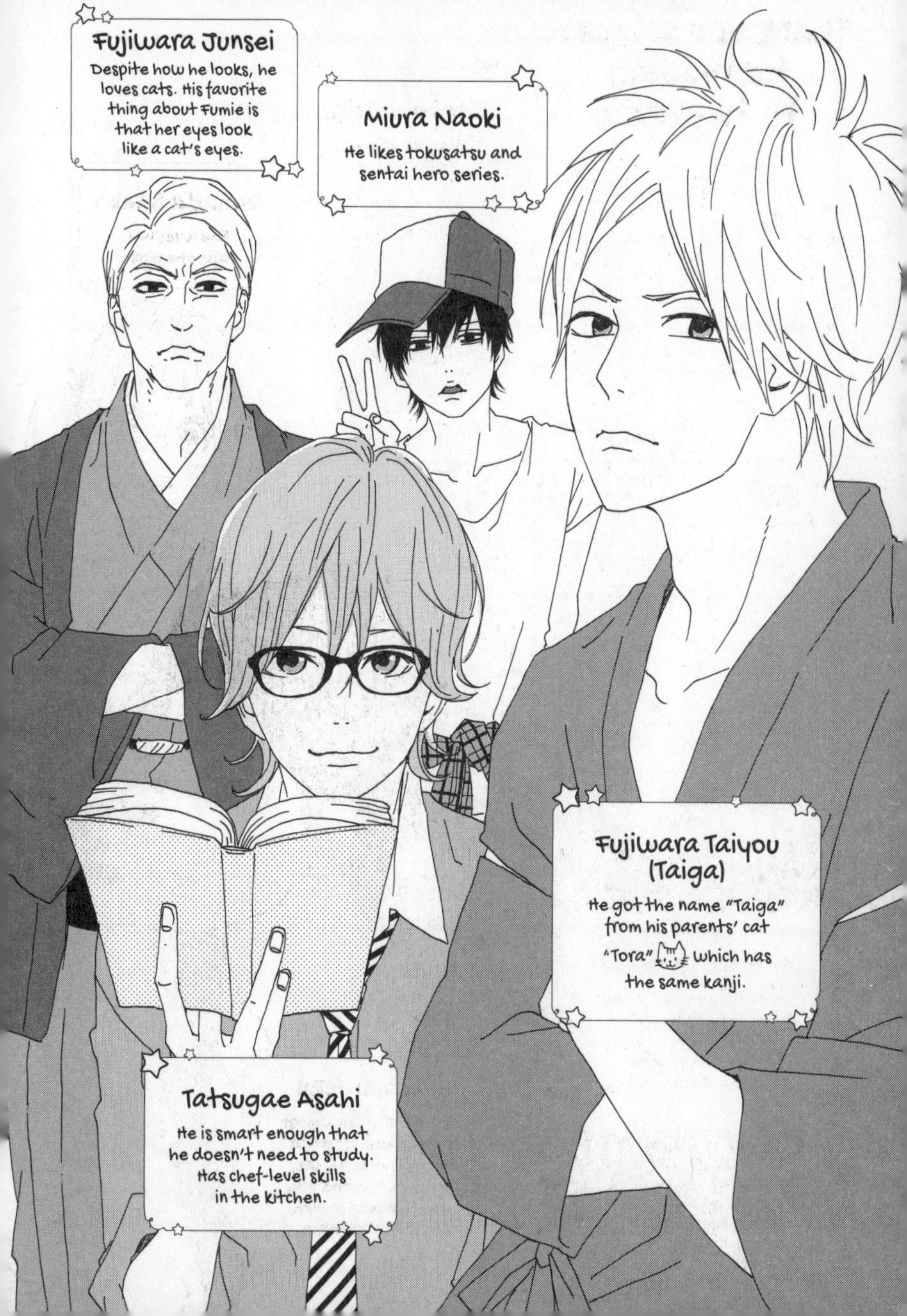
Fujiwara Junsei
Despite how he looks, he loves cats. His favorite thing about Fumie is that her eyes look like a cat's eyes.
Miura Naoki
He likes tokusatsu and sentai hero series.
Fujiwara Taiyou (Taiga)
He got the name "Taiga" from his parents' cat "Tora" which has the same kanji.
Tatsugae Asahi
He is smart enough that he doesn't need to study. Has chef-level skills in the kitchen.

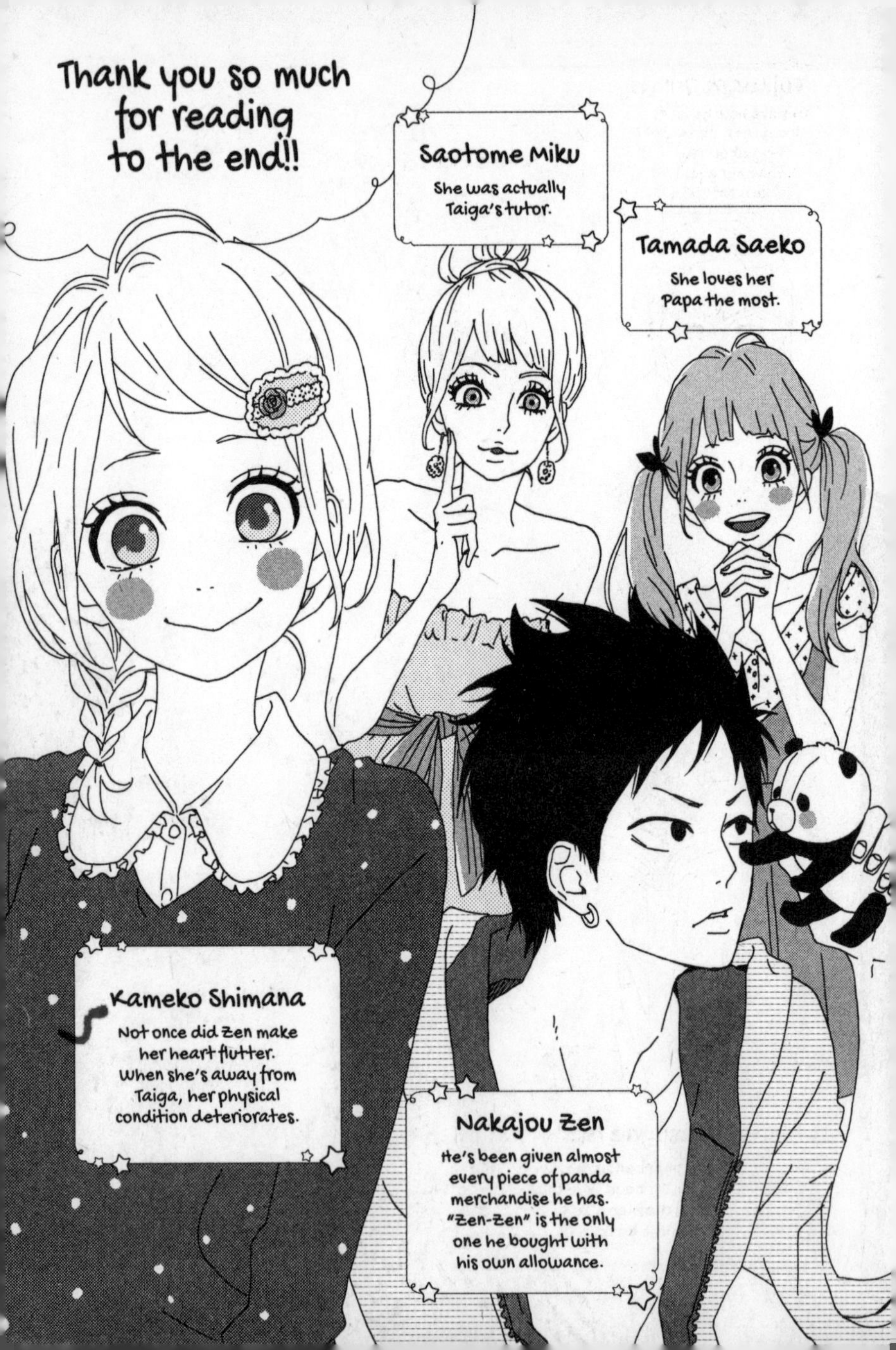
Thank you so much for reading to the end!!
Saotome Miku
She was actually Taiga's tutor.
Tamada Saeko
She loves her Papa the most.
Kameko Shimana
Not once did Zen make her heart flutter. When she's away from Taiga, her physical condition deteriorates.
Nakajou Zen
He's been given almost every piece of panda merchandise he has. "Zen-Zen" is the only one he bought with his own allowance.

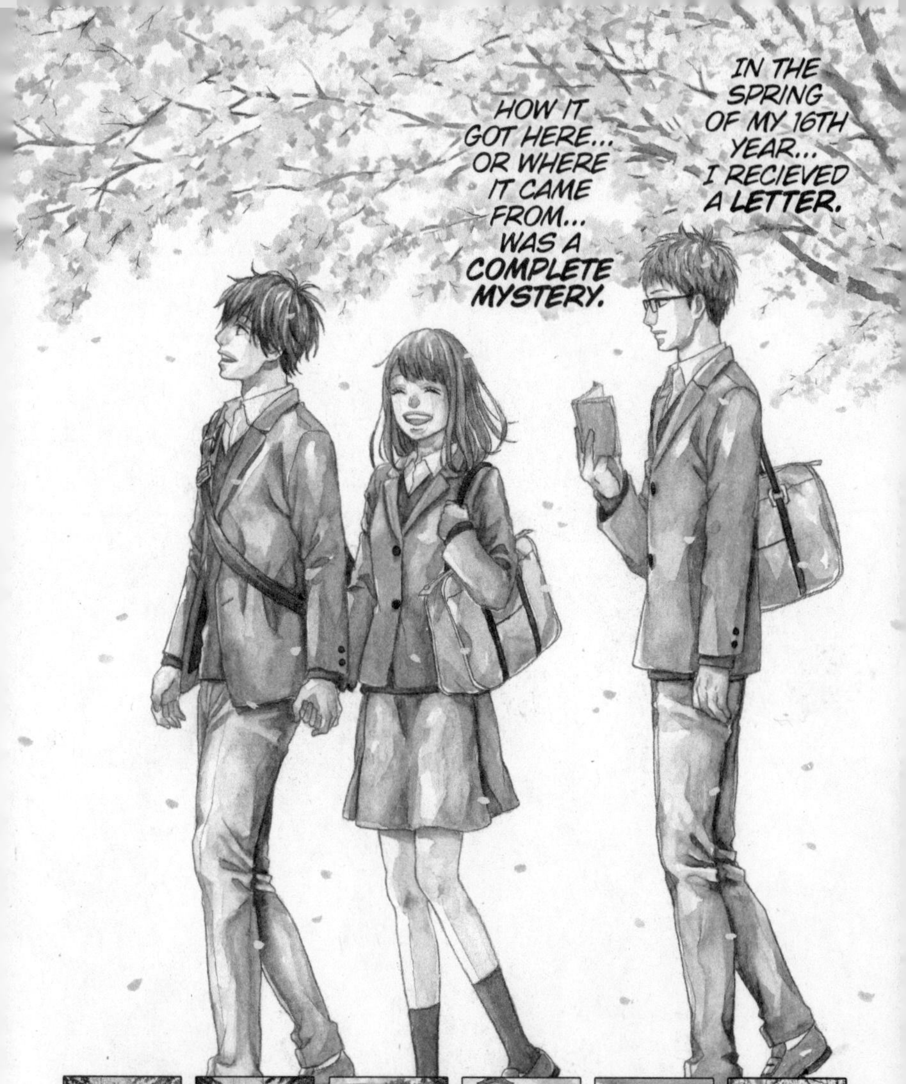
IN THE SPRING OF MY 16TH YEAR... I RECIEVED A **LETTER.**
HOW IT GOT HERE... OR WHERE IT CAME FROM... WAS A **COMPLETE MYSTERY.**
orange
orange
orange
orange
orange
orange

The complete five-volume series and sequel volume, *orange -future-*, are available now in both omnibus print and digital editions!

The *New York Times*' manga bestseller—a story of love
and friendship that transcends time and tragedy.

orange

story & art by ICHIGO TAKANO

Dreamin' Sun

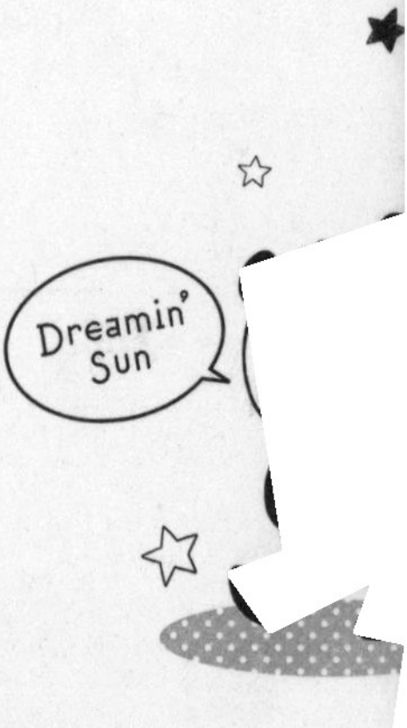
Dreamin' Sun

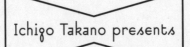

Ichigo Takano presents

Dreamin'

Sun

volume
ten